Lecture Notes in Computer Science 9922

Commenced Publication in 1973
Founding and Former Series Editors:
Gerhard Goos, Juris Hartmanis, and Jan van Leeuwen

Amund Skavhaug · Jérémie Guiochet
Friedemann Bitsch (Eds.)

Computer Safety, Reliability, and Security

35th International Conference, SAFECOMP 2016
Trondheim, Norway, September 21–23, 2016
Proceedings

 Springer

Editors
Amund Skavhaug
Norwegian University of Science and
  Technology
Trondheim
Norway

Jérémie Guiochet
University of Toulouse
Toulouse
France

Friedemann Bitsch
Thales Transportation Systems GmbH
Ditzingen
Germany

ISSN 0302-9743   ISSN 1611-3349   (electronic)
Lecture Notes in Computer Science
ISBN 978-3-319-45476-4   ISBN 978-3-319-45477-1   (eBook)
DOI 10.1007/978-3-319-45477-1

Library of Congress Control Number: 2015948709

LNCS Sublibrary: SL2 – Programming and Software Engineering

This Springer imprint is published by Springer Nature
The registered company is Springer International Publishing AG Switzerland

Preface

It is our pleasure to present the proceedings of the 35th International Conference on Computer Safety, Reliability, and Security (SAFECOMP 2016), held in Trondheim, Norway, in September 2016. Since 1979, when the conference was established by the European Workshop on Industrial Computer Systems, Technical Committee 7 on Reliability, Safety, and Security (EWICS TC7), it has contributed to the state of the art through the knowledge dissemination and discussions of important aspects of computer systems of our everyday life. With the proliferation of embedded systems, the omnipresence of the Internet of Things, and the commodity of advanced real-time control systems, our dependence on safe and correct behavior is ever increasing. Currently, we are witnessing the beginning of the era of truly autonomous systems, driverless cars being the most well-known phenomenon to the non-specialist, where the safety and correctness of their computer systems are already being discussed in the main-stream media. In this context, it is clear that the relevance of the SAFECOMP conference series is increasing.

The international Program Committee, consisting of 57 members from 16 countries, received 71 papers from 21 nations. Of these, 24 papers were selected to be presented at the conference.

The review process was thorough with at least 3 reviewers with ensured independency, and 20 of these reviewers met in person in Toulouse, France in April 2016 for the final discussion and selection. Our warm thanks go to the reviewers, who offered their time and competence in the Program Committee work. We are grateful for the support we received from LAAS-CNRS, who in its generosity hosted the PC meeting.

As has been the tradition for many years, the day before the main-track of the conference was dedicated to 6 workshops: DECSoS, ASSURE, SASSUR, CPSELabs, SAFADAPT, and TIPS. Papers from these are published in a separate LNCS volume.

We would like to express our gratitude to the many who have helped with the preparations and running of the conference, especially Friedemann Bitsch as publication chair, Elena Troubitsyna as publicity chair, Erwin Schoitsch as workshop chair, and not to be forgotten the local organization and support staff, Knut Reklev, Sverre Hendseth, and Adam L. Kleppe.

For its support, we would like to thank the Norwegian University of Science and Technology, represented by both the Department of Engineering Cybernetics and the Department for Production and Quality engineering.

Without the support from the EWICS TC7, headed by Francesca Saglietti, this event could not have happened. We wish the EWICS TC7 organization continued success, and we are looking forward to being part of this also in the future.

Finally, the most important persons to whom we would like to express our gratitude are the authors and participants. Your dedication, effort, and knowledge are the foundation of the scientific progress. We hope you had fruitful discussions, gained new insights, and generally had a memorable time in Trondheim.

September 2016   Amund Skavhaug
                                                                 Jérémie Guiochet

Organization

EWICS TC7 Chair

Francesca Saglietti   University of Erlangen-Nuremberg, Germany

General Chair

Amund Skavhaug   The Norwegian University of Science and Technology, Norway

Program Co-chairs

Jérémie Guiochet   LAAS-CNRS, University of Toulouse, France
Amund Skavhaug   The Norwegian University of Science and Technology, Norway

Publication Chair

Friedemann Bitsch   Thales Transportation Systems GmbH, Germany

Local Organizing Committee

Sverre Hendseth   The Norwegian University of Science and Technology, Norway
Knut Reklev   The Norwegian University of Science and Technology, Norway
Adam L. Kleppe   The Norwegian University of Science and Technology, Norway

Workshop Chair

Erwin Schoitsch   AIT Austrian Institute of Technology, Austria

Publicity Chair

Elena Troubitsyna   Åbo Akademi University, Finland

International Program Committee

Eric Alata   LAAS-CNRS, France
Friedemann Bitsch   Thales Transportation Systems GmbH, Germany

Sandro Bologna	Associazione Italiana esperti in Infrastrutture Critiche (AIIC), Italy
Andrea Bondavalli	University of Florence, Italy
Jens Braband	Siemens AG, Germany
António Casimiro	University of Lisbon, Portugal
Nick Chozos	ADELARD, London, UK
Domenico Cotroneo	Federico II University of Naples, Italy
Peter Daniel	EWICS TC7, UK
Ewen Denney	SGT/NASA Ames Research Center, USA
Felicita Di Giandomenico	ISTI-CNR, Italy
Wolfgang Ehrenberger	Hochschule Fulda – University of Applied Science, Germany
Francesco Flammini	Ansaldo STS Italy, Federico II University of Naples, Italy
Barbara Gallina	Mälardalen University, Sweden
Ilir Gashi	CSR, City University London, UK
Janusz Górski	Gdansk University of Technology, Poland
Lars Grunske	University of Stuttgart, Germany
Jérémie Guiochet	LAAS-CNRS, France
Wolfgang Halang	Fernuniversität Hagen, Germany
Poul Heegaard	The Norwegian University of Science and Technology, Norway
Maritta Heisel	University of Duisburg-Essen, Germany
Bjarne E. Helvik	The Norwegian University of Science and Technology, Norway
Chris Johnson	University of Glasgow, UK
Erland Jonsson	Chalmers University, Stockholm, Sweden
Mohamed Kaâniche	LAAS-CNRS, France
Karama Kanoun	LAAS-CNRS, France
Tim Kelly	University of York, UK
John Knight	University of Virginia, USA
Phil Koopman	Carnegie-Mellon University, USA
Floor Koornneef	Delft University of Technology, The Netherlands
Youssef Laarouchi	Electricité de France (EDF), France
Bev Littlewood	City University London, UK
Regina Moraes	Universidade Estadul de Campinas, Brazil
Takashi Nanya	Canon Inc., Japan
Odd Nordland	SINTEF ICT, Trondheim, Norway
Frank Ortmeier	Otto-von-Guericke Universität Magdeburg, Germany
Philippe Palanque	University of Toulouse, IRIT, France
Karthik Pattabiraman	The University of British Columbia, Canada
Michael Paulitsch	Thales Austria GmbH, Austria
Holger Pfeifer	fortiss GmbH, Germany
Alexander Romanovsky	Newcastle University, UK
John Rushby	SRI International, USA
Francesca Saglietti	University of Erlangen-Nuremberg, Germany

Christoph Schmitz	Zühlke Engineering AG, Switzerland
Erwin Schoitsch	AIT Austrian Institute of Technology, Austria
Walter Schön	Heudiasyc, Université de Technologie de Compiègne, France
Christel Seguin	Office National d'Etudes et Recherches Aérospatiales, France
Amund Skavhaug	The Norwegian University of Science and Technology, Norway
Mark-Alexander Sujan	University of Warwick, UK
Stefano Tonetta	Fondazione Bruno Kessler, Italy
Martin Törngren	KTH Royal Institute of Technology, Stockholm, Sweden
Mario Trapp	Fraunhofer Institute for Experimental Software Engineering, Germany
Elena Troubitsyna	Åbo Akademi University, Finland
Meine van der Meulen	DNV GL, Norway
Coen van Gulijk	University of Huddersfield, UK
Marcel Verhoef	European Space Agency, The Netherlands
Helene Waeselynck	LAAS-CNRS, France

Sub-reviewers

Karin Bernsmed	SINTEF ICT, Trondheim, Norway
John Filleau	Carnegie Mellon University, USA
Denis Hatebur	University of Duisburg-Essen, Germany
Alexei Iliasov	Newcastle University, UK
Viacheslav Izosimov	KTH Royal Institute of Technology, Stockholm, Sweden
Linas Laibinis	Åbo Akademi University, Finland
Paolo Lollini	University of Florence, Italy
Mathilde Machin	APSYS - Airbus, France
Naveen Mohan	KTH Royal Institute of Technology, Stockholm, Sweden
André Luiz de Oliveira	Universidade Estadual do Norte do Paraná, Brazil
Roberto Natella	Federico II University of Naples, Italy
Antonio Pecchia	Federico II University of Naples, Italy
José Rufino	University of Lisbon, Portugal
Inna Pereverzeva	Åbo Akademi University, Finland
Thomas Santen	Technische Universität Berlin, Germany
Christoph Schmittner	AIT Austrian Institute of Technology, Austria
Thierry Sotiropoulos	LAAS-CNRS, France
Milda Zizyte	Carnegie Mellon University, USA
Tommaso Zoppi	University of Florence, Italy

Sponsoring Institutions

European Workshop on Industrial Computer
Systems Reliability, Safety and Security

Norwegian University of Science and Technology

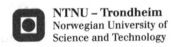

Laboratory for Analysis and Architecture
of Systems, Carnot Institute

Lecture Notes in Computer Science (LNCS),
Springer Science + Business Media

International Federation for Information Processing

Austrian Institute of Technology

Thales Transportation Systems GmbH

Austrian Association for Research in IT

Electronic Components and Systems
for European Leadership - Austria

ARTEMIS Industry Association

European Research Consortium for Informatics
and Mathematics

Informationstechnische Gesellschaft

German Computer Society

Austrian Computer Society

European Network of Clubs for Reliability
and Safety of Software-Intensive Systems

Verband österreichischer Software Industrie

Contents

Anomaly Detection and Resilience

Cyber Security

Fault Trees

Safety Analysis

Fault Injection

FISSC: A Fault Injection and Simulation Secure Collection

Louis Dureuil[1,2,3(✉)], Guillaume Petiot[1,3], Marie-Laure Potet[1,3],
Thanh-Ha Le[4], Aude Crohen[4], and Philippe de Choudens[1,2]

[1] University of Grenoble Alpes, 38000 Grenoble, France
[2] CEA, LETI, MINATEC Campus, 38054 Grenoble, France
{louis.dureuil,philippe.de.choudens}@cea.fr
[3] CNRS, VERIMAG, 38000 Grenoble, France
{louis.dureuil,marie-laure.potet}@imag.fr
[4] Safran Morpho, Paris, France
{thanh-ha.le,aude.crohen}@morpho.com

Abstract. Applications in secure components (such as smartcards, mobile phones or secure dongles) must be hardened against fault injection to guarantee security even in the presence of a malicious fault. Crafting applications robust against fault injection is an open problem for all actors of the secure application development life cycle, which prompted the development of many simulation tools. A major difficulty for these tools is the absence of representative codes, criteria and metrics to evaluate or compare obtained results. We present FISSC, the first public code collection dedicated to the analysis of code robustness against fault injection attacks. FISSC provides a framework of various robust code implementations and an approach for comparing tools based on predefined attack scenarios.

1 Introduction

1.1 Security Assessment Against Fault Injection Attacks

In 1997, Differential Fault Analysis (DFA) [6] demonstrated that unprotected cryptographic implementations are insecure against malicious fault injection, which is performed using specialized equipment such as a glitch generator, focused light (laser) or an electromagnetic injector [3]. Although fault attacks initially focused on cryptography, recent attacks target non-cryptographic properties of codes, such as modifying the control flow to skip security tests [16] or creating type confusion on Java cards in order to execute a malicious code [2].

Fault injections are modeled using various fault models, such as instruction skip [1], instruction replacement [10] or bitwise and byte-wise memory and register corruptions [6]. Fault models operate either at high-level (HL) on the source code or at low-level (LL) on the assembly or even the binary code. Both kinds of models are useful. HL models allow to perform faster and understandable analyses supplying a direct feedback about potential vulnerabilities. LL models

© Springer International Publishing Switzerland 2016
A. Skavhaug et al. (Eds.): SAFECOMP 2016, LNCS 9922, pp. 3–11, 2016.
DOI: 10.1007/978-3-319-45477-1_1

allow more accurate evaluations, as the results of fault injection directly depend on the compilation process and on the encoding of the binary.

Initially restricted to the domain of smartcards, fault attacks are nowadays taken into account in larger classes of secure components. For example the Protection Profile dedicated to *Trusted Execution Environment*[1] explicitly includes hardware attack paths such as power glitch fault injection. In the near future, developers of *Internet of Things* devices will use off-the-shelf components to build their systems, and will need means to protect them against fault attacks [8].

1.2   The Need for a Code Collection

In order to assist both the development and certification processes, several tools have been developed, either to analyze the robustness of applications against fault injection [4,5,7,8,10,11,13,14], or to harden applications by adding software countermeasures [9,12,15]. All these tools are dedicated to particular fault models and code levels. The main difficulty for these tools is the absence of representative and public codes allowing to evaluate and compare the relevance of their results. Partners of this paper are in this situation and have developed specific tools adapted to their needs: LAZART [14] an academic tool targeting multiple fault injection, EFS [4] an embedded LL simulator dedicated to developers and CELTIC [7] tailored for evaluators.

In this paper, we describe FISSC (Fault Injection and Simulation Secure Collection), the first public collection dedicated to the analysis of secure codes against fault injection. We intend to provide (1) a set of representative applications associated with predefined attack scenarios, (2) an inventory of classic and published countermeasures and programming practices embedded into a set of implementations, and (3) a methodology for the analysis and comparison of results of various tools involving different fault models and code levels.

In Sect. 2, we explain how high-level attack scenarios are produced through an example. We then present the organization and the content of this collection in Sect. 3. Lastly in Sect. 4, we propose an approach for comparing attacks found on several tools, illustrated with results obtained from CELTIC.

2   The VerifyPIN Example

Figure 1 gives an implementation of a VerifyPIN command, allowing to compare a user PIN to the card PIN under the control of a number of tries. The `byteArrayCompare` function implements the comparison of PINs. Both functions illustrate some classic countermeasures and programming features. For example the constants `BOOL_TRUE` and `BOOL_FALSE` encode booleans with values more robust than 0 and 1 that are very sensible to data fault injection. The loop of `byteArrayCompare` is in fixed time, in order to prevent timing attacks. Finally, to detect fault injection consisting in skipping comparison, a countermeasure checks whether i is equal to `size` after the loop. The `countermeasure` function raises the global flag `g_countermeasure` and returns.

---

[1] TEE Protection Profile. Tech. Rep. GPD_SPE_021. GlobalPlatform, november 2014.

```
 1  BOOL VerifyPIN() {                    15  BOOL byteArrayCompare(UBYTE* a1,
 2     g_authenticated = BOOL_FALSE;      16     UBYTE* a2, UBYTE size) {
 3     if(g_ptc > 0) {                    17     int i;
 4        if(byteArrayCompare(g_userPin,  18     BOOL status = BOOL_FALSE;
 5           g_cardPin, PIN_SIZE)         19     BOOL diff = BOOL_FALSE;
 6           == BOOL_TRUE) {              20     for(i = 0; i < size; i++) {
 7           g_ptc = 3;                   21        if(a1[i] != a2[i]) {
 8           g_authenticated = BOOL_TRUE; 22           diff = BOOL_TRUE; } }
 9           return BOOL_TRUE;            23     if(i != size) {
10        } else {                        24        countermeasure(); }
11           g_ptc--;                     25     if(diff == BOOL_FALSE) {
12           return BOOL_FALSE;           26        status = BOOL_TRUE;
13        }                               27     } else { status = BOOL_FALSE;
14     } return BOOL_FALSE; }             28     } return status; }
```

Fig. 1. Implementation of functions `VerifyPIN` and `byteArrayCompare`

To obtain high-level attack scenarios, we use the LAZART tool [14] which analyses the robustness of a source code (C-LLVM) against multiple control-flow fault injections (other types of faults can also be taken into account). The advantage of this approach is twofold: first, LAZART is based on a symbolic execution engine ensuring the coverage of all possible paths resulting from the chosen fault model; second, multiple injections encompass attacks that can be implemented as a single one in other fault models or low-level codes. Thus, according to the considered fault model, we obtain a set of significant high-level coarse-grained attack scenarios that can be easily understood by developers.

We apply LAZART to the VerifyPIN example to detect attacks where an attacker can authenticate itself with an invalid PIN without triggering a countermeasure. Successful attacks are detected with an oracle, i.e., a boolean condition on the C variables. Here: `g_countermeasure != 1 && g_authenticated == BOOL_TRUE`. We chose each byte of the user PIN distinct from its reference counterpart. Table 1 summarizes, for each vulnerability, the number of required faults, the targeted lines in the C code, and the effect of the faults on the application.

In FISSC, for each attack, we provide a file containing the chosen inputs and fault injection locations (in terms of basic blocks of the control flow graph) as well as a colored graph indicating how the control flow has been modified. Detailed results for this example can be found on the website.[2]

Table 1. High-level attacks found by LAZART and their effects

Number of faults	Fault injection locations	Effects
1	l. 25	Invert the result of the condition
1	l. 4	Invert the result of the condition
2	l. 20	Do not execute the loop
	l. 23	Do not trigger the countermeasure
4	l. 21 (four times)	Invert each byte check

---

[2] http://sertif-projet.forge.imag.fr/documents/VerifyPIN_2_results.pdf.

3   The FISSC Framework

As pointed out before, FISSC targets tools working at various code levels and high-level attack scenarios can be used as reference to interpret low-level attacks. Then, we supply codes at various levels and the preconized approach is described in Fig. 2 and illustrated in Sect. 4.

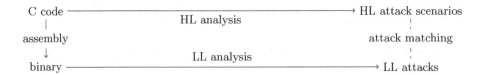

Fig. 2. Matching LL attacks with HL attack scenarios

In this current configuration, FISSC supports the C language and the ARM-v7 M (Cortex M4) assembly. We do not distribute binaries targeting a specific device, but they can be generated by completing the gcc linker scripts.

3.1   Contents and File Organization

The first release of FISSC contains small basic functions of cryptographic implementations (key copy, generation of random number, RSA) and a suite of VerifyPIN implementations of various robustness, detailed in Sect. 3.2. For these examples, Table 2 describes oracles determining attacks that are considered successful. For instance attacks against the VerifyPIN command target either to be authenticated with a wrong PIN or to get as many tries as wanted. Attacks against AESAddRoundKeyCopy try to assign a known value to the key in order to make the encryption algorithm deterministic. Attacks against GetChallenge try to prevent the random buffer generation, so that the challenge buffer is left unchanged. Attacks against CRT-RSA target the signature computation, so that the attacker can retrieve a prime factor p or q of N.

Table 2. Oracles in FISSC

Example	Oracle
VerifyPIN	`g_authenticated == 1`
VerifyPIN	`g_ptc >= 3`
AES KeyCopy	`g_key[0] = g_expect[0] || ... || g_key[N-1] = g_expect[N-1]`
GetChallenge	`g_challenge == g_previousChallenge`
CRT-RSA	`(g_cp == pow(m,dp)% p && g_cq != pow(m,dq)% q)`
	`|| (g_cp != pow(m,dp)% p && g_cq == pow(m,dq)% q)`

Each example is split into several C files, with a file containing the actual code, and other files providing the necessary environment (e.g., countermeasure, oracle, initialization) as well as an interface to embed the code on a device (types, NVM memory read/write functions). This modularity allows one to use the implementation while replacing parts of the analysis or interface environments.

3.2   The VerifyPIN Suite

Applications are hardened against fault injections by means of countermeasures (CM) and programming features (PF). Countermeasures denote specific code designed to detect abnormal behaviors. Programming Features denote implementation choices impacting fault injection sensitivity. For instance, introducing function calls or inlining them introduces instructions to pass parameters, which changes the attack surface for fault injections. Table 4 lists a subset of classic and published PF and CM we are taking into account. The objective of the suite is not to provide a fully robust implementation, but to observe the effect of the implemented CM and PF on the produced attack scenarios.

Table 3. PF/CM embedded in VerifyPIN suite

	HB	FTL	INL	BK	SC	DT	1	2	3	4	Σ
v0							2	0	0	1	3
v1	✓						2	0	0	1	3
v2	✓	✓			✓		2	1	0	1	4
v3	✓	✓	✓		✓		2	1	0	1	4
v4	✓	✓	✓	✓	✓		2	0	1	1	4
v5	✓	✓			✓	✓	0	4	4	1	9
v6	✓	✓	✓			✓	0	3	0	1	4
v7	✓	✓	✓		✓	✓	0	2	0	0	2

(# scenarios for i faults)

Table 4. List of CM/PF

PF	
INL	Inlined calls
FTL	Fixed time loop
CM	
HB	Hardened booleans
BK	Backup copy
DT	Double test
SC	Step counter

Table 3 gives the distribution of CM and PF in each implementation (v2 is the example of Fig. 1). Hardened booleans protect against faults modifying data-bytes. Fixed-time loops protect against temporal side-channel attacks. Step counters check the number of loop iterations. Inlining the `byteArrayCompare` function protects against faults changing the call to a NOP. Backup copy prevents against 1-fault attacks targeting the data. Double call to `byteArrayCompare` and double tests prevent single fault attacks, which become double fault attacks. Calling a function twice (v5) doubles the attack surface on this function. Step counters protect against all attacks disrupting the control flow integrity [9].

4   Comparing Tools

The HL scenarios and oracles defined in Sects. 2–3 allow for the comparison of tools in the FISCC framework. In particular, the successful attacks discovered by tools should cover the HL scenarios. In order to associate HL scenarios and attacks we propose several *Attack Matching* criteria. *Attack matching* consists in deciding whether some attacks found by a tool are related to attacks found by another tool. An attack is *unmatched* if it is not related to any other attack.

In [5], HL faults are compared with LL faults with the following criterion: attacks that lead to the same program output are considered as matching. This "functional" criterion is not always discriminating enough. For instance, codes like verifyPIN produce a very limited set of possible outputs ("authenticated" or not). We propose two additional criteria:

Matching by address. Match attacks that target the same address. To match LL and HL attacks, one must additionally locate the C address corresponding to the assembly address of the LL attack.

Fault Model Matching. Interpret faults in one fault model as faults in the other fault model. For instance, since conditional HL statements are usually compiled to cmp and jmp instructions, it makes sense to interpret corruptions of cmp or jmp instructions (in the *instruction replacement* fault model) as test inversions.

4.1   Case Study

We apply our criteria to compare the results of CELTIC and LAZART on the example of Fig. 1. In our experiments, CELTIC uses the *instruction replacement* fault model, where a single byte of the code is replaced by another value at runtime. Testing the possible values exhaustively, CELTIC finds 432 successful attacks. We then apply our two matching criteria to these results. Fig. 3 indicates the number of successful attacks per address of assembly code, and the (manually determined) correspondence between assembly addresses and C lines. The C lines *4*, *20*, *21*, *23* and *25* correspond to the scenarios found by LAZART in Table 1. They are matched *by address* with the attacks found by CELTIC. CELTIC attacks that target a jump or a compare instruction are also matched *by fault model*.

4.2   Interpretation

Fault model matching can be used to quickly identify HL-attacks amongst LL-attacks with only a hint of the correspondence between C and assembly, while address matching allows to precisely find the HL-attacks matched by the LL-attacks. Both matching criteria yield complementary results. For instance, attacks at address 0x41eb are matched only by address, while attacks at 0x41fd only by fault model.

Interestingly, some multiple fault scenarios of LAZART are implemented by single fault attacks in CELTIC. For instance, the 4-fault scenario of l.21 is implemented with the attacks at address 0x41b6. In the HL scenario the conditional test inside the loop is inverted 4 consecutive times. In the LL attacks, The corresponding jump instruction is actually not inverted, but its target is replaced so that it jumps to l.26 instead of l.22. These attacks are matched with our current criteria, although they are semantically very different. Lastly, 20 LL-attacks remain unmatched. They are subtle attacks that depend on the encoding of the

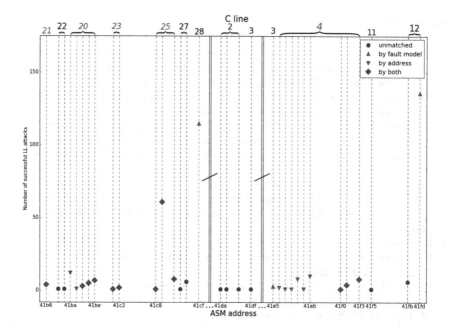

Fig. 3. Matching HL and LL attacks

binary or on a very specific byte being injected. For instance, at 0x41da, the value for BOOL_FALSE is replaced by the value for BOOL_TRUE. This is likely to be hard to achieve with actual attack equipment.

In this example, *attack matching* criteria allows to show that CELTIC attacks cover each HL-scenario. Other tools can use this approach to compare their results with those of CELTIC and the HL-scenario of LAZART. Their results should cover the HL-scenario, or offer explanations (for instance, due to the fault model) if the coverage is not complete.

5   Conclusion

FISSC is available on request.[3] It can be used by tool developers to evaluate their implementation against many fault models and it can be contributed to with new countermeasures (the first external contribution is the countermeasure of [9]). We plan to add more examples in the future releases of FISSC (e.g. hardened DES implementations) and to extend LAZART to simulate faults on data.

Acknowledgments. This work has been partially supported by the SERTIF project (ANR-14-ASTR-0003-01): http://sertif-projet.forge.imag.fr and by the LabEx PERSYVAL-Lab (ANR-11-LABX-0025).

---

[3] To request or contribute, send an e-mail to sertif-secure-collection@imag.fr.

References

1. Anderson, R., Kuhn, M.: Low cost attacks on tamper resistant devices. In: Christianson, B., Crispo, B., Lomas, M., Roe, M. (eds.) Security Protocols 1997. LNCS, vol. 1361, pp. 125–136. Springer, Heidelberg (1998)
2. Barbu, G., Thiebeauld, H., Guerin, V.: Attacks on Java card 3.0 combining fault and logical attacks. In: Gollmann, D., Lanet, J.-L., Iguchi-Cartigny, J. (eds.) CARDIS 2010. LNCS, vol. 6035, pp. 148–163. Springer, Heidelberg (2010)
3. Barenghi, A., Breveglieri, L., Koren, I., Naccache, D.: Fault injection attacks on cryptographic devices: theory, practice, and countermeasures. Proc. IEEE **100**(11), 3056–3076 (2012)
4. Berthier, M., Bringer, J., Chabanne, H., Le, T.-H., Rivière, L., Servant, V.: Idea: embedded fault injection simulator on smartcard. In: Jürjens, J., Piessens, F., Bielova, N. (eds.) ESSoS. LNCS, vol. 8364, pp. 222–229. Springer, Heidelberg (2014)
5. Berthomé, P., Heydemann, K., Kauffmann-Tourkestansky, X., Lalande, J.: High level model of control flow attacks for smart card functional security. In: ARES 2012, pp. 224–229. IEEE (2012)
6. Boneh, D., DeMillo, R.A., Lipton, R.J.: On the importance of checking cryptographic protocols for faults. In: Fumy, W. (ed.) EUROCRYPT 1997. LNCS, vol. 1233, pp. 37–51. Springer, Heidelberg (1997)
7. Dureuil, L., Potet, M.-L., de Choudens, P., Dumas, C., Clédière, J.: From code review to fault injection attacks: filling the gap using fault model inference. In: Homma, N., Medwed, M. (eds.) CARDIS 2015. LNCS, vol. 9514, pp. 107–124. Springer, Heidelberg (2015). doi:10.1007/978-3-319-31271-2_7
8. Holler, A., Krieg, A., Rauter, T., Iber, J., Kreiner, C.: Qemu-based fault injection for a system-level analysis of software countermeasures against fault attacks. In: Digital System Design (DSD), Euromicro 15. pp. 530–533. IEEE (2015)
9. Lalande, J., Heydemann, K., Berthomé, P.: Software countermeasures for control flow integrity of smart card C codes. In: Proceedings of the 19th European Symposium on Research in Computer Security, ESORICS 2014, pp. 200–218 (2014)
10. Machemie, J.B., Mazin, C., Lanet, J.L., Cartigny, J.: SmartCM a smart card fault injection simulator. In: IEEE International Workshop on Information Forensics and Security. IEEE (2011)
11. Meola, M.L., Walker, D.: Faulty logic: reasoning about fault tolerant programs. In: Gordon, A.D. (ed.) ESOP 2010. LNCS, vol. 6012, pp. 468–487. Springer, Heidelberg (2010)
12. Moro, N., Heydemann, K., Encrenaz, E., Robisson, B.: Formal verification of a software countermeasure against instruction skip attacks. J. Cryptographic Eng. **4**(3), 145–156 (2014)
13. Pattabiraman, K., Nakka, N., Kalbarczyk, Z., Iyer, R.: Discovering application-level insider attacks using symbolic execution. In: Gritzalis, D., Lopez, J. (eds.) SEC 2009. IFIP AICT, vol. 297, pp. 63–75. Springer, Heidelberg (2009)
14. Potet, M.L., Mounier, L., Puys, M., Dureuil, L.: Lazart: a symbolic approach for evaluation the robustness of secured codes against control flow injections. In: Seventh IEEE International Conference on Software Testing, Verification and Validation, ICST 2014, pp. 213–222. IEEE (2014)

15. Séré, A., Lanet, J.L., Iguchi-Cartigny, J.: Evaluation of countermeasures against fault attacks on smart cards. Int. J. Secur. Appl. **5**(2), 49–60 (2011)
16. Van Woudenberg, J.G., Witteman, M.F., Menarini, F.: Practical optical fault injection on secure microcontrollers. In: 2011 Workshop on Fault Diagnosis and Tolerance in Cryptography (FDTC), pp. 91–99. IEEE (2011)

FIDL: A Fault Injection Description Language for Compiler-Based SFI Tools

Maryam Raiyat Aliabadi[✉] and Karthik Pattabiraman

Electrical and Computer Engineering,
University of British Columbia, Vancouver BC, Canada
{raiyat,karthikp}@ece.ubc.ca

Abstract. Software Fault Injection (SFI) techniques play a pivotal role in evaluating the dependability properties of a software system. Evaluating the dependability of software system against multiple fault scenarios is challenging, due to the combinatorial explosion and the advent of new fault models. These necessitate SFI tools that are programmable and easily extensible. This paper proposes FIDL, which stands for fault injection description language, which allows compiler-based fault injection tools to be extended with new fault models. FIDL is an Aspect-Oriented Programming language that dynamically weaves the fault models into the code of the fault injector. We implement FIDL using the LLFI fault injection framework and measure its overheads. We find that FIDL significantly reduces the complexity of fault models by 10x on average, while incurring 4–18% implementation overhead, which in turn increases the execution time of the injector by at most 7 % across five programs.

1 Introduction

Evaluating the dependability properties of a software system is a major concern in practice. Software Fault Injection (SFI) techniques assess the effectiveness and coverage of fault-tolerance mechanisms, and help in investigating the corner cases [4,5,15]. Testers and dependability practitioners need to evaluate the software system's dependability against a wide variety of fault scenarios. Therefore, it is important to make it easy to develop and deploy new fault scenarios [18].

In this paper, we propose FIDL (Fault Injection Description Language)[1], a new language for defining fault scenarios for SFI. The choice of introducing a specialized language for software fault injection is motivated by three reasons. First, evaluating the dependability of software system against multiple fault scenarios is challenging - the challenge is combinatorial explosion of multiple failure modes [11] when dealing with different attributes of a fault model (e.g., fault types, fault locations and time slots). Second, due to the increasing complexity of software systems, the advent of new types of failure modes (due to residual software bugs) is inevitable [5]. Previous studies have shown that anticipating and modeling all types of failure modes a system may face is challenging [11]. Hence, SFI tools

---

[1] Pronounced *Fiddle* as it involves fiddling with the program.

© Springer International Publishing Switzerland 2016
A. Skavhaug et al. (Eds.): SAFECOMP 2016, LNCS 9922, pp. 12–23, 2016.
DOI: 10.1007/978-3-319-45477-1_2

need to have extensibility facilities that enable dependability practitioners to dynamically model new failure modes, with low effort. Third, decoupling the languages used for describing fault scenarios from the fault injection process enables SFI tool developers and application testers to assume distinct roles in their respective domains of expertise.

The main idea in FIDL is to use Aspect Oriented Programming (AOP) to weave the aspects of different fault models dynamically into the source program through compiler-based SFI tools. This is challenging because the language needs to capture the high-level abstractions for describing fault scenarios, while at the same time being capable of extending the SFI tool to inject the scenarios. Prior work has presented domain specific languages to drive the fault injection tool [3,6,11,16,18]. However, these languages provide neither high level abstractions for managing fault scenarios, nor dynamic extensibility of the associated SFI tools. *To the best of our knowledge, FIDL is the first language to provide high-level abstractions for writing fault injectors spanning a wide variety of software faults, for extending compiler-based SFI tools.*

Paper contributions: The main contributions of this paper are as follows:

- Proposed a fault injection description language (FIDL) which enables programmable compiler-based SFI tools.
- Built FIDLFI, a programmable software fault injection framework by adding FIDL to LLFI, an open-source, compiler-based framework for fault injections [1,14].
- Evaluated FIDL and FIDLFI on five programs. We find that FIDL reduces the complexity of fault models by 10x on average, while incurring 4 to 18 % implementation overhead, which in turn increases the time overhead by at most 6.7 % across programs compared to a native C++ implementation.

2   Background

We developed FIDL as an Aspect-Oriented Programming (AOP) language on the LLFI fault injection framework. In this section, we first provide a brief overview of LLFI. We then explain why we are motivated to develop an AOP language for extending and driving LLFI. Though we demonstrate FIDL in the context of LLFI, it can be applied to any compiler-based SFI tool.

2.1   LLFI

LLVM is a production, open-source compiler that allows a wide variety of static program analysis and transformations [13]. LLFI is an open source LLVM-based fault injection tool that injects faults into the LLVM Intermediate Representation (IR) level of application source code [21]. LLFI was originally developed for hardware fault injection. It injects a fault (e.g., bit flip) into a live register at every run of program in specific locations that are instrumented during compile time [14]. LLFI also allows user to track the fault propagation path, and map it back to the application source code.

Since its development, we have extended LLFI to inject different kinds of software faults in a program in addition to hardware faults [1]. This is the version of LLFI that we use in this paper for comparison with FIDL.

2.2 Aspect-Oriented Programming (AOP)

Object-Oriented Programming (OOP) is a well-known programming technique to decompose a system into sets of objects. However, it provides a static model of a system - thus any changes in the requirements of software system may have a big impact on development time. Aspect-Oriented Programming (AOP) presents a solution to the OOP challenge since it enables the developer to adopt the code that is needed to add secondary requirements such as logging, exception handling without needing to change the original static model [17]. In the following, we introduce the standard terminology defined in AOP [17].

- **Cross-cutting concerns:** are the secondary requirements of a system that cut across multiple abstracted entities of an OOP. AOP aims to encapsulate the cross-cutting concerns of a system into aspects and provide a modular system.
- **Advice:** is the additional code that is "joined" to specific points of program or at specific time.
- **Point-cut:** specifies the points in the program at which advice needs to be applied.
- **Aspect:** the combination of the point-cut and the advice is called an aspect. AOP allows multiple aspects to be described and unified into the system automatically.

3   Related Work

A wide variety of programmable fault injection tools based on SWIFI (Soft-Ware Implemented Fault Injection) techniques have been presented in prior work [3,6,11,11,12,16,18,23]. In this section, we aim to define where FIDL stands in relation to them. More particularly, we argue why *"Programmability"* is a necessity for fault injection tools.

Programmability, is defined as the ability of programming the fault injection mechanism for different test scenarios based on desired metrics of the tester [6,18]. Programmability has two aspects. The first is a unified description language that is independent of the language of the SFI tool [3]. This language is needed to accelerate the process of fault scenario development, and dynamically manage the injection space for a variety of fault types. The second aspect of programmability is providing high level abstractions in the language. The abstracted information keeps the fault description language as simple as possible. By removing the complexity of fault scenario's developing phases, high level abstraction enhances the usability of the tool [3,9,11,16].

There have been a number of languages for fault injection. FAIL* is a fault injection framework supported by a domain specific language that drives the fault load distributions for Grid middleware [18]. FIG is supported by a domain specific language that manages the errors injected to application/shared library boundary [3]. Orchestra and Genesis2 use scripts to describe how to inject failures into TCL layers and service level respectively [6,12]. LFI is supported by a XML-based language for introducing faults into the libraries [16]. EDFI is a LLVM-based tool supporting a hybrid (dynamic and static) fault model description in a user-controlled way through command line inputs [8]. However, the aforementioned languages do not provide high level abstractions, and hence developing a new fault model (or scenario) is non-trivial. PREFAIL proposes a programmable tool to write policies (a set of multiple-failure combinations) for testing cloud applications [11]. Although its supporting language provides high level abstractions, the abstracted modules only manage the failure locations, and do not provide any means to describe new failure types.

4   System Overview

In this paper, we present FIDLFI: a programmable fault injection framework, which improves upon the previous work in both extensibility and high level abstraction. FIDLFI enables programmability of compiler-based SFI tools, and consists of two components: a SFI engine to manage fault injection, and FIDL as SFI driver to manage fault scenarios. It enables testers to generate aggregate fault models in a systematic way, and examine the behavior of the Application Under Test (AUT) after introducing the fault models.

We built the FIDL language to be independent from the language used in the fault injector, which is C++. This enables decoupling the SFI engine and FIDL. Figure 1 indicates the FIDLFI architecture, and the way both pieces interact with each other. The tester describes a fault scenario (new failure mode or a set of multiple failure modes' combinations) in FIDL script, and feeds it into the FIDL core, where it is compiled into a fault model in the C/C++ language. The generated code is automatically integrated into the SFI engine's source code. It enables the SFI engine to test AUT using the generated fault model.

In the rest of this section, we first explain how we design aspects in FIDL to specify the fault model, and then, present the algorithm to weave the models into the fault injector.

Fig. 1. FIDLFI architecture

4.1 FIDL Structure

FIDL represents the fault models in a granular fashion. We reflected the granularity in the fault model by designing it in the form of distinguishable modules, in which the associated attributes are described. The main attributes of a fault model includes fault type (what to inject), and fault location (where/when to inject) that forms the basis of the model.

A FIDL script is formed of four core entities; Trigger, Trigger*, Target and Action, each of which represents a specific task toward fault model design. Once a FIDL script is executed, the FIDL algorithm creates two separate modules (fault trigger and fault injector). Trigger, Trigger* and Target are entities which are representative for responding to the *where to inject* question in fault model design. For simplicity, we call all three entities as *Triggers*. Triggers provide the required information for FIDL algorithm to generate fault trigger module. Triggers are like programmable monitors scattered all over the application in desired places to which FIDL can bind a request to perform a set of Actions. An Action entity represents what to be injected in targeted locations, and is translated to fault injector module by the FIDL algorithm.

We use the terms *instruction* and *register* to describe the entities, as this is what LLVM uses for its intermediate representation (IR) [13]. The FIDL language can be adapted for other compiler infrastructures which use different terms.

Trigger identifies the IR instructions of interest which have previously been defined based on the tester's primary metrics or static analysis results.

Trigger: <instruction name >

Trigger* selects a special subset of identified instructions based on the tester's secondary metrics. This entity enables the tester to filter the injection space to more specific locations. Trigger* is an optional feature that is used when the tester needs to narrow down the Trigger-defined instructions based on specific test purposes, e.g., if she aims to trigger the instructions which are located in tainted paths.

Trigger: <specific instruction indexes>*

Target identifies the desired register(s) in IR level (variable or function argument in the source code level).

Target: < function name :: register type >

Register type can be specified as one of the following options;

dst/RetVal/src (arg number)

in which *dst* and *src* stand for destination and source registers of selected instruction respectively, and *RetVal* refers to the return value of the corresponding instruction. For example *fread:: src 2* means *entry into 3rd source register of fread instruction*, and similarly *src 0* means *entry into 1st source register of every Trigger-defined instruction*.

Action defines what kind of mutation is to be done according to the expected faulty behavior or test objectives.

Action: Corrupt/Freeze/Delay/SetValue/ Perturb

Corrupt is defined as bit flipping the Data/Address variables. *Delay* and *Freeze* are defined as creating an artificial delay and creating an artificial loop respectively, and *Perturb* describes an erroneous behavior. If Action is specified as Perturb, it has to be followed by the name of a built-in injector of the SFI tool or a custom injector written in the C++ language.

Action : Perturb :: built-in/custom injector

4.2   Aspect Design

We design aspects (advice and point-cut) using FIDL scripts. FIDL scripts are very short, simple, and use abstract entities defined in the previous section. This allows testers to avoid dealing with the internal details of the SFI tool or the underlying compiler (LLVM in our case), and substitutes the complex fault model design process with a simple scripting process. As indicated in Fig. 2, FIDL core weaves the defined aspects into LLFI source code by compiling aspects into fault triggers and fault injectors, and automatically integrating them into LLFI.

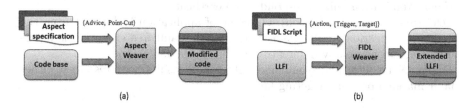

Fig. 2. (a) Aspect-oriented software development [7], (b) FIDL as an AOP-based language.

Algorithm 1 describes how FIDL designs aspects, and how it weaves the aspects into LLFI source code. For the instructions that belong to both Trigger and Trigger* sets (line 1), Algorithm 1 looks for the register(s) that are defined in Target (line 2). Every pair of instruction and corresponding register provides the required information for building PointCut (line 3). FIDL takes the Action description to build Advice (line 4), that is paired with PointCut to form a FIDL aspect (line 5). Now, Algorithm 1 walks through the AUT's code, and looks for the pairs of instruction and register(s) that match to those of PointCut (line 8). Then, it generates the fault trigger and fault injector's code in C++ (line 9, 10). Fault trigger is a LLVM pass that instruments the locations of code identified by PointCut during compile time, and fault injector is a C++ class that binds the Advice to the locations pointed to by PointCut during run time.

Algorithm 1. FIDL weaver description

1: **for all** $inst_i \in (Trigger \cap Trigger*)$ **do**
2:     **for all** $reg_j \in Target$ **do**
3:         $PointCut[i, j] \leftarrow [inst_i, reg_j]$
4:         $Advice \leftarrow Action$
5:         $Aspect \leftarrow [Advice, PointCut[i, j]]$
6: Iterate all basic blocks of AUT
7: **for all** $[inst_m, reg_n] \in AUT$ **do**
8:     **for all** $[inst_m, reg_n] = PointCut[i, j]$ **do**
9:         $FaultTrigger_k \leftarrow PointCut[i, j]$
10: Generate $FaultInjector$ from $Advice$

5   Evaluation Metrics

We propose three metrics for capturing the efficiency of our programmable fault injection framework, *(1) complexity, (2) time overhead, and (3) implementation overhead*. We apply these metrics to the SFI campaign that utilizes different fault models across multiple AUTs. For each metric, we compare the corresponding values in FIDL with the original fault injectors implemented in the LLFI framework (in C++ code). Before we explain the above metrics, we describe the possible outcomes of the fault injection experiment across AUTs as follows:

- *Crash*: Application is aborted due to an exception.
- *Hang*: Application fails to respond to a heartbeat.
- *SDC* (Silent Data Corruption): Outcome of application is different from the fault-free execution result (we assume that the fault-free execution is deterministic, and hence any differences are due to the fault).
- *Benign*: None of the above outcomes (observable results) with respect to either fault masking or non-triggering faults.

Complexity is defined as the effort needed to set up the injection campaign for a particular failure mode. Complexity is measured as time or man hours of uninterrupted work in developing a fault model. Because this is difficult to measure, we calculate instead, the number of source Lines Of Code (LOC) associated with a developed fault model [22]. We have used the above definition for measuring of both OFM's and FFM's complexities. *OFM (Original Fault Model)* is the fault model which is primarily developed as part of the LLFI framework in C++ language. *FFM (FIDL-generated Fault Model)* is the fault model which is translated from FIDL script to C++ code by the FIDL compiler (our tool).

Time Overhead is the extra execution time needed to perform fault-free (profiling) and faulty (fault injection) runs respectively compared to the execution time of AUT within our framework. To precisely measure the average time overhead of each SFI campaign, we only include those runs whose impact are SDCs, as the times taken by Crashes and Hangs depend on the exception handling overheads and the timeout detection mechanisms respectively, both of which are outside the purview of fault injections. We also exclude the benign results in time overhead calculations, because we do not want to measure time when the fault is masked as these do not add any overhead.

Implementation Overhead is the number of LOC introduced by the translation of the FIDL scripts into C++ code. The core of FIDL includes a FIDL compiler written in Python, and three general template files to translate FIDL scripts to respective fault trigger and fault injector modules. FIDL core's is less than 1000 (Lines of Code) LOC. However, FIDL uses general templates to generate fault models' source code, which introduces additional space overhead. To measure this overhead, for every given fault model, we compared the original LOC of OFMs and those of FIDL-generated ones.

6   Evaluation

6.1   Experimental Setup

Fault Models: Using FIDL, we implemented over 40 different fault models that had originally been implemented in LLFI as C++ code [2]. However, due to time constraints, we choose five fault models for our evaluation, namely *Buffer overflow, Memory leak, Data corruption, Wrong API and G-heartbleed* (Details in Table 1). We limited the number of applied fault models to 5, as for a given fault model, we need to perform a total of 20,000 runs (two types of campaigns (2*2000 runs) with and without FIDL, across 5 benchmarks) for obtaining statistically significant results, which takes a significant amount of time.

Table 1. Sample fault model description

Fault model	Description
Buffer overflow	The amount of data written in a local buffer exceeds the amount of memory allocated for it, and overwrites adjacent memory
Data corruption	The data is corrupted before or after processing
Memory leak	The allocated memory on the heap is not released though its not used further in the program
Wrong API	Common mistakes in handling the program APIs responsibility for performing certain tasks such as reading/writing files
G-heartbleed	A generalized model of the Heartbleed vulnerability, that is a type of buffer over-read bug happening in memcpy(), where the buffer size is maliciously enlarged and leads to information leakage [20]

---

[2] Available at: https://github.com/DependableSystemsLab/LLFI.

Target Injection: We selected five benchmarks from three benchmark suites, SPEC [10], Parboil [19], and Parsec [2]. We also selected the Nullhttpd web server to represent server applications. Table 2 indicates the characteristics of benchmark programs. The *Src-LOC* and *IR-LOC* columns refer to the number of lines of benchmark code in C and LLVM IR format respectively. In each benchmark, we inject 2000 faults for each fault model - we have verified that this is sufficient to get tight error bars at the 95 % confidence intervals.

Table 2. Characteristics of benchmark programs

Benchmark	Suite	Description	Src-LOC	IR-LOC
mcf	SPEC	Solves vehicle scheduling problems planning transportation	1960	5054
sad	Parboil	Sum of absolute differences kernel, used in MPEG video encoder	1243	3700
cutcp	Parboil	Computes the short range components of Coulombic potential at grid points	1645	4200
blackscholes	Parsec	Option pricing with Black-Scholes Partial Differential Equations	1198	3560
null httpd	Nulllogic	A multi-threaded web server for Linux and Windows	2067	6930

Research Questions: We address three questions in our evaluation.

RQ1: *How much does FIDL reduce the complexity of fault models?*
RQ2: *How much time overhead is imposed by FIDL?*
RQ3: *How much implementation overhead is imposed by FIDL?*

6.2   Experimental Results

Figure 4 shows the aggregate percentage of SDCs, crashes and benign fault injections (FI) observed across benchmarks for each of the fault models. We find that there is significant variation in the results depending on the fault model.

Complexity (RQ1): For each of the fault models, we quantitatively measure how much FIDL reduces the complexity of fault model development in our framework. Table 3 compares LOC of original fault models primarily developed in the C++ language, and fault models described in FIDL scripts. As can be seen, the LOC of FIDL scripts is much smaller than OFM ones, e.g., 10 LOC of FIDL script against 112 LOC of C++ code for developing G-heartbleed fault model. *Thus, FIDL considerably reduces the fault model complexity by 10X, or one order of magnitude, on average, across fault models.*

Time Overhead (RQ2): Our first goal of time overhead evaluation is measuring how much LLFI slows down AUTs' execution by itself, even without FIDL.

Table 3. Comparing the complexity of FIDL scripts with original and FIDL-generated fault models

Fault model	OFM (LOC)	FFM (LOC)	FIDL script (LOC)
Buffer overflow	68	96	9
Memory leak	68	71	11
Data corruption	61	64	8
Wrong API	109	111	11
G-Heartbleed	81	112	10

Given an OFM, we measured the average execution time for both profiling and fault injection steps, and computed the respective time overheads (TP and TF). We analyzed the results to figure out how time overhead varies for each fault model across benchmarks. We find that both TP and TF increase when the number of candidate locations for injecting the related fault increases, especially when the candidate location is inside a loop. For example, the number of memory de-allocation instances (*free()* calls) within *cutcp* and *mcf* benchmarks are 18 and 4 respectively, and as can be seen in Fig. 3(c), the associated TF and TP varies between 161–196 % and 59–115 % for these benchmarks. In this figure, the maximum and minimum time overhead are related to the *sad* and *blackscholes* with respective maximum and minimum number of *free()* calls.

Secondly, we aim to analyze how FIDL influences the time overhead. To do so, we repeated our experiments using FIDL-generated fault models, and measured the associated time overhead across benchmarks. As shown in Fig. 3, the time overhead either shows a small increase or does not change at all. We also find that there is a positive correlation between the increased amount of time overhead

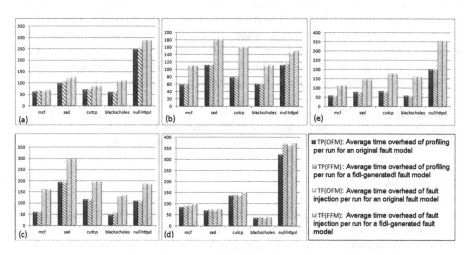

Fig. 3. Comparing Time overhead (%) of selected fault model across benchmarks; (a) buffer overflow, (b) data corruption, (c) memory leak, (d) G-heartbleed, (e) Wrong API.

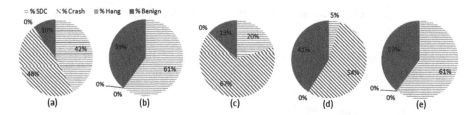

Fig. 4. Distribution (%) of aggregate impact types of sample fault models over 5 programs; (a) data corruption, (b) buffer overflow, (c) memory leak, (d) Wrong API, (e) G-heartbleed.

and the additional LOC that FFMs introduce. For example, the G-heartbleed fault model imposes the maximum increase in time overhead (6.7 %), and its implementation overhead has the highest value (21 LOC).

Implementation Overhead (RQ3): We measured FIDL-generated failure modes (*FFM*) to calculate the respective implementation overhead in terms of the additional LOC (Table 3). We find that the implementation overhead for the selected fault models varies between 3–18 percent. As mentioned earlier, we find that the associated time overhead for the respective fault model with maximum implementation overhead is 6.7 %, which is negligible.

7   Summary

In this paper, we proposed FIDL (fault injection description language) that enables the programmability of compiler-based Software Fault Injection (SFI) tools. FIDL uses Aspect-Oriented Programming (AOP) to dynamically weave new fault models into the SFI tool's source code, thus extending it. We compared the FIDL fault models with hand-written ones (in C++) across five applications and five fault models. Our results show that FIDL significantly reduces the complexity of fault models by about 10x, while incurring 4–18% implementation overhead, which in turn increases the execution time of the injector by atmost 7 % across five different programs, thus pointing to its practicality.

Acknowledgements. This work was supported by the Natural Sciences and Engineering Research Council of Canada (NSERC), and a gift from Cisco Systems. We thank Nematollah Bidokhti for his valuable comments on this work.

References

1. Aliabadi, M.R., Pattabiraman, K., Bidokhti, N.: Soft-LLFI: a comprehensive framework for software fault injection. In: ISSRE 2014, pp. 1–5 (2014)
2. Bienia, C., Kumar, S., Singh, J.P., Li, K.: The PARSEC benchmark suite: characterization and architecturalimplications. In: Parallel Architectures and Compilation Techniques, pp. 72–81 (2008)

3. Broadwell, P., Sastry, N., Traupman, J.: FIG: a prototype tool for online verification of recovery mechanisms. In: Workshop on Self-healing, Adaptive and Self-managed Systems (2002)
4. Cotroneo, D., Lanzaro, A., Natella, R., Barbosa, R.: Experimental analysis of binary-level software fault injection in complex software. In: EDCC 2012, pp. 162–172 (2012)
5. Cotroneo, D., Natella, R.: Fault injection for software certification. IEEE Trans. Secur. Priv. 11(4), 38–45 (2013)
6. Dawson, S., Jahanian, F., Mitton, T.: Experiments on six commercial TCP implementations using a software fault injection tool. Softw. Pract. Exper. 27(12), 1385–1410 (1997)
7. Filman, R., Elrad, T., Clarke, S., et al.: Aspect-Oriented Software Development. Addison-Wesley Professional, Boston (2004)
8. Giuffrida, C., Kuijsten, A., Tanenbaum, A.S.: EDFI: a dependable fault injection tool for dependability benchmarking experiments. In: PRDC 2013, pp. 31–40 (2013)
9. Gregg, B., Mauro, J.: DTrace: Dynamic Tracing in Oracle Solaris, Mac OS X, and FreeBSD. Prentice Hall Professional, Upper Saddle River (2011)
10. Henning, J.L.: SPEC CPU2000: measuring cpu performance in the new millennium. IEEE Trans. Comput. 33(7), 28–35 (2000)
11. Joshi, P., Gunawi, H.S., Sen, K.: PREFAIL: a programmable tool for multiple-failure injection. ACM SIGPLAN Not. 46, 171–188 (2011)
12. Juszczyk, L., Dustdar, S.: A programmble fault injection testbed generator for SOA. In: Weske, M., Yang, J., Fantinato, M., Maglio, P.P. (eds.) ICSOC 2010. LNCS, vol. 6470, pp. 411–425. Springer, Heidelberg (2010)
13. Lattner, C., Adve, V.: LLVM: a compilation framework for lifelong program analysis & transformation. In: CGO 2004, pp. 75–86 (2004)
14. Qining, L., Farahani, M., Wei, J., Thomas, A., Pattabiraman, K.: LLFI: an intermediate code-level fault injection tool for hardware faults. QRS 2015, 11–16 (2015)
15. Madeira, H., Costa, D., Vieira, M.: On the emulation of software faults by software fault injection. DSN 2000, 417–426 (2000)
16. Marinescu, P.D., George Candea, L.F.I.: A practical and general library-level fault injector. In: DSN 2009, pp. 379–388 (2009)
17. Murphy, G.C., Walker, R.J., Banlassad, E.L.A.: Evaluating emerging software development technologies: lessons learned from assessing aspect-oriented programming. IEEE Trans. Softw. Eng. 25(4), 438–455 (1999)
18. Schirmeier, H., Hoffmann, M., Kapitza, R., Lohmann, D., Spinczyk, O.: FAIL: towards a versatile fault-injection experiment framework. ARCS 2012, 1–5 (2012)
19. Stratton, J.A., Rodrigues, C., Sung, I.-J., Obeid, N., Chang, L.-W., Anssari, N., Liu, G.D., W Hwu, W.-M.: PARBOIL: a revised benchmark suite for scientific and commercial throughput computing. In: RHPC 2012 (2012)
20. Wang, J., Zhao, M., Zeng, Q., Wu, D., Liu, P.: Risk assessment of buffer heartbleed over-read vulnerabilities. In: DSN 2015 (2015)
21. Wei, J., Thomas, A., Li, G., Pattabiraman, K.: Quantifying the accuracy of high-level fault injection techniques for hardware faults. In: DSN 2014, pp. 375–382 (2014)
22. Winter, S., Sârbu, C., Suri, N., Murphy, B.: The impact of fault models on software robustness evaluations. In: ICSE 2011, pp. 51–60 (2011)
23. Zhou, F., Condit, J., Anderson, Z., Bagrak, I., Ennals, R., Harren, M., Necula, G., Brewer, E.: SafeDrive: safe and recoverable extensions using language-based techniques. In: OSDI, pp. 45–60 (2006)

Safety Assurance

Using Process Models in System Assurance

Richard Hawkins$^{(\boxtimes)}$, Thomas Richardson, and Tim Kelly

Department of Computer Science, The University of York, York YO10 5GH, UK
richard.hawkins@york.ac.uk

Abstract. When creating an assurance justification for a critical system, the focus is often on demonstrating technical properties of that system. Complete, compelling justifications also require consideration of the processes used to develop the system. Creating such justifications can be an onerous task for systems using complex processes and highly integrated tool chains. In this paper we describe how process models can be used to automatically generate the process justifications required in assurance cases for critical systems. We use an example case study to illustrate an implementation of the approach. We describe the advantages that this approach brings for system assurance and the development of critical systems.

1 Introduction and Motivation

Systems used to perform critical functions require justification that they exhibit the necessary properties (such as for safety or security). The assurance of a system requires the generation of evidence (from the development and analysis of the system) and also a reasoned and compelling justification that explains how the evidence demonstrates the required properties are met. The evidence and justifications are often presented in an assurance case. A compelling justification will always require both a technical risk argument (reasoning about assurance mitigations of the system) and confidence arguments (documenting the reasons for having confidence in the technical argument). Although both technical arguments and arguments of confidence are included in most assurance cases, we find that often the focus is on the technical aspects of assurance and that confidence is often dealt with in very general terms. In [8] we discuss the need for confidence arguments to be specific and explicit within an assurance case. The confidence argument should consider all the assertions made as part of the technical argument. In this paper we focus on one important aspect of this - demonstrating the trustworthiness of the artefacts used as evidence in the technical argument.

As an example, Fig. 1 shows a small extract from an assurance argument that uses evidence from formal verification to demonstrate than an assurance property of the system is satisfied. Figure 1 is represented using Goal Structuring Notation (GSN). In this paper we assume familiarity with GSN, for details on GSN syntax and semantics we refer readers to [5] and [11].

Figure 1 can be seen to present a technical argument (the left-hand leg), and also a claim that there is sufficient confidence in the verification results that are

© Springer International Publishing Switzerland 2016
A. Skavhaug et al. (Eds.): SAFECOMP 2016, LNCS 9922, pp. 27–38, 2016.
DOI: 10.1007/978-3-319-45477-1_3

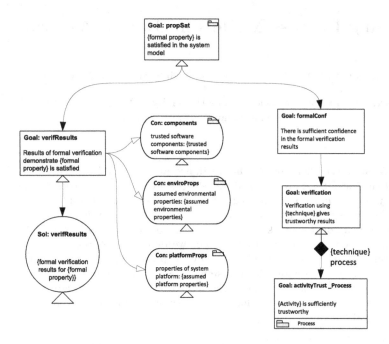

Fig. 1. Example assurance argument pattern

presented in that technical argument (Goal: formalConf). The level of confidence required in the verification results is determined by both the assurance required for the system as a whole, and the role of those verification results in the overall system argument. This issue of establishing confidence in an evidence artefact is a complex one. As discussed in [20], both the appropriateness of the artefact in supporting the argument claim and the trustworthiness of that artefact must be considered. In this paper we focus on the trustworthiness of the artefact. The notion of evidence trustworthiness has been widely discussed, such as in the Structured Assurance Case Metamodel standard (SACM) [16]. Trustworthiness (sometimes also referred to as evidence integrity) relates to the likelihood that the artefact contains errors. It has long been understood that the processes used to generate an artefact are one of the most important factors in determining how trustworthy an artefact is. This is discussed further in work such as [18], and is also seen in standards such as [9] and tool qualification levels in [10]. The basis for such an approach is that a trustworthy artefact is more likely to result form the application of a rigorous, systematic process undertaken by suitable participants using appropriate techniques and incorporating thorough evaluation. This includes consideration of the assessment and qualification of tools used as part of a tool chain. In Fig. 1 it is seen how the claim 'Goal: formalConf' can be supported by reasoning over the trustworthiness of the verification results

(Goal: verification), and then in turn by arguing over the formal verification process that generated that result (Goal: activityTrust_Process)[1].

Modern critical systems often require the use of complex processes involving the integration of multiple development tools and techniques. Creating a compelling justification for each process adopted can be a huge challenge, and indeed this may be a reason why this is often overlooked in favour of more general demonstrations of process compliance. We believe that it should be possible to make the generation of confidence arguments from processes easier and more systematic. This paper therefore provides the following solution:

"Using process models generated as part of system development, and a set of confidence argument patterns, the required confidence arguments for assurance artefacts can be automatically generated."

Firstly, in Sect. 2 we discuss the process models, in Sect. 3 we describe the confidence argument patterns, finally in Sect. 4 we describe how the process models and argument patterns can be linked together to create the required confidence arguments for the target system. We use an example throughout to illustrate our approach.

2   Process Models

Our approach permits the use of any process model in order to generate the process argument. This provides important flexibility for system developers to use any existing process models and tooling. A defined meta-model must however be provided for all models used (in order to create a weaving model for instantiation - see Sect. 4) and the process models must be valid instances of the defined meta-model. It should be noted that for most commonly used process modelling approaches such as SPEM [13] meta-models already exist. For the purposes of our example we have chosen to use the process meta-model that is summarised in Fig. 2, which is based upon that created as part of the OPENCOSS project[2]. We used the OPENCOSS process meta-model [2] as the basis for this since it has been developed based upon a cross-domain consideration of safety standards and processes and with input from industrial partners from many industries.

Here we provide a summary of the main elements of the meta-model in Fig. 2. Processes entail Activities, which may themselves entail other Activities (subactivities). Any activity may have related Participants (which could be a Person, Tool or Organisation (see Fig. 3)). Activities may require and produce Artefacts. Any artefact may be defined as a ManageableAssuraceAsset (defined as part of the evidence meta-model (see Fig. 3)) for which evaluations (AssuranceAssetEvaluation) may be created (such as review or testing of the generated artefact). Activities may also be associated with a particular Technique that is used to carry out that activity.

In Fig. 4 we show an example process model created from the meta-model described above. The example process used is the process of formally checking

---

[1] As described later, we use the term 'Activity' to refer to the relevant process.

[2] See http://www.opencoss-project.eu/.

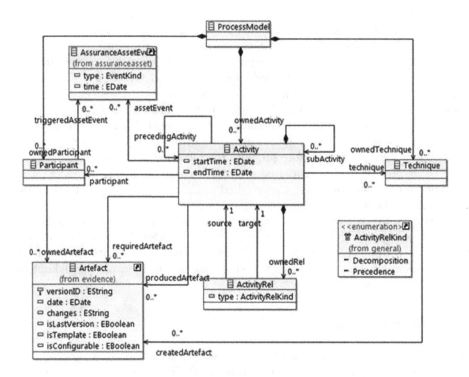

Fig. 2. EMF [19] core meta-model of processes

contracts specified using OCRA [14]. The results of the contract checking can be used to provide evidence as part of an assurance justification for the system by demonstrating that important security properties hold. As seen in Fig. 4, the contract checking activity can be broken down to two sub-activities. Firstly the system model specified in AADL [15] must be translated to an OCRA specification. The second sub-activity is to perform the refinement check on the OCRA specification. The translation activity uses a tool called Compass [1], that has been evaluated for its correctness through testing. This activity requires the AADL specification, and produces a specification in the form of OCRA contracts. The contract specification is evaluated using consistency checking. The refinement activity requires the OCRA contract specification and uses another tool, the OCRA tool, in order to do the refinement. This tool has also been tested.

3   Confidence Argument Patterns

Patterns are widely used in software engineering as a way of abstracting the fundamental design strategies from the details of particular designs [4]. The use of patterns as a way of documenting and reusing successful assurance argument structures was pioneered by Kelly [11]. Assurance argument patterns provide

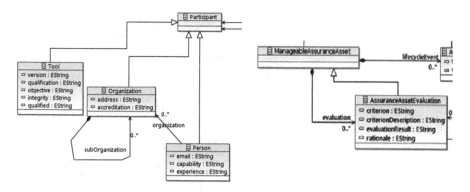

Fig. 3. Sub-types of Participant available in the process meta-model (left) and Extract from the evidence meta-model used in creating process models (right)

a way of capturing the required form of an assurance argument in a manner that is abstract from the details of a particular argument. It is then possible to use the patterns to create specific arguments by instantiating the patterns in a manner appropriate to the application. Assurance argument patterns are a very useful technique as they can help to ensure a consistent approach is applied when similar assurance claims are required in different systems. It also provides a way of sharing experience across projects.

Figure 5 shows an assurance argument pattern we have developed that can be used to argue the trustworthiness of a process activity. This could be used to support the argument we presented in Fig. 1. This argument pattern could be instantiated for an activity using information in a process model such as that shown in Fig. 4.

This argument structure can be seen to make claims over the trustworthiness of the participants of the activity, the required and produced artefacts, the techniques used and the sub-activities. For each of these elements of the process, the argument shows they are sufficiently trustworthy through consideration of their demonstrable attributes. The notion of what is sufficiently trustworthy for a process element is driven firstly by the confidence required in the artefact being generated. As discussed in Sect. 1, this is determined by the assurance required for the system as a whole, and the role of the artefact in the overall system argument. Errors in some evidence artefacts will have less impact on the assurance of the system, and the level of confidence required in such cases is correspondingly reduced.

The trustworthiness of the process must reflect the confidence required in the artefact itself. For each element of the process, it is necessary to take account of the role that the process element itself plays as part of the process to generate the artefact. For example, errors in a tool that generates an input file for an activity may be mitigated by other elements of the process, such as manual review of that input file or the provision of multiple inputs. In such cases the level of trust required for that element may be reduced. What this means is that the claim

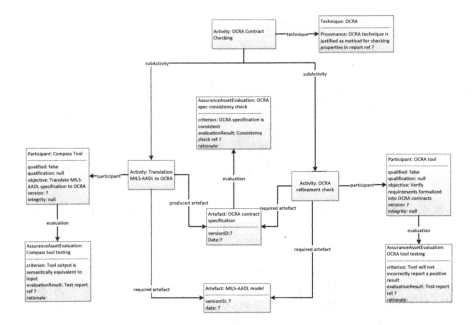

Fig. 4. Process model for OCRA contract checking

that the element is sufficiently trustworthy must be interpreted for each element based upon a consideration of its role in the process. In some domains, and some standards, the notion of sufficiently trustworthy evidence is codified, such as requirements for testing and review to be performed by independent persons in DO-178C [17] and accepted and established notions of competency and tool qualification. Where such guidance exists this can also be used to help ensure proportionality in the process argument.

We have created argument patterns for all the process elements considered in the argument pattern in Fig. 5, full details of these patterns are provided in [3]. Figure 6 shows one of these patterns, the argument pattern for creating arguments regarding the artefacts required by a process. This argument uses the evaluations performed on the artefact, plus attributes of the artefact, such as its version number and defined evaluation criterion, to form the confidence argument. The argument patterns for all of the elements of a process can similarly be instantiated from a process model such as the one in Fig. 4.

4   Instantiating Argument Patterns

Instantiating an assurance argument pattern involves identifying the necessary information relating to the target system, required to choose and instantiate the assurance claims and to provide the required evidence. In this sense the instantiable elements of the patterns define requirements for information. It is

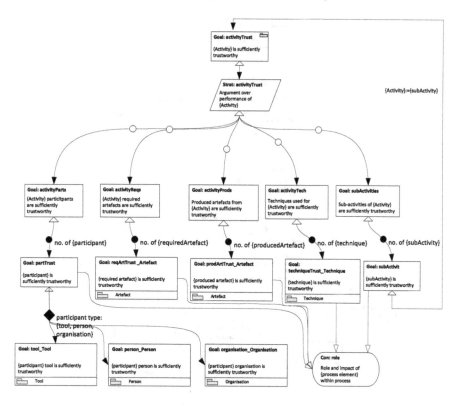

Fig. 5. Assurance argument pattern for confidence arguments

possible to manually obtain this information and instantiate the argument patterns; this is current practice. A manual approach however is often not ideal. The instantiation is often repetitive and mechanistic in nature and prone to human error. Manual instantiation can also be time consuming and inconsistent. In [7] we described a model-based approach to automated instantiation of assurance argument patterns, based upon the specification of a weaving model that describes the dependencies between abstract elements of the argument pattern and elements of various system models for the target system. At instantiation, information is extracted from the relevant model elements of the target system to create the assurance argument. Our previous work on applying our approach ([6,7]) has focussed predominantly on the automated instantiation of the technical argument. To move to a more complete automation of the assurance case, automation of the confidence argument is also required. Below we describe how the process model and confidence argument patterns presented can be used to create an assurance argument for a claim regarding a formal property of our example system as part of an assurance case for that system. Firstly we identify a claim we wish to support as part of the assurance case for the example system. In this case a claim is required for each formal property specified as

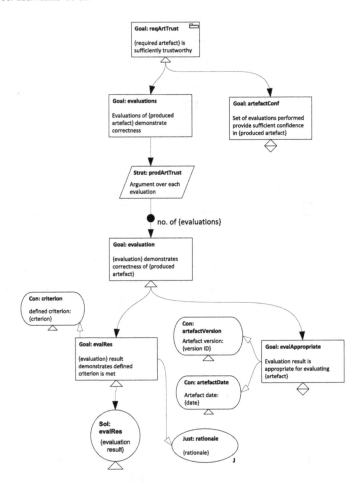

Fig. 6. Assurance argument pattern for artefacts

part of the AADL specification of the system. One such claim is shown in Fig. 7, which follows the form presented in Fig. 1. In this case the formal property to be satisfied is "always (outL > high_bound)". This is one of a number of specified properties of the AADL model required in order to guarantee the security of the system. The result of an OCRA contract check is used to demonstrate this property. Following the structure of Fig. 1, the trustworthiness of the OCRA contract checking must be demonstrated for this argument to be compelling (Goal: activityTrust_Process). The OCRA checking process model in Fig. 4 can be used in conjunction with the confidence argument patterns to create an argument to support this claim. An extract showing just the top level of the resulting argument is shown in Fig. 8. This argument structure instantiation is completed using the patterns for each aspect of the model such as Fig. 6.

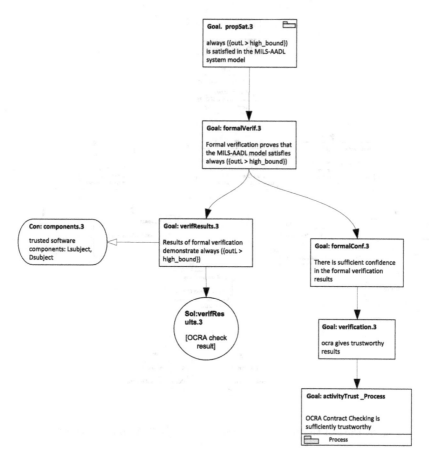

Fig. 7. Part of the assurance argument for an example system

To make the process of instantiating the confidence argument patterns from the process models for a system easier and less error prone it is possible to make use of the model-based assurance case tool that we have developed to automatically generate the confidence argument from the process model. Below we briefly describe how the tool works.

– Argument patterns are created in machine-readable format using a graphical editor that creates a model in an XML form from a graphical representation of the argument pattern in GSN. We refer to these files (that are compliant with a GSN meta-model) as GSNML files.
– A weaving model is created to define links between elements in other models. In this case links are specified between GSN pattern models and the system or process models. The weaving model is then used as the specification for model transformations to generate the output model (instantiated assurance argument). The current version of the tool uses an interim solution for creating

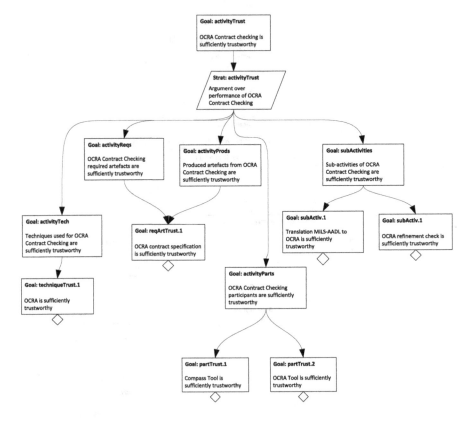

Fig. 8. Part of the confidence argument for OCRA contract checking

weaving models that involves creating the weaving models graphically and importing them to the tool as graphML files.

- The MBAC (Model Based Assurance Case) program is executed. This is an Epsilon Object Language (eol) program [12] that runs on the Eclipse platform. It takes the GSNML argument pattern files, the system and process models and corresponding meta-models, and the weaving model as inputs. The output is a GSN argument model for the target system that has been instantiated using information extracted from the system models.
- The argument model is generated as a GSNML file. This GSNML file can then be used to present information to the user in a number of ways. Firstly, the argument model can be represented graphically as a GSN structure. Secondly, the model can be queried in order to provide a particular view on the assurance case. For example it is possible to just select those argument elements that remain undeveloped, requiring additional support from the system developer. Finally an instantiation table can also be generated that summarises how the pattern has been instantiated in tabular form, rather than having to consult the entire argument structure.

Using the model-based assurance case tool described above it becomes possible to:

- Automatically select the appropriate process model relevant to the evidence artefact cited in the assurance argument.
- Automatically populate the confidence argument pattern using information extracted from the process model.

It is important to note that when adopting this approach, thorough review of the assurance argument is still, as always, essential. However, rather than focussing review on the correctness of each argument created, the review effort can instead be focussed on the sufficiency of the pattern structure and the validity of the weaving model. Both of these, once reviewed can then be re-used for each instantiation. Another important focus for review becomes whether the role of each element of the process has been correctly interpreted, and whether what has been generated corresponds to this interpretation. We believe that in contrast to needing to review for correctness each time, this shift in focus helps to achieve more value from the review effort.

5   Conclusions

When creating an assurance justification for a system, the focus is often on the technical aspects of the assurance argument. The important confidence aspects are often addressed only in very general terms. Assurance cases are improved through provision of more focussed confidence arguments that address the integrity of specific artefacts through justification of the processes used. Creating such confidence arguments can be an onerous task for systems using complex processes and highly integrated tool chains. In this paper we have described how compelling confidence arguments can be developed directly from existing process models with the help of confidence argument patterns. We have described how existing tools can be used to automatically generate these arguments.

Acknowledgements. This work was part funded by the European Union FP7 D-MILS project (www.d-mils.org).

References

1. The COMPASS Project Web Site. http://compass.informatik.rwth-aachen.de/
2. Opencoss Consortium. Common Certification Language: Conceptual Model D4.4 version 1.4 (2015). http://www.opencoss-project.eu/
3. Integration of Formal Evidence and Expression in MILS Assurance Case. Technical report D4.3, D-MILS Project, March 2015. http://www.d-mils.org/page/results
4. Gamma, E., Johnson, R., Helm, R., Vlissides, J., Patterns, D.: Elements of Reusable Object-Oriented Software. Addison-Wesley, Boston (1994)
5. Goal Structuring Notation Working Group: GSN Community Standard Volume 1 (2011)

6. Hawkins, R., Habli, I., Kelly, T.: The need for a weaving model in assurance case automation. Ada User J. **36**(3), 187–191

7. Hawkins, R., Habli, I., Kolovos, D., Paige, R., Kelly, T.: Weaving an assurance case from design: a model-based approach. In: Proceedings of the 16th IEEE International Symposium on High Assurance Systems Engineering (2015)

8. Hawkins, R.D., Kelly, T.P., Knight, J., Graydon, P.: A new approach to creating clear safety arguments. In: Dale, C., Anderson, T. (eds.) Advances in Systems Safety, pp. 3–23. Springer, London (2011)

9. IEC: IEC 61508 - Functional Safety of Electrical/Electronic/Programmable Electronic Safety-Related Systems. Technical report IEC 61508, The International Electrotechnical Commission (1998)

10. ISO: ISO 26262 - Road Vehicles Functional Safety. Technical report ISO 26262, ISO, Geneva, Switzerland (2011)

11. Kelly, T.: Arguing safety a systematic approach to safety case management. Ph.D. thesis, The University of York

12. Kolovos, D., Rose, L., Garcia-Dominguez, A., Paige, R.: The Epsilon book (2013). http://www.eclipse.org/epsilon/doc/book/

13. Object Management Group. Software and Systems Process Engineering Metamodel Specification (SPEM) version 2.0 (2008)

14. The Othello Contract Refinement Analysis (OCRA) Tool. https://es.fbk.eu/tools/ocra

15. International Society of Automotive Engineers. Architecture Analysis and Design Language Annex (AADL), vol. 1. SAE Standard AS 5506/1, SAE, June 2006

16. Object Management Group (OMG). Structured Assurance Case Metamodel (SACM), Version 1.0 (2013)

17. RTCA. DO-178C - Software Considerations in Airborne Systems and Equipment Certification. Technical report DO-178C, RTCA (2011)

18. Nair, S., Walkinshaw, N., Kelly, T., de la Vara, J.L.: An evidential reasoning approach for assessing confidence in safety evidence. In: Proceedings of the 26th IEEE International Symposium on Software Reliability Engineering (ISSRE 2015) (2015)

19. Steinberg, D., Budinsky, F., Paternostro, M., Merks, E.: EMF: Eclipse Modeling Framework, 2nd edn. Addison-Wesley, Boston (2008)

20. Sun, L.: Establishing confidence in safety assessment evidence. Ph.D. thesis, University of York (2012)

The Indispensable Role of Rationale
in Safety Standards

John C. Knight[(⊠)] and Jonathan Rowanhill

Dependable Computing, Charlottesville, VA, USA
{john.knight,jonathan.rowanhill}
@dependablecomputing.com

Abstract. In this paper, we argue that standards, especially those intended to support critical applications, should define explicitly both the properties expected to accrue from use of the standard and an explicit rationale that justifies the contents of the standard. Current standards do not include an explicit, comprehensive rationale. Without a rationale, the use, maintenance, and revision of standards is unnecessarily difficult. We introduce a new concept for standards, the rationalized standard. A rationalized standard combines: (a) an explicit goal defining a property desired for conformant systems, (b) guidance that, if followed correctly, should yield an entity with the property stated in the goal, and (c) the rationale showing the reasoning why there is assurance with reasonable confidence that a conformant entity will have the property defined by the goal. We illustrate the utility of an explicit rationale using an existing safety standard, ISO 26262.

Keywords: Standards · System safety · Rigorous argument

1 Introduction

Safety standards such as ARP 4754 [1], ARP 4761 [2], IEC 61508 [3], and Mil Std 882E [4] have served the community well. They provide a repository of expert knowledge, foster consistency in the community, and document the expectations that arise when regulating agencies use standards conformance as a basis for approval. The role of a standard as a knowledge repository is especially important, because the knowledge usually originates from many experts and is subject to analysis and synthesis before becoming part of the standard. No single engineer or a small group is likely to have the composite background and experience of those who developed an officially accepted safety standard.

Despite their value, safety standards have been criticized in a variety of ways [5–7]. Standards have difficulty addressing the needs of individual systems or particular circumstances, and rarely define precisely what conformance will mean or how it will be assessed.

The most serious weakness with existing standards, however, is that, in almost all cases, conformance to a safety standard does not lead to assurance that the conforming system has any specific property or properties other than those required to demonstrate conformance. A conforming system is viewed as generally suitable for its intended use,

© Springer International Publishing Switzerland 2016
A. Skavhaug et al. (Eds.): SAFECOMP 2016, LNCS 9922, pp. 39–50, 2016.
DOI: 10.1007/978-3-319-45477-1_4

but use of a conforming system is based on an assumption that the system has one or more specific, implied but unstated properties.

At the heart of this problem is the fact that standards almost never include explicit documentation of the *rationale* for their contents. Developers produce evidence artifacts defined by the standard, and conformance experts examine these artifacts. With no explicit rationale for the evidence, both developers and conformance experts have to rely on their own knowledge of why the standard calls for certain forms of evidence and can do little more than check the form of the evidence produced. Frequently, conformance reduces to an almost meaningless checklist activity that ignores the technical *intent* of the standard.

In this paper, we introduce the *rationalized standard*. A rationalized standard combines: (a) an explicit *goal* defining a property desired for conformant systems, (b) *guidance* that, if followed correctly, should yield an entity with the property stated in the goal, and (c) the *rationale* showing the reasoning why there is assurance with reasonable confidence that a conformant entity will have the property defined by the goal.

The intent of a rationalized standard is *not* to simply improve the rigor of a standard; the intent is to change the relationship between a standard and the associated prerequisite knowledge in a fundamental way. Changing this relationship leads to a new and rigorous mechanism for using a standard.

The focus of this paper is safety standards although we note that the analysis is applicable to standards in general. This paper is organized as follows. In the next section we discuss the detailed circumstances of current standards, and in Sect. 3 we present the details of rationalized standards. In Sect. 4 we illustrate the potential value of an explicit rationale by examining an existing safety standard, and in Sect. 5 we present our conclusions.

2   Current Standards

2.1   Development of Standards

An overview of the way in which existing standards are developed and applied is shown in Fig. 1. Most standards are developed by committees. A group of experts, the authors of the standard, convene based upon a perceived demand for a standard in the associated technical area. Each expert brings his or her own knowledge, both tacit and explicit, to the committee's deliberations.

The content of the evolving standard is the result of group meetings, discussions, drafts of the standard, white papers, etc. During these deliberations, individual elements of the standard are proposed, examined, refined, and either accepted or rejected resulting in a collective view of what the standard should contain. This view is then refined into a documented entity consisting of rules and guidelines. These rules and guidelines in turn define evidence that must be provided by developers using the standard to demonstrate conformance. The *intent* is that conformance to the framework will assure particular qualities of engineering entities such as development processes, development artifacts, or complete systems. But the rationale for the content of the standard, though it existed, at least in the minds of the authoring committee members, is not available to either developers or conformance experts. In fact, the rationale was essentially discarded once development of the standard was complete and the committee disbanded.

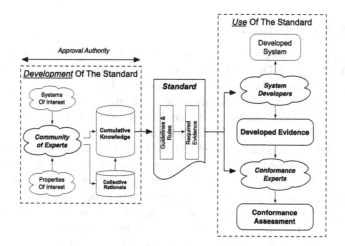

Fig. 1. Standards development and use as currently practiced.

2.2 Using Standards

Once developed, standards are put to use. No matter how careful the development process was, questions arise about interpretation, applicability, conformance, etc. To illustrate the difficulties that arise over time with current, static standards we examine a standard that was widely used for software assurance in avionics systems until recently, RTCA DO-178B [8]. Our use of this particular standard as an example is not intended to be critical of DO-178B in any way.

DO-178B was published in 1992 and replaced by DO-178C [9] only in 2012. During the twenty years that DO-178B was in effect, several documents were produced to supplement the standard including:

DO-248B. This guidance document is entitled "Final Annual Report for Clarification of DO-178B 'Software Considerations In Airborne Systems And Equipment Certification'" and was published in 2001 [10]. It was developed in response to hundreds of questions about DO-178B.

FAA Order 8110.49. This FAA order is entitled "Software Approval Guidelines". It provides a great deal of guidance on the software approval process, i.e., how compliance with DO-178B should be judged.

Certification Authorities Software Team (CAST) Position Papers. CAST papers are neither official policy nor guidance and are provided for educational and informational purposes. Nevertheless, they do play a role in supplementing the DO-178B standard. Twenty six CAST papers have been written to support DO-178B.

FAA Advisory Circular 20-148. This document is entitled "Reusable Software Components" and provides guidance for software reuse in the context of DO-178B.

Clearly the need for clarification in many different areas arose when the DO-178B standard was applied. We hypothesize that having an explicit rationale would have reduced the need for supplementary material substantially.

2.3 Maintenance of Standards

As is clear from the example in the previous section of the supplementary material that has been developed for DO-178B, those using a standard are likely to find defects, omissions or limitations. In addition, advances in technology will occur that could bring value to developers, but such advances are often prohibited because an existing standard does not address the new technology. Both of these circumstances motivate the need over time to modify the standard in some way.

Modification of a standard is closely related to developing the standard in the first place. The key difference between the development and subsequent modification of a standard is that the latter activity has one additional input, the standard itself.

Modifying a standard successfully requires a deep understanding of the standard and all of the technology that the standard references. Thus, as with development, modifications are: (a) often undertaken by a committee of experts, and (b) occur infrequently because of the difficulties and resource levels required.

Clearly, those undertaking a modification to a standard require access to the "why" of the content and the existing form of the standard in order to understand fully the ramifications of a modification. In other words, those undertaking a modification require access to the usually unavailable rationale for the original standard.

3 Rationalized Standards

3.1 The Concept

We conclude from the previous section that the explicit rationale for a standard as an integral part of the standard could provide great value. How then could the rationale be included in a standard? The rationale cannot merely be a new section added to an existing standard structure with no other change. The overall structure used for standards needs to be revised to both accommodate and take advantage of the introduction of the rationale.

In this section we introduce the *rationalized standard*. A rationalized standard emerges from recognition that the rationale for a standard is the *fundamental* content of the standard. The rationale is neither precursory nor supplementary; it argues, from first principles backed by sound evidence, why a set of proscriptive and prescriptive guidance will assure with reasonable confidence that an engineering entity holds a certain property that is stated explicitly.

The explicit rationale moves the rationale from the realm of *informality* and *oral tradition* into the realm of *rigor* and *written tradition*. Furthermore, it *models* the guidance of the standard as part of the rationale. The introduction of the rationale would restructure the associated standard and integrate revised versions of much of the existing material. Thus, the rationale need not lead to a major increase in the length of the standard, although the practical effect on length would have to be determined by experiment.

Figure 2 shows the three key components of a rationalized standard. At the top of the figure is the *Desired Property* (or properties) to be assured for a conformant system. At the bottom of the figure is the *Guidance* that defines conformance. In between is the *Reasoning* for why conformance engenders belief in the Desired Property.

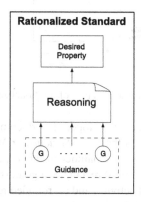

Fig. 2. The three key components of a rationalized standard.

The guidance specifies a set of items of evidence that must be obtained about the subject system by the system's developers. If the evidence is supplied and is sufficient, i.e., the subject system is determined to be conformant, then the reasoning leads to belief in the desired property. Ensuring that the reasoning is adequate to justify this belief is the responsibility of the authors of the standard.

The manner in which a rationalized standard would be used is shown in Fig. 3. Developers reference the reasoning in the standard in order to determine the suitability of the standard for their application and to map the evidence specifications in the guidance to their application. Conformance assessment requires judgment as to whether the evidence supplied meets the specification in the guidance.

3.2   Defining Reasoning

A convenient way to document reasoning is as a rigorous argument, and a hierarchical structure known as a *goal structure* is an effective way to represent an argument. A goal structure begins with a top-level goal that is decomposed into sub-goals such that belief in the top-level goal is justified by belief in the sub-goals using a documented strategy that links the sub-goals to the top-level goal. In the case of a standard, the top-level goal is the desired property. Each sub-goal in the goal structure is then decomposed into sub-goals that are further decomposed, and so on until leaf sub-goals are reached. A leaf sub-goal is a goal for which belief can be justified directly by supplied evidence.

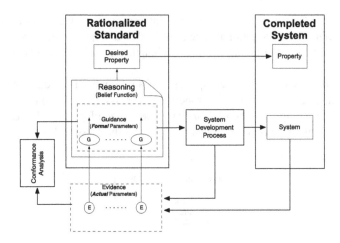

Fig. 3. Practical application of a rationalized standard.

Various notations have been developed for documenting arguments, and one notation that is in common use is the *Goal Structuring Notation* (GSN) [11]. We use GSN to document arguments in the remainder of this paper. The syntactic elements of GSN that we use in this paper are: (a) rectangle: a goal, (b) circle: an item of evidence such as results of a software test activity, and (c) rounded rectangle: an item of context – rigorous arguments are defined for a specific context such as the system's planned operating environment(s).

3.3   Defining Guidance

Recall that guidance is the specification of evidence that, if supplied and determined to be sufficient, justifies belief in the associated leaf goal. There are two forms that guidance can take in this case:

1. A statement of the leaf sub-goal and the required level of confidence that the evidence will justify belief in the sub-goal.
2. A statement of the explicit evidence that is required for the sub-goal.

As an example, suppose that, as part of the rationale for a safety standard, a leaf sub-goal is that the system software will ensure real-time task schedulability with an ultra-high level of assurance. This sub-goal derives from the overall safety goal of the system, and safety will be compromised without ultra-high assurance of schedulability.

Stating the sub-goal in order to define the evidence requirement (guidance form 1 above) is insufficient, because the level of confidence required is so high. The evidence needed for this sub-goal will not be sufficient if, for example, developers chose testing as an appropriate form of evidence. In this case, the rationale will specify specific forms of evidence. For example, the use of a static form of scheduling such as a time-triggered protocol together with a proof of the static schedule.

The structure shown in Fig. 2 is similar to an assurance case [12]. This similarity is not a coincidence. In essence what is required of a standard is an assurance case that will document the reason for belief that a conformant system has a desired property. The difference between a rationalized standard and a traditional assurance case is that the former has to be reusable whereas the latter is system specific.

4 Analysis of a Safety Standard

In order to illustrate the concept of a rationalized standard, we examine a small piece of an existing safety standard, ISO 26262 [13]. Our use of this particular standard as an example is not intended to be critical of ISO 26262 in any way.

ISO 26262 was published in 2011 and is organized into ten parts. Our examples come from Part 6 entitled: "Product development at the software level". For simplicity, we limit our examples to Automotive Safety Integrity Level (ASIL) D, the highest integrity level.

4.1 Example Element

Section 5.4.7 of ISO 26262 Part 6 has no specific title but is part of Section 5.4 entitled "Requirements and recommendations". Section 5.4.7 addresses, in part, software design and implementation correctness. The majority of the content of Section 5.4.7 is a table listing eight techniques, the use of which the standard defines as "highly recommend" for ASIL D applications. The bulk of that table is reproduced here as Table 1 and the following footnotes.

Table 1. ISO 26262 Part 6 Section 5.4.7

Topics to be covered by modelling and coding guidelines	ASIL D
1a	Enforcement of low complexity[a]	Highly recommended
1b	Use of language subsets[b]	Highly recommended
1c	Enforcement of strong typing[c]	Highly recommended
1d	Use of defensive implementation techniques	Highly recommended
1e	Use of established design principles	Highly recommended
1f	Use of unambiguous graphical representation	Highly recommended
1g	Use of style guides	Highly recommended
1h	Use of naming conventions	Highly recommended

Footnotes:

[a]An appropriate compromise of this topic with other methods in this part of ISO 26262 may be required.

[b]Exclusion of ambiguously defined language constructs which may be interpreted differently by different modellers, programmers, code generators or compilers.

Exclusion of language constructs which from experience easily lead to mistakes, for example assignments in conditions or identical naming of local and global variables.

Exclusion of language constructs which could result in unhandled run-time errors.

[c]The objective of method 1c is to impose principles of strong typing where these are not inherent in the language.

4.2 Analysis of Example Element

To begin the analysis, we attempted to reconstruct the rationale for the example element. Although no rationale is included in ISO 26262, we examined the subject element and tried to identify: (a) the properties that conformance to the element should yield, (b) the evidence that should be produced, and (c) the reason for belief that the properties follow from conformance.

The intent of ISO 26262 Part 6, Section 5.4.7 is stated as:

> *"To support the correctness of the design and implementation, the design and coding guidelines for the modelling, or programming languages, shall address the topics listed in* Table 1."

We infer that the property intended is "the correctness of the design and implementation". The intended strategy is for the user to apply coding and design guidelines from Table 1, with the user providing suitable evidence. How this guidance helps fulfill correctness of design and implementation is not presented and is left to the reader's intuition. For example, line 1b in Table 1 ("Use of language subsets") gives examples of the type of issue that might be avoided by restricting the use of certain language features but defines neither a sub-goal for this guidance nor a complete set of properties that are desired from this guidance.

Presently, ISO 26262 is built around the philosophy of "organized containers of best practice". Table 1 is a container of techniques related to "correctness of design and implementation" by a common theme of software tools and techniques. But it is neither exhaustive nor definitive with respect to "correctness", "design", or "implementation", nor tools or techniques. Other related containers, organized by *themes*, are presented elsewhere in ISO 26262. Collectively, the standard implies (but does not state) that the thematic containers, when taken as a whole, will yield adequately safe software.

An example of the difficulties that arise with implicit arguments occurs with item 1b and footnote b – they should be *reversed*. The statement of "how" (use a language subset) is placed before the statement of "what" (avoid specific classes of fault). In practice there might be other techniques that could avoid the fault classes.

As a second example, consider that Line 1c in Table 1, "Enforcement of strong typing". This line merely indicates "how" one could reduce software faults, with no indication of "why" strong typing impacts the subject system. An implied community understanding of the utility of strong typing does not facilitate a comprehensive and uniform understanding of the role that it plays.

The standard does not define the evidence that is expected in order to conform to the guidelines. Evidence is crucial if rigorous (possibly independent) conformance checking is to be undertaken. The standard needs to either define evidence that would be considered sufficient or define precise specifications of sufficient evidence.

The standard notes:

"Coding guidelines are usually different for different programming languages."

This observation is correct but does not preclude requiring, for a specific use of the standard, the development of one or more sub-goals for the associated guidance together with an appropriate language subset definition. Some languages are in common use and could be addressed specifically by the standard as an example.

Finally, we note that terms such as "complexity", "language subset" and "naming convention" have intuitive meanings, but intuition is not sufficient in dealing with challenging issues such as software correctness. ISO 26262 Part 1 is composed entirely of the definitions of terms but does not include definitions of these terms.

In summary, the important observations about this example are:

The properties of the software that are expected to follow from conformance to the guidance i.e., why the guidance should be observed, are not stated precisely.

The specific items of evidence that should be produced in order to justify conformance are neither defined nor specified.

The rationale for the guidance, i.e., why following the guidance implies a desired software property, is not stated. The standard is organized around collections of best practice and does not convey how these practices lead to a useful property.

The purpose of a rationalized standard is to provide a structure within which all of these issues are dealt with, so that a standard conveys why things add up, not just what adds up.

4.3   Rationalized Standard Fragment

Developing the rationale for the properties in the set listed in Table 1 is a tempting approach. But the existing ISO 26262 implied rationale is structurally weak for the reasons stated in Sect. 4.2. For example, important techniques could be missed, because they cut *across* themes.

A potential improvement would be to organize the rationale along a more compelling axis as shown in Fig. 4. In this organization, the top-level goal of the rationale is *fitness for use* in the target application, where fitness for use could reasonably be defined as: (a) the software meets stated requirements, and (b) the software avoids states that could lead to an identified system hazard. Combined, these indicate that the software does what is expected and prevents known hazards, and could be judged to be adequately safe. We note that avoiding identified hazards is an example of a cross-cutting theme related to "why" the system is safe. With this framing of the top-level goal, a decomposition into sub-goals is carried out based on best practices.

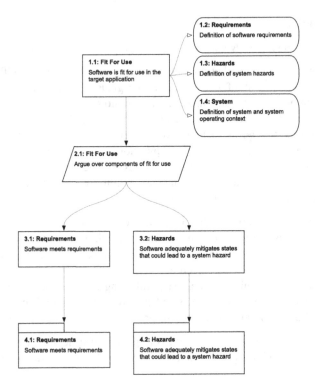

Fig. 4. Top-level rationale arguing fitness for use defined using the Goal Structuring Notation

The lowest level of the goal structure for the refined rationale shown in Fig. 4 consists of two modules (4.1 and 4.2). A module is merely a means of encapsulating an argument fragment that is defined elsewhere. Rather than showing the content of these modules in GSN, for purposes of illustration, we provide an informal, text description of a possible goal structure for the "Requirements" module.

The goal "Software meets requirements" (the Requirements module) might be refined to two sub-goals: "Software meets functional requirements" and "Software meets non-functional requirements". An effective way to argue that a software entity meets functional requirements is to argue: (a) that the defined functionality is provided, and (b) the absence of faults in the software. Thus, the sub-goal "Software meets functional requirements" might be refined into a set of sub-goals; one for each element of functionality and one for each element in a taxonomy of fault classes. Each fault class would be addressed in the standard's guidance by suitable techniques of fault avoidance or fault elimination. This finally brings the goal structure down to a suitably low level of abstraction that specific techniques such as those in Table 1 can be introduced.

An example of this type of rationale is shown in Fig. 5. The black "dot" on the inference linking nodes 4.1 and 5.1 indicates repetition; a means of abstraction in the rationale. The associated guidance should be applied to each functional element of the applicant system, as provided by the user.

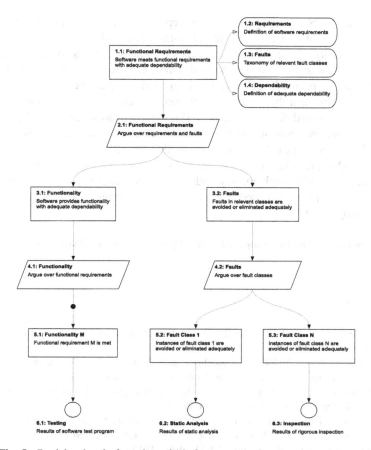

Fig. 5. Partial rationale for sub-goal "Software meets functional requirements"

5   Conclusion

Despite the value of existing safety standards, introducing an explicit rationale into a standard has the potential to improve the clarity, utility, and adaptability of standards considerably. These improvements emerge because the rationale for a standard becomes explicit information, retaining analyzable knowledge about the standard. The rationale enables incremental change as well as comparison and fitness with other rationales. Communities of practice can interact analytically with both the justification for the standard and with demonstration of conformance.

A rationale is intended to shed light on the "why" of a standard, material that is routinely discarded once a standard is published. The net result of explicit rationale, therefore, should be a significant increase in the efficacy of the application of standards, their maintenance and enhancement, and the associated conformance assessment.

Introducing the rationale to a standard might seem likely to increase its length. This could happen, but the impression we have formed from analyzing ISO 26262 is that the rationale will replace large volumes of text rather than merely be an addition. Although we have used GSN in this paper, textual representations of arguments have been developed and might be well suited to rationalized standards.

The availability of the rationale facilitates community discussion about the technical content of the standard and possible desirable enhancements. Valid and desirable enhancements are inevitable and would be integrated into periodic, controlled releases.

Finally, we note that the rationale is not meant to introduce prescriptive techniques that would be required for conformance. The evidence documented in the rationale would constrain developers only to the extent that would be necessary to ensure that the associated goals were met. Standards such as ISO 26262 already include recommendations for techniques and thus associated evidence. All that the rationale would do is to structure and justify such recommendations. Using alternative techniques would certainly be appropriate provided developers created a refined rationale that justified their technological choices.

Acknowledgment. This work supported in part by NASA Contract NNL13AA08C.

References

1. SAE International. ARP4754: Guidelines for Development of Civil Aircraft and Systems (2010)
2. SAE International. ARP4761: Guidelines and Methods for Conducting the Safety Assessment Process on Civil Airborne Systems and Equipment (1996)
3. IEC 61508: Functional safety of electrical/electronic/programmable electronic safety-related systems, International Electrotechnical Commission (1998)
4. Mil-Std-882E. Department of Defense Standard Practice System Safety (2012)
5. Fenton, N.E., Neil, M.: A strategy for improving safety related software engineering standards. IEEE Trans. Softw. Eng. **24**(11), 1002–1013 (1998)
6. Knight, J.: Safety standards – a new approach. In: 22nd Safety-Critical Systems Symposium, Brighton, UK (2014)
7. Laporte, C.Y., O'Connor, R.V., Paucar, L.H.G., Gerancon, B.: An innovative approach in developing standard professionals by involving software engineering students in implementing and improving international standards. Stand. Eng.: J. Soc. Stand. Prof. **67** (2), 1–9 (2015)
8. RTCA Inc.: DO-178B, Software Considerations in Airborne Systems and Equipment Certification (1992)
9. RTCA Inc.: DO-178C, Software Considerations in Airborne Systems and Equipment Certification (2012)
10. RTCA Inc.: DO-248B, Final Annual Report for Clarification of DO-178B Software Considerations in Airborne Systems and Equipment Certification (2001)
11. Kelly, T., Weaver, R.: The goal structuring notation–a safety argument notation. In: Proceedings DSN 2004 Workshop on Assurance Cases, Florence, Italy (2004)
12. Software Engineering Institute, Assurance cases, Carnegie Mellon University. http://www.sei.cmu.edu/dependability/tools/assurancecase/
13. International Organization for Standardization, ISO 26262: Road vehicles–functional safety (2011)

Composition of Safety Argument Patterns

Ewen Denney[⊠] and Ganesh Pai[⊠]

SGT/NASA Ames Research Center, Moffett Field, CA 94035, USA
{ewen.denney,ganesh.pai}@nasa.gov

Abstract. Argument structure patterns can be used to represent classes
of safety arguments. Such patterns can become quite complex, making
use of loops and choices, posing a potential challenge for comprehen-
sion and evaluation, offsetting the likely gains that might follow from
creating arguments using them. We show how complex patterns can be
constructed by *composition* of simpler patterns. We provide a formal
basis for pattern composition and show that this notion satisfies certain
desirable properties. Furthermore, we show that it is always possible to
construct complex patterns by omposition in this way. We motivate this
work with example patterns extracted from real aviation safety cases,
and illustrate the application of the theory on the same.

Keywords: Argumentation · Composition · Patterns · Safety cases ·
Unmanned aircraft systems

1   Introduction

Over the past few years, we have been involved in engineering a number of
real safety cases for unmanned aircraft system (UAS) operations: initially, those
concerning NASA Earth science missions [1] and, more recently, increasingly
complex aeronautics research missions[1]. Our previous safety cases have successfully undergone review and approval by the Federal Aviation Administration
(FAA), the US civil aviation regulator, while the more recent ones are either
undergoing FAA review, or are in development.

The current set of guidelines governing UAS operational approval [2] does not
explicitly require the use of argumentation in a safety case. However, the guidelines do require that an explanation be supplied for how the hazard mitigation
measures specified in the safety case are expected to reduce risk. Indeed, we have
found argumentation to be largely useful for that purpose and, using our methodology for developing assurance arguments [3], we have slowly begun including
structured arguments in the safety case (reports) to organize and document the
reasons why the intended operations can be expected to be acceptably safe.

Based on our previous, and ongoing effort, and the experience gained, a number of observations follow to motivate the work in this paper. Firstly, many of the

---

[1] As part of NASA's UAS traffic management (UTM) effort: http://utm.arc.nasa.
gov/.

© Springer International Publishing Switzerland 2016
A. Skavhaug et al. (Eds.): SAFECOMP 2016, LNCS 9922, pp. 51–63, 2016.
DOI: 10.1007/978-3-319-45477-1_5

UAS operations have been the first of their kind conducted in civil airspace.[2] Individually, they have unique mission-specific constraints and safety requirements; so, much of the associated safety reasoning is also tailored to the mission. Taking the various operations together, we have been able to identify similarities amongst the associated hazard control mechanisms and safety systems, e.g., ground-based surveillance, safe separation measures, a suite of avoidance maneuvers, emergency procedures for off-nominal situations, etc. That, in turn, has allowed us to develop both domain-independent and domain-specific patterns of safety reasoning – clarifying how the identified Safety measures contribute to risk reduction – which we have specified as argument structure patterns in the Goal Structuring Notation(GSN) using our tool, AdvoCATE [4].

Next, going forward we want to design the required safety systems for future UAS missions by carefully leveraging as many reusable safety assets that have a successful operational history, as possible. In conjunction, we want to apply our argument development methodology, and construct the corresponding safety case(s) from a combination of the relevant safety reasoning patterns, and tailored arguments, as appropriate. Intuitively, there is a need for exploring how patterns (and/or arguments) can be combined.

Third, as mission complexity grows, the associated safety cases can also be expected to become larger and more complex. In fact, that has indeed been our own experience. The way in which argument patterns are composed, and the results of such composition, can be thought of as providing a view of the overall *architecture* of the safety case and, thereby, an insight into the 'big picture' of how the safety measures contribute to managing risk. Moreover, by using argument patterns and their composition to the extent possible, we expect to be able to generate large parts of the arguments through automatic pattern instantiation [5]. We further anticipate that this will allow us to better manage the complexity of the safety cases we create while also amortizing the effort expended in their development.

As such, the main goal (and contribution) of this paper is a (preliminary) formulation of the formal foundations for composing GSN argument patterns. First, we give a running example to illustrate the intuition underlying the theory (Sect. 2). Specifically, we give some simple patterns which we extracted from the UAS safety cases we authored. Then, on the basis of this example, we formalize the notion of composition (Sect. 3), after which we illustrate how we have applied composition in practice (Sect. 4). We conclude this paper contrasting our work with related research, and identifying avenues for future research (Sect. 5).

2   Illustrative Example

For what follows, we assume familiarity with GSN for specifying arguments/patterns, and refer interested readers to [5] and [6] for details on GSN syntax and semantics. We have extracted a number of simple patterns of safety reasoning from the initial UAS safety cases we created. Figure 1 shows a selection

---

[2] To our knowledge, at least in the US, and within a non-military context.

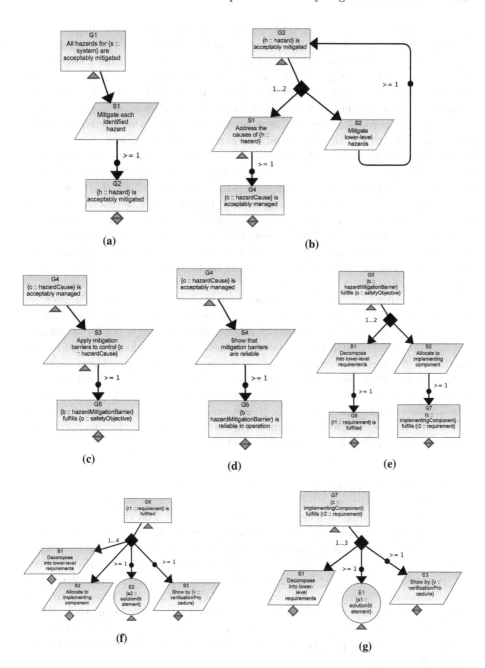

Fig. 1. A selection of simple, domain-independent GSN argument patterns extracted from real UAS safety cases, representing part of the reasoning underlying (*i*) risk reduction with the use of mitigation barriers and (*ii*) how mitigation barriers satisfy their applicable safety objectives. We will subsequently compose these patterns (see Fig. 2, which composes the latter three, and Fig. 4, which composes the former four).

of those patterns, given using GSN pattern syntax[3] and representing, respectively: hazard enumeration (Fig. 1a); mitigating a specific hazard by enumerating its causes or by hierarchical decomposition over its constituent lower-level hazards (Fig. 1b); managing a hazard cause by invoking multiple hazard mitigation barriers, each of which meets a particular safety objective that, in turn, specifies the requirement to be fulfilled to manage that hazard cause (Fig. 1c); managing a hazard cause by also showing that the applicable barriers are reliable in operation (Fig. 1d); hierarchical decomposition of a safety objective into lower-level requirements, or its allocation to specific components of a mitigation barrier (Fig. 1e); and supporting a safety objective by applying a verification procedure, via direct evidential support, reapplying hierarchical decomposition, or by reallocation to lower-level components (Figs. 1f and g, respectively). Note that these patterns do not encode a comprehensive collection of risk reduction measures, but reflect part of the approach that we have used successfully in the safety cases we authored. Moreover, the individual structures are variations on well-known safety argument patterns, such as *hazard-directed breakdown*, and *requirements breakdown* [5].

By examining Fig. 1, we can see that there is an intuitive notion of *sequential composition* where patterns are joined in a *top-down* way so that a leaf node of one pattern is the root of another. Similarly, there is also a notion of *parallel composition*, where patterns can be thought of as being placed alongside one another, and joined to reconcile common nodes and links. Using these patterns as the running example, we subsequently describe (Sect. 4) how we have composed patterns to supply safety rationale in a recently authored UAS safety case. The instance arguments of those patterns explain how the barriers of ground-based surveillance, and avoidance meet their safety objectives for managing the collision hazard posed by air proximity events.

3   Pattern Composition

We now formalize what it means to compose patterns. The goal is to develop a principled approach to composing arbitrary patterns, generalizing the intuition (as above) underlying the composition of the simple patterns of Fig. 1, to arbitrary (and larger) patterns. There are several subtleties that must be addressed, e.g., reconciling overlapping fragments, and determining when a composition will be well-formed. Moreover, we manually created the composition when we applied it in practice; however, we want to automate the functionality in our tool, Advo-CATE. We build on our previous work, using the following (slightly modified) definition of argument patterns from [5], and omit the conditions described there for brevity.

---

[3] Due to space constraints, and for figure legibility, we omit the contextual nodes (i.e., assumptions, justifications, and context) that provide additional clarification of the associated reasoning, from the patterns in Fig. 1. Also note that, in some cases, the strategies in these patterns include the safety measures used to achieve a goal in addition to the standard GSN strategies that provide inference explanations.

Definition 1 (Argument Pattern). *An* argument pattern *(or* pattern, *for short), P, is a tuple* $\langle N, l, p, \mathfrak{m}, \mathfrak{c}, \rightarrow \rangle$, *where* $\langle N, \rightarrow \rangle$ *is a directed hypergraph*[4] *in which each hyperedge has a single source and possibly multiple targets, and comprising a set of nodes, N, a family of labeling functions, l_X, where $X \in \{t, d, m, s\}$, giving the node fields* type, description, metadata, *and* status; *and* $\rightarrow$ *is the connector relation between nodes.*

Let $\{\mathcal{G}, \mathcal{S}, \mathcal{E}, \mathcal{A}, \mathcal{J}, \mathcal{C}\}$ be the node types goal, strategy, evidence, assumption, justification, *and* context *respectively. Then, $l_t : N \rightarrow \{\mathcal{G}, \mathcal{S}, \mathcal{E}, \mathcal{A}, \mathcal{J}, \mathcal{C}\}$ gives node types, $l_d : N \rightarrow$ string gives node descriptions, $l_m : N \rightarrow A^*$ gives node instance attributes, and $l_s : N \rightarrow \mathcal{P}(\{tbd, tbi\})$ gives node development status.*

There are additional (partial) labeling functions: p is a parameter label on nodes, $p : N \rightharpoonup Id \times T$, giving the parameter identifier and type; $\mathfrak{m} : N^2 \rightharpoonup \mathbb{N}^2$ gives the multiplicity range on a link between two nodes, with $\langle L, H \rangle$ representing the range from L to H; $\mathfrak{c} : N \times \mathcal{P}(N) \rightharpoonup \mathbb{N}^2$, gives the range on the choice attached to a given node, where $\mathfrak{c}(x, \mathbf{y})$ is the choice between child legs $\mathbf{y}$ with parent node x. Here, n is simply the number of legs in the choice, and so can be omitted.

The links of the hypergraph, $a \rightarrow \mathbf{b}$, where a is a single node and $\mathbf{b}$ is a set of nodes, represent choices. We write $a \rightarrow b$ when $a \rightarrow \mathbf{b}$ and $b \in \mathbf{b}$, and $a \rightarrow \{b, c\}$ when a is the parent of a choice between b and c. A pattern node n is a *data node*, if it has a parameter, i.e., $n \in dom(p)$. Otherwise, a node is *boilerplate*.

3.1   Composition

There are various alternative ways in which composition can be defined. The simplest definition, however, which works for our driving examples, is to take the union of all links in the respective patterns, using shared identifiers as the points at which to join. This is a *conjunctive* interpretation of composition, where we require fragments in *both* patterns to be satisfied. We will require that data be equivalent on corresponding nodes, and call such patterns *conflict-free*. For multiplicities on corresponding links and choices, however, it is not possible to reconcile distinct ranges without either losing information[5] or making ad hoc combinations. We thus adopt the simple solution of also assuming that there are no conflicts between corresponding multiplicities.

Definition 2 (Conflict-free Patterns). *The two patterns $P_1 = \langle N_1, l_1, p_1, \mathfrak{m}_1, \mathfrak{c}_1, \rightarrow_1 \rangle$ and $P_2 = \langle N_2, l_2, p_2, \mathfrak{m}_2, \mathfrak{c}_2, \rightarrow_2 \rangle$ are conflict-free whenever $l_1|_{N_1 \cap N_2} = l_2|_{N_1 \cap N_2}$ and $p_1|_{N_1 \cap N_2} = p_2|_{N_1 \cap N_2}$. If $x, y \in N_1 \cap N_2$ and $x \rightarrow_i y$ (i = 1, 2) then $\mathfrak{m}_1(x, y) = \mathfrak{m}_2(x, y)$, and if $x \in N_1 \cap N_2$, $\mathbf{y} \subseteq N_1 \cap N_2$, and $x \rightarrow_i \mathbf{y}$ (i = 1, 2) then $\mathfrak{c}_1(x, \mathbf{y}) = \mathfrak{c}_2(x, \mathbf{y})$.*

Henceforth, we will use P_1 and P_2 as metavariables for patterns representing the above tuples.

---

[4] A graph where edges connect multiple vertices.

[5] There is no single range that corresponds to the union of possibilities represented by two distinct ranges. This could be addressed, however, by generalizing annotations from ranges to logical constraints that can express dependencies between nodes.

Definition 3 (Pattern Composition). *Let P_1 and P_2 be conflict-free patterns. Then, $P_1 \parallel P_2 = \langle N_1 \cup N_2, l'', p'', \mathfrak{m}'', \mathfrak{c}'', \rightarrow'' \rangle$ where i) $l'' = l_1 \cup l_2$; ii) $x \rightarrow'' y$ iff $x \rightarrow_1 y$ or $x \rightarrow_2 y$; iii) $\mathfrak{m}'' = \mathfrak{m}_1 \cup \mathfrak{m}_2$; and iv) $\mathfrak{c}'' = \mathfrak{c}_1 \cup \mathfrak{c}_2$.*

It can be seen that this is a well-formed pattern. The definition is simple but subtle, since the merging of the links can introduce recursion. Note also that when composing a choice $A \rightarrow \{B, C\}$ with $A \rightarrow B$ we retain both links, rather than merging them. Also, choices can be interwoven in, for example, $A \rightarrow \{B, C\} \parallel A \rightarrow \{C, D\}$. However, duplicates are removed in $A \rightarrow B \parallel (A \rightarrow B, A \rightarrow C)$. Now, clearly $\parallel$ is commutative and associative modulo renaming of the node identifiers, and so composition can be defined over sets of patterns.

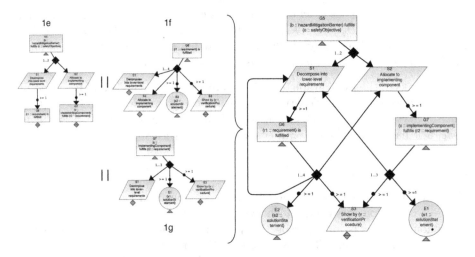

Fig. 2. Parallel composition ($\parallel$) of the *elementary* patterns of Figs. 1e–g (repeated here, above left) giving a *compound* pattern (above right).

Figure 2 shows a *compound* pattern – a variation on the *requirements breakdown pattern* [5] – the result of the (parallel) composition of its reasoning elements, which are themselves the *elementary* patterns in Figs. 1e–g. The elementary pattern in Fig. 1e describes how the claim that a hazard mitigation barrier fulfills a specific safety objective (goal node G5) is supported by decomposition into lower-level requirements, or by allocation to an implementing component of the technical system embodying the barrier (strategy nodes S1 and S2 respectively). The patterns in Figs. 1f and g, respectively, show how the resulting leaf claims (of Fig. 1e) – that a particular requirement is fulfilled (goal node G6), or that the allocated component fulfills a corresponding requirement (goal node G7) – are each either supported directly by relevant evidence items (solution nodes E1 and E2, respectively), or developed using an appropriate verification procedure (strategy node S3). Additionally, each of those claims can be further supported, again, by hierarchical decomposition (strategy S1).

Upon composing these elementary patterns, if there are repeated nodes (or fragments) we retain one copy and discard other copies, after which we resolve the relations between all the pattern nodes (as specified in Definition 3). Note, in Fig. 2, that the abstraction for iteration (i.e., the loop link from the choice following goal node G6, to strategy node S1) follows as a natural consequence of composition.

3.2 Correctness

We now discuss in what sense the pattern composition is *correct*.[6] Intuitively, a pattern represents a set of traces, or paths, and the composition should, in some sense, be a conservative combination of the paths in the component patterns. Since we have defined the composition as the union of (single-step) links, this is trivially true so, instead, we ask whether interesting properties are preserved. In [5], we defined various properties of patterns. It can be shown that composition preserves some of those properties, while for others, we need additional conditions. We will discuss two such properties now:

(i) We say that a pattern is *unambiguous* when for all paths $s_1, s_2 : A \rightarrow B^*$ such that every internal node is boilerplate, we have $s_1 = s_2$, and that a pattern is *complete* when every leaf node is a data node.

(ii) We say that $a \rightarrow^{must} b$, when every loop-free path from a that is sufficiently long must eventually pass through some $b \in \mathbf{b}$. Then, an argument pattern is *well-founded* when, for all pattern nodes a, and sets of nodes $\mathbf{b}$, such that $a \notin \mathbf{b}$, if $a \rightarrow^{must} \mathbf{b}$ then it is not the case that for all $b \in \mathbf{b}$, $b \rightarrow^{must} a$.

Theorem 1 (Property Preservation). *Let P_1 and P_2 be patterns.*

(i) *If P_1 and P_2 are complete and unambiguous, then if there are not distinct paths of boilerplate nodes such that $A \rightarrow^* B$ in both patterns, the composition is complete and unambiguous.*

(ii) *If P_1 and P_2 are well-founded and, in addition, if whenever $A \rightarrow^* B$ in P_1 and $B \rightarrow^* A$ in P_2, then $\exists C . B \rightarrow C$ in either P_1 or P_2, and $C \not\rightarrow^* A$ in either P_1 or P_2, then the composition is well-founded.*

The preservation theorem thus tells us that (with some additional 'compatibility' conditions) composition of 'good' patterns gives us a good pattern. We would now like to formulate a dual theorem, that any pattern can be constructed from elementary patterns.

Definition 4 (Elementary Pattern). *A pattern is elementary (or loop-free) if for all nodes A, B, if $A \rightarrow^* B$ then $B \not\rightarrow^* A$.*

---

[6] Proofs of the theorems in the rest of this paper have been omitted due to space constraints.

Prima facie, however, it is a trivial observation that it is always possible to construct a pattern by composition of elementary patterns, since we can simply compose fragments consisting of all the separate links (and hyperlinks). Instead, we need to show that a pattern can be factorized into a collection of elementary patterns which are maximal in some sense. We make two observations:

(i) 'tight' loops between a node and its child can only be composed from non-pattern fragments. Thus we either allow such loops in the factors or, as we do here, simply exclude them from the statement of the theorem;

(ii) the factors need not actually be unique. Even if we limit ourselves to maximal factors, it is still possible to move branches between factors, so any characterization of uniqueness needs to be modulo an equivalence under such rearrangements.

Hence we define an equivalence relation on pairs of patterns, $p_1, p_2 \sim p_3, p_4$ when we can rearrange a branch in p_1, p_2 to get p_3, p_4 and then extend this in the obvious way to arbitrary sets of patterns. In other words, pruning a branch b from p_1 gives p_3, and grafting it on p_2 gives p_4.

Theorem 2 (Pattern Factorization). *All patterns with no tight loops can be expressed as a maximal composition of elementary patterns. That is, if p is a pattern with no tight loops, then $\exists p_1 \cdots p_n \cdot p_i$ elementary and $p = p_1 \parallel \cdots \parallel p_n$, such that $\forall q_1 \cdots q_m \cdot p = q_1 \parallel \cdots \parallel q_m \Rightarrow$ there exists a partition $I_{i \ldots n}$ of $\{1, \ldots, m\}$ with for each $I_i = \{x_1, \ldots, x_{n_i}\}$, $r_i = q_{x_i} \parallel \cdots q_{x_{n_i}}$, such that we have $r_1, \ldots r_n \sim p_1, \ldots, p_n$.*

That is, any factorization $\{q_i\}$ of p can be partitioned so that each subset of the partition corresponds to a single factor p_i, modulo rearranging.

3.3   General Composition

Rather than use overlapping node identifiers to determine composition points, we want to be able to compose *arbitrary* patterns, placing no assumptions on identifiers. We thus generalize the above definition so that nodes of P_1 and P_2 may or may not overlap. Without loss of generality, however, we will typically assume that they are disjoint.

Since the overlap between two patterns need not, itself, be a pattern, we need to generalize to *pre-patterns*. A pre-pattern has the same type of data (i.e., nodes, links, labels, etc.) as a pattern but need not respect the well-formedness rules. We define embeddings as mapping between pre-patterns that preserve structure. To express that embeddings do not introduce loops, we first define $a \le b$ if for all paths from the root $s : r \to^* b$, we have $a \in s$, and $a < b$ when $a \le b$ and $a \ne b$.

Definition 5 (Pre-pattern Mappings & Embeddings). *Let A and B be (pre-)patterns. We say that $e : A \to B$ is a (pre-)pattern mapping if it maps nodes to nodes and whenever $A \to B$ then $e(A) < e(B)$, i.e., all paths to*

$e(B)$ *must pass through* $e(A)$, *and* $e(A) \neq e(B)$. *A* pre-pattern embedding *is a* pre-pattern mapping *that preserves data, that is, 1)* $l_x^B(e(a)) = l_x^A(a)$ *for* $x \in \{t, d, m, s\}$; *2) If* $\mathfrak{m}^A(x, y) = m$ *then for some link* $x' \to y'$ *in* $e(x) \to^* e(y)$ *we have* $\mathfrak{m}^B(x', y') = m$. *Similarly for* $\mathfrak{c}^A(x, \mathbf{y}) = c$. *If* e *is an embedding from* A *to* B *we write this as* $e : A \hookrightarrow B$.

To define compositions more generally we make use of some simple category theory[7] and, in particular, the notion of *pushout*. A pushout encodes the minimal (and thus unique) object which combines two objects in a specific way. We define this within the *category of pre-patterns*, $\mathcal{PrePat}$, which has pre-patterns for objects and pre-pattern embeddings for morphisms. We are now in a position to define general compositions.

Definition 6 (General Composition). *Let* C *be a pre-pattern, and* $e_1 : C \hookrightarrow P_1$, $e_2 : C \hookrightarrow P_2$ *(a so-called* span*) be pre-pattern embeddings. Then the pushout of* e_1 *and* e_2, *which we write as* $P_1 \parallel_{e_1, e_2} P_2$, *gives us the general composition of* P_1 *and* P_2.

Note that the notion of context-freedom is now generalized by e_1 and e_2 being embeddings. Next, since $\mathcal{PrePat}$ is not co-complete (as co-equalizers do not exist, in general), we rely on an explicit construction to show that pushouts exist.

Theorem 3 (Well-definedness of General Composition). *The general composition of* P_1 *and* P_2 *is well-defined. That is, pushouts exist in* $\mathcal{PrePat}$ *and, moreover, if* P_1 *and* P_2 *are patterns, then* $P_1 \parallel_{e_1, e_2} P_2$ *is also a pattern.*

We define the pushout $\langle N, l, p, \mathfrak{m}, \mathfrak{c}, \to \rangle$ as follows. Let P_1 and P_2 be pre-patterns, and $e_1 : C \hookrightarrow P_1$, $e_2 : C \hookrightarrow P_2$ the common embeddings. We sketch the construction of the pushout (omitting the definitions of l, $\mathfrak{m}$, and $\mathfrak{c}$ to save space): $N = N_c \oplus N_1 \backslash ran(e_1) \oplus N_2 \backslash ran(e_2)$, i.e., disjoint union of the node sets minus ranges of the embeddings. Also,

$$
x \to y \Leftrightarrow \begin{cases} x = x_i, y = y_i \in N_i, \nexists z \in C . e_i(z) \in \{x, y\} \text{ and } x_i \to_i y_i \\ x = x_i \in N_i, y \in C, \text{ and } x_i \to_i e_i(y) \\ y = y_i \in N_i, x \in C, \text{ and } e_i(x) \to_i y_i. \end{cases}
$$

Finally, we observe that the general definition is equivalent to Definition 3 in the following sense.

Corollary 1 (Equivalence of Composition). *Let* P_1 *and* P_2 *be patterns. There exists a span giving a general composition of* P_1 *and* P_2 *which is isomorphic to* $P_1 \parallel P_2$. *Define the span* $e_1 : C \hookrightarrow P_1$, $e_2 : C \hookrightarrow P_2$ *as: i)* $N_c = N_1 \cap N_2$; *ii)* $l_c, p_c, \mathfrak{m}_c, \mathfrak{c}_c, \to_c$ *are the obvious restrictions to* N_c; *and iii)* $e_1(n) = e_2(n) = n$. *Then,* $P_1 \parallel_{e_1, e_2} P_2 \cong P_1 \parallel P_2$.

---

[7] For basic concepts of category theory, we refer the reader to an introductory textbook, such as [7].

4   Application

We have used the elementary patterns identified in Fig. 1 (and others) along with their combinations to explain the required safety rationale – by creating *instance arguments* of the combined patterns – in a more recent UAS safety case to provide assurance of safe operations. We are also applying them to other safety cases currently in development. In brief, our approach is as follows.

First, we select the patterns that we can meaningfully compose into larger patterns to address specific concerns, e.g., how a hazard is managed by the combination of different mitigation barriers, how a specific barrier meets its safety objectives, etc. Then we examine the composed pattern to determine the extent to which it is applicable, e.g., whether it is (internally) complete

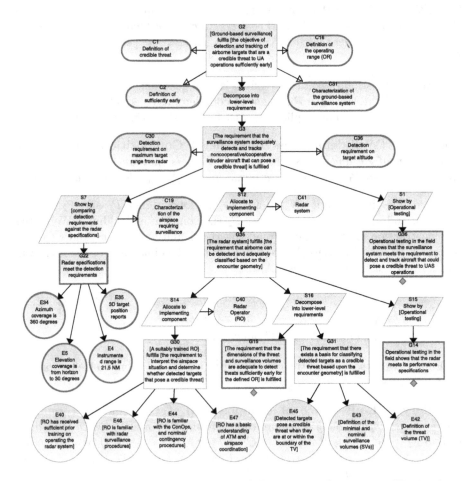

Fig. 3. Fragment of the instance argument of the compound pattern in Fig. 2, when instantiated for the surveillance barrier, and appended with tailored argument elements (shown by the goal, context, and solution nodes highlighted with a thick border).

or whether additional reasoning content is required in the pattern. Here, there may be a need to define additional domain- or application-specific patterns. Thereafter, we instantiate the patterns and examine the instance arguments to determine the extent to which the instance provides the assurance required. Again, there may be a need to define additional argument elements or bespoke arguments to *complete* the overall reasoning. The result comprises argument structures that supply the required safety rationale, e.g., how specific mitigation barriers meet their safety objectives and contribute to reducing risk.

Figure 3 shows a fragment of one such argument structure resulting from this approach. In particular, the nodes *not* highlighted by the thick border in the figure are a fragment of the instance argument of the composed pattern in Fig. 2, instantiated with respect to the ground-based surveillance barrier. The argument is intended to show how the barrier meets its safety objective (root goal node G2, in Fig. 3). The highlighted (goal, context, and solution) nodes are additional argument elements/fragments that we subsequently introduced to complete the argument, and to address the concerns/essential information that the pattern did not include. Note that the instance argument also includes contextual nodes of the pattern that we had previously omitted (e.g., the context nodes C37 and C41). We similarly instantiated the pattern in Fig. 2) with respect to the avoidance barrier (not given here).

Figure 4 shows the (structure of the) compound pattern which explains the contribution of hazard mitigation barriers to managing hazard causes and, in turn, to mitigating the identified hazards. This pattern is produced from the general composition (see Sect. 3.3) of the patterns in Figs. 1a–d. Intuitively, it can also be seen as the result of a sequence of simpler compositions, in particular the (sequential) composition of the patterns in Figs. 1a and b which, in turn, is

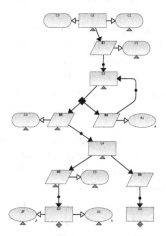

Fig. 4. Result of the composition of the elementary patterns in Figs. 1a–d. Note that this figure primarily illustrates the compound pattern *structure*, also indicating the contextual nodes not shown earlier. For node/link content, see Figs. 1a–d.

(sequentially) composed with the parallel composition of the patterns in Figs. 1c and d. Similarly, the compound pattern of Fig. 2 can, in fact, be sequentially composed with the compound pattern of Fig. 4. The result, another compound pattern, is equivalent to the general composition of all the elementary patterns in Fig. 1. The instance argument for that pattern[8], which includes the argument fragment shown in Fig. 3, explains the role of all applicable mitigation barriers in reducing the likelihood of the different identified hazards during the UAS mission, e.g., a near midair collision (NMAC), or air proximity event (AIRPROX).

5   Related Work and Conclusions

Compositional approaches to safety case construction have been considered in [8], however the focus there is on composing modular arguments. A catalogue of GSN patterns for software safety assurance has been supplied in [9], along with the assertion that the patterns link together to form a single software safety argument upon instantiation. Thus, that work (implicitly) alludes to the capability and utility of pattern composition, although it stops short of describing what composition means, and providing examples for the same. Similarly, [10] gives generic patterns of reasoning empirically identified from real safety cases – -i.e., so called *building blocks*, given in the Claims-Argument-Evidence (CAE) notation – with the explicit intent to combine them into *composite blocks* – analogous to hierarchical (argument) nodes [11] – and *templates*, which are closer to the compound patterns presented here. This work also asserts the capability and utility of composition, but only gives examples of building blocks as opposed to the templates produced from their composition. Moreover, little has been said about what composition means, and what modifications, if any, result to template semantics, and their graphical structure, in relation to their constituent building blocks.

In this paper we have continued our ongoing line of work on developing formal foundations to support automation in safety case development, in which argument structures are a first class object of study. We are now using our preliminary theory of pattern composition to provide a formal basis for implementing a suite of features in our tool, AdvoCATE, including automated refactoring of patterns, identifying reusable pattern components, and composing them in an automated (or interactive) way.

Although we currently manually create patterns for instantiation, composition lets us incrementally construct larger patterns of safety reasoning by combining smaller patterns (extracted from, say, legacy safety cases). When combined with automated pattern instantiation [5], we can increase the level of useful automation that can be brought to bear when creating larger, more complex safety cases. The value addition for creating arguments this way, we believe, is that patterns give the *type* of an instance argument, providing a richer abstraction than argumentation schemes [12], for example, and allowing us to determine

---

[8] Due to space constraints, neither this compound pattern nor its instance are given here.

whether larger arguments can be sensibly combined by examining abstract, and relatively smaller, structures. Moreover, though there are differences, similar techniques could be used for merging and refactoring of argument fragments themselves. An interesting avenue of inquiry for future work is to determine what a suitable representation of *argument architecture* should be. Modular structure has been proposed for this [13], but here we have suggested that patterns and their combination can serve as such an architecture. It might also be useful to represent 'glue' argumentation that connects patterns, or refinements between domain-independent and domain-specific patterns.

Acknowledgement. This work was funded by the SASO project under the Airspace Operations and Safety Program of NASA ARMD.

References

1. Berthold, R., Denney, E., Fladeland, M., Pai, G., Storms, B., Sumich, M.: Assuring ground-based detect and avoid for UAS operations. In: 33rd IEEE/AIAA Digital Avionics Systems Conference (DASC 2015), pp. 6A1-1–6A1-16, October 2014
2. Federal Aviation Administration (FAA): Flight Standards Information Management System, vol. 16, Unmanned Aircraft Systems. Order 8900.1, June 2014
3. Denney, E., Pai, G.: A methodology for the development of assurance arguments for unmanned aircraft systems. In: 33rd International System Safety Conference (ISSC 2015), August 2015
4. Denney, E., Pai, G., Pohl, J.: AdvoCATE: an assurance case automation toolset. In: Ortmeier, F., Daniel, P. (eds.) SAFECOMP Workshops 2012. LNCS, vol. 7613, pp. 8–21. Springer, Heidelberg (2012)
5. Denney, E., Pai, G.: A formal basis for safety case patterns. In: Bitsch, F., Guiochet, J., Kaâniche, M. (eds.) SAFECOMP. LNCS, vol. 8153, pp. 21–32. Springer, Heidelberg (2013)
6. Goal Structuring Notation Working Group: GSN Community Standard Version 1. http://www.goalstructuringnotation.info/
7. Pierce, B.C.: Basic Category Theory for Computer Scientists. MIT Press, Cambridge (1991)
8. Kelly, T.: Concepts and principles of compositional safety case construction. Technical report COMSA/2001/1/1, University of York (2001)
9. Hawkins, R., Kelly, T.: A systematic approach for developing software safety arguments. In: 27th International System Safety Conference (ISSC 2009) (2009)
10. Bloomfield, R., Netkachova, K.: Building blocks for assurance cases. In: 2014 IEEE ISSRE Workshops, (ISSREW), pp. 186–191, November 2014
11. Denney, E., Pai, G., Whiteside, I.: Formal foundations for hierarchical safety cases. In: 16th IEEE International Symposium High Assurance Systems Engineering (HASE 2015), pp. 52–59, January 2015
12. Walton, D., Reed, C.: Argumentation schemes and defeasible inferences. In: Workshop on Computational Models of Natural Argument, 15th European Conference on Artificial Intelligence, pp. 11–20 (2002)
13. Industrial Avionics Working Group: Modular Software Safety Case Process GSN - MSSC 203 Issue 1, November 2012

Formal Verification

Formal Analysis of Security Properties on the OPC-UA SCADA Protocol

Maxime Puys[1]([✉]), Marie-Laure Potet[1], and Pascal Lafourcade[1,2]

[1] Verimag, University of Grenoble Alpes, Saint-Martin-D'hères, France
{maxime.puys,marie-laure.potet}@imag.fr
[2] LIMOS, University of Clermont Auvergne, Campus des Cézeaux, Aubière, France
pascal.lafourcade@udamail.fr

Abstract. Industrial systems are publicly the target of cyberattacks since Stuxnet [1]. Nowadays they are increasingly communicating over insecure media such as Internet. Due to their interaction with the real world, it is crucial to prove the security of their protocols. In this paper, we formally study the security of one of the most used industrial protocols: OPC-UA. Using ProVerif, a well known cryptographic protocol verification tool, we are able to check secrecy and authentication properties. We find several attacks on the protocols and provide countermeasures.

1 Introduction

Industrial systems also called SCADA (*Supervisory Control And Data Acquisition*) have been known to be targeted by cyberattacks since the famous Stuxnet case [1] in 2010. Due to the criticality of their interaction with the real world, these systems can potentially be really harmful for humans and environment. The frequency of such attacks is increasing to become one of the priorities for governmental agencies, *e.g.* [2] from the US National Institute of Standards and Technology (NIST) or [3] from the French *Agence Nationale de la Sécurité des Systèmes d'Information* (ANSSI).

Industrial systems differ from other systems because of the long lifetime of the devices and their difficulty to be patched in case of vulnerabilities. Such specificities encourage to carefully check standards and applications before deploying them. As it already appeared for business IT's protocols for twenty years, automated verification is crucial in order to discover flaws in the specifications of protocols before assessing implementations. However, the lack of formal verification of industrial protocols has been emphasized in 2006 by Igure *et al.* [4] and in 2009 by Patel et al. [5]. They particularly argued that automated protocol verification help to understand most of the vulnerabilities of a protocol before changing its standards in order to minimize the number of revisions which costs time and money.

State-of-the-Art. Most of the works on the security of industrial protocols only rely on specifications written in human language rather than using formal methods. In 2004, Clarke *et al.* [6] discussed the security of DNP3 (*Distributed*

© Springer International Publishing Switzerland 2016
A. Skavhaug et al. (Eds.): SAFECOMP 2016, LNCS 9922, pp. 67–75, 2016.
DOI: 10.1007/978-3-319-45477-1_6

Network Protocol) and ICCP (*Inter-Control Center Communications Protocol*). In 2005, Dzung *et al.* [7] proposed a detailed survey on the security in SCADA systems including informal analysis on the security properties offered by various industrial protocols: OPC (*Open Platform Communications*), MMS (*Manufacturing Message Specification*), IEC 61850, ICCP and EtherNet/IP. In 2006, in the technical documentation of OPC-UA (*OPC Unified Architecture*) the authors detailed the security measures of the protocol (specially in part 2, 4 and 6). In 2015, Wanying *et al.* [8] summarized the security offered by MODBUS, DNP3 and OPC-UA.

On the other hand, some works propose new versions of existing protocols to make them secure against malicious adversaries. In 2007, Patel *et al.* [9] studied the security of DNP3 and proposed two ways of enhancing it through digital signatures and challenge-response models. In 2009, Fovino *et al.* [10] proposed a secure version of MODBUS relying on well-known cryptographic primitives such as RSA and SHA2. In 2013, Hayes *et al.* [11] designed another secure MODBUS protocol using hash-based message authentication codes and built on STCP (*Stream Transmission Control Protocol*). To the best of our knowledge, Graham *et al.* [12] is the only work directly using formal methods to prove the security of industrial protocols or find attack against them. They proposed a formal verification of DNP3 using OFMC [13] (Open-Source Fixed-Point Model-Checker) and SPEAR II [14] (Security Protocol Engineering and Analysis Resource).

Contributions. We propose a formal analysis of the security of the sub-protocols involved in the OPC-UA handshake, namely OPC-UA *OpenSecureChannel* and OPC-UA *CreateSession*. These sub-protocols are crucial for the security since the first aims at authenticating a client and a server and deriving secret keys while the second allows the client to send his credentials to the server. To perform our security analysis, we use one of the most efficient tools in the domain of cryptographic protocol verification according to [15], namely ProVerif developed by Blanchet *et al.* [16]. It considers the classical Dolev-Yao intruder model [17] who controls the network, listens, stops, forges, replays or modifies some messages according to its knowledge. The perfect encryption hypothesis is assumed, meaning that it is not possible to decrypt a ciphertext without its encryption key or to forge a signature without knowing the secret key. ProVerif can verify security properties of a protocol such as secrecy and authentication. The first property ensures that a secret message cannot be discovered by an unauthorized agent (including the intruder). The authentication property means that one participant of the protocol is guaranteed to communicate with another one. Modeling credential in ProVerif is not common and requires to understand the assumptions made in the protocol in order to model it correctly. We follow the official OPC-UA standards in our models and checked it against a free implementation called *FreeOpcUa*[1]. Finally, using ProVerif, we automatically find attacks against both sub-protocols and provide simple realistic countermeasures. All sources we developed are available[2].

---

[1] https://freeopcua.github.io/.

[2] http://indusprotoverif.forge.imag.fr/PPL16.tar.gz.

Outline. In Sect. 2, we analyze the security of OPC-UA *OpenSecureChannel* and OPC-UA *CreateSession* in Sect. 3. Finally, we conclude in Sect. 4.

2   OPC-UA OpenSecureChannel

The *OpenSecureChannel* sub-protocol aims to authenticate a client and a server and allows them to exchange two secret nonces (random numbers) that will be used to derive shared keys for the later communications. Moreover, OPC-UA can be used with three security modes, namely *None*, *Sign* and *SignAndEncrypt*.

- *SignAndEncrypt*: messages are signed $\{h(m)\}_{sk(X)}$ and encrypted $\{m\}_{pk(X)}$, where h is an hash function, $sk(X)$ the secret key associated to X and $pk(X)$ the public key of X. This mode claims to provide secrecy of communication using symmetric and asymmetric encryption, but also both authentication and integrity through digital signatures.
- *Sign*: it is the same as SignAndEncrypt but messages are only signed $\{h(m)\}_{sk(x)}$, and not encrypted.
- *None*: using this mode, the *OpenSecureChannel* sub-protocol does not serve much purpose as it does not provide any security but is used for compatibility.

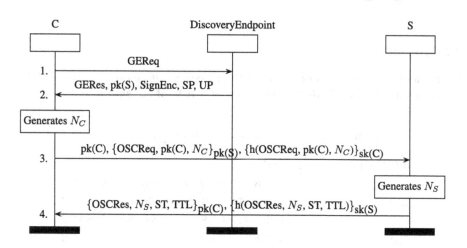

Fig. 1. OPC-UA *OpenSecureChannel* sub-protocol in mode SignAndEncrypt.

This protocol is described in Fig. 1. In message 1, C requests information on S with *GEReq* meaning *GetEndpointRequest*. In message 2, *DiscoveryEndpoint* answers with server's public key and possible security levels and where *GERes* stands for *GetEndpointResponse*, *SP* for *SecurityPolicy* and *UP* for *UserPolicy*. Both *SP* and *UP* are used for cryptographic primitive negotiations. In message 3, C sends a nonce N_C to S with *OSReq* standing for *OpenSecureChannelRequest*.

Finally in message 4, S answers a nonce N_S to C with *OSCRes* for *OpenSecureChannelResponse*, *ST* for *SecurityToken* (a unique identifier for the channel) and *TTL* for *TimeToLive* (its life-time). The four terms *GEReq*, *GERes*, *OSCReq* and *OSCRes* indicate the purpose of each message of the protocol. At the end of this protocol, both C and S derive four keys (K_{CS}, $KSig_{CS}$, K_{SC} and $KSig_{SC}$) by hashing the nonces with a function named P_hash, similar as in TLS [18]: $(K_{CS}, KSig_{CS}) = P\_hash(N_C, N_S)$ and $(K_{SC}, KSig_{SC}) = P\_hash(N_S, N_C)$.

2.1 Modeling

Normally, a *GetEnpointRequest* would be answered by a list of session endpoints with possibly different security modes. We suppose that the client always accepts the security mode proposed. Client's and server's certificates are modeled by their public keys. Moreover, thanks to the perfect encryption hypothesis, we can abstract the cryptographic primitives used. We consider an intruder whose public key would be accepted by a legitimate client or server. Such an intruder could for instance represent a legitimate device that has been corrupted through a virus or that is controlled by a malicious operator. We consider the following security objectives: (i) the secrecy of the keys obtained by C (denominated by K_{CS} and $KSig_{CS}$), (ii) the secrecy of the keys obtained by S (denominated by K_{SC} and $KSig_{SC}$), (iii) the authentication of C on N_C and (iv) the authentication of S on N_S.

2.2 Results

We model in ProVerif this protocol for the three security modes of OPC-UA for each objective proposed. Results provided by ProVerif are shown in Table 1.

Table 1. Results for *OpenSecureChannel* sub-protocol

OPC-UA security mode	Objectives			
	Sec K_{CS}	Sec K_{SC}	Auth N_S	Auth N_C
None	UNSAFE	UNSAFE	UNSAFE	UNSAFE
Sign	UNSAFE	UNSAFE	UNSAFE	UNSAFE
SignEnc	SAFE	SAFE	UNSAFE	UNSAFE

Obviously, as the security mode None does not provide any security, all objectives can be attacked. Moreover, as nonces are exchanged in plaintext in security mode Sign, the keys are leaked. Finally, in the case of Sign and SignAndEncrypt, the intruder reroutes messages to mount attacks on authentication in order to bypass replay protections such as timestamps as the packet's destination is changed rather than being replayed later. Figure 2 shows an attack on the authentication of C using N_C. This attack is possible because the standard

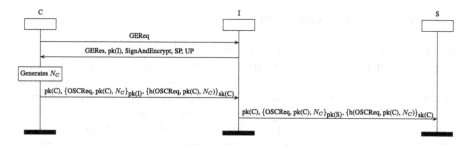

Fig. 2. Attack on N_C: I usurps C when speaking to S.

OPC-UA protocol does not require explicitly to give the identity of the receiver of a message. Thus it allows the intruder to send to S the signed message C sent to him similarly as the *man-in-the-middle* attack on the Needham-Schroeder protocol [19].

2.3   Fixed Version

We propose a fixed version of the *OpenSecureChannel* sub-protocol using one of the classical counter-measures for communication protocols proposed in [20]. It consists in explicitly adding the public key of the receiver to the messages and thus avoiding an intruder to reroute signed messages to usurp hosts, as presented in Sect. 2.2. This resolves the authentication problem but, as ProVerif confirms, attacks on secrecy are still present. In order to solve the remaining secrecy attacks, we use the key wrapping [21] mechanism present in the OPC-UA standards [22–25]. All occurrences of N_C are replaced by $\{N_C\}_{pk(S)}$ in message 3 and all occurrences of N_S in message 4 by $\{N_S\}_{pk(C)}$. Thus in security mode Sign, all the entire messages are signed but only the nonces are encrypted. More formally, message 3 and 4 of Fig. 1 are replaced by:

3. $C \rightarrow S : \big\{\text{OSCReq, pk(C)}, \{N_C\}_{pk(S)}, \mathbf{pk(S)}\big\}_{pk(S)}, \big\{\text{h(OSCReq, pk(C)}, \{N_C\}_{pk(S)}, \mathbf{pk(S)})\big\}_{sk(C)}$
4. $S \rightarrow C : \big\{\text{OSCRes}, \{N_S\}_{pk(C)}, \text{ST, TTL}, \mathbf{pk(C)}\big\}_{pk(C)}, \big\{\text{h(OSCRes}, \{N_S\}_{pk(C)}, \text{ST, TTL}, \mathbf{pk(C)})\big\}_{sk(S)}$

We also use ProVerif to confirm the security of the protocol with all our counter-measures. The results are presented in Table 2 and show that both authentication and secrecy are now secure for security modes Sign and SignAndEncrypt. As nonces are encrypted in security mode Sign, keys remain secret.

Table 2. Results for fixed *OpenSecureChannel* sub-protocol

OPC-UA security mode	Objectives			
	Sec K_{CS}	Sec K_{SC}	Auth N_S	Auth N_C
None	UNSAFE	UNSAFE	UNSAFE	UNSAFE
Sign	SAFE	SAFE	SAFE	SAFE
SignEnc	SAFE	SAFE	SAFE	SAFE

3   OPC-UA CreateSession

The OPC-UA *CreateSession* sub-protocol allows a client to send credentials (*e.g.* a login and a password) over an already created Secure Channel. This sub-protocol is presented in Fig. 3. This protocol follows the security mode that was chosen during the *OpenSecureChannel* sub-protocol and uses the symmetric keys derived, thus encryption becomes symmetric and signature relies on a *Message Authentication Code* (MAC). Then messages sent by C are encrypted using K_{CS} (resp. signed with $KSig_{CS}$) and messages sent by S are encrypted with K_{SC} (resp. signed with $KSig_{SC}$). More formally, in message 1, C sends a nonce as a challenge to S with *CSReq* meaning *CreateSessionRequest*. In message 2, S answers with $Sig_{N_C} = \{pk(C), N_C\}_{sk(S)}$ and *CSRes* for *CreateSessionResponse*. The message Sig_{N_C} is the response of C's challenge and requires S to sign with its private (asymmetric) key to prove that he is the same as in the *OpenSecureChannel* sub-protocol. For this particular use, the OPC-UA standard explicitly asks to add C's public key to the signature (which confirms the counter-measure given in Sect. 2.3). In message 3, C answers S's challenge with Sig_{N_S} and sends his credentials to S with *ASReq* for *ActivateSessionRequest*. Finally, in message 4, S confirms to C that the session is created with *ASRes* for *ActivateSessionResponse* and N_{S2} a fresh nonce as a challenge that C should use to refresh the session when it is timed-out. Again, *CSReq*, *CSRes*, *ASReq* and *ASRes* indicate the purpose of each message of the protocol.

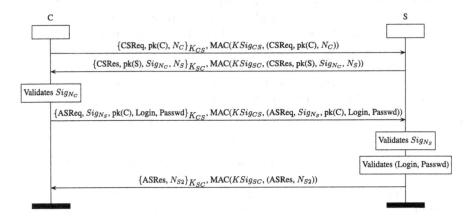

Fig. 3. OPC-UA *CreateSession* sub-protocol

3.1   Modeling

As this protocol involves logins and passwords, we assume that C uses a different password for each server he speaks with. On the contrary, as mentioned in Sect. 2.1, we consider an intruder that can play a legitimate device that has been corrupted and would obtain the credentials of the client just by playing the protocol with him. Modeling of credentials is still not common in ProVerif. We use two functions: *Login* and *Passwd*. The first one takes as parameter the public key of a host in order to associate his login with him. This function is public for everybody. The function *Passwd* takes as parameter the private key of its owner to make it secret, but also the public key of the server to model a different password for each server. Then we provide the following equation: `verifyCreds(pk(S),Login(pk(C)),Passwd(sk(C),pk(S))) = true`. It allows the server to verify if a password and a login are matching and if the password is the one he knows (using his public key). According to our results for the *OpenSecureChannel* sub-protocol, the secrecy of the symmetric keys in security mode Sign depends on if the protocol uses key wrapping. Again, as the OPC-UA standard is not clear on how to use the mechanism in this mode, we check with and without this security. This means that if keys are compromised, then the intruder has access to it. We consider four security objectives: (i) the secrecy of the password, (ii) the authentication of C on his password, (iii) the authentication of C on $Sign_{N_S}$ and (iv) the authentication of S on $Sign_{N_C}$.

3.2   Results

Results without key wrapping (thus with keys leaked in security mode Sign, cf. Table 1) are presented in Table 3. Again, all objectives are attacked in security mode None. Also the secrecy of the password cannot hold even in security mode Sign since it will be sent by the client in plaintext during a legitimate exchange. However, both challenge-response nonces ensure authentication since the private keys are used instead of the symmetric keys. An attack on the authentication on *Passwd* in security mode Sign is found by the tool. In this attacks the intruder replaces the credentials of C by other valid credentials and recalculates the MAC of the message using the leaked keys.

Table 3. Results for OPC-UA *CreateSession* sub-protocol

OPC-UA security mode	Objectives			
	Sec *Passwd*	Auth *Passwd*	Auth $Sign_{N_S}$	Auth $Sign_{N_C}$
None	UNSAFE	UNSAFE	UNSAFE	UNSAFE
Sign	UNSAFE	UNSAFE	SAFE	SAFE
SignEnc	SAFE	SAFE	SAFE	SAFE

If we consider that key wrapping is used in the *OpenSecureChannel* sub-protocol (thus without keys leaked in security mode Sign) then according to ProVerif results the authentication on C's password becomes secure. This analysis shows that the use of key wrapping is crucial in security mode Sign. Thus it should be clearly said in the OPC-UA standard since missing this feature completely breaks the security of Sign mode. Moreover, C's credential should also be encrypted when exchanged in Sign mode to ensure their confidentiality. Finally, we check the source code of the free implementation of OPC-UA (*FreeOpcUa*). This implementation is secure since it forces encryption of secrets even in security mode Sign.

4 Conclusion

We provided a formal verification of the industry standard communication protocol OPC-UA, relying its official specifications [22–25]. We used ProVerif a tool for automatic cryptographic protocol verification. Protocol modelings were tedious tasks since specifications are often elusive to allow interoperability. Particularly due to unclear statements on the use of cryptography with security mode Sign, we studied the protocol with and without counter-measures and proved the need of encryption for secrets to ensure messages security properties. We also found attacks on authentication and provided realistic counter-measures. We chose to focus on the two sub-protocols involved in the security handshake as they represent the core of the protocol's security. In the future, we aim at testing the attacks we found on official implementations which are proprietary in order to check if they filled the gap as did *FreeOpcUa*.

Acknowledgements. This work has been partially funded by the CNRS PEPS SISC ASSI 2016, the LabEx PERSYVAL-Lab (ANR-11-LABX-0025), the ARAMIS project (PIA P3342-146798) and "Digital trust" Chair from the University of Auvergne Foundation.

References

1. Langner, R.: Stuxnet: dissecting a cyberwarfare weapon. IEEE Secur. Priv. **9**(3), 49–51 (2011)
2. Stouffer, K., Falco, J., Karen, S.: Guide to industrial control systems (ICS) security. NIST Spec. Publ. **800**(82), 16–16 (2011)
3. ANSSI. Managing cybersecurity for ICS, June 2012
4. Igure, V.M., Laughter, S.A., Williams, R.D.: Security issues in SCADA networks. Comput. Secur. **25**(7), 498–506 (2006)
5. Patel, S.C., Bhatt, G.D., Graham, J.H.: Improving the cyber security of SCADA communication networks. Commun. ACM **52**(7), 139–142 (2009)
6. Clarke, G.R., Reynders, D., Wright, E.: Practical modern SCADA protocols: DNP3, 60870.5 and related systems. Newnes (2004)
7. Dzung, D., Naedele, M., von Hoff, T.P., Crevatin, M.: Security for industrial communication systems. Proc. IEEE **93**(6), 1152–1177 (2005)
8. Wanying, Q., Weimin, W., Surong, Z., Yan, Z.: The study of security issues for the industrial control systems communication protocols. In: JIMET 2015 (2015)
9. Patel, S.C., Yu, Y.: Analysis of SCADA security models. Int. Manag. Rev. **3**(2), 68 (2007)
10. Fovino, I., Carcano, A., Masera, M., Trombetta, A.: Design and implementation of a secure MODBUS protocol. In: IFIP AICT 2009 (2009)

11. Hayes, G., El-Khatib, K.: Securing MODBUS transactions using hash-based message authentication codes and stream transmission control protocol. In: ICCIT 2013, June 2013
12. Graham, J.H., Patel, S.C.: Correctness proofs for SCADA communication protocols. In: WM-SCI 2005 (2005)
13. Basin, D., Mödersheim, S., Viganò, L.: An on-the-fly model-checker for security protocol analysis. In: Snekkenes, E., Gollmann, D. (eds.) ESORICS 2003. LNCS, vol. 2808, pp. 253–270. Springer, Heidelberg (2003)
14. Saul, E., Hutchison, A.: SPEAR II - the security protocol engineering and analysis resource (1999)
15. Lafourcade, P., Puys, M.: Performance evaluations of cryptographic protocols verification tools dealing with algebraic properties. In: Garcia-Alfaro, J., et al. (eds.) FPS 2015. LNCS, vol. 9482, pp. 137–155. Springer, Heidelberg (2016). doi:10.1007/978-3-319-30303-1_9
16. Blanchet, B.: An efficient cryptographic protocol verifier based on Prolog rules. In: CSF 2001 (2001)
17. Dolev, D., Yao, A.C.: On the security of public key protocols. IEEE Trans. Inf. Theory **29**(2), 198–208 (1981)
18. Dierks, T., Rescorla, E.: The transport layer security (TLS) protocol, version 1.2. IETFRFC 5246, August 2008
19. Lowe, G.: Breaking and fixing the Needham-Schroeder public-key protocol using FDR. In: TACAS 1996 (1996)
20. Abadi, M., Needham, R.: Prudent engineering practice for cryptographic protocols. IEEE Trans. Softw. Eng. **22**(1), 6 (1996)
21. Focardi, R., Luccio, F.L., Steel, G.: An introduction to security api analysis. In: Aldini, A., Gorrieri, R. (eds.) FOSAD 2011. LNCS, vol. 6858, pp. 35–65. Springer, Heidelberg (2011)
22. Mahnke, W., Leitner, S., Damm, M.: OPC Unified Architecture. Springer, Heidelberg (2009)
23. OPC Unified Architecture. Part 2: Security model, April 2013
24. OPC Unified Architecture. Part 4: Services, August 2012
25. OPC Unified Architecture. Part 6: Mappings, August 2012

A Dedicated Algorithm for Verification of Interlocking Systems

Quentin Cappart[⊠] and Pierre Schaus

Université catholique de Louvain, Louvain-La-Neuve, Belgium
{quentin.cappart,pierre.schaus}@uclouvain.be

Abstract. A railway interlocking is the system ensuring a safe train traffic inside a station by monitoring and controlling signalling components. Modern interlockings are controlled by a generic software that uses data, called application data, reflecting the layout of the station under control and defining which actions the interlocking can perform. The safety of the train traffic relies thereby on application data correctness, errors inside them can lead to unexpected events, such as collisions or derailments. Automatising and improving the verification process of application data is an active field of research. Most of this research is based on model checking, which performs an exhaustive verification of the system but which suffers from scalability issues. In this paper, we propose to use our knowledge of the system in order to design a polynomial verification algorithm that can detect all the possible safety issues provided that an assumption of monotonicity hold.

1 Introduction

In the railway domain, an interlocking is the subsystem that is responsible for ensuring a safe and fluid train traffic by controlling active track components of a station. Among these components, there are the signals, defining when trains can move, and the points, that guide trains from track to track. Modern interlockings, like Solid State Interlocking [1], are computerised systems composed of a generic software taking data, called application data, as input. They describe the actions that the interlocking must perform [2]. The main requirement to consider when designing an interlocking is the safety. A correct interlocking must never allow critical situations such as derailments or collisions. To this purpose, an interlocking must satisfy the highest safety integrity level as stated by Standard EN 50128 of CENELEC [3]. Although the generic software is developed in accordance with these requirements, the reliability of an interlocking is also dependant of the correctness of its application data which are particular to each station. However, preparation of application data is still nowadays done by tools that do not guarantee the required level of safety. Furthermore, the verification of their correctness, as well as their validation, is mainly done manually through a physic simulator that reproduces the behaviour of the interlocking on real infrastructures. In addition to the high cost of this process, it is also error prone

© Springer International Publishing Switzerland 2016
A. Skavhaug et al. (Eds.): SAFECOMP 2016, LNCS 9922, pp. 76–87, 2016.
DOI: 10.1007/978-3-319-45477-1_7

because there is no guarantee that all the situations that could end-up in a safety issue have been tested by the simulator.

To overcome this lack, research has been carried out in order to improve this verification process [4–7]. Most of it is based on model checking [8]. The goal is to perform an exhaustive verification of the system. It is done in three steps. First, the application data and the station layout are translated into a model reflecting the interlocking behaviour. Secondly, the requirements that the interlocking must ensure in order to prevent any safety issue are formalised. Finally, the model checker verifies that no reachable state of the model violates the safety requirements. The main advantage of this method is its exhaustiveness: if a requirement is not satisfied, the model checker will always detect it. However, this method suffers from the state space explosion problem. The number of reachable states exponentially grows as the size of the model grows and the model checker algorithm might not return a result within a reasonable time in practice. Different methods to limit it have been proposed. Winter et al. [9] suggest to keep the model as simple as possible by abstracting some parameters, such as the trains speed or length. Besides, improvements can also be done on the model checking algorithms. Different studies propose to use symbolic model checking instead of classical approaches [6,7]. Variable ordering can also be considered in order to speed up the verification [10]. Cappart et al. [11] propose to limit the verification to a set of likely scenarios through a discrete event simulation. Furthermore, Limbree et al. [12] propose a compositional approach and use modern model checking algorithms, such as IC3 or k-liveness for the verification. However, despite the good performances obtained, their method still requires manual work for modelling each station individually and defining their decomposition through contracts.

All of these improvements are generic and although they can be applied for any model checking application, they do not take advantage of the intrinsic specificities of the considered system. In this paper, we propose to use our knowledge of the railway field in order to design an efficient dedicated verification algorithm. The contributions of this paper are as follows:

- An extension of the model presented by Cappart et al. [11]. Concretely, we add the bidirectional locking functionality [2] that prevents head to head collisions on platforms. We also add the differentiation between a route command and a route activation.
- The introduction of a polynomial algorithm verifying that the interlocking will never cause derailments or collisions provided that an assumption of monotonicity hold. It also verifies that each train will reach its correct destination. Furthermore, its performances are also analysed through several experimentations done on three instances.

This paper is structured around a typical medium sized Belgian station (the same as [11]). The next section describes the interlocking components, explains how it works, and illustrates its behaviour on the case study. Section 3 presents the verification algorithm and states under which assumptions it can be used. Performances are finally discussed in Sect. 4.

2   Interlocking Principles

The role of an interlocking is to ensure a safe train traffic inside a station. This section explains how it is done in practice for the Belgian interlockings and illustrates the process on a case study, Braine l'Alleud Station.

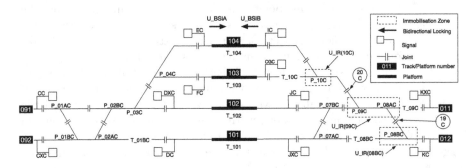

Fig. 1. Layout of Braine l'Alleud Station.

A representation of its track layout with its related components is shown on Fig. 1. This figure recaps all the component types that are used in our model. Firstly, there are the physical components of the track layout:

- The **tracks** (e.g. Track 101) are the railway structures where trains can move. A track can be a **platform** if trains can stop on it to pick up passengers.
- The **track segments** (e.g. T_01BC) are the portions of tracks where a train can be detected. They are delimited by the **joints**.
- The **points** (e.g. P_01AC) are the movable devices that allow trains to move from one track to another. According to Belgian convention, they can be in a normal position (left) or in a reverse position (right).
- The **signals** (e.g. CXC) are the devices used to control the train traffic. They are set on a proceed state (green) if a train can safely move into the station or in a stop state (red) otherwise.

Braine l'Alleud Station is composed of 4 tracks, 17 track segments, 4 platforms, 12 points and 12 signals. The physical components are controlled and monitored by the interlocking. For instance, the system can detect that a train is waiting on Track segment T_01AC in front of Signal CC and then puts this signal to a proceed state if this action will not cause any safety issue. Generally speaking, the interlocking must known which actions can be done and under which conditions. Such information can be defined in different ways according to the type of interlocking considered. Since 1992, Belgian railway stations have used SSI format [1] for their interlockings. Such interlockings use a route based paradigm. A **route** is the path that a train is supposed to follow inside a station. It is named according to its origin and its destination place. Signals are often used as a reference for the origins whereas tracks or platforms are used for destinations. For instance, Route R_CXC_101 starts from Signal CXC and ends on Platform 101. When a train is approaching to a station, a signalman performs a route request to the interlocking in order to ask if the route can be commanded. It is a **route command**. If this request is fulfilled, all the requested components are locked but the train cannot use the route yet because the start signal is still on a stop state. The start signal goes to a proceed state only after the activation of the route. **Route activations** are periodically tried by the interlocking after that the route has been commanded. Once the route activation has been accepted, the train can finally use its route. The interlocking handles such requests and accepts or rejects it according to the station state. To manage the requests, logical components are used:

- The **subroutes** are the contiguous segments that the trains must follow inside a route. When a route is commanded for a train, a set of subroutes is locked. When not requested, subroutes are in a free state. They are defined by this syntax: U_origin_dest. For instance, U_19C_20C is the subroute from Joint 19 C to Joint 20C.

- The **immobilisation zones** are the variables materialising the immobilisation of a set of points. When they are locked, their attached points cannot be moved. They are represented in the application data by the name U_IR.

- The **bidirectional locking** is the mechanism used to prevent head to head collisions on platforms. Each bidirectional locking consists of two variables (U_BSIA and U_BSIB) which can prevent the activation of a route coming from the left or the right of the platform. For instance, when U_BSIA(104) is locked, no route going to the Platform 104 from the right can be activated.

There are 32 possible routes in Braine l'Alleud. To manage it, 48 subroutes, 10 immobilisation zones and 4 bidirectional locking mechanisms are used. With both the physical and logical components, a route based interlocking controls the train traffic by monitoring the station, setting routes, activating them, locking components and releasing them. To illustrate how it works, let us consider the scenario where a train is coming from Track 012 and has to go to Platform 103:

- Firstly, when the train is waiting at Signal KC, the interlocking verifies whether the request for Route R_KC_103 can be granted. Listing 1.1 presents the request according to the application data of Braine l'Alleud.

```
1  *Q_R(KC_103)
2     if    R_KC_103 xs , // xs: unset
3           P_08BC cfr, P_08AC cfr, P_09C cfr, P_10C cfn,
4           U_IR(08BC) f, U_IR(09C) f, U_IR(10C) // f: free
5     then  R_KC_103 s // s: set
6           P_08BC cr, P_08AC cr, P_09C cr, P_10C cn,
7           U_IR(08BC) l, U_IR(09C) l, U_IR(10C) l,
8           U_KC_19C l, U_19C_20C l, U_20C_CGC l // l: locked
```

Listing 1.1. Request for commanding Route R_KC_103.

The request is accepted only if Route R_KC_103 is not already set (line 2), if some points are free to be commanded to the reverse (cfr) or normal (cfn) position (line 3) and if some immobilisation zones are not locked (line 4). If all the conditions are satisfied, R_KC_103 is set (line 5), the points are controlled to the reverse (cr) or normal (cn) position (line 6) and some components as the immobilisation zones (line 7) or subroutes (line 8) are locked. At this step, Route R_KC_103 is set, or commanded, but not yet activated. Its start signal is still on a stop state and the train can thereby not enter in the station yet.

- Before moving a point, the interlocking must verify that this action can safely be executed. Listing 1.2 illustrates such conditions for Point P_08AC.

```
1  *P_08ACN U_IR(09C) f // condition for normal (N) position
2  *P_08ACR U_IR(09C) f // condition for reverse (R) position
```

Listing 1.2. Conditions allowing Point P_08AC to move.

- Directly after the acceptance of the request of Listing 1.1, the interlocking checks if a bidirectional locking must be used in order to prevent routes going to Platform 103 from the left to be activated. It is shown on Listing 1.3.

```
1  if U_BSIA(103) f then U_BSIB(103) 1
```

Listing 1.3. Request for setting the bidirectional locking of Platform 103.

- Once R_KC_103 has been commanded, the interlocking checks if it can safely activate the route and so gives the train an authority to move.

```
1  *R_KC_103
2     if    P_08BC cdr, P_08AC cdr, P_09C cdr, P_10C cdn,
3           U_IR(08BC) 1, U_IR(09C) 1, U_IR(10C) 1,
4           T_08BC c, T_09C c, T_10C c, T_103 c, // c: clear
5           U_BSIA(103) f
6     then  U_BSIB(103) 1, KC proceed
```

Listing 1.4. Request for activating Route R_KC_103.

Listing 1.4 states that R_KC_103 can be activated only if the points are commanded and detected in the requested position (cdn and cdr on line 2), if the immobilisation zones are locked (line 3), if there is no train on some track segments (line 4) and if the bidirectional locking for trains coming from right to Platform 103 is free (line 5). The route activation results on locking the paired bidirectional locking and on setting Signal KC on a proceed state (line 6). At this step, the train can finally move into the station.

- When they are not used, locked components can be released. It is done according to the progress of the train on its route. After each train movement, the interlocking checks if a releasing event can be triggered. Listing 1.5 states the conditions for releasing Subroute U_20C_CGC. If all the conditions are fulfilled, the requested components are thoroughly released.

```
1  U_20C_CGC f if U_KXC_20C f, U_19C_20C f, T_10C c
```

Listing 1.5. Conditions for releasing Subroute U_20C_CGC.

This process briefly describes the life cycle of a route and how it is managed by the interlocking. To be more precise, application data also contain other information but it is either not related to the safety or abstracted in our model. Cappart et al. [11] designed a model aiming to reproduce the interlocking behaviour through a discrete event simulation. However they did not consider the bidirectional locking conditions and the differentiation between a route command and a route activation. In this paper, we enrich their model by adding these functionalities. Errors in application data can lead to disastrous situations. For instance, if the bidirectional locking is not properly checked before activating route R_KC_103 (line 5 missing from Listing 1.4), two routes going to the same platform from a different side can be activated together which will potentially cause a head to head collision. There is thereby a real need of efficient and reliable methods to verify the application data correctness.

3 Verification Algorithm

This section describes the method that we have designed to verify that an interlocking will never cause any safety issue in a station. However, we need to define first what is exactly a safety issue and how it can be detected. Different authors [5,13,14] identified two types of safety issues: collisions and derailments. According to Busard et al. [13], there are three requirements that must hold in order to avoid safety issues. Beyond the safety, a correct interlocking must also ensure that trains will always reach their destination. We have then four requirements:

(1) A same track segment cannot have two trains or more on it at the same time. Otherwise, a collision will occur.
(2) A point cannot move if there is a train on it in order to avoid derailments.
(3) A point must always be set on a position allowing trains to continue their path in order to avoid derailments.
(4) Each train following a route must reach the destination stated by the route.

Much research has been carried out in order to verify automatically if an interlocking always satisfies these properties. However, current methods present some shortcomings. Model checking approaches suffer from the state space explosion problem and the discrete event simulation [11] does not provide enough guarantees that all the errors leading to safety issues will be detected. The approach described in this paper tackles the problem with a different perspective. Instead of limiting our knowledge of the system only for its modelling, we propose to use it for designing the verification algorithm. Specificities of the system can be used to identify what are the scenarios that can lead to safety issues and to distinguish them from others that are either redundant or that never happen in practice. The state space is then pruned and the verification is more efficient. This approach is related to model checking. Indeed, an automatic and exhaustive verification is still performed, but now this verification is restricted to a limited state space that increases polynomially in function of the number of routes and track segments. The rest of this section describes our algorithm and states the assumption under which it can be used.

Initialisation. This paragraph presents the variables and the conventions used in our dedicated algorithm. For a station S, we define $ROUTES$ as the set of all routes, $TRACK\_SEGMENTS$ as the set of all track segments, $POINTS$ as the set of all points and $COMPONENTS$ as the set of all physical components in S. The algorithm returns `True` if S satisfies the requirements and `False` otherwise. For all routes r, we define $r.origin$ as the origin of r, $r.destination$ as its destination, $r.isCommanded$ and $r.isActivated$ as boolean values defining if r is commanded and activated. We also define $t.position$ as the current position of a train t, $p.state$ as the state (normal or reverse) of a point p and $c.isLocked$ as a boolean value defining whether a component c is locked.

No Conflictual Pair of Routes. The idea behind this algorithm is to verify that no issue occurs in any situation, and for that, only pairs of routes are considered. The correctness of this algorithm is then based on the assumption that testing only pairs of routes is sufficient for detecting all the issues. It is related to the **monotonicity** of the application data.

Proposition 1. *The application data are monotonic. If a route cannot be commanded given a particular station state, it will not be able to be commanded for a more constrained station state. The same rule must also apply for the components releasing.*

Proof. In other words, if a route r_1 cannot be commanded when a route r_2 is commanded, it cannot be commanded if r_2 and a third route r_3 are commanded together. Such a scenario can only occur if conditions for route commands (Listing 1.1) require components to be locked instead of being free. It is because the station becomes more constrained each time a component is locked for a route. In some cases, the application data are not monotonic. This situation happens when the itinerary of a train is not only determined by a single route but by a sequence of n routes $[r_1, \ldots, r_n]$. In this case, a route r_i with $i \in]1, n]$ can only be set if r_{i-1} is also set. Route r_i requires then a more constrained state for its command. However, the property of monotonicity can be easily checked through a static analysis. To do so, one can simply read sequentially the application data and check separately each condition. Furthermore, applying the notion of monotonicity to the set of itineraries instead of routes can also be done.   □

Proposition 2. *Considering only pairs of routes is sufficient to verify the safety of an interlocking based on the application data format described previously provided that they are monotonic.*

Proof. We have to prove that all the requirements can be verified by using at most two routes. An issue can occur if the first route is not properly set, such a case only requires routes taken separately and is then trivially proved, or if the command or activation of another route interacts with components already locked for the first route. We need to prove that considering two routes is sufficient to detect all of these issues. Let us consider C, the set of all the components, either physical or logical, of the station and $C_i \subseteq C$, the set of components used or locked by Route r_i. Let us take two arbitrary routes, r_1 and r_2. There are two possible situations:

- $C_1 \cap C_2 = \emptyset$: the two routes have no component in common and are then completely disjoint. No issue can happen between them.
- $C_1 \cap C_2 \neq \emptyset$: the routes have at least a component in common. If the interlocking allows both routes to be set at the same time, an issue can happen.

Any issue can be represented as an intersection between such sets. An intersection is formed by at least two routes. Two routes are then sufficient to detect any safety issue provided that commanding a third route will not relax C_1 or C_2 by releasing some components thereafter. According to Proposition 1, the application data must be monotonic to avoid that. In this case, testing only all the pairs of routes is thus sufficient to cover all the conflictual scenarios.   □

This kind of assumption is also considered in [15] where the verification is limited to two trains. Algorithm 1 presents how we performed the verification by considering all the pairs of routes. The `command` and `activate` instructions (lines 5 and 7) correspond to the requests defined in the application data, like Listings 1.1 and 1.4. The bidirectional locking request (Listing 1.3) is also done through `command` instruction. They return `True` if the request is fulfilled and `False` otherwise. Furthermore, if they are accepted, all the attached actions modifying the station state are executed. `move` instruction (lines 20 and 23) moves a train to the next track segment as defined by the points state. If a point is misplaced, the train will either derail or pursue its movements until it leaves the station.

First, each pair of routes are considered (lines 1–2). The goal is to move a train t_1 from the origin of a route to its destination (lines 10–28) and for each position of t_1, we will try to command and to activate another route (lines 12 and 17). We also try to command r_2 directly after that r_1 has been commanded (line 6). Such a case can happen in real situations. If r_2 is successfully commanded and activated (line 18), we move a train t_2 until it reaches the destination of the route (lines 19–22). When a particular position of t_1 has been tested, t_1 goes to its next position (line 23) and the interlocking will try to release all the locked components (lines 27–28). Releasing conditions are described in the application data such as in Listing 1.5. Through the iterations on the positions of t_1, we memorize the fact that the other route, r_2, has been commanded or activated (lines 12 and 17). Indeed, because of the succession of release actions, the command and the activation can occur at different moments during the route life cycle. When a pair of routes has been entirely tested, the station is reinitialised

---

Algorithm 1. No conflictual pair of routes

---

1 **for** $r_1 \in ROUTES$ **do**
2   **for** $r_2 \in ROUTES$ *such that* $r_2 \neq r_1$ **do**
3   place a train t_1 at $r_1.origin$
4   place a train t_2 at $r_2.origin$
5        $r_1.isCommanded \leftarrow$ command r_1
6        $r_2.isCommanded \leftarrow$ command r_2
7        $r_1.isActivated \leftarrow$ activate r_1
8   **if** *not* $r_1.isActivated$ **then**
9   **return False**
10   **while** $t_1.position \neq r_1.destination$ **do**
11   **if** *not* $r_2.isCommanded$ **then**
12             $r_2.isCommanded \leftarrow$ command r_2
13   **if** $r_2.isCommanded$ *and not* $r_2.isActivated$ **then**
14   **for** $p \in POINTS$ *such that* $t_1.position = p$ **do**
15   **if** $p.state \neq previous(p.state)$ **then**
16   **return False**
17             $r_2.isActivated \leftarrow$ activate r_2
18   **if** $r_2.isCommanded$ *and* $r_2.isActivated$ **then**
19   **while** $t_2.position \neq r_2.destination$ **do**
20   move t_2
21   **if** $t_1.position = t_2.position$ **then**
22   **return False**
23   move t_1
24   **if** $t_1.position \notin TRACK\_SEGMENTS$ **then**
25   **return False**
26   remove t_2 from S
27   **for** $c \in COMPONENTS$ *such that* $c.isLocked$ **do**
28   release c
29   reinitialise S
30 **return True**

(line 29) in order to have an empty station before testing the next pair. It is done through **reinitialise** instruction which releases all the locked components and removes all the trains of the station.

Detection of Issues. Requirement (1) is tested after each movement of t_2 by testing that its position can never be the same as t_1 (lines 21–22). Requirement (2) is tested each time r_2 has been commanded. If the current position of t_1 is a point, the point cannot move after the command of r_2 (lines 14–16). It is done by comparing its state with its previous one through the operator **previous**. Requirements (3) and (4) are tested on lines 24 and 25. If r_1 cannot be activated (lines 8–9), we consider that we have a fluidity issue because no other route is already activated (not presented as a requirement).

Time Complexity. Each pair of routes must be tested, as well as all the possible configurations of positions between two trains. We have thereby the theoretical bound $\mathcal{O}(r^2t^2)$ with r the number of routes and t the number of track segments. The verification of Braine l'Alleud Station took **148 s** on a MacBook Pro 2.6 GHz Intel Core i5 processor and with a RAM of 16 Go 1600 MHz DDR3 using a 64-Bit HotSpot(TM) JVM 1.8 on Yosemite 10.10.5.

4   Experiments

Several kinds of errors have been introduced in the application data in order to test the adequacy of our algorithm and all of them have been successfully detected in Braine l'Alleud:

- Incorrect or missing conditions on a route command (Listing 1.1).
- Conditions missing for releasing a component (Listing 1.5).
- Route activation not consistent with the related route command or condition verifying the vacancy of a track segment is missing (Listing 1.4).
- Bidirectional locking not properly locked (Listings 1.3 and 1.4).

In order to analyse the scalability of our algorithm, we perform three experimentations. Firstly, we compare the execution time required to verify different numbers of routes in the station. A complete verification requires to consider all the possible routes. Indeed, limiting the number of routes only produces a partial verification. Secondly, in addition to Braine l'Alleud (17 tracks segments and 32 routes) we test our algorithm on a smaller instance, Nameche

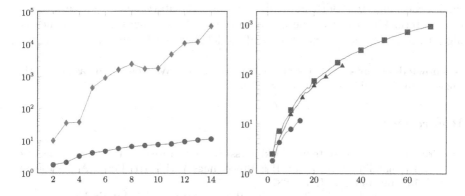

Fig. 2. Execution time (in seconds) in function of the number of routes in Nameche (●), Braine l'Alleud (■) and Courtrai (▲) by using our algorithm and the model checking approach of Busard et al. [13] for Nameche (♦).

(13 tracks segments and 14 routes), and a larger one, a subpart of Courtrai (19 track segments and 70 routes). Finally, we compare our method with the approach of Busard et al. [13] that have performed a model checking verification of Nameche. Figure 2 recaps the execution time of the different experimentations. Let us notice that the y-scale is logarithmic. As we can see, our algorithm runs faster ($\approx$ 4 orders of magnitude for 14 routes) than the model checking approach, even for larger instances and more routes. Furthermore, the algorithm scales well for larger instances: a verification of all the routes is performed in less than 3 min for Braine l'Alleud and in less than 16 min for Courtrai. The experimentations have been performed on the same computer as in the previous section.

5   Conclusion

Much research has been carried out in order to automatically verify the correctness of an interlocking system. Up to now, most of it tackles the problem with a model checking approach or, more recently, using a discrete event simulation. Both of them have some limitations. On the one hand, model checking suffers from the state space explosion problem, and on the other hand, simulation does not provide sufficient guarantees that the system is correct. In this paper, we proposed another approach. The idea was to use our knowledge of the system not only to model it, but also to design the verification algorithm. Concretely, we implemented a dedicated polynomial algorithm that can verify the safety of a medium size station in less than three minutes and that can scale on larger stations provided that an assumption of monotonicity hold. We also shown their validity by introducing several errors in the application that were successfully detected. The method proposed in this paper only deals with the verification of safety. Availability properties, stating that the trains will always progress in the station, are not considered. However, whereas Standard EN50128 [3] strongly recommends the use of exhaustive methods for the verification of safety, the verification of availability can be based on non exhaustive methods as statistical model checking [16]. Both methods are complementary and a full verification of an interlocking can then be based on a hybrid approach using the dedicated algorithm for the safety and statistical model checking for the availability.

Acknowledgements. This research is financed by the Walloon Region as part of the Logistics in Wallonia competitiveness pole.

References

1. Cribbens, A.: Solid-state interlocking (ssi): an integrated electronic signalling system for mainline railways. In: IEE Proceedings B (Electric Power Applications), vol. 134, pp. 148–158. IET (1987)
2. Theeg, G., Anders, E., Vlasenko, S.: Railway Signalling & Interlocking: International Compendium. Eurailpress, Hamburg (2009)
3. Cenelec, E.: 50128. Railway Applications-Communication, Signaling and Processing Systems-Software for Railway Control and Protection Systems (2011)

4. Vu, L.H., Haxthausen, A.E., Peleska, J.: Formal modeling and verification of inter-locking systems featuring sequential release. In: Artho, C., Ölveczky, P.C. (eds.) FTSCS 2014. CCIS, vol. 476, pp. 223–238. Springer, Heidelberg (2015)
5. Winter, K.: Model checking railway interlocking systems. Aust. Comput. Sci. Com-mun. **24**, 303–310 (2002)
6. Eisner, C.: Using symbolic model checking to verify the railway stations of Hoorn-Kersenboogerd and Heerhugowaard. In: Pierre, L., Kropf, T. (eds.) CHARME 1999. LNCS, vol. 1703, pp. 99–109. Springer, Heidelberg (1999)
7. Huber, M., King, S.: Towards an integrated model checker for railway signalling data. In: Eriksson, L.-H., Lindsay, P.A. (eds.) FME 2002. LNCS, vol. 2391, pp. 204–223. Springer, Heidelberg (2002)
8. Clarke, E.M., Klieber, W., Nováček, M., Zuliani, P.: Model checking and the state explosion problem. In: Meyer, B., Nordio, M. (eds.) LASER 2011. LNCS, vol. 7682, pp. 1–30. Springer, Heidelberg (2012)
9. Winter, K., Johnston, W., Robinson, P., Strooper, P., Van Den Berg, L.: Tool support for checking railway interlocking designs. In: Proceedings of the 10th Aus-tralian Workshop on Safety Critical Systems and Software, vol. 55, pp. 101–107. Australian Computer Society, Inc. (2006)
10. Winter, K.: Optimising ordering strategies for symbolic model checking of railway interlockings. In: Steffen, B., Margaria, T. (eds.) ISoLA 2012, Part II. LNCS, vol. 7610, pp. 246–260. Springer, Heidelberg (2012)
11. Cappart, Q., Limbrée, C., Schaus, P., Legay, A.: Verification by discrete simula-tion of interlocking systems. In: 29th Annual European Simulation and Modelling Conference 2015, ESM 2015, pp. 402–409 (2015)
12. Limbree, C., Cappart, Q., Pecheur, C., Tonetta, S.: Verification of interlocking systems using statistical model checking. arXiv preprint arXiv:1605.06245 (2016)
13. Busard, S., Cappart, Q., Limbrée, C., Pecheur, C., Schaus, P.: Verification of rail-way interlocking systems. In: Proceedings 4th International Workshop on Engi-neering Safety and Security Systems, ESSS, pp. 19–31 (2015)
14. Anunchai, S.: Verification of railway interlocking tables using coloured pertri nets. In: Proceedings of the 10th Workshop and Tutorial on Practical Use of Coloured Petri Nets and the CPN Tools (2009)
15. Moller, F., Nguyen, H.N., Roggenbach, M., Schneider, S., Treharne, H.: Defining and model checking abstractions of complex railway models using CSP||B. In: Biere, A., Nahir, A., Vos, T. (eds.) HVC. LNCS, vol. 7857, pp. 193–208. Springer, Heidelberg (2013)
16. Cappart, Q., Limbrée, C., Schaus, P., Quilbeuf, J., Traonouez, L.M., Legay, A.: Verification of interlocking systems using statistical model checking. arXiv preprint arXiv:1605.02529 (2016)

Catalogue of System and Software Properties

Victor Bos[1]($\boxtimes$), Harold Bruintjes[2]($\boxtimes$), and Stefano Tonetta[3]($\boxtimes$)

[1] SSF, Espoo, Finland
victor.bos@ssf.fi
[2] RWTH, Aachen, Germany
h.bruintjes@cs.rwth-aachen.de
[3] FBK, Trento, Italy
tonettas@fbk.eu

Abstract. The use of formal methods has been recognized in different domains as a potential means for early validation and verification. However, correctly specifying formal properties is difficult due to the ambiguity of the typical textual requirements and the complexity of the formal languages. To address this, we define the Catalogue of System and Software Properties. Starting from a taxonomy of requirements extracted from space standards, we derive a list of design attributes divided per requirement type. We map these design attributes to AADL system architectures and properties, for which we define formal semantics and properties. We exemplify the approach using AADL models taken from the space domain.

1 Introduction

In many sectors such as transportation, space and health, the criticality of the software systems requires a high level of confidence and operational integrity. Formal methods allow early discovery of potential issues which otherwise may be discovered only during the (software) system integration and validation phases. In formal methods, the correctness and validity of design models is expressed in terms of formal properties. Therefore, their proper definition becomes a cornerstone of the early validation. The process of adequate properties specification poses multiple challenges. Requirements, being the main source of the properties to be specified, are often not trivial to be formalized due to the current practice of using natural language specifications. Furthermore, the formal properties may be very complex, which hinders the specification and the use of the formal methods.

We start from the observation that, as the design is being expanded and refined, design attributes are being specified either to perform specific analysis such as schedulability or to configure standard functions such as the monitoring of critical values. However, these design attributes are typically not formalized in the language used for system-level early verification and validation and no consistency is therefore checked with the previous analysis. This is a missed opportunity, as formalizing such design attributes can increase the consistency of the models and decrease the cost of specifying formal properties.

© Springer International Publishing Switzerland 2016
A. Skavhaug et al. (Eds.): SAFECOMP 2016, LNCS 9922, pp. 88–101, 2016.
DOI: 10.1007/978-3-319-45477-1_8

In this paper, we describe the Catalogue of System and Software Properties (CSSP). This is a predefined set of design properties already formalized into a mixture of temporal, real-time, and probabilistic logics. We extracted the design properties by analyzing standards and requirements documents in the space domain and creating a taxonomy of requirements with a list of design attributes divided per requirement type. We defined a property set for AADL (Architecture Analysis & Design Language [1]), which can be used to specify such design attributes on a system architecture. By assigning values to the design attributes in this way, a predefined formal property is specified. These formal properties can then be analyzed for consistency among different levels of the architecture, be used as assumptions or guarantees of components for contract-based design, and be model checked on a behavioral model of the components. We extended the COMPASS tool to support this property set, automatically associating design attributes to formal properties. We exemplify the approach on the AADL model of a space system.

Related Work. Similar approaches make use of predefined patterns, either by defining a fixed set of patterns with placeholders, or by defining a grammar to construct such patterns from well defined rules. Well-known approaches for patterns are proposed in [2] (qualitative properties), [3,4] (real-time properties), and [5] (probabilistic). Recently a combination of such patterns, derived by a grammar was published in [6]. More domain specific patterns are known as well, such as for security [7] and epistemic properties [8]. Patterns are used also in contract based approach: in [9], a number of predefined patterns are defined to specify contract assumptions and guarantees.

All these approaches have in common that patterns are defined with a number of placeholders which accept (formal) propositions describing a certain state of the system. This is in contrast with the CSSP, which rather assigns values to predefined design attributes of the system, from which then formal properties are derived. So, the CSSP distinguishes itself from pattern-based approaches in two ways: first, it contains a predefined set of formal properties systematically derived from requirement categories; second, the formal properties are not instantiated by replacing the pattern placeholders with arbitrary expressions, but rather by assigning values to various attributes of the system. Clearly, in this way, the CSSP is very limited in expressiveness. The advantage is that the designer does not need to choose a pattern and invent an instantiation.

2   Scope and Known Limitations

In the paper, we analyze the typical types of system requirements and we list a set of design attributes that are often used to specify a related detailed characteristic on the design. In order to have a systematic approach, we list these design attributes using a classification of requirement types. The classification is derived from ECSS (European Cooperation for Space Standardization) documents related to requirements engineering, in particular from [10–15]. The classification intends to cover all different levels of abstraction in space missions:

Mission Level defining the mission objectives, products, and services; *System-of-System Level* covering aggregates of ground segment, space segment, launch segment and support segment; *System Level* covering single satellites, launchers, and data processing centers; *Sub-System Level* covering, e.g., electrical power, attitude control, structure, thermal control, and software; and finally *Equipment Level* covering, e.g., valves, batteries and individual electronic boxes.

Some remarks follow. First, we do not consider this classification as complete but just a means to derive the design attributes. The taxonomy is biased by the very specific domain (space) of the documents. Moreover, despite the documents coming from the same domain, we found conflicting descriptions of requirement types. Therefore, the resulting taxonomy has been influenced by our knowledge and experience.

Second, we focus the attention on technical requirements, which specify characteristics of systems (products or services) to be developed. In [11], the term Technical Requirement is defined as the "required technical capability of the product in terms of performances, interfaces and operations". So, we do not consider requirements such as verification, usage, portability, and usability requirements. We also exclude from the present analysis security requirements, which are left for future work.

Third, in the description of requirement classes below, the term system refers to the subject for which requirements specify characteristics. In this sense, a system covers products and services. Moreover, it should not be confused with the system abstraction level. The term system (as the subject of requirements) applies to all abstraction levels.

3   Requirements Taxonomy and Design Attributes

1 *Context Requirements* specify the context in which the system is supposed to work. They specify assumptions about external entities such as physical phenomena, external systems and resources. For instance, if the system is software, its context is usually specified in terms of resources like processing power and memory. Context Requirements include both Environmental Requirements and Physical Requirements, defined in [10] respectively as "Requirements that define the context in which the system operates" and "Requirements that establish the boundary conditions to ensure physical compatibility and that are not defined by the interface requirements, design and construction requirements, or referenced drawings".

Typical design attributes associated to context requirements are the *allocated processor and memory* units, the *processing capacity*, the *clock frequency, endianness, memory sizes*, and *addressable memory units*.

2 *Configuration Requirements* specify the product's internal composition in terms of sub-systems and connections. For instance, for a satellite, the Configuration Requirements define the power system, the thermal control system, the attitude control system, the payload systems, and all connections between them. In [10], Configuration Requirements are defined as Requirements related to the composition of the product or its organization.

In this case, typical design attributes are the *list of sub-systems*, the *type of sub-systems*, the *connections between sub-systems*, and the *redundancy scheme* for sub-systems (identification of nominal and redundant sub-systems).

3 *Interface Requirements* define the data or services that a system provides to or requires from other systems. Depending on the system being specified, such data/services can be physical, thermal, electrical, or software.

Typical physical design attributes are *area, volume, alignment, stiffness, tolerance, geometry, flatness, fixation, mass* and *inertia*; electrical design attributes are *voltage, current,* and *margins for electrically induced effects* on nearby components; thermal design attributes are *temperature* and *thermal resistance* (conductibility) of materials; software design attributes are *events* or *functions*.

4 *Functional requirements* specify what a system should do. In [10], the following example of a functional requirement is given: "The product shall analyze the surface of Mars and transmit the data so that it is at the disposal of the scientific community". Although, in [10], Mission Requirements are identified as separate class, we identify Mission Requirements as Functional Requirements at the Mission abstraction level, as they specify "what the mission should do".

  4.1 *Input/Output Functional Requirements* describe the relation between input/output of the system. Typical design attributes associated to input/output functional requirements are the output that is generated in *response* to an input of the component, the maximum *reaction time* that can elapse between the received input and the generated output, and the *input that is required to generate an output*.

  4.2 *Mode Requirements* specify modes and mode transitions of a system. The mode (also known as phase) represents a configuration of a system determining how the system shall respond to inputs in that configuration. In addition transitions allow systems to switch between modes. Mode Requirements can also specify mode invariants, i.e., constraints on the values of variables. For instance, a single star tracker unit has one or more tracking modes. During a tracking mode, the star tracker constantly computes its attitude based on locations of detected stars. A Mode Requirement specifies an invariant on the attitude so that when the difference between successive attitudes is too large, the star tracker is said to have lost its "tracking lock" and will have to switch to another mode.

  Typical design attributes associated to mode requirements are the list of *modes, mode transitions, transition triggers,* and *mode invariants*.

  4.3 *Data-Handling Requirements* specify the operations the system has to perform on data. This includes acquisition, processing, generation, and storage of data as well as refreshing and deletion of old data. For instance, for an Attitude and Orbit Control Subsystem (AOCS), data-handling requirements specify that the system estimates the spacecrafts current attitude and orbit from sensor inputs, determines the desired future attitude and orbit, and generates control commands for the actuators.

Typical design attributes associated to data-handling requirements are *input data rates, output data rates, volatile data, persistent data, processing steps, output data generation.*

4.4 *Monitoring Requirements* specify the system parameters to be checked, the values against which to check, and the frequency at which to perform the check. In addition, monitoring requirements specify all actions needed depending on the outcome of a check.

Typical design attributes associated to monitoring requirements are *monitored parameters* (the parameters that have to be checked), *monitor range* (values against which to check, e.g., ranges or enumerated values), *check frequency, parameter check response actions* (specify what the system shall do after a check has been performed), *parameter check response result* (success or failure), and *monitoring state* (enabled or disabled).

4.5 *Operational Requirements* specify rules according to which connected systems shall communicate. This includes requirements specifying what commands an operator shall issue to a system and what feedback is given in return. In [10], Operational Requirements are defined as: "Requirements related to the system operability".

Operational requirements include requirements on the observability of the system, on the commanding of the system, and on the protocols for system-to-system communications.

Typical design attributes related to observability are the *report format* (i.e., the format of the data the system has to generate), the *data frequency* (when data has to be generated at a certain frequency), *event data* (when data has to be generated only when a certain event occurs), and *observation mode* (enabled or disabled); associated to commandability, there are the *list of commands*, the *type of commands, command conditions* (i.e., the conditions under when commands can be invoked), and *command responses* (i.e., the response a system shall send to the operator upon reception of a command); related to protocol, there are the *type of messages* (commands to the system, information from the system, acknowledgment), the *format of the messages* (headers, payload, source, target, ...), *message rate* (minimum, maximum, average), *response time* of acknowledgment (maximum time between reception of the original input message and the transmission of the acknowledgment), and *communication windows* (i.e., the period during which communication via a particular interface is possible).

5 *Quality Requirements* specify the manner in which a system must perform as well as the characteristics it should have in order for developers, maintainers, and users to be able to perform their tasks involving the system.

5.1 *Performance Requirements* specify how well the system is supposed to perform with respect to certain indicators.

Typical design attributes are *jitter, latency, response times, deadlines, throughput, processing capacity, CPU load, communication capacity,* and *memory capacity.*

5.2 *Dependability Requirements* specify the degree to which the system can reasonably be relied upon. In [16], dependability is defined as "the extent to which the fulfillment of a required function can be justifiably trusted." An important concept related to dependability, especially in the space domain, is Fault Detection, Isolation, and Recovery (FDIR). The FDIR requirements describe what failures must be detected and what to do when a failure has been detected. For instance, if a failure occurs in equipment which has redundancy, it might be possible to switch from the nominal to redundant equipment configuration and continue with nominal operations.

We identify therefore the following design attributes: the *kind of failures* that might occur, the *tolerance of failures* (how often the failure may occur), the *failure detection delay*, and the *recovery actions*.

5.3 *Reliability Requirements.* Reliability is defined as the probability that a system (i.e., product or service) will perform a required function under stated conditions for a stated period of time. In [16], reliability is defined as "the ability of an item to perform a required function under given conditions for a given time interval." For instance, the description of a space mission may state that after reaching a correct orbit, a 1 year nominal mission starts during which scientific data is gathered. Consequently, at the start of the nominal mission, the reliability shall be sufficiently high to ensure a 1 year nominal operation.

A measure for reliability of a system is the Mean Time To Failure, $MTTF$, which is the mean operational time (up time) of a system before any failure occurs.

5.4 *Availability Requirements.* Availability is defined as the proportion of time for which the system (product or service) is able to perform its function in its intended environment. Availability takes into account both the operational time and the repair time.

Consequently, even if a system is not very reliable (i.e., it has a high probability of failure), short repair times of the system might be sufficient to achieve the desired availability. In [16], availability is defined as the "ability of an item to be in a state to perform a required function under given conditions at a given instant of time or over a given time interval, assuming that the required external resources are provided".

In general, *availability* can be seen as the fraction of time the system spends on average in an operational (i.e. *not failed*) state along its life cycle.

5.5 *Maintainability Requirements* specify the acceptable efforts needed to restore a system after a failure has occurred. In [16], maintainability is defined as the "ease of performing maintenance on a product." It can be expressed as the probability that a maintenance action on a product can be carried out within a defined time interval, using stated procedures and resources. A measure for maintainability is the Mean Time To Repair, $MTTR$, that indicates the average time needed to restore the system operation after a failure has occurred.

5.6 *Safety Requirements* specify system hazards and the acceptable risk of such hazard occurring. Hazards can be, e.g., loss of lives, injuries, loss of the mission, loss systems, and loss of equipment. Safety Requirements define all hazards relevant to the system. A typical design attribute is the *tolerance of failures* of the system.

4   The CSSP

The CSSP is based on models specified in AADL [1]. In AADL, a system is described in terms of components, which may contain other systems as subcomponents. Each system may specify a number of event, data or event data ports on its interface. Communication between systems and subsystems occurs via port connections.

The configuration of the system is determined by modes and mode transitions. At any given moment, each system is in a given mode, and based on events may move to another mode as specified by mode transitions.

The CSSP is specified as an AADL property set, which provides the language constructs to associate values to specific model's elements. For example, the CSSP contains the AADL property **Period**, which is applicable to event or event data ports; thus, every port of this kind in the architectural model can have a value associated with it that represents its period. The formal properties provided by the CSSP are determined by the value associated to the corresponding AADL properties.

A design attribute is then specified in terms of these property values or can be formalized by means of using certain structures in the AADL model (such as subcomponents and port connections).

4.1   Formalization of the CSSP

The formal semantics of CSSP formal properties relies on the behavioral semantics which have been defined for the SLIM language [17], a subset of AADL extended with behavioral models. In these semantics, event ports allow instantaneous event synchronization and data ports allow the continuous synchronization of data. Event data ports provide a mix where an event may be fired with an associated data value. Finally, SLIM models are described either by a real-time automaton, with *clock* values continuously increasing over time, or a probabilistic Markov chain, based on exponential distributions associated with events.

The logic used to define most CSSP formal properties is variant of MTL [18], where the atoms are predicates over the event and data ports, and modes of the AADL model. In particular, we use the following notations: $F_{\leq u}\phi$ is true when ϕ is true within the following u time units; $O_{\leq u}\phi$ is true when ϕ is true within the preceding u time units; $\triangleright_{[a,b]} \phi$ is true when the next time ϕ is true is within $[a,b]$ time units; $\mathbb{D}_{[a,b]}\phi$ is the strict version of $\triangleright_{[a,b]} \phi$ that does not consider the occurrence of ϕ at the current time; $change(x)$ is true when the value of x changes; $rise(b)$ is true when the expression b becomes true; the variable mode refs to the active mode of the current state; for an event data port p, $\mathsf{data}(p)$ holds the value of data passed with p after p occurs; for an event port p, $\sharp p$ is the number of occurrences of p in the past history. A more formal definition of the semantics can be found in [17].

Apart from MTL properties, we have ExpectedTime and Long-run average (abbreviated to LRA), which are described in [19] and rely on the probabilistic semantics of SLIM. The expected time is derived from the average sojourn time of a state in the system, and generates the mean time until reaching any state given as its parameter. The long-run average gives the fraction of time spent in states given as its parameter.

The list of formal properties that form the CSSP is shown in the following Table. The first column shows the CSSP formal properties. Each property is parametrized with an element from the input AADL model, indicated by the second column. In the third column the formalization is shown, which is para- metrized by one or more AADL properties specified for the specified element. The formal property is defined if and only if all AADL properties inside the for- mal definition have a value in the model. For time intervals, if the upper bound is not set, it is assumed to be ∞.

Some properties can be expressed as an arbitrary arithmetic expression over data ports, data components and uninterpreted functions. This is a language feature specific to COMPASS. In the CSSP property set, they are encoded as strings, see [17] for details.

Name	element	Formal property
PersistentProperty(p)	data	$G(change(p) \rightarrow \mathbf{Change}(p))$
Specifies that the value of p changes only on the **Change**(p) event.		
ModeInhibitedProperty(m)	mode	$G(\text{mode} = m \rightarrow \bigwedge_{e \in \mathbf{ModeInhibited}(m)} !e)$
Specifies that the events in **ModeInhibited**(m) cannot occur in mode m.		
ModeInvariantProperty(m)	mode	$G(\text{mode} = m \rightarrow \mathbf{ModeInvariant}(m))$
Specifies a generic invariant for mode m.		
MonitorProperty(p)	event data	$G((p \wedge \text{mode} \in \mathbf{MonitorEnabled}(p) \wedge (data(p) \notin \mathbf{MonitorRange}(p))) \rightarrow F_{\leq u} \mathbf{MonitorResponse}(p))$
where $u = \mathbf{MonitorDelay}(p)$. Specifies that the event **MonitorResponse**(p) is fired if the value of p falls outside the specified **MonitorRange**(p).		
CompleteAlarm-Property(p)	event (data)	$G(rise(\text{mode} \in \mathbf{FailureCondition}(p)) \rightarrow F_{\leq u} p)$
where $u = \mathbf{AlarmDelay}(p)$. Specifies that if failure configuration **FailureCondition**(p) is entered, the alarm event p follows.		
CorrectAlarmProperty(p)	event (data)	$G(p \rightarrow O_{\leq u} rise(\text{mode} \in \mathbf{FailureCondition}(p)))$
where $u = \mathbf{AlarmDelay}(p)$. Specifies that if the alarm event p occurs, it was preceded by entering the failure configuration **FailureCondition**(p).		
RecoveryProperty(p)	event (data)	$G(p \rightarrow F_{\leq u} \text{mode} \notin \mathbf{FailureCondition}(p))$
where $u = \mathbf{RecoveryDelay}(p)$. Specifies that upon event p, eventually the failure configura- tion **FailureCondition**(p) is recovered.		

CompleteTimeout-Property(p)	event (data)	$G(F_{\leq u}(\textbf{TimeoutCondition}(p) \rightarrow p \lor \textbf{Timeout-Reset}(p)))$
where $u = \textbf{Timeout}(p)$. Specifies that if p does not occur within $\textbf{Timeout}(p)$, the alarm $\textbf{TimeoutReset}(p)$ must occur		
CorrectTimeout-Property(p)	event (data)	$G(\textbf{TimeoutCondition}(p) \land O_{\leq u} \textbf{TimeoutReset}(p) \rightarrow !p)$
where $u = \textbf{Timeout}(p)$. Specifies that if the alarm $\textbf{TimeoutReset}(p)$ occurs, the event p did not occur.		
FunctionProperty(p)	data	$G(p = \textbf{Function}(p))$
	event data	$G(p \rightarrow data(p) = \textbf{Function}(p))$
Specifies the value of p remains within the associated function $\textbf{Function}(p)$ (an expression).		
InvariantProperty(p)	data	$G(p \in \textbf{InvariantRange}(p))$
	event data	$G(p \rightarrow data(p) \in \textbf{InvariantRange}(p))$
Specifies the value of p remains within the associated range of values.		
ReactionProperty(p)	event (data)	$G((p \land \text{mode} \in \textbf{ReactionCondition}(p)) \rightarrow F_{\in I} \textbf{Reaction}(p))$
where $I = [\textbf{ReactionMinDelay}(p), \textbf{ReactionMaxDelay}(p)]$. Specifies the event p is followed by $\textbf{Reaction}(p)$ provided the mode is in $\textbf{ReactionCondition}(p)$.		
PrecededByProperty(p)	event (data)	$p \rightarrow O_{\in I} \textbf{PrecededBy}(p)$
where $I = [\textbf{PrecededMinDelay}(p), \textbf{PrecededMaxDelay}(p)]$. Specifies the event p is preceded by $\textbf{PrecededBy}(p)$		
PeriodProperty(p)	event (data)	$(F_{\leq v}!enabled \lor \triangleright_{[v,v+j]} p) \land G(rise(enabled) \rightarrow (F_{\leq v}!enabled \lor \triangleright_{[v,v+j]} p)) \land G((p \land enabled) \rightarrow (F_{\leq u}!enabled \lor \triangleright_{[u,u+j]} p))$
where $u = \textbf{PeriodInterval}(p)$, $v = \textbf{PeriodOffset}$, $j = \textbf{PeriodJitter}$, $enabled = \text{mode} \in \textbf{PeriodEnabled}$. Specifies the event p occurs within the specified period and optional offset.		
ThroughputRatio(p)	event (data)	$\textbf{PeriodInterval}(p) = \textbf{ThroughputRatio}(p) * \textbf{PeriodInterval}(\textbf{ThroughputInput}(p))$
Specifies the throughput of event p as an ratio of the throughput of $\textbf{ThroughputInput}(p)$.		
ToleranceProperty(p)	port	$G(\sharp p <= \textbf{Tolerance}(p))$
Specifies the tolerated number of failure events $\textbf{Tolerance}(p)$. This is generally an assumption for other properties.		
MTTF(x)	event, component	$\text{ExpectedTime}(\text{mode} \in \textbf{FailureCondition}(x))$
The expected time (mean time) until $\textbf{FailureCondition}(x)$ holds.		
MTTR(x)	event, component	$\text{ExpectedTime}(\text{mode} \notin \textbf{FailureCondition}(x))$ with starting state $= \textbf{FailureCondition}(x)$
The expected time (mean time) until $\textbf{FailureCondition}(x)$ no longer holds.		
Availability(s)	system	$\text{LRA}(\text{mode} \notin \textbf{FailureCondition}(s))$
The availability specified as the *long-run average* of s being in a nominal mode.		

4.2   Coverage of the Design Attributes

In the next Table we summarize how the design attributes are formalized using AADL and the CSSP property set. For each design property, the associated CSSP parameter(s) or AADL structure are listed that allows its formalization.

Design Attributes	CSSP parameters or structure
allocated processor and memory	Connected component of category **processor** or **memory**.
processing capacity, clock frequency, endianness, memory size, addressable memory units	**InvariantRange** or **Function** property associated to corresponding connected feature. E.g., the system as an input port called processing capacity connected to the processor and **InvariantRange**=1(MHz)..5(MHz) applied to such a port.
list of sub-systems, type of sub-systems, connections between sub-systems	Modeled as AADL subcomponents and port connections between components.
redundancy scheme, memory protection mechanism	The sub-system architecture establishes the available redundancy. System modes identify the current sub-system configuration. E.g., the system has 2 identical CPUs, CPU A and CPU B, fully cross-strapped with 2 identical memory modules, mem A and mem B. In nom-nom mode, CPU A and mem A are used. In nom-red mode, CPU A and mem B are used.
area, volume, alignment, stiffness, tolerance, geometry, flatness, fixation, mass, inertia, voltage, current, margins for electrically induced effects, temperature and thermal resistance.	A (constant) **Function** property associated to corresponding connected feature. E.g., the system type has an output port called voltage and has set 50(Volts) as **Function** applied this port.
response to inputs and *reaction time*	**Reaction** and **ReactionLatency** associated to input event or event data ports.
events or specific *functions*	Modeled as AADL event ports.
The *input that is required to generate an output*	**PrecededBy** associated to output event or event data ports.
modes, mode transitions, transition triggers	Modeled as AADL modes, mode transitions and transition triggers (event ports).
mode invariants	**ModeInvariant** associated with an AADL mode.
input data rates, output data rates	**PeriodInterval** associated to input/output event data ports.
volatile data	Default semantics (no formalization is required).
persistent data	**Change** event associated to a data port of an AADL component modeling a persistent memory.
processing steps	Modeled as AADL modes and mode transitions.
output data generation	Modeled as event data ports.
monitored parameters, monitor range	The parameters are modeled as event ports, the range is specified with **MonitorRange** for the parameter ports.
monitoring state check frequency	**MonitorEnabled** associated to the parameter port. **MonitorDelay** associated to parameter port (an upper bound on the response time implies a lower bound in the check frequency).
parameter check response actions	**MonitorResponse** associated to parameter port.
parameter check response result	**Function** associated to the output event port set as **MonitorResponse** of the parameter port.

event data	Either by modeling the data port as event data port, or by specifying **PrecededBy** if data generation is triggered by a previous event.
report format	An AADL data component type is used as type of an output event data port of the system and the AADL data component implementation is used to specify the format.
data frequency	Specified by **PeriodInterval** associated to output event data port.
observation mode	**PeriodEnabled** mode associated to an event data port that models the observation event.
list of commands	Modeled as AADL data component types.
type of commands	Modeled as the AADL data type of ports.
command conditions	**PeriodEnabled** mode associated to an event data port that models the command event.
command responses	**Response** associated to command port.
type of messages	AADL implementation of the command data component.
format of the messages	AADL implementation of the command data component.
message rate, jitter	**PeriodInterval** and **PeriodJitter** associated to the command port.
response time, latency, deadline	**ResponseLatency** associated to the command port.
communication windows	**PeriodEnabled** mode associated to an event data port that models the AADL modes in which communication can occur.
throughput	Specify **ThroughputInput** and **ThroughputRatio** to define throughput in terms of input events.
CPU load, communication capacity, memory capacity	AADL connection with input port of processor and **MonitorRange** property associated to connected output port of the system.
kind of failures	Specify **FailureCondition** to determine the failure configuration.
the failure detection delay	Specify **AlarmDelay**.
recovery actions	Specify **Reaction** to indicate the recovery event after an error event.
MTTF, MTTR	Specify **FailureCondition** to determine the time to reach the failed state.
availability	Specify **FailureCondition** in which the system is not available.
tolerance of failures	**ToleratedError** on some input events representing faults or **InvariantRange** on an input data (e.g. the number of good pixels in the CCD of a star tracker must be higher than a certain threshold).

4.3   COMPASS Tool Support

The CSSP has been implemented in the COMPASS toolset [20, 21], where it is possible for a user to specify the CSSP property values for a SLIM model (the input language of COMPASS). Such properties are automatically translated by COMPASS into their formal counterparts, which are then analyzed by the toolset. Furthermore, it is possible to specify contracts based on these properties, for which consistency and refinement checks can be made [22].

4.4   Example

To provide a better understanding of the use of the CSSP, we give an example based on a standard watchdog. This example and a more complete case study, modeling additionally an AOCS and a Startracker, using different kinds

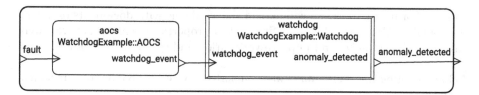

Fig. 1. Watchdog example

of CSSP properties is available at http://compass.informatik.rwth-aachen.de/ publications/safecomp2016/.

The AADL architecture is shown in Fig. 1. The AOCS process periodically sends a signal to the watchdog when running in nominal mode "alive". In addition it has a failure mode "dead" in which the signal is not sent. The watchdog raises an alarm if it does not receive the signal. To formalize this, we can set the following AADL properties:

Timeout(anomaly_detected)   => 1 Sec;
TimeoutReset(anomaly_detected)   => reference(watchdog_event);
PeriodInterval(watchdog_event)   => 1 Sec;
PeriodEnabled(watchdog_event)   => (reference(alive));
ModeInhibited(dead)   => (reference(watchdog_event));
Reaction(fault)   => reference(anomaly_detected);
ReactionMaxDelay(anomaly_detected) => 3 Sec;

These properties automatically specify the formal properties *Complete-TimeoutProperty*(watchdog.anomaly_detected), *PeriodProperty*(aocs.watchdog_event), *ModeInhibitedProperty*(aocs.watchdog_event), and *ReactionProperty*(fault), as defined in Sect. 4.1. Moreover, COMPASS can automatically verify that *ModeInhibitedProperty*(aocs.watchdog_event) and *CompleteTimeoutProperty*(watchdog.anomaly_detected) entail (logically) *ReactionProperty*(anomaly_detected).

5   Conclusions and Future Work

This paper provides an important contribution to close the gap between formal methods and the standard practices in system and software design. It describes an extension of AADL that defines a catalogue of AADL properties with a precise formal semantics and provides a mapping from standard design attributes typically used in system and software design to the AADL properties. This allows the designer to easily apply model checking techniques to verify the component behaviors or to check the consistency among the properties specified at different abstraction levels. To cover a wise range of properties we collaborated with space engineers analyzing standards and requirement documents taken from the space domain. For future work, we will extend the catalogue with documents of different domains. Moreover, this predefined set of properties opens up new research directions to customize and improve verification and synthesis techniques.

Acknowledgments. This work was supported by ESA/ESTEC (contract no. 4000111828).

References

1. As-2 Embedded Computing Systems Committee SAE: Architecture Analysis & Design Language (AADL). SAE Standards n° AS5506B, September 2012
2. Dwyer, M.B., Avrunin, G.S., Corbett, J.C.: Property specification patterns for finite-state verification. In: Formal Methods in Software Practice, pp. 7–15. ACM (1998)
3. Bellini, P., Nesi, P., Rogai, D.: Expressing and organizing real-time specification patterns via temporal logics. J. Syst. Softw. **82**(2), 183–196 (2009)
4. Konrad, S., Cheng, B.H.: Real-time specification patterns. In: Software Engineering, pp. 372–381. ACM (2005)
5. Grunske, L.: Specification patterns for probabilistic quality properties. In: Software Engineering, pp. 31–40. IEEE (2008)
6. Autili, M., Grunske, L., Lumpe, M., Pelliccione, P., Tang, A.: Aligning qualitative, real-time, and probabilistic property specification patterns using a structured English grammar. IEEE Trans. Softw. Eng. **41**(7), 620–638 (2015)
7. Cheng, B., Konrad, S., Campbell, L., Wassermann, R.: Using security patterns to model and analyze security requirements, pp. 13–22. In: RHAS (2003)
8. Bozzano, M., Cimatti, A., Gario, M., Tonetta, S.: Formal design of fault detection and identification components using temporal epistemic logic. In: Ábrahám, E., Havelund, K. (eds.) TACAS 2014 (ETAPS). LNCS, vol. 8413, pp. 326–340. Springer, Heidelberg (2014)
9. Gafni, V., Benveniste, A., Caillaud, B., Graph, S., Josko, B.: Contract specification language (CSL). Speeds D2 (2008)
10. ECSS Std ECSS-E-ST-10-06-C Space Engineering - Technical requirements specification. Technical report third issue, ESA-ESTEC, Requirements & Standards Division, March 2009
11. ECSS Std ECSS-E-ST-10C Space Engineering - System engineering general requirements. Technical report third issue, ESA-ESTEC, Requirements & Standards Division, March 2009
12. ECSS Std ECSS-E-ST-40C Space Engineering - Software. Technical report third issue, ESA-ESTEC, Requirements & Standards Division, March 2009
13. ECSS Std ECSS-E-HB-40A Space Engineering - Software Engineering Handbook. Technical report first issue, ESA-ESTEC, Requirements & Standards Division, December 2013
14. ECSS Std ECSS-E-ST-60-30C Space Engineering - Satellite attitude and orbit control system (AOCS) requirements. Technical report first issue, ESA-ESTEC, Requirements & Standards Division, August 2013
15. ECSS Std ECSS-E-HB-10-02A Space engineering - Verification guidelines. Technical report first issue, ESA-ESTEC, Requirements & Standards Division, December 2015

16. ECSS Std ECSS-S-ST-00-01C ECSS System–Glossary of terms. Technical report third issue, ESA-ESTEC, Requirements & Standards Division, October 2012
17. Bozzano, M., Bruintjes, H., Nguyen, V.Y., Noll, T., Tonetta, S.: SLIM 3.0 - syntax and semantics. Technical report, RWTH Aachen, Fondazione Bruno Kesseler (2016)
18. Koymans, R.: Specifying real-time properties with metric temporal logic. Real-Time Syst. **2**(4), 255–299 (1990)
19. Guck, D., Han, T., Katoen, J.P., Neuhäußer, M.R.: Quantitative timed analysis of interactive Markov chains. In: Goodloe, A.E., Person, S. (eds.) NFM 2012. LNCS, vol. 7226, pp. 8–23. Springer, Heidelberg (2012)
20. COMPASS Project. http://compass.informatik.rwth-aachen.de. Accessed 11 Mar 2016
21. Noll, T.: Safety, dependability and performance analysis of aerospace systems. In: Artho, C., Ölveczky, P.C. (eds.) FTSCS 2014. CCIS, vol. 476, pp. 17–31. Springer, Heidelberg (2015)
22. Cimatti, A., Tonetta, S.: A property-based proof system for contract-based design. In: Software Engineering and Advanced Applications, pp. 21–28. IEEE (2012)

A High-Assurance, High-Performance Hardware-Based Cross-Domain System

David Hardin[1]($\boxtimes$), Konrad Slind[1], Mark Bortz[1], James Potts[1], and Scott Owens[2]

[1] Rockwell Collins Advanced Technology Center, Cedar Rapids, USA
david.hardin@rockwellcollins.com
[2] University of Kent, Canterbury, UK

Abstract. Guardol is a domain-specific language focused on the creation of high-assurance cross-domain systems (*i.e.*, network guards). The Guardol system generates executable code from Guardol programs while also providing formal property specification and automated verification support. Guardol programs and specifications are translated to higher order logic, then deductively transformed to a form suitable for code generation. Recently, we extended Guardol to support regular expressions; this has enabled the creation of a class of fast and secure hardware guards. We justify the regular expression extension via proof that the extension compiles to the original language while preserving key correctness properties. In this paper, we detail the verified compilation of regular expression guards written in Guardol, producing Ada, Java, ML, and VHDL. We have compiled a regular expression guard written in Guardol to VHDL, then synthesized and tested the guard on a low-SWAP (Size, Weight, And Power) embedded FPGA-based hardware guard platform; performance of the FPGA guard core exceeded the data payload rate for UDP/IP packets on Gigabit Ethernet, while consuming less than 1 % of FPGA resources.

1 Introduction

As critical systems become increasingly internetworked, they become ever more vulnerable to cyber attacks. Experience with the public Internet has shown that high-profile vulnerabilities, such as HeartBleed, MyDoom, Sobig.F, Confiker, and ShellShock, continue to crop up, outpacing the ability of the off-the-shelf software development community to "plug the leaks". These vulnerabilities are pernicious in that they are generally very low-level, and are "a needle in a haystack," existing within a software corpus of millions of lines of code. In the case of the public Internet, patches can be developed rather quickly (on the order of days to weeks), and distributed throughout the Internet in a matter of days. Critical networked embedded systems typically utilize the same sorts of operating systems and applications as in the public Internet, but do not embrace rapid update cycles; a shipboard system, for example, may go years between upgrades, leaving many known vulnerabilities unpatched for long stretches of time.

© Springer International Publishing Switzerland 2016
A. Skavhaug et al. (Eds.): SAFECOMP 2016, LNCS 9922, pp. 102–113, 2016.
DOI: 10.1007/978-3-319-45477-1_9

Cross-domain systems, or *guards*, can provide a line of defense against cyber attack for critical applications in areas such as military communications and avionics. A cross-domain system mediates information sharing between safety/security domains according to a specified policy. Figure 1 depicts a guard controlling information flow between two networks. Guards are similar in principle to firewalls, but focus more on application-level filtering, and undergo more rigorous accreditation.

Fig. 1. Idealized two-way guard

In a typical guard, both the "low side" and "high side" networks terminate at the guard, and only certain protocols are allowed to transit the guard from one side to the other, and then only if the protocol headers are valid. Further, user-programmable logic allows the guard to either accept, reject, or modify data payloads carried by the allowed protocols, based on a user-defined policy. In theory, cross-domain systems provide a very high "cyber-wall" to any would-be attacker. However, most cross-domain systems are architected as applications hosted on the same sorts of operating systems and hardware platforms that have shown to be so vulnerable to cyber attack. Thus, an attacker can exploit a known vulnerability in the cross-domain system operating system (NB: the operating systems for most cross-domain systems tend to be older versions, and are infrequently updated) in order to bypass the guard logic entirely.

It is possible, however, to architect a cross-domain system in such a way that the core guard logic is not bypassable. This type of guard architecture is embodied by the Rockwell Collins Turnstile guard [5]. In the Turnstile architecture, the network interfaces for the "low side" and "high side" networks are allocated to their own CPUs and operating systems, and the core guard logic is implemented on a third, separate high-assurance processing platform. Data movement amongst processing platforms is mediated by hardware, and a high degree of assurance is provided that the guard logic is NEAT (Non-bypassable, Evaluatable, Always invoked, and Tamper-proof). In the Turnstile architecture, this NEAT property is established through the use of the Rockwell Collins AAMP7G microprocessor, which has earned a United States Department of Defense MILS certification, stating that it is capable of simultaneously processing Unclassified through Top Secret Codeword information [24]. Turnstile has been accredited to DCID 6/3 PL 5 (the highest level), and is UCDSMO listed [20].

The advantages of this approach are apparent; since the AAMP7G is a highly trustworthy platform with a hardware-based separation kernel, it is much less vulnerable to the usual sorts of cyber attacks. A potential disadvantage comes in terms of absolute performance. The AAMP7G is an embedded CPU with a typical 150 MHz internal clock, so an AAMP7G-based guard would not be appropriate for high-throughput applications. However, one could implement the basic Turnstile architecture, replacing the AAMP7G with a hardware-based guard engine, and achieve both extremely high performance, as well as a very low vulnerability to typical cyber attacks.

1.1   Guardol for Cross-Domain Systems

Most guards are programmed using proprietary rule languages. These languages are limited in their capabilities; lack portability from one guard vendor to another; exhibit unpredictable performance; and do not provide assurance that the rulesets written by operators satisfy higher-level security properties. The Guardol system [10] is designed to overcome these limitations. The Guardol language is a domain-specific language for expressing portable, high-assurance guard logic, as well as the specification and proof of guard properties. The Guardol system generates source code from Guardol programs for several target languages, and also provides formal specification and automated verification support. Guard programs and specifications are translated to higher order logic, then deductively transformed to a form suitable for a SMT-style decision procedure for recursive functions over algebraic datatypes. The result is that difficult properties of Guardol programs can be proved fully automatically. In recent work, we have added support for regular expressions, in the form of a formally verified compiler from regular expressions to Deterministic Finite-state Automata (DFAs), using the Derivatives approach due to Brzozowski [6]. We have established the mathematical correctness of the compilation from Guardol regular expressions to DFA arrays utilizing the HOL4 theorem prover.

Guardol is primarily a sequential imperative language, with non-side-effecting expressions; assignment; arrays; traditional control flow operators such as if statements, for and while loops; and procedures with in out parameters. To this extent, Guardol is quite similar to traditional imperative languages such as Ada [1]. To this base we add datatype declaration facilities similar to those found in SML [16]. Recursive programs over such datatypes are supported by ML-style pattern-matching. This hybrid language approach supports writing elegant programs over complex data structures, while also providing standard programming constructs familiar to most developers.

An example Guardol function that demonstrates the use of the ML-style match operator appears below. The function inserts a tree into a priority queue.

```
function ins(t: in Tree, tlist: in TreeList) returns Output: TreeList = {
  match tlist {
    'Nil => Output := 'Cons [hd: t, tl: 'Nil];
    'Cons c =>
      if t.rank < c.hd.rank then
        Output := 'Cons [hd: t, tl: tlist];
      else
        Output := ins(link(t, c.hd), c.tl);
  }
}
```

Guardol's verification support centers around property specifications, expressed in Guardol syntax. A specification that priority queue rank order is preserved by the insertion function ins above is given by:

```
spec rank_ordered_ins = {
  var t : Tree;
      list : TreeList;
  in
    if rank_ordered(list) then
      check rank_ordered(ins(t, list));
    else skip;
}
```

This property specification is automatically verified by the Guardol toolchain.

1.2   Guardol and Hardware-Based Guards

When we contemplated generating hardware guard logic from Guardol source, we realized that not all legal Guardol programs would be able to be translated to a hardware description language such as VHDL [11], at least not in the short term. But, a great deal of practical Guardol functionality would be directly translatable, including regular expressions. Indeed, due to the nature of the compiled output for regular expressions (repeated array indexing), very high assurance regular expression matching in VHDL targeting a modern FPGA could be achieved, resulting in very high-performance programmable hardware-based guards. We have validated these initial feasibility and performance claims for Guardol-derived hardware guards utilizing regular expressions, as will be discussed in Sect. 6.

In the hardware-based guard workflow, a guard logic developer expresses the desired guard behavior in Guardol, which is much simpler than VHDL, and does not require knowledge of hardware. The guard logic developer utilizes the Eclipse-based Guardol Interactive Development Environment (IDE). The Guardol toolchain then translates the user's Guardol program into VHDL, while also translating any property specifications that the user wishes to prove into a form that can be handled by the SMT backend. The Guardol SMT backend then attempts to prove these properties, and provide results to the user. The VHDL is then be compiled to a "bit file" using standard VHDL compilation tools provided by the FPGA vendor. Finally, this bit file is loaded onto the guard platform using a standard JTAG interface, which typically connects to the user's computer via USB.

In this paper, we describe the development of a proof-of-concept system that supports this workflow. In particular, we describe how we crafted a high-assurance hardware-based cross-domain system prototype in which the Guardol language was used to express the guard functionality, and the Guardol toolchain was used to generate VHDL as well as produce proofs of guard correctness. Finally, we report on measured performance and FPGA resource consumption for a Guardol-based hardware guard prototype.

2   The Guardol Toolchain

The Guardol toolchain architecture is illustrated in Fig. 2. A guard program is created, edited, and typechecked in the Guardol IDE before being sent to HOL4 theorem prover [22], operating in fully automated fashion, for formal modeling. HOL4 defines the Guardol abstract syntax tree form, as well as the operational semantics of the language. From this semantic model, the program can be reasoned about formally; and Ada, Java, CakeML [13], or VHDL code can be generated from it.

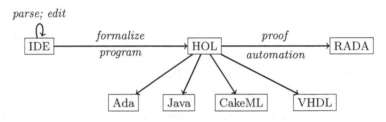

Fig. 2. Guardol toolchain

2.1   Guardol IDE

The Guardol IDE is used to create, edit, and typecheck Guardol programs, as well as to initiate code generation and formal analysis. The Guardol IDE is based on Xtext, an Eclipse-hosted IDE generator [7]. Xtext uses ANTLR [18] to express the Guardol grammar and builds an IDE around the resulting parser.

2.2   Verification

The verification path provides automated proof for Guardol property specifications. We use HOL4 to give a semantics to Guardol evaluation. Decompilation into logic formally transforms specifications about Guardol program evaluation into properties of HOL functions (which have no evaluation semantics). HOL4 is also used as a semantical conduit to RADA, our automated SMT-based tool for reasoning about catamorphisms ("fold" functions) [19].

Figure 3 illustrates the heart of the verification path. A package defining types $\tau_1, \ldots, \tau_j$, and programs $p_1, \ldots, p_k$, along with property specifications $s_1, \ldots, s_\ell$ to be proved is mapped directly to HOL. The "decompilation into logic" phase then formally reduces the programs and property specifications into their denotations in logic. Thus programs $p_1, \ldots, p_k$ translate to logic functions $f_1, \ldots, f_k$ and specifications $s_1, \ldots, s_\ell$ translate to logic goals (formulae) $g_1, \ldots, g_\ell$. Any inductive goals are processed using induction schemes derived from the definition of $f_1, \ldots, f_k$ before being shipped off to the RADA decision procedure, if needed.

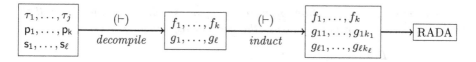

Fig. 3. Guardol verification path

The Guardol verifier has been able to automatically prove complex properties of recursive functions over unbounded algebraic datatypes, *e.g.*, properties of priority queues and red-black search trees [19].

3   Adding Regular Expressions to Guardol

We have extended the Guardol language with a new primitive expression

$$\mathsf{regex\_match}(rlit, s)$$

which takes a regular expression literal[1] *rlit*, and a string expression *s*, and returns a boolean result. In the Guardol toolchain, our intent is to ensure that the code generation path and the verification path agree on the semantics of the programs and specifications being handled. In the case of regular expressions, this manifests in a *proof translation* and a *code translation*, which are related by a formally proved correctness theorem.

3.1   Proof Translation

In the proof translation, $\mathsf{regex\_match}(rlit, s)$ maps to $s \in \mathcal{L}(r)$, where $r = \mathsf{parse}(rlit)$ is the regexp corresponding to *rlit*. Therefore, reasoning about the regex_match expression will be based on the set-theoretic formal language semantics of r.

Definition 1 (Language of an Extended Regular Expression). *The semantics of regular expressions, $\mathcal{L}(-)$, maps from a regular expression to a formal language (set of strings). Strings are represented as lists of characters. The abstract syntax of regular expressions can be given by the following ML-style datatype declaration.*

```
regexp ::= Epsilon             ; empty string
         | Symbs of charset     ; set of characters
         | Or of regexp regexp  ; disjunction
         | Cat of regexp regexp ; concatenation
         | Star of regexp       ; Kleene star
         | Not of regexp        ; complement     (non-standard)
         | And of regexp regexp ; intersection   (non-standard)
```

---

[1] Regular expression literals in Guardol largely conform to the syntax found in the Python programming language.

Complement and intersection operators support succinct specifications; their inclusion does not formally increase the class of regular languages.

$$
\begin{aligned}
&\mathcal{L}(\mathsf{Epsilon}) && = \{\varepsilon\} \\
&\mathcal{L}(\mathsf{Symbs}\ P) && = \{[x] \mid x \in P\} && ;\text{strings of length 1} \\
&\mathcal{L}(\mathsf{Or}\ r_1\ r_2) && = \mathcal{L}(r_1) \cup \mathcal{L}(r_2) \\
&\mathcal{L}(\mathsf{Cat}\ r_1\ r_2) && = \mathcal{L}(r_1) \cdot \mathcal{L}(r_2) && ;\text{concatenation} \\
&\mathcal{L}(\mathsf{Star}\ r) && = (\mathcal{L}(r))^* && ;\text{Kleene star} \\
&\mathcal{L}(\mathsf{Not}\ r) && = \overline{\mathcal{L}(r)} && ;\text{complement} \\
&\mathcal{L}(\mathsf{And}\ r_1\ r_2) && = \mathcal{L}(r_1) \cap \mathcal{L}(r_2)
\end{aligned}
$$

3.2 Code Translation

The code translation maps regex_match($rlit, s$) to the application of a DFA to s. In particular, regex_match($rlit, s$) maps to a function call Exec_DFA(D,s) where Exec_DFA is defined, in Guardol syntax, as

```
function Exec_DFA (d:DFA, s:string) returns verdict:bool = {
var q : int;
in
  q := d.init;
  for (i=0; i < length(s); i++) { q := d.trans(q,s[i]); }
  verdict := d.final(q);
}
```

The DFA type is a record comprising the components of the automaton. An abstract presentation is as follows:

```
type DFA =
 [init  : state                    ; start state
  trans : state * char -> state    ; transition table
  final : state -> bool            ; final states]
```

The transition function, which takes a pair (q, c) consisting of the current state (q) and the current character in the string (c), and returns the next state, is represented by a two-dimensional array. Thus matching a string is very quick, since there is one array indexing operation per character position in the string. Similarly, the final states are also represented in an array, with constant-time lookup, so the final check to see if the string is accepted takes essentially one computation step.

Regular Expression Compilation. A variety of means exist to translate a regular expression to a corresponding DFA. We chose one from Brzozowski [6], who proposed an algorithm that compiles regular expressions directly to DFAs, avoiding low-level automata constructions and treating non-standard—but useful—boolean operations such as negation and intersection uniformly. The core of the algorithm is an elegant quotient construction identifying regular expressions with DFA states. Recent work [17] has shown that his method often generates minimal DFAs and can be extended to large character sets and character classes.

We have formalized and proved correct a version of Brzozowski's algorithm in HOL4. The complete HOL4 proof that the array-based DFA code generated by the Brzozowski method implements the meaning of regular expressions is provided in the HOL4 distribution, culminating in the following theorem :

Theorem 1 (Correctness of regexp compilation).

1. ⊢ (compile_regexp r = (*state_numbering, delta, accepts*)) ∧
2. (lookup regexp_compare (normalize r)*state_numbering* = SOME *start_state*) ∧
3. dom_Brz_alt empty [normalize r]
   ⇒
4.   ∀s. EVERY(λc. ORD c < alphabet_size) s
5.   ⇒ (exec_dfa *accepts delta start_state* s = regexp_lang r s)

In words:

1. *Suppose regexp r is compiled to state_numbering (a map from regexps to states), delta (a state transition table), and accepts (a list of the accepting states)—together these comprise the DFA;*
2. *the original regexp r (normalized) corresponds to the start state of the DFA; and*
3. *the regexp compilation terminates; then*
4. *for any string s made solely from characters in the alphabet,*
5. *the result of running the DFA on s delivers a verdict that agrees with the semantics of r (regexp_lang is the HOL4 name for $\mathcal{L}(-)$ and exec_dfa is the HOL4 name for Exec_Dfa).*

Termination. Notice that the theorem above is constrained to apply when the input is "terminating". This is formalized in the dom_Brz_alt predicate, which returns true just when the regexp compiler terminates. This predicate, and the compiler itself, have been defined using the approach of Greve and Slind [9], which allows the definition of partial recursive functions while also supporting deferred termination proofs and executability of the defined function. This allows our compiler to be introduced into the logic and proved correct, while deferring the proof of termination.

Assurance Levels. The formal regexp compiler can be applied in several ways. First, it can be executed "inside the logic" in order to build the desired DFA for a given regexp, delivering a corresponding formal theorem for that problem instance. This can be thought of as an *ultra high assurance* DFA generator. Alternatively, we have generated CakeML [13] source code from the HOL4 definitions of the regexp compiler and compiled them with CakeML. In this approach, Theorem 1 pairs with the correctness of the CakeML compiler in a "once-and-forall" fashion to produce a very high assurance formally verified DFA generator, where the correctness extends to the execution of the DFA at the binary level. Another choice would be to take the generated CakeML, which is in a subset of Standard ML, and compile it with an off-the-shelf ML compiler. This would result in a higher performance DFA generator, at the price of some loss in assurance at the binary executable level.

4   Guardol VHDL Code Generation

In order to perform VHDL code generation for regular expression-based Guardol programs, the key task is to generate VHDL for the Exec_DFA function. Syntactically, VHDL is quite similar to Ada, the previous primary target language for Guardol code generation. Semantically, however, the two languages are quite different. While the Ada developer thinks in terms of traditional imperative programming language idioms for the most part, with occasional forays into concurrency if tasking is being used, the VHDL developer must think first and foremost about parallel execution. Ada variables become VHDL signals; Boolean types become std_logic types; Integer types become std_logic_vector types; Strings become RAM entities; and loops with control variables become parallel processes with sensitivity lists.

This yields a hardware implementation that provides examination of one byte of input packet data, and one DFA transition, per clock of the state machine. Here our choice of compilation to a DFA (vs. NFA) form is doubly fortuitous, as it yields simple (i.e., no backtracking) state machine hardware that provides predictable performance, regardless of the complexity of the regular expression.

5   FPGA-Based Guard Architecture and Implementation

Figure 4 illustrates the FPGA architecture for our prototype hardware guard.

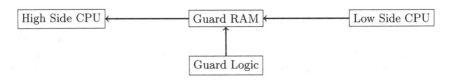

Fig. 4. Hardware guard FPGA architecture.

Low Side and High Side networking are handled separately by CPU cores that are resident in the FPGA (note that for higher-performance applications, the cores could be external to the FPGA). A core may be either a hard core, or a soft core. Upon receipt of a packet on the correct port, the Low Side writes the packet into the Guard RAM. The Guardol-derived Guard Logic inspects the packet, and renders a pass/fail verdict on it. If the packet passes the Guard Logic inspection, it is transferred to the High Side CPU. To create a two-way guard, one would merely replicate the Guard RAM and Guard Logic blocks, and connect these new blocks to the High Side CPU and Low Side CPU, reversing the dataflows.

6 Results

To summarize our achievements on this project:

1. We have successfully generated VHDL code for a Guardol program employing regular expression pattern matching, and have synthesized this VHDL for a Xilinx Zynq FPGA. The regular expression guard logic (mainly the DFA traverser) and DFA tables consume less than 1 % of the FPGA's registers and LUTs.
2. We have incorporated this VHDL code into a compact Rockwell Collins-designed hardware-based prototype guard circuit board measuring 8 cm by 15 cm, and dissipating only 7.5 W, allowing power-over-Ethernet operation.
3. We have measured the performance of Guardol-derived regular expression guard VHDL code on our prototype hardware. The FPGA guard core can process 964,000,000 bits/sec at a system clock rate of 167 MHz, which exceeds the payload data rate of UDP/IP over Gigabit Ethernet. This level of performance was achieved using a modest clock rate on an FPGA that was designed for embedded, not high-performance, applications. Successful synthesis of the guard core is possible for this same FPGA up to a system clock of 250 MHz.
4. We have proven that the regular expression extension compiles to the original Guardol language while preserving key correctness properties. We have formally shown that the Brzozowski regular expression compiler is correct with respect to the standard formal language semantics of regular expressions.
5. We have produced high-assurance guards for several representative security-critical applications, such as a regular expression-based guard for complex JSON-based application data packets. Recently, we have begun to explore utilizing Guardol and the Guardol toolchain to produce high-assurance, high-speed, low-SWAP bus monitors for CAN bus, MIL-STD-1553, *etc.*

7 Related Work

Guardol is one of several verification-enhanced programming languages; other such languages include SPARK/Ada [3], Dafny [14], the Leon subset of the Scala programming language [4], as well as certain C dialects [15,23].[2] Guardol is unique amongst these in that it is a domain-specific language. Elements of the Leon environment motivated our work; in particular, its SMT-based solver for catamorphisms was a starting point for our RADA algorithm. One significant difference between the Guardol toolchain and the Leon environment is our use of HOL4 as a formal Intermediate Verification Language (IVL), as described further in [21]. An example of a verification-enhanced version of C that is similar in spirit to our work is Appel's Hoare Logic for Leroy's CompCert C [2], which is derived from the operational semantics of CompCert C [15]. Properties of C

---

[2] Note that any logic capable of expressing computable functions, *e.g.*, ACL2 [12] or higher order logic, can be regarded as a verification-enhanced programming language; our emphasis here is on more conventional programming languages.

code can be extended down to low-level code by use of the correctness proof of the CompCert compiler. Several domain-specific languages for hardware description are documented in the literature. One such language is Kansas Lava [8], a Haskell-hosted Embedded DSL. Kansas Lava is much more expressive for hardware design than is Guardol, but Kansas Lava lacks a formal IVL that enables proofs of correctness of the sort described in this paper.

8   Conclusion

We have extended the Guardol domain-specific language for cross-domain systems to support regular expressions; this has enabled the creation of a class of fast and secure hardware guards. We take advantage of the fact that the Guardol toolchain translates Guardol source to higher order logic, then deductively transforms it to a form suitable for code generation, to prove that the regular expression extension compiles to the original language while preserving key correctness properties. We have accomplished verified compilation of regular expression guards written in Guardol, producing Ada, Java, ML, and VHDL. We have compiled a regular expression guard written in Guardol to VHDL, then synthesized and tested the guard on a low-SWAP (Size, Weight, And Power) embedded FPGA-based hardware guard platform; performance of the FPGA guard core exceeds the data payload rate for UDP/IP packets on Gigabit Ethernet, while consuming less than 1 % of FPGA resources. We have thus demonstrated that a verification-enhanced domain-specific language for cross-domain systems can readily generate efficient and high-performance hardware-based guards, resulting in a very high degree of assurance for critical applications.

References

1. Ada Working Group (ISO WG 9). Ada Reference Manual: Language and Standard Libraries (2012)
2. Appel, A.W.: Program Logics for Certified Compilers. Cambridge University Press, Cambridge (2014)
3. Barnes, J.: High Integrity Software: The SPARK Approach to Safety and Security. Addison-Wesley, Boston (2003)
4. Blanc, R., Kuncak, V., Kneuss, E., Suter, P.: An overview of the Leon verification system: verification by translation to recursive functions. In: Proceedings of the 4th Workshop on Scala, SCALA 2013, New York, NY, USA, pp. 1:1–1:10. ACM (2013)
5. Bortz, M., Wilding, M., Marek, J., Hardin, D., Hiratzka, T.D., Limondin, P.: High-assurance architecture for routing of information between networks of differing security level. United States Patent 8,161,529, April 2012
6. Brzozowski, J.: Derivatives of regular expressions. J. ACM **11**(4), 481–494 (1964)
7. Eysholdt, M., Behrens, H.: Xtext: implement your language faster than the quick and dirty way. In: Proceedings of the ACM International Conference on Object Oriented Programming Systems Languages and Applications Companion, SPLASH 2010, pp. 307–309. ACM (2010)

8. Gill, A., Bull, T., Kimmell, G., Perrins, E., Komp, E., Werling, B.: Introducing Kansas Lava. In: Scholz, S.-B., Morazán, M.T. (eds.) IFL 2009. LNCS, vol. 6041, pp. 18–35. Springer, Heidelberg (2010)

9. Greve, D., Slind, K.: A step-indexing approach to partial functions. In: Proceedings of the Eleventh International Workshop on the ACL2 Theorem Prover and its Applications. Electronic Proceedings in Theoretical Computer Science, vol. 114, pp. 42–53 (2013)

10. Hardin, D., Slind, K., Whalen, M., Pham, T.H.: The Guardol language and verification system. In: Flanagan, C., König, B. (eds.) TACAS 2012. LNCS, vol. 7214, pp. 18–32. Springer, Heidelberg (2012)

11. Institute of Electrical and Electronics Engineers: IEEE Standard VHDL Language Reference Manual (2000)

12. Kaufmann, M., Manolios, P., Moore, J.S.: Computer-Aided Reasoning: An Approach. Texts and Monographs in Computer Science. Kluwer Academic, Boston (2000)

13. Kumar, R., Myreen, M.O., Norrish, M., Owens, S.: CakeML: a verified implementation of ML. In: POPL 2014: Proceedings of the 41st ACM SIGPLAN-SIGACT Symposium on Principles of Programming Languages, pp. 179–191. ACM Press, January 2014

14. Leino, K. Rustan M.: Developing verified programs with Dafny. In: Proceedings of the International Conference on Software Engineering, ICSE 2013, Piscataway, NJ, USA, pp. 1488–1490. IEEE Press (2013)

15. Leroy, X.: Formal verification of a realistic compiler. Commun. ACM **52**(7), 107–115 (2009)

16. Milner, R., Tofte, M., Harper, R., MacQueen, D.: The Definition of Standard ML (Revised). The MIT Press, Cambridge (1997)

17. Owens, S., Reppy, J., Turon, A.: Regular-expression derivatives re-examined. J. Funct. Program. **19**(2), 173–190 (2009)

18. Parr, T., Fisher, K.: LL(*): the foundation of the ANTLR parser generator. In: Proceedings of the 32nd ACM SIGPLAN Conference on Programming Language Design and Implementation, PLDI 2011, pp. 425–436 (2011)

19. Pham, T.H., Gacek, A., Whalen, M.W.: Reasoning about algebraic data types with abstractions. J. Autom. Reasoning (2016, to appear)

20. Rockwell Collins: Rockwell Collins Turnstile Selected for UCDMO's Baseline List of Validated Cross Domain Products, March 2012

21. Slind, K., Hardin, D., Davis, J., Owens, S.: Benefits of using logic as an intermediate verification language. In: Review (2016)

22. Slind, K., Norrish, M.: A brief overview of HOL4. In: Mohamed, O.A., Muñoz, C., Tahar, S. (eds.) TPHOLs 2008. LNCS, vol. 5170, pp. 28–32. Springer, Heidelberg (2008)

23. Tuch, H., Klein, G., Norrish, M.: Types, bytes, and separation logic. In: Proceedings of the 34th Annual ACM SIGPLAN-SIGACT Symposium on Principles of Programming Languages, POPL 2007, New York, NY, USA, pp. 97–108, ACM (2007)

24. Wilding, M., Greve, D., Richards, R., Hardin, D.: Formal verification of partition management for the AAMP7G microprocessor. In: Hardin, D. (ed.) Design and Verification of Microprocessor Systems for High-Assurance Applications, pp. 175–192. Springer, New York (2010)

Automotive

Using STPA in an ISO 26262 Compliant Process

Archana Mallya[1], Vera Pantelic[1(✉)], Morayo Adedjouma[2], Mark Lawford[1],
and Alan Wassyng[1]

[1] McMaster Centre for Software Certification,
Department of Computing and Software, McMaster University,
Hamilton, ON, Canada
{mallya,pantelv,lawford,wassyng}@mcmaster.ca
[2] CEA LIST, LISE, Gif-sur-Yvette Cedex, France
morayo.adedjouma@cea.fr

Abstract. ISO 26262 is the de facto standard for automotive functional safety, and every automotive Original Equipment Manufacturer (OEM), as well as their major suppliers, are striving to ensure that their development processes are ISO 26262 compliant. ISO 26262 mandates both hazard analysis and risk assessment. Systems Theoretic Process Analysis (STPA) is a relatively new hazard analysis technique, that promises to overcome some limitations of traditional hazard analysis techniques. In this paper, we analyze how STPA can be used in an ISO 26262 compliant process. We also provide an excerpt of our application of STPA on an automotive subsystem as per the concept phase of ISO 26262.

Keywords: Hazard analysis · Risk assessment · STPA · ISO 26262 · ASILs · Automotive industry · Battery Management System

1 Introduction

Systems Theoretic Process Analysis (STPA) [6] is a relatively novel hazard analysis technique, geared towards modern, software-intensive complex systems in which analyzing the interacting subsystems as separate entities could give misleading results. Recently, STPA has gained popularity in the automotive domain (e.g., [2,4,8]). Also, ISO 26262 [5] has become the de facto standard for automotive functional safety. Given the industry's gradual shift to compliance with ISO 26262, the topic of STPA's application in an ISO 26262 compliant process is highly relevant to enabling greater acceptance of STPA in the industry. The key difference between *STPA* and the *Hazard Analysis and Risk Assessment (HARA)* process of ISO 26262 is the risk assessment. While STPA has proven itself as an effective hazard analysis technique across industries, it does not—nor was it intended to—include risk analysis.

In this paper, we carefully explore how to use STPA to satisfy the hazard analysis requirements of the concept phase of development as per ISO 26262, and how to augment STPA with an appropriate risk analysis. First, we provide a detailed comparison of the standard and the technique: we note the major

A. Skavhaug et al. (Eds.): SAFECOMP 2016, LNCS 9922, pp. 117–129, 2016.
DOI: 10.1007/978-3-319-45477-1_10

similarities and differences in the philosophical underpinnings of the two, and provide a comparison of their key terms. Then, we build on the comparisons to check if and how every relevant artefact as required/recommended by ISO 26262 can be generated/supported by applying STPA. Finally, we illustrate the application of the approach on a real-world automotive subsystem provided by our industrial partner, a large automotive OEM.

Although the topic of using STPA in an ISO 26262 compliant process has been the subject of study [4], or at least its significance has been recognized [3,8], to the best of the authors' knowledge, this paper represents the first detailed account of the topic. The closest to an investigation of the topic is presented in [4], where the author suggests that HAZOP (Hazard and Operability), STPA and FMEA (Failure Mode and Effects Analysis) could be used in the concept phase of development as per ISO 26262. Although [4] provides a rough, high-level view on the topic, our work presents a detailed analysis of the topic with illustrative examples. Also, Hommes [3] suggests investigating the effectiveness of STPA in the automotive domain as the ISO 26262 recommended hazard analysis techniques are not sufficient to handle the growing complexity of modern software intensive safety-critical systems.

This paper is organized as follows. Section 2 provides relevant background. Section 3 provides a comparison of the terminologies of STPA and ISO 26262, while Sect. 4 presents guidelines on how to use STPA in an ISO 26262 compliant process, illustrated with an excerpt from an automotive subsystem. Section 5 concludes the paper and provides suggestions for future work.

This paper is based on the Master's thesis of the first author [7], and we refer the reader to it for further details.

2 Preliminaries

In this section, we provide a brief introduction to STPA and ISO 26262.

2.1 Systems Theoretic Process Analysis (STPA)

STPA is based on the accident causation model called STAMP (Systems-Theoretic Accident Model and Processes), built on systems theory and systems engineering [6]. The main ideas behind systems theory are: (1) Emergence and Hierarchy and, (2) Communication and Control [6]. Safety is considered an *emergent* system property: the safety of the whole system cannot be guaranteed just by proving that the system's individual components are safe. Further, systems are modeled as a *hierarchy* of organizational levels, where each level is more detailed than the one above. Also, accidents are treated as a dynamic *control problem* (as opposed to the classical approach viewing accidents as caused by component failures only): accidents occur when inadequate or inappropriate control actions (commands issued by system's controllers) violate the safety constraints of the system.

The STPA technique follows three steps: Preliminary step (Step 0), Step 1 and Step 2. Step 0 deals with the identification of accidents, associated hazards, safety constraints as a negation of those hazards, and drawing of the control structure (a functional abstraction of the system). Step 1 identifies the ways in which unsafe control actions could lead to accidents, and the corresponding safety constraints. Step 2, causal factor analysis, involves identifying the causes of previously identified unsafe control actions along with the corresponding safety constraints. The detailed steps to perform STPA are described in Sect. 4.

STPA promises to address some limitations of traditional hazard analysis techniques as it accounts for the interactions between the subsystems and the dynamics between the system and its environment, along with management issues and human factors. There exists related work in various domains that presents cases where STPA identified hazards previously not identified by ISO 26262 recommended hazard analysis techniques (a detailed review of the literature can be found in [7]). For example, Song [10] applied STPA on the Nuclear Darlington Shutdown system and compared the results with the original FMEA results. The author found that, when compared with FMEA, STPA identified more hazards, failure modes and causal factors, including inadequate control algorithms, missing feedback and an incorrect logic model [10].

There have been varied opinions on the ease of use of STPA and the learning curve involved. There is no strong evidence to suggest that STPA is harder to use than traditional hazard analysis techniques. According to the controlled experiment presented in [1], there is no significant difference in the ease of use and understandability between STPA, FMEA and FTA (Fault Tree Analysis).

2.2 ISO 26262 Standard

ISO 26262, published in late 2011, addresses functional safety of road vehicles, and applies to electric, electronic and software components within the vehicle [5]. ISO 26262 consists of ten parts, and our work focuses on the Hazard Analysis and Risk Assessment (HARA) clause of Part 3 of [5].

The *Item Definition* is a necessary prerequisite for the HARA. The *item* is defined as "system", "or array of systems to implement a function at the vehicle level, to which ISO 26262 is applied", [Part 1 of [5]]. It contains the requirements for the item under study, its dependencies and its interactions with the environment and other items. The HARA comprises Situation Analysis, Hazard Identification, Classification of *Hazardous Events*, and Determination of *Automotive Safety Integrity Levels (ASILs)* and *Safety Goals*. The Situation Analysis determines "the operational situations and operating modes in which an item's malfunctioning behaviour will result in a hazardous event". The *Operational situation* is defined as a "scenario that can occur during a vehicle's life" (e.g., driving), while the *operating mode* is a "perceivable functional state of an item or element" (e.g., system off, degraded operation, emergency operation), [Part 1 of [5]]. The Hazard Identification step involves identifying the *vehicle level hazards*, the *hazardous events* and *consequences of hazardous events*. Hazardous events are determined by considering the hazards in different operational situations identified during the situation analysis. In the Classification of Hazardous Events step, the hazardous events are classified using impact factors *Severity (S)*, *Probability of Exposure (E)* and *Controllability (C)*. The severity is estimated based on the extent of potential harm to each person potentially at risk. The parameter ranges from S0 to S3. The probability of exposure is the duration or the frequency of occurrence of the operational situations and is valued from E0 to E4. The controllability factor, ranged from C0 to C3, is an estimation of the ability of the driver or other persons potentially at risk to control the hazardous event. ASIL levels help determine the stringency of the requirements and the safety measures needed to avoid what the standard considers to be unreasonable risks. The Determination of ASILs for each hazardous event is based on the estimated values of the severity, probability of exposure and controllability parameters in accordance with Table 4 of Part 3 of [5], and range from ASIL A to ASIL D (highest criticality). Another class called Quality Management (QM) exists to denote there is no safety requirement to comply with. For each hazardous event with an assigned ASIL, a safety goal shall be determined as a top-level safety requirement for the item. The ASIL identified for a hazardous event shall also be assigned to the corresponding safety goal.

Then, the Functional Safety Concept (FSC) clause helps derive the *Functional Safety Requirements (FSRs)* from the item's safety goals based on preliminary architectural assumptions. The standard suggests using traditional safety analyses like FMEA, FTA, and HAZOP to support the FSR specification.

3   STPA and ISO 26262

In this section, we first compare the foundations of STPA and ISO 26262, and then compare their central terminologies. Table 1 presents definitions of central terms used by STPA as defined in [6] and ISO 26262, as defined in Part 1 of [5].

3.1   STPA and ISO 26262: Comparing Foundations

Both ISO 26262 and STPA are based on a systems engineering framework in which a system is considered to be more than merely the sum of its parts. Top-down analysis and development are common to both. However, while ISO 26262 emphasizes the importance of considering the context of a system in achieving safety (including the role of safety management and safety culture), there seems to be no consensus whether ISO 26262 considers a driver to be a part of the hazard analysis of an item. STPA on the other hand, includes all relevant aspects of the system's environment, including the driver.

The key difference between STPA and the HARA process of ISO 26262 is the risk assessment process. Risk assessment as per ISO 26262 involves determining the impact factors: Severity (S), Probability of Exposure (E) and Controllability (C). While ISO 26262 justifiably avoids using probabilities of failure of system components to estimate risk (estimating the probability of failures in modern

Table 1. Definitions of terms in STPA and ISO 26262

Term	STPA [6]	ISO 26262 [Part 1 of [5]]
Hazard	A system state or set of conditions that, together with a particular set of worst-case environmental conditions, will lead to an accident (loss)	Potential source of harm caused by malfunctioning behaviour of the item
Malfunctioning behaviour	No explicit definition	Failure or unintended behaviour of an item with respect to its design intent
Failure	No explicit definition. Note: A failure in engineering can be defined as the non-performance or inability of a component (or a system) to perform its intended function	Termination of the ability of an element, to perform a function as required. Note: Incorrect specification is a source of failure
Accident	An undesired or unplanned event that results in a loss, including loss of human life or human injury, property damage, environmental pollution, mission loss, etc.	No explicit definition
Harm	No explicit definition	Physical injury or damage to the health of persons
Hazardous event	No explicit definition	Combination of a hazard and an operational situation

systems is very hard given the prevalence of non-random failures and the lack of historical information), determining E and C factors is still rather subjective and not yet standardized in the industry. Although SAE J2980 presents a recommended practice to "provide guidance for identifying and classifying hazardous events, which are as per [5]", its current focus is limited to collision related hazards and not the wider scope of ISO 26262 [9]. Although some authors suggest using only severity for risk estimation [3], an ISO 26262 compliant process requires that S, E and C factors are determined and used.

3.2 STPA and ISO 26262: Comparing Basic Terminologies

Important terms are italicized in this section and defined in Table 1.

Starting from the definition of term *hazard*, the most notable difference between the definitions of the term is that STPA does not limit *hazards* to those caused by *malfunctioning behaviour*, while ISO 26262 does. Due to ISO 26262's ambiguity in the definition of the term of *malfunctioning behaviour* (both "design intent" and "unintended behaviour" are undefined in the standard), it is hard to determine what exactly the term is intended to mean. However, it seems that ISO 26262, by including "unintended behaviour of an item with respect to its design intent" in the definition of *malfunctioning behaviour*, departs from the notion that only component failures lead to accidents, but also includes unintended interactions of the system components often reflected in flawed requirements.

ISO 26262 does not have an explicit definition of *accident*. However, STPA's *accident* defines unacceptable losses; hence, it is very closely related to ISO 26262's *harm*. We note that STPA's concept of loss not only includes human injury or loss of human life, but also property damage, pollution, mission loss, etc., and hence is more general than ISO 26262's which considers only injury to people. We note, however, that STPA is meant for different stakeholders to adapt it as it suits them. Further, the consequences of hazardous events of ISO 26262, identified by considering the consequences of the *hazard* in various operational situations, could be mapped to *accidents* of STPA. However, STPA's *accidents* are more general in nature—ISO 26262's consequences tend to be more fine-grained, since they are determined for different operational situations of the *hazard*.

4   Using STPA in an ISO 26262 Compliant Process

The foundation and terminology comparison presented in Sect. 3 lays the groundwork for our approach of using STPA in an ISO 26262 compliant process. In this section, we explore how every relevant artefact as required/recommended by ISO 26262 can be generated/supported by applying STPA. We illustrate the approach on a simplified version of the Battery Management System (BMS) of a Plug-in Hybrid Electric Vehicle (PHEV). Not all the details of the analysis and the control structure are shown due to their proprietary nature.

A PHEV is a hybrid electric vehicle (a vehicle combining Internal Combustion Engine (ICE) propulsion with electric propulsion) that has energy storage devices like rechargeable batteries that can be charged by connecting to the electrical grid using a plug. These rechargeable batteries are monitored and protected by the BMS. The primary functions of the example BMS are to: (1) enable charging and discharging of the battery back by closing the contactors; or disable charging and discharging of the battery back by opening the contactors, (2) provide accurate information on charge and discharge to the HPC (Hybrid Powertrain Controller) system, (3) equalize cell charge using passive cell balancing, (4) heat/cool the battery pack, (5) isolate the battery in case of emergency.

Figure 1 shows the STPA results (as shown on the right hand side of the figure) that can help generate the outputs required by the concept phase of ISO 26262 (as shown on the left hand side of the figure), illustrated with examples. The grey dashed box includes blocks numbered i2 to i10 corresponding to all the subclauses of the HARA. Rectangles denote outputs (artefacts) obtained as a result of either following the requirements of ISO 26262 or performing STPA steps. An oval inside a rectangle represents the output of HARA that is itself required to determine the output represented by the encompassing rectangle. The solid arrows from STPA blocks to ISO 26262 blocks denote that the specific STPA output can completely support the corresponding ISO 26262 block output, while the dashed arrows denote that the specific STPA output can partially support the corresponding ISO 26262 block output. The dotted arrows are used to represent cases where a result of STPA can help provide additional support in generating an output of ISO 26262. The numbers in the form of w-x-y-z point to the specific subclause of the standard where the requirements are specified. w corresponds to the specific part of the ISO 26262 standard, x corresponds to the specific clause and y-z corresponds to the subclauses where the requirements of the clauses and subclauses are mentioned.

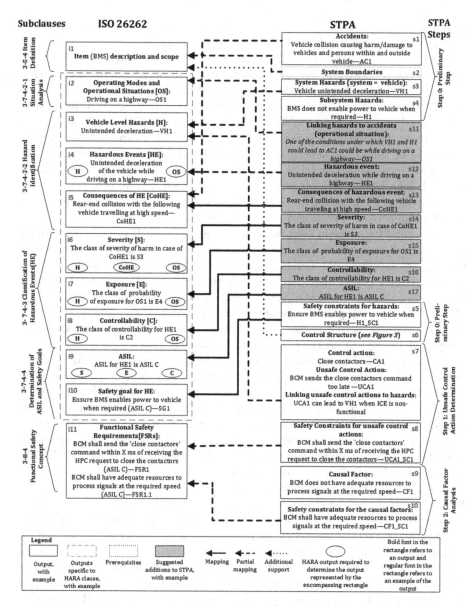

Fig. 1. STPA in compliance with ISO 26262, illustrated with excerpt of BMS example

As shown in Fig. 1, there exist outputs of the original STPA that have been mapped to ISO 26262's outputs represented by blocks i1, i2, i3, i5, i10 and i11. However, ISO 26262's outputs represented by blocks i4, i6, i7, i8 and i9 have no corresponding outputs of the original STPA—instead, we augment STPA's outputs with a set of new outputs (shaded rectangles in the figure) and present guidelines on how they can be generated. The mappings from Fig. 1 are discussed next in the sequence in which STPA is performed.

First, in the initial step of STPA (Step 0), accidents, related hazards, corresponding safety constraints, and the control structure of the system under analysis are defined. *Accidents* of STPA are mapped to the standard's *consequences of hazardous events* (s1 → i5 mapping). However, *accidents* are typically not as fine-grained as *consequences of hazardous events*, since STPA does not consider *accidents* in different *operational situations*. Thus, STPA can *partially* support derivation of the *consequences of hazardous events*. However, *consequences of hazardous events* are only to be determined later in the STPA process compliant with ISO 26262 after *hazardous events* have been determined. An example of a vehicle accident would be *AC1: Vehicle collision causing harm/damage to vehicles and persons within and outside vehicle.*

Next in STPA, vehicle level hazards are determined. If the hazards cannot be eliminated or controlled at the system level, the corresponding component hazards are identified. An example of a system (vehicle) level hazard for *AC1* is *VH1: Vehicle experiences unintended deceleration*, which maps to the vehicle level hazard (block i3) of ISO 26262. A corresponding BMS-level hazard is *H1: BMS does not enable power to vehicle when required*. *H1* is a refinement of *VH1* as *H1* is hazardous in the case when ICE is non-functional so the vehicle is completely dependent on the power from the battery pack.

In an ISO 26262-compliant process, *operational situations* should be documented. This is why, in our approach, we explicitly document *operational situations* during the process of linking hazards to accidents (block s11). When analyzing in what situations the hazards *VH1* and *H1* could lead to *AC1*, we can come up with situations like *driving on a highway, snow, ice on road, etc.* To help analysts in determining operational situations, the standard presents examples of operational situations (the examples have been summarized in [7]). As mentioned in ISO 26262, an overly detailed list of *operational situations* might result in "a very granular classification of *hazardous events*" and could eventually lead to "an inappropriate lowering" of an *ASIL* [Part 3 of [5]].

Once we have the list of *operational situations* and *hazards*, we can derive the *hazardous event* (block s12), as it is the combination of a *hazard* and an *operational situation*. Thus, we augment STPA to include this step (block s12). For *VH1*, a hazardous event identified is *HE1: Unintended deceleration while driving on highway*. It is at this point when the *consequence of hazardous event* is determined (block s13). For example, the consequence of *HE1* would be *CoHE1: Rear-end collision with the following vehicle travelling at high speed.*

Classification of hazardous events and *determination of ASILs* are the main subclauses of the concept phase of ISO 26262 that do not have a corresponding step in STPA. As per ISO 26262, the severity of potential harm is estimated using injury scales like the Abbreviated Injury Scale (AIS) and Maximum AIS in accordance with the Table 1 of Part 3 of [5]. According to ISO 26262, the *severity* is determined for a hazardous event, based on the *consequence of the hazardous event*. Using the results obtained from blocks i2, i3 and i5, i.e., *operational sit-*

uations, hazards and consequences of hazardous events, we can estimate the S impact factor (block i6) as per ISO 26262. For *HE1*, the class of severity of harm is *S3* (Life-threatening injuries). Further, the class of probability of exposure for driving on a highway is *E4* (greater than 10 % of average operating time). Then, the class of controllability for unintended deceleration while driving on a highway is *C2*, i.e. 90 % or more of all drivers or other traffic participants are usually able to avoid harm. The impact factors *S3*, *E4*, and *C2* were estimated based on Tables 1, 2, and 3 of Part 3 of [5], respectively. *ASILs* are then determined using the values of *S, E and C* from previous blocks and using Table 4 of Part 3 of [5]. The ASIL for the above chosen impact factors is *ASIL C*.

For each of the hazardous events with an assigned ASIL, a *safety goal* is determined. *Safety constraints* (block s5) derived as the negation of hazards in STPA's Step 0 can be used to support the *safety goal* determination subclause of ISO 26262 (as shown by the mapping s5 → i10), as the safety goals are high-level requirements. An example of a safety constraint for *H1* is *H1_SC1: Ensure BMS enables power to the vehicle when required*, corresponding to ISO 26262's *safety goal*, denoted *SG1*. *SG1* is then assigned *ASIL C*, as determined for *HE1*.

The next task in STPA is the development of *control structure* (block s6) as a graphical representation of the functional model of the system [6]. Building from the vehicle view, a control structure for the entire vehicle (including driver and environment) is first built so that hazards due to interactions between the components can be identified (Fig. 2). Thus, an STPA control structure gives a holistic view of the entire system under study. We then zoom in on the BMS itself, with the control structure as given in Fig. 3. The *HPC (Hybrid Powertrain Controller)*, the contactors, the battery pack and the 12 V battery are the external systems that interact with the BMS. Other systems in the BMS environment are the fan/pump components for the thermal management system, the on-board charger, and the external charger. The components of the BMS are shown inside the shaded dashed box in Fig. 3, namely, the *BCM (Battery Control Module)*, *BMM (Battery Monitoring Module)*, and the history log and cells specification module. The components and arrows as shown in Fig. 3 were identified based on the general functionalities of a BMS elicited through literature review and with the help of domain experts. The *control structure*, as a control-oriented diagram depicting the functionalities of an item, is additional information to help an analyst in accomplishing part of the item definition output. Thus it represents a valuable diagram that complements the existing item definition (block i1)—hence the dotted s6 → i1 mapping in Fig. 1.

In STPA Step 1, the control actions from the control structure are categorized into four categories, i.e., four ways in which a control action can be unsafe (see Table 2). The control action selected for Step 1 of this example application is *CA1: Close contactors*. This control action is sent by the BMS after it receives the authorization or a request to close the contactors from the HPC. When the contactors are closed in the driving mode, the battery pack can receive power from HPC from regenerative braking and the HPC can receive power from the battery pack. Let us consider the control action *CA1: Close contactors* under the category 'Safe control action is provided too late, too early, wrong

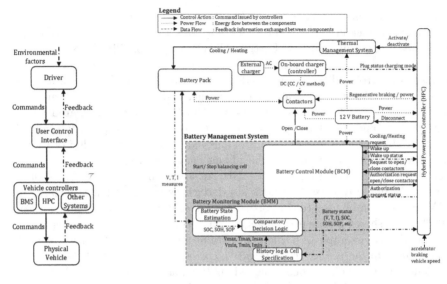

Fig. 2. High level control structure

Fig. 3. Detailed BMS control structure [7]

order'. An example of unsafe control action would be *UCA1: BCM sends the close contactors command too late*. When analyzing the ways in which a control action can be unsafe and linking them to the hazards, the analyst has to identify the context which makes the control action hazardous. In this case, the *UCA1* can lead to *VH1: Vehicle experiences unintended deceleration*, when the *ICE is non-functional*. The assumption is that the HPC has already requested the BMS to close the contactors and that the HPC gives the command only when safe to do so. When linking UCAs to the hazards of Step 0, one can sometimes identify hazards that were not previously identified. Hence, Step 1 can be linked to the hazard identification step of ISO 26262 as well (see mapping s7 → i3). Step 1 also involves translating the UCAs into safety constraints and further refining the safety constraints from Step 0 (block s8). An example of a safety constraint for *UCA1* is *UCA1_SC1: BCM shall send the 'Close contactors' command within X ms of receiving the HPC request to close the contactors*. Since this safety constraint of Step 1 describes what needs to be done to achieve the *safety goal*, it represents ISO 26262's *functional safety requirement* (denoted by s8 → i11).

Causal factor analysis (Step 2) of STPA involves examining the control loop of control actions and identifying the causes of unsafe controls (block s9 from Fig. 1). The control loop includes the controller that initiates the control action, the actuator, the sensor, and the controlled process [6]. A unique control loop is identified and used for all identified Unsafe Control Actions (UCAs) of the selected control action. Then, a causal factors analysis diagram is defined for the UCAs based on the guide words provided by STPA [6]. Part of our causal factor

Table 2. Excerpt of results of STPA Step 1 for CA1: close contactors

Control action	Required control action not provided	Unsafe control action provided	Safe control action provided too late, too early, wrong order	Continuous safe control action provided too long or stopped too soon
CA1:Close contactors	...	...	UCA1:BCM sends the close contactors command too late [VH1]	...

analysis for *UCA1* is shown in Fig. 4. Specific causes of UCAs that may lead to hazards are shown in *italics*.

For the loop in Fig. 4, the BCM, as a controller, should issue the control action *Close Contactors* to the actuators that will realize the command. The controlled process in the loop is the battery pack. During the causal factors analysis we assume that the HPC has already sent the request to close the contactors. For the sake of simplicity, in Fig. 4, we have only shown a few of the causal factors of the contactors, the battery pack, the BMM, the BCM including its process model and the ones between the BCM and the contactors. Other causal factors (e.g., 12 V power disconnected) are not shown here. The causal factors identified in STPA Step 2 can help fulfill one of the objectives of the safety analyses as per ISO 26262 (Clause 8 of Part 9 of ISO 26262), i.e., to identify the "causes that could lead to the violation of a safety goal or safety requirement". Once the causes are identified, the analyst needs to identify the

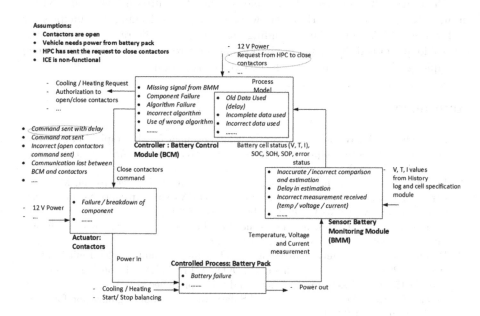

Fig. 4. Causal factor analysis for control action, CA1: Close contactors

safety constraints to mitigate or eliminate those causes. One of the causes which could result in *UCA1* is *BCM does not have adequate resources to process signals at the required speed*. An example of a Step 2 safety constraint identified for *CF1* is *CF1_SC1: BCM shall have adequate resources to process signals at the required speed*. This Step 2 safety constraint represents a *functional safety requirement* of ISO 26262—hence the mapping s10 → i11. While the level of details needed when defining the safety constraints during STPA is not pre-determined, ISO 26262 specifies the characteristics and parameters that a safety requirement should include, e.g., the fault tolerant time interval if available, the safe state, the operating mode, etc.

5   Conclusion and Future Work

While STPA represents a promising hazard analysis technique that addresses some limitations of traditional techniques, it does not attempt to provide the risk analysis component sometimes included in traditional hazard analysis techniques. By careful investigation of the requirements of the HARA clause of Part 3 of ISO 26262, we conclude that STPA does not interfere with the ISO 26262's risk analysis in any way—instead, STPA was shown to only require modest augmentation in order to be used in a HARA process compliant with ISO 26262. Thus, the augmented STPA presented here can support all the outputs of ISO 26262 generated as a result of satisfying the standard's HARA requirements. Consequently, we can utilize STPA's advantages in an ISO 26262-compliant process.

There are now a number of examples in the literature on how to use STPA in an automotive context. However, what seems to be lacking is principles for performing STPA. For example, finding an appropriate abstraction level for the control loop seems to be extremely important. Future work on documenting such principles and their rationale would be extremely useful.

References

1. Abdulkhaleq, A., Wagner, S.: A controlled experiment for the empirical evaluation of safety analysis techniques for safety-critical software. In: EASE 2015, pp. 16:1–16:10. ACM (2015)
2. D'Ambrosio, J., Debouk, R., Hartfelder, D., Sundaram, P., Vernacchia, M., Wagner, S., Thomas, J., Placke, S.: Application of STPA to an automotive shift-by-wire system. In: STAMP Workshop, Cambridge, MA (2014)
3. Hommes, Q.V.E.: Review and assessment of the ISO 26262 Draft Road Vehicle - Functional Safety. SAE technical paper (2012)
4. Hommes, Q.V.E.: Safety analysis approaches for automotive electronic control-systems (2015). http://www.nhtsa.gov/DOT/NHTSA/NVS/Public%20Meetings/SAE/2015/2015SAE-Hommes-SafetyAnalysisApproaches.pdf
5. ISO 26262: Road Vehicles - Functional Safety. International Organization for Standardization (ISO) (2011)
6. Leveson, N.G.: Engineering a Safer World: Systems Thinking Applied to Safety (Engineering Systems). The MIT Press, Cambridge (2012)

7. Mallya, A.: Using STPA in an ISO 26262 compliant process. M.A.Sc., McMaster University, Canada, October 2015
8. NHTSA: Request for comment on automotive electronic control systems safety and security (2014). https://federalregister.gov/a/2014-23805
9. SAE J2980: Considerations for ISO 26262 ASIL Hazard Classification, SAE International (2015)
10. Song, Y.: Applying system-theoretic accident model and processes (STAMP) to hazard analysis. M.A.Sc., McMaster University, Canada (2012)

A Review of Threat Analysis and Risk Assessment Methods in the Automotive Context

Georg Macher[1(✉)], Eric Armengaud[1], Eugen Brenner[2], and Christian Kreiner[2]

[1] AVL List GmbH, Graz, Austria
{georg.macher,eric.armengaud}@avl.com
[2] Institute for Technical Informatics, Graz University of Technology, Graz, Austria
{brenner,christian.kreiner}@tugraz.at

Abstract. Consumer demands for advanced automotive assistant systems and connectivity of cars to the internet make cyber-security an important requirement for vehicle providers. As vehicle providers gear up for the cyber security challenges, they can leverage experiences from many other domains, but nevertheless, must face several unique challenges. Thus, several security standards are well established and do not need to be created from scratch. The recently released SAE J3061 guidebook for cyber-physical vehicle systems provides information and high-level principles for automotive organizations to identify and assess cyber-security threats and design cyber-security aware systems.

In the course of this document, a review of available threat analysis methods and the recommendations of the SAE J3061 guidebook regarding threat analysis and risk assessment method (TARA) is given. The aim of this work is to provide a position statement for the discussion of available analysis methods and their applicability for early development phases in context of ISO 26262 and SAE J3061.

Keywords: TARA · ISO 26262 · SAE J3061 · Automotive · Security analysis

1 Introduction

Numerous industrial sectors are currently confronted with massive difficulties originating from managing the increasing complexity of systems. The automotive industry, for instance, has an annual increase rate of software-implemented functions of about 30 % [1]. This rate is only higher for avionics systems and the Internet of Things [9]. New challenges regarding the manageability of systems are emerging caused by the increasing gap between cross-domain expertise required and the pervasiveness of novel technologies and software functions. In the automotive domain this evolution became challenging with the advent of multi-core processors, advanced driving assistance systems and automated driving functionalities, and the thus broadening societal sensitivity for security and safety properties (remote hacking and control of cars). Management of extra-functional properties (e.g. timing, safety, security, memory consumption, etc.) is still one of

A. Skavhaug et al. (Eds.): SAFECOMP 2016, LNCS 9922, pp. 130–141, 2016.
DOI: 10.1007/978-3-319-45477-1_11

the core challenges faced by developers of embedded systems [14]. Appropriate systematic approaches to support the development of these properties are thus required. Standards and guidelines, such as ISO 26262 [6] in the automotive safety and more recently SAE J3061 [15] in automotive security domain, have been established to provide guidance during the development of dependable systems and are currently reviewed for similarities and alignment.

In the course of this document, a review of available threat analysis methods and the recommendations of the SAE J3061 guidebook regarding threat analysis and risk assessment method (TARA) is given. The aim of this work is to provide a position statement for the discussion of available analysis methods and their applicability for early development phases in context of ISO 26262 and SAE J3061.

We provide an overview of the recommendations of the SAE J3061 guidebook regarding threat analysis and risk assessment method (TARA) for this paper together with a review of available threat analysis methods. The aim of this work is to provide an evaluation of available analysis methods for the discussion of their applicability for early development phases in the context of ISO 26262 and SAE J3061.

This paper is organized as follows: Sect. 2 reviews the recommendations of the SAE J3061 guidebook regarding threat analysis and risk assessment method (TARA). Based on this review, Sect. 3 analyzes the TARA approaches available in the automotive domain. In Sect. 4 an evaluation of the applicability of the analysis methods for early development phases in context of ISO 26262 and SAE J3061 is provided. Finally, Sect. 5 concludes the work.

2   SAE J3061 Guidebook TARA Recommendations

Safety and security engineering are very closely related disciplines. They both focus on system-wide features and could greatly benefit from one another if adequate interactions are defined. Safety engineering is already an integral part of automotive engineering and safety standards, such as the road vehicles functional safety norm ISO 26262 [6] and its basic norm IEC 61508 [2], are well established in the automotive industry. Safety assessment techniques, such as failure mode and effects analysis (FMEA) [3] and fault tree analysis(FTA) [4], are also specified, standardized, and integrated in the automotive development process landscape.

IEC 61508 Ed 2.0 provides a first approach of integrating safety and security; security threats are to be considered during hazard analysis in the form of a security threat analysis. However, this threat analysis is not specified in more details in the standard and Ed 3.0 is about to be more elaborated on security-aware safety topics. Also ISO 26262 Ed 2.0, which is still in progress, is likely to include recommendations for fitting security standards and appropriate security measure implementations.

The recently published SAE J3061 [15] guideline establishes a set of high-level guiding principles for cyber-security by:

– defining a complete lifecycle process framework
– providing information on some common existing tools and methods
– supporting basic guiding principles on cyber-security
– summarizing further standard development activities

SAE J3061 states that cyber-security engineering requires an appropriate lifecycle process, which is defined analogous to the process framework described in ISO 26262. Further, no restrictions are given on whether to maintain separate processes for safety and security engineering with appropriate levels of interaction or to attempt direct integration of the two processes. Apart from that, the guidebook recommends an initial assessment of potential threats and an estimation of risks for systems that may be considered cyber-security relevant or are safety-related systems, to determine whether there are cyber-security threats that can potentially lead to safety violations.

In paragraph 3.88 of SAE J3061 TARA is defined as: *'an analysis technique that is applied in the concept phase to help identify potential threats to a feature and to assess the risk associated with the identified threats...'* [15]

In paragraph 8.3.3 of SAE J3061 this threat analysis and risk assessment (TARA) method is further specified as a method identifying threats and assessing the risk and residual risk of the identified threats by following three steps:

1. Threat Identification
2. Risk Assessment (includes classification of the risk associated with a particular threat)
3. Risk Analysis, which ranks threats according to their risk level

Beyond this the guidebook does not give any restrictions on how to excerpt the TARA analysis. *'It is left to an organization to determine which TARA method is appropriate for their purposes, and to determine what an acceptable level of risk means ...'* [15]

Appendices A–C of the SAE J3061 provide an overview of the techniques for threat analysis and risk assessments and threat modeling and vulnerability analysis. These TARA methods proposals will also be analyzed in the following section of this document, and are:

– EVITA method
– TVRA
– OCTAVE
– HEAVENS security model
– Attack trees
– SW vulnerability analysis

3   TARA Approaches Available for the Automotive Domain

This section of the document analyzes the TARA approaches available in the automotive domain. Some TARA approach suggestions are already given by

Feature: Remote Vehicle Disable					Severity				Attack Potential								Risk					
Threat ID	Function	Potential Item Threats	Potential Vehicle Level Threat	Potential Worst-Case Threat Scenario	Financial	Operational	Privacy	Safety	Elpsd Time	Expertise	Knowledge	Window of Opportunity	Equipment Required	Attack Probability Total	Attack Prob.	Controllability (Safety)	Financial	Operational	Privacy	Safety	Cybersecurity Goal ID	Cybersecurity Goals

Fig. 1. The EVITA method using THROP spreadsheet example (from [15])

Appendix A of the SAE J3061 guidebook [15]. This section thus mentions those TARA approaches already introduced by SAE J3061 (recommended or not-recommended) and those not mentioned in the guidebook separately. Additionally, SAE J3061 already mentions a limited applicability of some of the methods introduced for the automotive domain. These methods are only mentioned briefly in this document for the sake of completeness and are not further detailed.

3.1 TARA Approaches Recommended in SAE J3061

The EVITA Method is part of a European Commission funded research project (EVITA - E-Safety Vehicle Intrusion Protected Applications) and is an adaptation of ISO 26262 HAZOP analysis for security engineering. The method is named threat and operability analysis (THROP) and considers potential threats for a particular feature from a functional perspective. Threats are defined at the functional level based on the primary functions of the analyzed feature using attack trees. Thus, THROP first identifies the primary functions of the feature, second applies guide-words to identify potential threats and third determines potential worst-case scenario outcomes from the potential malicious behavior. Figure 1 shows a THROP spreadsheet example.

The risk level determination is also adopted from ISO 26262 (ASIL determination) based on a combination of severity, attack probability, and controllability measures. The severity classification separates different aspects of the consequences of security threats (operational, safety, privacy, and financial); as shown in Fig. 2. Similar to the determination of the ASIL, controllability, severity, and attack probability are mapped to a qualitative risk levels (R0 to R7 and R7+) for classification of the security threats. This risk level determination reveals some issues of the approach: (a) the classification of severity as standardized in ISO 26262 is adopted and thus no longer conforms to the ISO 26262 standard, (b) the classification of safety-related threats and non-safety-related (operational, privacy, and financial) threats differs and could thus lead to imbalance of efforts and (c) the sufficient accuracy of attack potential measures and expression as probabilities is still an open issue, as also the combination of these probabilities by summing, minimum, and maximum operations.

Nevertheless, the classification of attack potentials and the analysis based on threat trees is suitable at feature or system level and thus applicable for embedded automotive systems. Although not explicitly mentioned this method

Security threat severity class	Aspects of security threats			
	Safety (S_S)	Privacy (S_p)	Financial (S_F)	Operational (S_o)
0	No injuries.	No unauthorized access to data.	No financial loss.	No impact on operational performance.
1	Light or moderate injuries.	Anonymous data only (no specific driver of vehicle data).	Low-level loss (~€10).	Impact not discernible to driver.
2	Severe injuries (survival probable). Light/moderate injuries for multiple vehicles.	Identification of vehicle or driver. Anonymous data for multiple vehicles.	Moderate loss (~€100). Low losses for multiple vehicles.	Driver aware of performance degradation. Indiscernible impacts for multiple vehicles.
3	Life threatening (survival uncertain) or fatal injuries. Severe injuries for multiple vehicles.	Driver or vehicle tracking. Identification of driver or vehicle, for multiple vehicles.	Heavy loss (~1000). Moderate losses for multiple vehicles.	Significant impact on performance. Noticeable impact for multiple vehicles.
4	Life threatening or fatal injuries for multiple vehicles.	Driver or vehicle tracking for multiple vehicles.	Heavy losses for multiple vehicles.	Significant impact for multiple vehicles.

Fig. 2. The EVITA severity classification scheme (from [11])

seems to be the method that is most recommended in the SAE J3061 guidebook for an initial assessment of potential threats and estimation of risks for cyber-security relevant or safety-related systems.

HEAVENS Security Model analyzes threats based on Microsoft's STRIDE [8] approach and ranks the threats based on a risk assessment. This risk assessment consists of three steps: (a) determination of threat level (TL), (b) determination of impact level (IL), and (c) determination of security level (SL), which corresponds to the final risk ranking.

The determination of the threat level (TL), which corresponds to a 'likelihood estimation', is based on four parameters (expertise of the attacker, knowledge about the system, window of opportunity, and equipment), which are individually estimated using values between 0 and 3 (referring to the different levels: none, low, medium, and high).

The threat impact level (IL) estimates the impact on four categories (safety, financial, operational, and privacy and legislation). For the IL quantification the impact level of the attack on these four categories is parametrized with no impact (value 0), low (value 1), medium (value 10), or high impact (value 100). The summation of the values of the impact parameters is then quantified via 5 IL values (no impact for 0, low for 1–19, medium 20–99, high 100–999 and critical ≥ 1000)

The threat level factors (TL) and threat impact level (IL) further derive the security level (SL) and thus the ranking of risks. This approach clearly benefits from the structured and systematic STRIDE approach to exploit threats, but requires a huge amount of work to analyze and determine the SL of individual threats; which implies lots of discussion potential for each individual IL and TL factor of each single threat.

3.2   TARA Approaches Also Proposed in SAE J3061

The methods mentioned in this section are also proposed by the SAE J3061 guide book, but are not recommended for application in the automotive context. Thus, these methods are only mentioned in this document for the sake of completeness.

TVRA Threat, vulnerabilities, and implementation risks analysis (TVRA) identifies assets in the system and their associated threats by modeling the likelihood and impact of attacks. The analysis was developed for data - and telecommunication networks and is scarcely applicable for cyber physical systems in vehicles.

OCTAVE Stands for Operationally Critical Threat, Asset, and Vulnerability Evaluation and is a process-driven threat assessment methodology. OCTAVE focuses on bringing together stake holders of security through a progressive series of workshops; thus this approach is best suited for enterprise information security risk assessments but not readily applicable for embedded automotive systems.

Attack Tree Analysis (ATA) is analogous to the safety fault tree analysis (FTA) and thus adequate for exploiting combinations of threats (attack patterns), but requires more details of the system design (thus not appropriate for an initial TARA at early development phases).

SW Vulnerability Analysis, as the name implies, examines software code for known software constructs that should be avoided to prevent from potential vulnerabilities. This method aims at SW development level and is thus inappropriate for early development phases.

3.3   TARA Approaches Not Mentioned by SAE J3061

FMVEA Method is based on an FMEA as described in IEC 60812 [3]. Schmittner et. al [13] present this failure mode and failure effect model for safety and security cause-effect analysis. This work categorizes threats via quantification of threat agents (respectively attacker), threat modes (via STRIDE model), threat effects and attack probabilities. A general limitation of this analysis is the restriction to analyze only single causes of an effect and multi-stage attacks could be overlooked, thus the combination of FTA and ATA for supporting the FMVEA is considered. Nevertheless, the FMVEA method is based on the FMEA (safety pendant) and is thus in-appropriate for early development phases (TARA).

SAHARA Method [7] quantifies the security impact on dependable safety-related system development on system level. The SAHARA method combines the automotive HARA [6] with the security domain STRIDE approach [8] to trace impacts of security issues on safety concepts on the system level.

Table 1. Classification examples of knowledge 'K', resources 'R', and threat 'T' value of security threats

Level	Knowledge example	Resources example	Threat criticality example
0	Average driver, unknown internals	No tools required	No impact
1	Basic understanding of internals	Standard tools, screwdriver	Annoying, partially reduced service
2	Internals disclose, focused interests	Non-standard tools, sniffer, oscilloscope	Damage of goods, invoice manipulation, privacy
3		Advanced tools, simulator, flasher	Life-threatening possible

For the safety analysis an ISO 26262 conform HARA analysis can be performed in a conventional manner. Also a security focused analysis of possible attack vectors of the system can be done using the STRIDE approach independently from the safety team. For a combined approach, the SAHARA method combines the outcome of this security analysis with the outcomes of the safety analysis. Thus, the ASIL quantification concept is applied to the STRIDE analysis outcomes. Threats are quantified aligned with ASIL analysis, according to the resources (R), know-how (K) required to exert the threat, and the threats criticality (T). Table 1 shows the determination schemes for the different elements.

These three factors determine the resulting security level (SecL). The SecL determination is based on the ASIL determination approach and is calculated according to (1).

$$SecL = \begin{cases} 4 & \text{if } 5 - K - R + T \geq 7 \\ 3 & \text{if } 5 - K - R + T = 6 \\ 2 & \text{if } 5 - K - R + T = 5 \\ 1 & \text{if } 5 - K - R + T = 4 \\ 1 & \text{if } T = 3, K = 2, R = 3 \\ 0 & \text{if } 5 - K - R + T < 4 \ or \ T = 0 \end{cases} \qquad (1)$$

The SAHARA quantification scheme is less complex and requires less analysis effort and fewer details of the analyzed system than other proposed approaches. This quantification enables the possibility for determining limits on resources allocated to prevent the system from a specific threat (risk management for security threats) and the quantification of the threats impact on safety goals (threat level 3) or not (all others).

SHIELD is a methodology for assessing security, privacy, and dependability (SPD) of embedded systems and part of a European collaboration of the same name. SHIELD is a multi-metric approach to evaluate the system's SPD level and compares it with use case goals for SPD. The main objective of the methodology is to evaluate multiple system configurations and select those which address or achieve the established requirements. To achieve this aim a triplet is composed of the system's security, privacy and dependability levels (each element is described by a value in a range between 0 and 100). This approach implies a high discussion potential for each of the triplets, due to the lack of a guidance on how to estimate the security, privacy, and dependability values. Additionally, the method becomes increasingly suitable the more details and variants of a system exist and is therefore not optimally applicable for the early design phase TARA analysis.

CHASSIS also combines safety and security methods for a combined safety and security assessments approach. The approach relies on modeling misuse cases and misuse sequence diagrams within a UML behavior diagram, which implies additional modeling expenses for the early development phase. CHASSIS aims at unifying safety and security in the trade-off analysis, to define whether there are features that are mutually dependent or independent of each other. The activity specifies the safety/security requirements by structuring the harm information in the form of HAZOP tables and in combination with the BDMP technique (see next paragraph). Thus, the CHASSIS approach also requires a higher level of detail that is given at the TARA analysis stage.

Boolean Logic Driven Markov Processes (BDMP) represent an approach where fault tree and attack tree analysis are combined and extended with temporal connections. In addition to its logical structuring, this method also enables activation of top events based on triggers or the state of basic events. Furthermore, leave nodes have failure in operation or failure in demand fault behaviors, which extends the abilities of the FTA and ATA depiction of threats. Nevertheless, BDMP is in-appropriate for an early development phase TARA.

Threat Matrix approach proposed by US Department of Transportation [10] is used to consolidate threat data. The threat matrix is spreadsheet based, allowing the matrix to be sorted by various categories as needed. Categories of severity, sophistication level, and likelihood are indicated as high, medium, or low based on expert opinion. Other categories of the matrix are, among others, attack zone safety relation, system involved, vulnerability exploited, attack vector, access method, attack type, and resources required. Thus the threat matrix is another variation of the FMEA approach, which is geared towards the establishment of a threat database but is not the best approach for the early development phase TARA.

Binary Risk Analysis (BRA) [12] is a lightweight qualitative open license risk assessment and included, among others, by OCTAVE and NIST SP800-30. The BRA determines the asset and the threat a system must be protected from and quantizes their impacts by following these steps:

1. Answering the ten (yes/no) questions
2. Mapping the answers to each of the five 2×2 matrices which give a metric for individual attack and system features
3. Using the results from the five 2×2 matrices to select results from three 3×3 matrices (representing attack effectiveness, threat likelihood and impact).
4. Using these factors to final get the risk metric from a final 3x3 matrix.

The Binary Risk Analysis can be used for: (a) a quick risk conversations to enable discussion of a specific risk in just a few minutes, (b) helping to identify where perceptions about risk elements differ. Nevertheless, the Binary Risk Analysis is neither a full risk management methodology nor a quantitative analysis based on statistics and monetary values, nor does it eliminate subjectivity completely from the analysis. BRA is also not a threat discovery or threat risk assessment techniques on its own, which is a requirement for TARA in the early development phases.

4   Evaluation of Methods in ISO 26262 and SAE J3061 Context

This section briefly evaluates the applicability of the analysis methods presented in the previous section for early development phases in context of ISO 26262 and SAE J3061. Table 2 summarizes all the presented methods and the earliest suitable development phase, assets and drawbacks of the methods. As can be seen in the table, in addition to the SAE J3061 recommended EVITA method, two other methods (SAHARA and BRA) are well suited for an early concept analysis (TARA). These methods were already available at the release date of SAE J3061, but are not mentioned in the guide book. Besides this, SAE J3061 recommends two methods (TVRA and OCTAVE), which are scarcely applicable for TARA of embedded automotive systems and no hints are given for application in the automotive context.

Thus, in the context of the EMC^2 project[1] and in cooperation with the experts of the SOQRATES working group[2] an analysis of the 13 methods referred to has been performed and evaluated based on an electric steering column lock use-case for a connected vehicle. This safety-critical and security-related use-case application revealed the four most applicable TARA methods (EVITA method, HEAVENS, SAHARA and BRA) for early development phase analysis of the system. Additionally, if a combined approach for safety and security engineering is utilized the methods SAHARA (for combined analysis of security and safety of the development concept), BDMP (combination of FTA and ATA) and FMVEA (combination of security and safety FMEA) are recommended for use. The following paragraphs provide a brief extract of the use-case application outcomes:

TVRA not applicable for automotive application.

---

[1] http://www.artemis-emc2.eu/.
[2] http://www.soqrates.de/.

OCTAVE not applicable for automotive application.

Attack tree security pendant to FTA and thus for identification of nested attacks. Detailed system design required, thus not applicable for concept evaluation, but recommended for system design analysis.

SW vulnerability only applicable for SW codes, thus not applicable for concept evaluation.

FMVEA security pendant to FMEA. More details of the system design required, thus recommended for system design analysis. Best suitable for a combined safety and security engineering process landscape.

SHIELD guidance for estimation of security, privacy and dependability value triplet missing. The purpose of the analysis is the evaluation of different system configurations, but due to the lack of quantitative determination for the evaluation of the triplets mostly leading to long discussions.

CHASSIS relies on modeling of use-cases and misuse sequences, and is thus appropriate for identification of nested attacks but not applicable for early concept evaluation. Method might only be applied when detailed modeling of use-cases and sequences are available.

BDMP Combination of ATA and FTA, is thus not applicable for concept development evaluation. It is best suited for a combined safety and security engineering process landscape.

Threat Matrix Variant for providing input for establishing a database. Not recommended for concept analysis due to confusing size of table and thus not easy to focus on identification of new threats or threat vectors.

EVITA is a suitable approach for concept evaluation, but requires too many details for classification. These details are estimated based on concept design and thus involves the disadvantage of a huge potential for discussion. The separation of functional, safety, privacy and operational severity adds further potential for discussion but does not result in a significant difference in the resulting risk level. There is too much classification effort based on estimations for the concept evaluation phase.

HEAVENS involves less classification efforts requirements than the EVITA method. The STRIDE threat modeling approach brings additional support structuring for the estimation of threat scenarios.

SAHARA achieves easy classification of threats in combination with STRIDE threat modeling. It was evolved from HARA and STRIDE, thus originally focusing on safety, but redesigned for security evaluation. The basic classification aligned with ASIL classification and is thus optimal for use in combined security and safety engineering processes.

BRA brings easy classification by means of 10 binary decisions in the form of questions. Nevertheless, the resulting risks are only classified as high, medium or low and a conservative analysis trend leads to threat classification solely of high risks. Additionally, no structured estimation of threat scenarios is given and the resulting threat classification is too rudimentary for concept development phases.

Table 2. Evaluation of TARA methods and applicability for concept phase analysis

	Method Name	First applicable Phase	Advantages for Application in Concept Phase	Disadvantages
SAE J3061 recommended	EVITA method	concept phase	classification separates different aspects of the consequences of security threats (operational, safety, privacy, and financial)	classification of severity is adopted and thus not conforming the ISO 26262 standard; classification of safety-related and non-safety-related threats differs and could thus lead to in-balances; accuracy of attack potential measures and expression as probabilities is still an open issues
	TVRA	n.a.		models the likelihood and impact of attacks; complex 10 step approach; developed for data - and telecommunication networks; hardly applicable for cyber physical systems in vehicles
	OCTAVE	n.a.	bringing together stake holders thru series of workshops	approach is best suited for enterprise information security risk assessments; hardly applicable for cyber physical systems in vehicles
	HEAVENS model	system phase	based on Microsoft's STRIDE approach; determination of threat level (TL), impact level (IL), and security level (SL) for classification of threats	requires a high amount of work to analyze and determine the SL of individual threats; implies lots of discussion potential for each individual factor of each single threat
	ATA	system phase	identification of threats in hierarchical manner; adequate for exploiting combinations of threats (attack patterns)	requires more details of the system design to be more accurate, thus better suitable for system phase analysis
	SW vulnerability analysis	SW phase		examines software code to prevent from potential vulnerabilities; in-appropriate for early development phases
not in SAE J3061	FMVEA	system phase	quantification of attacker, threat modes (via STRIDE model), threat effects and attack probabilities	analysis is restricted to single causes of an effect and multi-stage attacks could be easily overlooked; based on the FMEA and thus in-appropriate for concept phase
	SAHARA	concept phase	threat analysis via STRIDE model; security and safety analysis possible in combined and independent manner; easy quantification scheme; no adapation of standardized quantification scheme for safety; requires less analysis efforts and details of the analyzed system	multi-stage attacks could be overlooked; no specific quantification for car fleet attacks; strong relationship to safety engineering
	SHIELD	system phase	evaluate multiple system configurations; only evaluates system's security, privacy and dependability level	implies a high discussion potential for each triplet, due to a missing guidance on how to estimate the security, privacy, and dependability values; not optimally applicable for early design phase TARA analysis
	CHASSIS	concept phase	HAZOP tables and in combination with the BDMP technique	requires a higher level of details as given at conept analysis stage; requires modeling of misuse cases and misuse sequence diagrams
	BDMP	system phase	fault tree and attack tree analysis are combined and extended with temporal connections	based on ATA and FTA and thus less appropriate for concept phase
	Threat Matrix	system phase		spreadsheet and text based; variant of FMEA geared towards establishment of database; not a preferable approach for concept analysis
	BRA	concept phase	threat impact determination via 10 yes/no questions; quick risk conversations to enable discussion of a specific risk	not a full risk management methodology; quantitative analysis not based on statistics or monetary values; not a threat discovery or threat risk assessment techniques by its own, which is required for TARA in early development phases.

5   Conclusion

In conclusion, this work highlights how security standards, such as IEC 62443 [5], or security guidelines, such as SAE J3061 [15], are currently still incomplete or not directly applicable in practice. Their current state is often fragmented, and each typically assumes that their open issues are covered by other guidelines or standards. For this reason a review of novel work by researchers and research projects is highly recommended. This work is thus solely focused on the evaluation of the analysis methods available (presented in SAE J3061 and other research projects) for threat analysis and risk assessment (TARA) method at concept phase. The work briefly summarizes a review of 13 TARA methods done in the context of the EMC^2 project and in cooperation with the experts of the SOQRATES working group. This review, based on a safety critical and security related automotive use-case (electric steering column lock) revealed the four most applicable TARA methods (EVITA method, HEAVENS, SAHARA and BRA) for early development phase analysis of the system. Additionally, it discovers a set of recommended techniques for a combined approach of safety and security engineering processes.

Acknowledgments. This work is supported by the EMC^2 project. The research leading to these results has received funding from the ARTEMIS Joint Undertaking under grant agreement nr 621429 (project EMC^2).

References

1. Ebert, C., Jones, C.: Embedded software: facts, figures, and future. IEEE Comput. Soc. **09**, 42–52 (2009). ISSN: 0018–9162
2. ISO - International Organization for Standardization. IEC 61508 functional safety of electrical/electronic/programmable electronic safety-related systems
3. ISO - International Organization for Standardization. IEC 60812 analysis techniques for system reliability - procedure for failure mode and effects analysis (FMEA) (2006)
4. ISO - International Organization for Standardization. IEC 61025 fault tree analysis (FTA), December 2006
5. ISO - International Organization for Standardization. IEC 62443 - industrial communication networks. Network and system security (2009)
6. ISO - International Organization for Standardization. ISO 26262 road vehicles functional safety part 1–10 (2011)
7. Macher, G., Sporer, H., Berlach, R., Armengaud, E., Kreiner, C.: SAHARA: a security-aware hazard and risk analysis method. In: 2015 Design, Automation Test in Europe Conference Exhibition (DATE), pp. 621–624, March 2015
8. Microsoft Corporation. The STRIDE Threat Model (2005)
9. Miller, M.: The Internet of Things: How Smart TVs, Smart Cars, Smart Homes, and Smart Cities are Changing the World. Que, Indianapolis (2015)
10. National Highway Traffic Safety Administration. Characterization of Potential Security Threats in Modern Automobiles - A Composite Modeling Approach, October 2014
11. Petschnigg, C., Deutschmann, M., Osterhues, A., Steden, L., Botta, S., Krasikau, M., Tverdyshev, S., Diemer, J., Ahrendts, L., Thiele, D., Bernardeschi, C., Natale, M.D., Dini, G., Sun, Y.: D2.1 architecture models and patterns for safety and security (alpha). Report ICT-644080-D2.1, SAFURE Project Partners, February 2016
12. Sapiro, B.: Binary Risk Analysis. Creative Commons License. 1st edn
13. Schmittner, C., Gruber, T., Puschner, P., Schoitsch, E.: Security application of failure mode and effect analysis (FMEA). In: Bondavalli, A., Di Giandomenico, F. (eds.) SAFECOMP 2014. LNCS, vol. 8666, pp. 310–325. Springer, Heidelberg (2014)
14. Sentilles, S., Štěpán, P., Carlson, J., Crnković, I.: Integration of extra-functional properties in component models. In: Lewis, G.A., Poernomo, I., Hofmeister, C. (eds.) CBSE 2009. LNCS, vol. 5582, pp. 173–190. Springer, Heidelberg (2009)
15. Vehicle Electrical System Security Committee. SAE J3061 Cybersecurity Guidebook for Cyber-Physical Automotive Systems

Anomaly Detection and Resilience

Context-Awareness to Improve Anomaly Detection in Dynamic Service Oriented Architectures

Tommaso Zoppi[(✉)], Andrea Ceccarelli, and Andrea Bondavalli

University of Florence, Viale Morgagni 65, Florence, Italy
{tommaso.zoppi,andrea.ceccarelli,bondavalli}@unifi.it

Abstract. Revealing anomalies to support error detection in software-intensive systems is a promising approach when traditional detection mechanisms are considered inadequate or not applicable. The core of anomaly detection lies in the definition of the expected behavior of the observed system. Unfortunately, the behavior of complex and dynamic systems is particularly difficult to understand. To improve the accuracy of anomaly detection in such systems, in this paper we present a context-aware anomaly detection framework which acquires information on the running services to calibrate the anomaly detection. To cope with system dynamicity, our framework avoids instrumenting probes into the application layer of the observed system monitoring multiple underlying layers instead. Experimental evaluation shows that the detection accuracy is increased considerably through context-awareness and multiple layers monitoring. Results are compared to state-of-the-art anomaly detectors exercised in demanding more static contexts.

Keywords: Anomaly detection · Monitoring · Service Oriented Architecture · SOA · Context aware · Multi-layer

1 Introduction

Complex software-intensive systems include several different components, software layers and services. Often, these systems are characterized by a dynamic behavior related to changes in their services, connections or components themselves. In particular, *Service-Oriented Architectures* (SOAs) may aggregate proprietary as well as *Off-The-Shelf* (OTS) services, hiding their implementation details. It is a matter of fact that SOA dynamicity and information hiding obstacle monitoring solutions that directly observe the SOA services [19]. This collides with the increasing interest in using these systems for (safety) critical applications, and raises a call for adequate solutions to monitoring and error detection [1, 21].

Anomaly detection aims to find patterns in monitored data that do not conform to the expected behavior [1]. Such patterns are changes in the trends of indicators such as memory usage or network data exchange characterizing the behavior of the system caused by specific and non-random factors. As an example, anomalies can be due to a system overload, adversarial intrusion attempts, malware activity or manifestation of

A. Skavhaug et al. (Eds.): SAFECOMP 2016, LNCS 9922, pp. 145–158, 2016.
DOI: 10.1007/978-3-319-45477-1_12

errors. Anomaly detection was proved [7] to be effective, highlighting anomalies and timely triggering reaction strategies to finally improve system safety or security.

Investigating dynamic contexts makes the definition of normal (and consequently anomalous) behavior a complex challenge: currently, there are no clear state-of-the-art answers on applying anomaly detection in highly dynamic contexts. Focusing on SOAs, anomaly detection usually requires a reconfiguration step to define the nominal behavior when services are updated, added or removed from the SOA [1]. It follows that anomaly detectors may be reconfigured frequently, reducing their effectiveness and with a negative impact on the SOA execution.

In this paper we present an anomaly detection framework that aims to tackle the challenges above. We tune the monitoring system to observe the underlying layers (e.g., operating system, middleware and network) instead of directly instrumenting the services with monitoring probes. This allows detecting anomalies due to errors or failures that manifest in the services without directly observing them [22]. Therefore, this *multi-layer* approach turned out very suitable to cope with dynamicity of complex systems, at the cost of a calibration time to reconfigure the parameters of the anomaly detector when changes of the components of the complex system are detected. This approach was previously proved effective on systems with reduced dynamicity respect to complex systems [14], while experimental results showed that a more accurate definition of the context was needed in highly dynamic systems [6] to improve detection accuracy. In this study we consider knowledge of basic information on the context - referred as *context-awareness* - that can be easily retrieved from integration modules of SOAs. This knowledge helps defining more precisely the expected behavior of the dynamic target system, resulting in more accurate definition of anomalies and, consequently, a more effective anomaly detection process. In fact, our multi-layer monitoring structure makes available a wide set of indicators, and the most relevant ones for anomaly detection purposes are identified depending on the current context. Consequently they are observed, with corresponding monitoring probes, building time series that are analyzed for anomaly detection purposes.

Summarizing, our main findings are: (i) describing how context-awareness on the SOA services can be used to improve detection; (ii) defining a methodology and the associated framework for anomaly detection in dynamic contexts using context-awareness; (iii) structuring a multi-layer anomaly detection module observing *operating system*, *middleware* (*Java Virtual Machine*, JVM) and *network* layers, (iv) assessing the whole solution on a case study, showing the obtained detection accuracy, which is presented using well-known metrics and (v) compare our detection system with state-of-the-art [2, 3, 14] solutions exercised in less dynamic contexts.

The paper is structured as follows. Section 2 motivates the use of context-awareness, which is at the basis of our work. Section 3 describes the resulting anomaly detection framework and the devised methodology. Section 4 presents the experimental evaluation. State of the art on related approaches and comparison are explored in Sect. 5. Section 6 concludes the paper.

2   Learning from the Past

This work stems from studies by the same authors [6, 14] who devised multi-layer anomaly detection [22] strategies to perform error detection using the *Statistical Predictor and Safety Margin* (SPS, [9]) algorithm. SPS is able to detect anomalies without requiring offline training; this was proved to be very performing in less dynamic contexts [14], where the authors applied SPS to detect the activation of software faults in an *Air Traffic Management* (ATM) system. Observing only OS indicators, SPS allowed implementing an anomaly detector which performed error detection with high precision. Therefore we adapted this promising approach to work in a more dynamic context [6], where we instantiated the multi-layer anomaly detection strategy on the prototype of the Secure! [8] SOA. The results achieved showed that analysing such a dynamic system without adequate knowledge on its behavior reduces the efficiency of the whole solution. Despite the observed data stream was rapidly processed, we obtained a detection time - the time interval between the manifestation of the error and its detection - of 40 s with a high number of false positives and negatives.

We explain these outcomes as follows. SPS detects changes in a stream of observations identifying variations with respect to a *predicted* trend: when an observation does not comply with the predicted trend, an alert is raised. If the system has high dynamicity due to frequent changes or updates of the system components, or due to variations of user behavior or workload, such trend may be difficult to identify and thus predict. Consequently, our ability in identifying anomalies is affected because boundaries between normal and anomalous behavior cannot be defined properly.

2.1   Considering Context-Awareness

We previously highlighted the need of acquiring more information on the target system, still maintaining the main benefits of the abovementioned approach. Consequently, we investigate which information on SOA services we can obtain in absence of details on the services internals and without requiring user context (i.e., user profile, user location). In SOAs, the different services share common information through an *Enterprise Service Bus* (*ESB*, [15]) that is in charge of (i) integrating and standardizing common functionalities, and (ii) collecting data about the services. This means that static (e.g., services description available in *Service Level Agreements* - SLAs) or runtime (e.g., the time instant a service is requested or replies, or the expected resources usage) information can be retrieved using knowledge given by ESB. Consequently, having access to the ESB provides knowledge on the set of generic services running at any time t. We refer to this information as *context-awareness* of the considered SOA; note that we do not require information on the user context, contrary to what is typically done in the state-of-the-art on context-awareness [16, 17].

We can exploit this information to define more precisely the boundaries between normal and anomalous behavior of the SOA. For example, consider a user that invokes a *store file* service at time t. We can combine context-awareness with information on the usual behavior of the service, which here regards data transfer. Therefore, if the *store file* service is invoked at time t, we expect the exchange of data during almost the entire execution of the service. If we observe no data exchange, we can reveal that something anomalous is happening.

2.2 Enhancing Detection Capabilities

Collect Services Information. Let us start from the example of the *store file* service. Our objective is to characterize the normal behavior the service, building a *fingerprint* of its usage. More in details, we need a description of the expected behavior of the service, meaning that we need to describe the *usual trend of the observed indicators* (examples of indicators are in Tables 2 and 3) while the service is invoked. In such a way, we can understand if the current observation complies or not with the expectations. This information can be retrieved in a SOA by observing the ESB and producing a new service fingerprint when the addition, update or removal of a service is detected. In several cases it is also possible to obtain a static characterization of the services looking at their SLA, where each service is defined from its owner or developer for the final user. We remark that we do not consider any assumption about the services except their connection with the ESB: consequently, we can obtain services information from any kind of service running in the SOA platform.

Integrate Information in the Anomaly Detector. Summarizing, information about the services can be obtained (i) statically, looking at SLAs, (ii) at runtime, invoking services for testing purposes or (iii) combining both approaches. In this paper we explore the second approach, discussing this choice in Sect. 3.2. This information needs to be aggregated and maintained (e.g., in a database) together with the calculated statistical indexes (e.g., mean, median), whenever applicable, to support the anomaly detection solutions.

3 Description of the Anomaly Detection Framework

3.1 Architectural Overview

In Fig. 1 we depict a high level view of the framework. Starting from the upper left part of the figure, the framework can be described as follows. The user executes a *workload*, which is a sequence of invocations of SOA services hosted on the *Target Machine*. In this machine *probes* are running, observing the indicators coming from 3 different system layers: (i) *OS*, (ii) *middleware* and (iii) *network*. These probes collect data, providing a *snapshot* of the target system composed by the observation of indicators retrieved at a defined time instant. The probes forward the snapshot to the *communication handler*, which encapsulates and sends the snapshot to the *communication handler* of the *Detector Machine*. Data is analyzed on a separate machine, the Detector Machine (which includes a *Complex Event Processor* - CEP [18]). This allows (i) not being intrusive on the Target Machine, and (ii) connecting more Target Machines to the same Detector Machine (obviously the number of Target Machines is limited by the computational resources of the Detector Machine). The communication handler of the

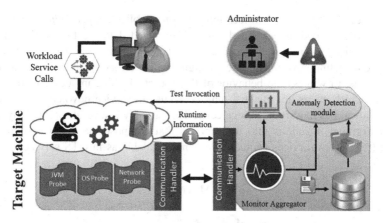

Fig. 1. High-level view of the resulting multi-layer monitoring and anomaly detection framework

Detector Machine collects and sends these data to the *monitor aggregator*, which merges them with *runtime information* (e.g., list of service calls) obtained from the ESB. This allows storing context-awareness information in the database. Looking at *runtime information*, the monitor aggregator can detect changes in the SOA and notify the administrator that up-to-date services information is needed to appropriately tune the anomaly detector. The administrator is in charge of running tests (*test invocation*) to gather novel information on such services.

The snapshots collected when SOA is opened to users are sent to the *anomaly detection module*, which can query the database for services information and analyzes each observed snapshot to detect anomalies. If an anomaly is detected, the *system administrator,* which takes countermeasures and applies reaction strategies (which are outside from the scope of this work and will not be elaborated further), is notified.

3.2   Methodology to Exercise the Framework

The framework is instantiated specifying (i) the *workload* we expect will be exercised on the target system, (ii) the way (static/runtime) the administrator prefers to obtain services information described in Sect. 2.2, (iii) the monitored layers on the Target Machine and the number of probes per layer, and (iv) the *number of preliminary runs* necessary to devise the detection strategy elaborated in Sect. 3.3. The methodology is composed of two phases: *Training the Anomaly Detector* and *Runtime Execution*.

Training the Anomaly Detector. This phase is organized in 3 steps. In the first step, *services information* characterizing the fingerprint of the investigated services can be obtained statically (e.g., from SLA) or at runtime (through the *test invocation* in Fig. 1). In our implementation, we chose this second option because it allows retrieving accurate information on the trend of the individual indicators; static information as SLA usually defines only general service characteristics and requirements.

In the second step, once services information is collected, *preliminary runs* using the expected workload are executed, and the retrieved data – a time series for each monitored indicator - are stored in the database. These data are complemented with data collected conducting error injection campaigns, where errors are injected in one of the SOA services, to witness the behavior of the Target Machine in such situations. The service in which errors are injected may be a custom service devoted exclusively to testing, allowing to modify its source code. This strategy can result particularly useful when performing injections into the services that compose the target system is not feasible (e.g., when services source code is not available as in OTS services).

Target Machine

Fig. 2. Methodology: SOA hosted on target machine is available to users until a service update is detected from the *runtime information*. In that case, the training phase starts collecting services information and executing preliminary runs; the user needs to wait until it completes. Then the SOA is again available to users.

In the third step, services information and preliminary runs data are used by the anomaly detection module to tune its parameters, automatically choosing the configuration that maximizes detection efficiency for the current SOA (see Sect. 3.3).

We remark that we figured out two ways of obtaining the data in the first two steps: (i) execute online tests before the user start working, or (ii) copy the platform on another virtual machine and execute the tests on the spare machine in a controlled experimental environment. The first solution will force the user to wait until tests complete (see Fig. 2), and consequently may reduce the availability of the SOA to the users. The second option requires additional resources to maintain and execute a copy of the Target Machine. In the rest of the paper we considered the first option: we collect context information through online tests before the SOA is opened to users. The induced delays on service delivery are measured in Sect. 4.1.

In some cases, to avoid downtime, it may be considered to postpone the execution of tests to low peak load periods such as at night. Obviously, delaying the execution of the tests (instead of running them immediately after services changes) implies that the anomaly detection module works with previous services information until the next training phase. This services information is now out of date: it is easy to note that this will negatively impact the accuracy of the anomaly detection module.

Runtime Execution. Once the anomaly detector is trained, the system is opened to users. *Monitor aggregator* merges each snapshot observed by the *probing system* with *runtime information*, and it sends them to the anomaly detection module. This module provides a numeric anomaly score (see Sect. 3.3). If the score reaches a specified threshold *alpha,* an anomaly alert is risen and the administrator is notified. If during this phase a service update is detected, a new *training phase* is scheduled and it will be executed depending on the policies defined by the administrator (see Fig. 2).

3.3   Insights on the Anomaly Detection Module

Periodically (e.g., once per second), the *monitor aggregator* provides a *snapshot* of the observed system, composed of the quantities retrieved from the indicators. For each indicator, two quantities are sent: (i) *value*: the current observation read by the probes, and (ii) *diff*: the difference among the current and previous *value*.

This allows building a set of *anomaly checkers* as follows. An anomaly checker is assigned to the *value* or to the *diff* quantity of an indicator, i.e., two anomaly checkers can be created for each indicators. More precisely, each anomaly checker observes a specific time series made with the observations of the *value* or the *diff* quantity of a given indicator. Each anomaly checker decides if the quantity of the indicator is anomalous or normal following rules as described in the section below. The anomaly score for an observed snapshot is built combining the individual outcomes of the selected anomaly checkers; an anomaly is raised only if the *alpha* threshold is met.

Anomaly Checkers. For each indicator, we build three types of *anomaly checkers*:

- *Historical*: for a given indicator, this module compares the *value* or *diff* quantity with the expectations defined in services information. If this quantity is outside of the interval defined by *average* $\pm$ *standard deviation* in service information for that indicator, an anomaly is raised.
- *SPS*: for a given data series (*value*, *diff*) of an indicator, this module applies an instance of the SPS algorithm described in [9, 14].
- *Remote call*: this checker observes the response time and the HTTP response code for each service invocation. If the response code is not correct (e.g., HTTP Success 2*xx*) or if the response time is not in the range of the acceptability interval defined by services information, an alert is raised.

For example, let us consider a set of 50 indicators. We obtain 201 possible anomaly checkers: 1 *remote call* checker and 200 anomaly checkers from the 50 indicators, organized in 4 anomaly checkers for each indicator (*historical* on *value/diff* data series, *SPS* on *value/diff* data series). The checkers to be used are selected during the training phase, analysing their scores for *specified metrics* (see below). As a result, the most performing checkers are selected (i) choosing the *n* checkers with the highest score, or (ii) considering checkers with a score greater than a threshold δ.

Specified Metrics. The anomaly checkers are evaluated during the training phase using measures based on indexes representing the correct detections - *true positives*

(TP), *true negatives* (TN) - and the wrong ones i.e., missed detections (*false negatives*, FN) or false detections (*false positives*, FP). More complex measures based on the abovementioned ones are *precision*, *recall* and *F-Score(β)* [12]. Especially in the *F-Score(β)*, varying the parameter β it becomes possible to weight the *precision* w.r.t the *recall* (note that *F-Score(1)* is referred as *F-Measure*). Considering that we are targeting safety-critical systems, we prefer to reduce the amount of missed detections (FN), even at the cost of a higher rate of FP. For this reason, we selected as reference metric the *F-Score(2)*, which considers the recall more relevant than the precision: the F-Score(2) for each anomaly checker is computed, and checkers are selected accordingly (choosing the n best, or those whose F-Score(2) > δ).

4   Experimental Evaluation.

We describe the experimental evaluation of the framework. To the purposes of the evaluation, we run an *automatic controller* that checks input data and manages the communications among the different modules of the Target Machine and Detector Machine. This facilitates the automatic execution of the experimental campaigns without requiring user intervention. All data are available at [20].

Table 1. Execution time of tests and workload.

Workload		Single test (s)	
Name	Type	avg	std
getCredentials	Serv. test	8.88	0.60
createFolder	Serv. test	10.71	0.69
addFiles	Serv. test	10.04	2.01
addEventCalendar	Serv. test	11.38	1.87
All tests	Test all	92.98	7.37
All services	Workload	86.04	4.87

4.1   Set-Up of the Target and the Detector Machine

We conducted an experimental campaign using as target system one of the four virtual machines that host the Secure! crisis management system [8], which is built on the Liferay [13] portal, and uses Liferay services such as authentication mechanisms, file storage, calendar management. We identified 11 different services that can be invoked by the Secure! users. To simulate a set of possible user actions, we created the *All Services* workload calling a sequence of services, with a time interval of 1 s and overall lasting approximately 85 s (see Table 1).

Target and Detector Machines are virtual machines that run on a rack server with 3 Intel Xeon E5-2620@ 2.00 GHz processors. The Target Machine runs the Secure! prototype and it is instrumented with the probing system which reads 1 snapshot per second. Following our methodology in Sect. 3.2, after defining the *expected workload* we execute tests to collect *services information*. In Table 1 we compute the time required to obtain services information: we report the time needed to test a single service and all the 11 services (*All Tests*). The execution of these tests forces the users to wait until the SOA is available again. When the SOA has to be deployed for its first time, this only implies that deploy is delayed to wait for the tests completion. Once the

SOA is deployed and available to users, it is expected that only few services will be updated each time, requiring only specific tests and consequently only short periods of unavailability. Consequently, except for the time needed for the initial test of all the services, the framework scales well also with a wider pool of services running on the SOA.

Regarding the most relevant anomaly checkers, we set $n = 20$, meaning that the 20 best anomaly checkers are selected following the *F-Score(2)* metric. Finally, we set *alpha* = 50 %, meaning that an alert is raised if at least half of the anomaly checkers detect an anomaly for the considered snapshot. We want to point out that we considered a basic setup for the monitored indicators, the best checkers and the *alpha* parameter. A more detailed sensitivity analysis exploring all the possible settings will be performed as future work targeting the identification of the most performing setup of these parameters for the scenario under investigation.

4.2 Experiments Description

We inject the following errors: (i) a memory consumption error (filling a Java *LinkedList*), and (ii) a wrong network usage (fetching *HTML* text data from an external web page). We executed 60 preliminary runs in which we inject the memory consumption error and other 60 in which we inject the network error in our services. The validation experiments are organized as follows: in 40 runs we inject the memory error, while in the other 40 runs the network error is injected, considering different *Liferay* services involved by the workload as injection points. Regarding the probing system, we observe 55 indicators [6, 22] from three different layers: 23 from the *CentOS* operating system, 25 from the middleware (the *JVM* [24]) and 7 from the *Network*. As explained in Sect. 3.3, we select the 20 most performing anomaly checkers (and consequently, the most relevant indicators) out of a set of 221 options.

4.3 Discussion of the Results

We show the results of the anomaly detection framework. We first comment on the indicators and the anomaly checkers: in Tables 2 and 3 we can observe the most performing anomaly checkers for each of the two error injections. Intuitively, the memory error injection can be detected observing indicators related to *Cpu* and *Java* memory; indeed, this can be verified considering the first three checkers selected in the training phase (Table 2). Similarly, concerning the network error, we expect to observe anomalies in the network layer (see *Tcp_Listen* in Table 3) or in the OS structures that process the incoming data flow (e.g., *Buffers* in Table 3).

In line *(iv)* of Table 4 we show the results for the anomaly detection module: it behaves far better than the single anomaly checkers, because it uses a set of them. Moreover, despite the scores of the checkers are on average better for the experiments with network error, the detection capabilities of the framework are worse compared to the experiments with memory consumption injection. It follows that combining "better" anomaly checkers does not always lead to better scores for our anomaly detector.

Table 2. 10 most performing anomaly checkers for the experiments with memory error injected

Indicator		Data type	FScore
Name	Layer	(check)	(2)
SysCpuLoad	OS	Diff (Hist)	0.37
SysCpuLoad	OS	Value (Hist)	0.35
ActVirtMPag	JVM	Value (SPS)	0.33
I/O Wait Proc	OS	Value (SPS)	0.31
Active Files	OS	Value (SPS)	0.30
Tcp_Syn	NET	Value (SPS)	0.28
Tcp_Listen	NET	Diff (SPS)	0.27
ProcCpuLoad	OS	Value (Hist)	0.26
ProcCpuLoad	OS	Diff (Hist)	0.25
Cached Mem	JVM	Value (SPS)	0.25

Table 3. 10 most performing anomaly checkers for the experiments with network error injected

Indicator		Data type	FScore
Name	Layer	(check)	(2)
Buffers	OS	Value (SPS)	0.45
PageIn	OS	Value (SPS)	0.42
Tcp_Listen	NET	Value (SPS)	0.40
PageIn	OS	Diff (SPS)	0.34
Cached Mem	JVM	Value (Hist)	0.33
Active files	OS	Value (SPS)	0.31
User Procs.	OS	Value (SPS)	0.30
Tcp_Syn	NET	Value (Hist)	0.29
ActVirt pages	JVM	Diff (Hist)	0.29
PageOut	OS	Value (SPS)	0.28

Table 4. Anomaly detection module performance

Detector setup				Anom. checks	Memory experiment			Network experiment		
#	Layers	Data	C-Aw		Precision	Recall	FScore (2)	Precision	Recall	FScore (2)
i	OS, JVM	value	NO	48	16.1 %	59.5 %	37.6 %	35.1 %	44.3 %	42.1 %
ii	OS, JVM, Net	value	NO	55	19.1 %	65.6 %	44.1 %	43.8 %	55.0 %	52.3 %
iii	OS, JVM, Net	value, diff	NO	110	22.7 %	78.3 %	52.5 %	29.2 %	72.2 %	55.7 %
iv	**OS, JVM, Net**	**value, diff**	**YES**	**221**	**33.5 %**	**95.8 %**	**69.8 %**	**50.0 %**	**86.7 %**	**75.6 %**

This efficiency strongly depends on the synergy between checkers: if a checker is not able to detect an error while another one is (e.g., they are related to indicators coming from different areas of the monitored system), this can *fix* the missed detection giving the framework the ability to answer correctly. In this study we considered each checker as a separate detector, and consequently the best checkers are chosen depending only on their score, without taking care of their characteristics. A possible improvement could be achieved considering the best *n* checkers for each monitored layer: in such a way, we are sure to consider checkers that observe different parts of the system, raising the likelihood of detecting anomalies.

In the experiments considered as validation set we obtained anomaly alerts in 95.8 % of the runs when the memory error is injected: the missed detections are the remaining 4.2 %. Regarding the 40 validation experiments with the network error injection, instead, we obtained a correct error detection in the 86.7 % of the runs.

It should be noted that with this configuration the framework provides an anomaly evaluation of the observed snapshot in 32.10 ± 5.99 ms. This is the time needed by our framework to process each snapshot coming from the Target Machine.

Precision and Recall Varying Modules We comment on the performances of the anomaly detector varying the modules and the anomaly checkers. From the top of Table 4 we summarize precision, recall and F-Scores obtained (i) using the framework in [6], (ii) introducing the network layer, (iii) including the *diff* data series in addition to the default (*value*) for each indicator and (iv) considering services information in combination with context awareness. Table 4 shows how using context awareness significantly raises the *F-Score*. Furthermore, as expected, introducing network probes significantly improves the *F-Score* in experiments with network errors.

Other framework configurations can be selected bringing to a higher balance between precision and recall. For example, considering *F-Measure* instead of *F-Score* (2) as reference metric we obtain a different set of anomaly checkers, ultimately resulting in precision of 41.0 % and 80.2 %, with recall of 58.3 % and 73.3 % respectively for the experiments with memory and network error injection.

5   State of the Art and Comparison with Other Solutions

Anomaly detectors have been proposed as error detectors [10] or failure predictors [2], based on the hypothesis that the activation of a fault (for error detection) or an error (for failure prediction) manifests as increasingly unstable performance-related behavior before escalating into a failure. The anomaly detector is in charge to observe these fluctuations providing a response to the administrator as soon as it can, triggering proactive recovery or dumping critical data. Reviewing state of the art it is possible to notice that the most used layers are the network [2, 3] and the operating system [6, 11]. This is not surprising since most of the systems include these layers: building solutions which fetch data from these layers allow building frameworks that fit in a very wide range of contexts. Regarding context-awareness, as highlighted in [16], in service-oriented architectures it usually refers to knowledge of the user environment to improve the performances of web services. For example, the *Akogrimo* project [17] aims at supporting mobile users to access data, knowledge, and computational services on the Grid focusing on user-context (such as user location and environmental information). In our work we refer to a server-side context-awareness, meaning that we do not require user information taking into account only runtime information about the services that are running in the SOA.

A detailed overview of anomaly detection frameworks can be found in [1]. Here we focus on three anomaly detection frameworks [2, 3, 14] addressing error detection/ failure prediction where the authors reported the measurements for detection accuracy metrics (i.e., *precision* and *recall*). They observe indicators from multiple layers as the framework presented here does. We remark that these studies are exercised on *systems with low dynamicity*. *Tiresias* [3] predicts crash failures trough the observation of network, OS and application metrics by applying an anomaly detection strategy that is instantiated on each different monitored parameter. In *CASPER* [2], instead, the authors use different detection modules based on symptoms aggregated trough *Complex Event Processing* techniques based on the non-intrusive observation of network traffic parameters. Lastly, in [14] the authors aimed to detect anomalies due to the manifestation of hang, crash and content failure errors in an ATM system looking at OS indicators, exercising the framework on *Windows* and *Linux* kernels.

In Table 5 we reported the anomaly detection performance extracted from the surveyed studies. Detection performances (we show precision, recall and F-Score(2)) are strongly influenced by the characteristics of the target system: with low dynamicity it is easier to define a normal behavior, resulting in a significantly lower number of false detections (see [2, 3, 14] in Table 5). Finally, looking at the performances of our framework we achieved a recall index that is competitive considering highly dynamic systems. Precision is low, meaning many false positives are generated, but in our setting we favoured recall since our aim is to minimize missed detections.

Table 5. Comparing performance indexes with similar studies.

	System under test			Precision	Recall	FScore (2)
	Characteristics	Dynamicity	Layers			
[14] (best UNIX)	ATM system	Very low	OS	97.0 %	100.0 %	99.3 %
CASPER [2]	ATM system	Very low	Net	88.5 %	76.5 %	78.6 %
TIRESIAS [3]	Emulab distrib. env.	Low	OS, Net	97.5 %	n.p.	n.p.
Our Work - Memory	Secure! SOA	High	Net, OS, JVM	**33.5 %**	**95.8 %**	**69.8 %**
Our Work - Network				**50.0 %**	**86.7 %**	**75.6 %**

6   Conclusions and Future Works

In this paper we presented an anomaly detection framework for dynamic systems and especially SOAs. Assuming knowledge of the services that are running at time *t* on the observed machine gave us the opportunity to consider additional information that resulted fundamental to improve our anomaly detection capabilities.

As future works a sensitivity analysis directed to find the best *alpha* setup, a larger error model comprising *Liferay* software bugs, and an estimation of detection time varying number and type of observed layers will be investigated, along with strategies to reduce false positives. To further explore our context, we will focus on how changes in the user workload – and not in the services – can influence our detection capabilities and which strategies can be applied to maintain our solution working effectively. The basic failure model we considered for the experiments will be expanded including other items, to test the capabilities of the framework in different contexts.

Lastly, analysis aimed to understand the applicability of this solution when multiple SOA services are called simultaneously by different users will be investigated.

Acknowledgements. This work has been partially supported by the Joint Program Initiative (JPI) Urban Europe via the IRENE project, by the European FP7-ICT-2013-10-610535 AMADEOS project and by the European FP7-IRSES DEVASSES.

References

1. Chandola, V., Banerjee, A., Kumar, V.: Anomaly detection: a survey. ACM Comput. Surv. (CSUR) **41**(3), 15 (2009)
2. Baldoni, R., Montanari, L., Rizzuto, M.: On-line failure prediction in safety-critical systems. Future Gener. Comput. Syst. **45**, 123–132 (2015)
3. Williams, A.W., Pertet, S.M., Narasimhan, P.: Tiresias: black-box failure prediction in distributed systems. In: Parallel and Distributed Processing Symposium, IPDPS 2007. IEEE (2007)
4. Tanenbaum, A.S., Van Steen, M.: Distributed Systems. Prentice-Hall, Upper saddle River (2007)
5. Bose, S., Bharathimurugan, S., Kannan, A.: Multi-layer integrated anomaly intrusion detection system for mobile adhoc networks. In: 2007 International Conference on Signal Processing, Communications and Networking, ICSCN 2007. IEEE (2007)
6. Ceccarelli, A., Zoppi, T., Itria, M., Bondavalli, A.: A multi-layer anomaly detector for dynamic service-based systems. In: Koornneef, F. (ed.) SAFECOMP 2015. LNCS, vol. 9337, pp. 166–180. Springer, Heidelberg (2015). doi:10.1007/978-3-319-24255-2_13
7. Jyothsna, V., Rama Prasad, V.V., Munivara Prasad, K.: A review of anomaly based intrusion detection systems. Int. J. Comput. Appl. **28**(7), 26–35 (2011)
8. Secure! project. http://secure.eng.it/ Accessed 1 Mar 2016
9. Bondavalli, A., et al.: Resilient estimation of synchronisation uncertainty through software clocks. Int. J. Crit. Comput.-Based Syst. **4**(4), 301–322 (2013)
10. Modi, C., et al.: A survey of intrusion detection techniques in cloud. J. Netw. Comput. Appl. **36**(1), 42–57 (2013)
11. Shabtai, A., et al.: "Andromaly": a behavioral malware detection framework for android devices. J. Intell. Inf. Syst. **38**(1), 161–190 (2012)
12. Sokolova, M., Japkowicz, N., Szpakowicz, S.: Beyond accuracy, F-score and ROC: a family of discriminant measures for performance evaluation. In: Sattar, A., Kang, B. (eds.) AI 2006, pp. 1015–1021. Springer, Heidelberg (2006)
13. Liferay. http://www.liferay.com Accessed 1 Mar 2016
14. Bovenzi, A., et al.: An OS-level framework for anomaly detection in complex software systems. IEEE Trans. Dependable Secure Comput. **12**(3), 366–372 (2015)
15. Erl, T.: SOA: Principles of Service Design, vol. 1. Prentice Hall, Upper Saddle River (2008)
16. Truong, H.-L., Dustdar, S.: A survey on context-aware web service systems. Int. J. Web Inf. Syst. **5**(1), 5–31 (2009)
17. Loos, C.: E-health with mobile grids: the akogrimo heart monitoring and emergency scenario. Akogrimo White Paper (2006). online
18. Esper Team and EsperTech Inc.: Esper reference version 4.9.0. Technical report (2012)
19. Valls, M.G., Iago, R.L., Villar, L.F.: iLAND: an enhanced middleware for real-time reconfiguration of service oriented distributed real-time systems. IEEE Trans. Ind. Inf. **9**(1), 228–236 (2013)
20. rclserver.dsi.unifi.it/owncloud/public.php?service=files&t=89f4b993136bda20ae9cfb3f32 ac62da

21. Thramboulidis, K., Doukas, G., Koumoutsos, G.: A SOA-based embedded systems development environment for industrial automation. EURASIP J. Embed. Syst. **2008**, 1–15 (2008). Article no. 3
22. Bondavalli, A., et al.: Differential analysis of operating system indicators for anomaly detection in dependable systems: an experimental study. Measurement **80**, 229–240 (2016)
23. Zoppi, T.: Multi-layer anomaly detection in complex dynamic critical systems. In: Dependable Systems and Networks – Student Forum Session, DSN (2015)
24. Cotroneo, D., et al.: Failure classification and analysis of the java virtual machine, ICDCS 2006. In: 26th IEEE International Conference on Distributed Computing Systems. IEEE (2006)

Towards Modelling Adaptive Fault Tolerance
for Resilient Computing Analysis

William Excoffon[1([⊠])], Jean-Charles Fabre[2], and Michael Lauer[3]

[1] LAAS-CNRS, Université de Toulouse, CNRS, Toulouse, France
william.excoffon@laas.fr
[2] INP, Toulouse, France
[3] UPS, Toulouse, France

Abstract. Fast evolution of computing systems is a hot topic today that is becoming a real challenge for safety critical embedded systems. For both maintenance and functionalities reasons, over-the-air updates are very attractive for embedded systems manufacturers in many application domains. The challenge here is to maintain dependability properties when facing changes. This is exactly the definition of resilient computing we consider in this work. The implementation of resilient computing relies on fault tolerance design patterns (FTDP) that comply with various types of non-functional assumptions (behavioural assumptions, fault model assumptions, temporal assumptions, resources assumptions, etc.). Despite changes in operation, the efficiency of the fault tolerance mechanisms (instance of a FTDP) depends on the strict compliance with such assumptions. The objective of the paper is to provide a model to simplify the analysis of resilient systems, in particular focusing on adaptive fault tolerant computing. Simple measures are illustrated on evolution scenarii.

1 Introduction and Problem Statement

Evolution during operational life is inevitable in many systems today. A system that remains dependable when facing changes (new threats, change in the fault model, updates of applications) is called resilient. The persistence of dependability when facing changes defines the concept of resilience [1]. Resilient computing encompasses several aspects, among which *evolvability*, i.e., the capacity of a system to evolve during its operational life. In practice, dependability relies on fault-tolerant computing at runtime, based on *Fault Tolerance Design Patterns* (FTDPs) instances attached to the application. As such, one key challenge of resilient computing is the capacity to maintain a consistent relation between assumptions and FTDP implementation in operation. The considered assumptions focus on fault model and application characteristics.

The fault model is obviously a key parameter for the selection of an adequate *Fault Tolerance Design Pattern*. It often includes both hardware and software faults, but also undesirable events that may affect the correct behaviour of the application. The role of the safety analysis (e.g. using FMECA – *Failure Mode, Effects and Criticality Analysis*) is to identify the failure modes and ultimately to define the safety mechanisms preventing the violation of safety properties. Such safety mechanisms rely on basic error detection and recovery mechanisms, namely fault tolerance techniques following

© Springer International Publishing Switzerland 2016
A. Skavhaug et al. (Eds.): SAFECOMP 2016, LNCS 9922, pp. 159–171, 2016.
DOI: 10.1007/978-3-319-45477-1_13

IFIP WG10.4 terminology. A safety mechanism can be based on a single FTDP or several combined together.

During the operational life of a system, several situations may occur. For instance, new threats may have an impact on the fault model (electromagnetic perturbations, obsolescence of HW components, software aging, etc.). A modification of the fault model has consequences on the assumptions of FTDPs, and thus on the validity of the initial selection of a fault tolerance mechanism. The coverage of the assumptions is definitely a key parameter to guarantee the validity of a FTDP as discussed in [2].

Other assumptions may also affect the validity of a FTDP when facing system evolution. Application updates may change the assumptions used for the initial selection of a FTDP. For instance, determinism, activation profile, state handing issues have a strong impact on the selection of a FTDP, e.g. a duplex strategy variant (cold, warm, hot and by the way the underlying inter-replica protocols). This means that a change in the assumptions (fault model, applications characteristics, available resources) may imply a change of FTDP to maintain system dependability.

The first question we address in this work is the following: *To what extent a FTDP remains valid when the fault model or the application characteristics change in operation?* The second question of interest is: *What type of indicators can be used to adjust and make FTDP instances consistent with actual assumptions in operation?*

So, why modelling Adaptive Fault Tolerant Computing? To answer both questions given above, we need a simple formalism to describe the configuration of the dependable system in operation and its evolution. Events and variables in this formalism will help us to formally define the changes, analyse their side effects on dependability mechanisms, and compute some measures regarding the resilience of the system.

In Sect. 2, we clarify the link between resilient and adaptive fault tolerant computing and also our terminology. Section 3 focuses on the assumptions of *Fault Tolerance Design Patterns* as the corner stone of the analysis proposed in this paper. A classification of conventional FTDP is proposed to illustrate the starting point of the work. In Sect. 4, we use several scenarii to illustrate some resilient computing situations. These examples will be used in the paper as a *guiding thread* to illustrate our modelling approach. Section 5 describes the model, the events and the measures that can be obtained. Section 6 illustrates our simple modelling approach, the triggers and the measures on the scenarii. Section 7 concludes the paper.

2 Resilience and Adaptive Fault Tolerant Computing

Various changes in operation may have an impact on dependability, the root of the definition of Resilience in computer system engineering. Such changes may trigger modifications of the system configuration, including *Fault Tolerance Mechanisms* (FTM), in the large (complete reload) or in the small (subtle *over-the-air* updates).

2.1   Basic Principles for AFT

The need for *Adaptive Fault Tolerance (AFT)* arises from the dynamically changing fault tolerance requirements and from the inefficiency of allocating a fixed amount of resources to fault tolerance mechanisms throughout the service life of a system, as stated in [3]. AFT is gaining more importance with the increasing concern for lowering the amount of energy consumed by cyber-physical systems and the amount of heat they generate [4]. On-line adaptation of fault tolerance mechanisms has attracted research efforts for some time now. Most of the solutions [5–7] tackle adaptation in a pre-programmed manner: all mechanisms necessary during the service life of the system are deployed from the beginning. An alternative to pre-programmed adaptation consists in viewing a system as a collection of fine-grain components that can be manipulated at runtime [8], a sort of *Lego System* implementing both application and safety/dependability mechanisms, enabling over-the-air updates.

A system configuration includes application components linked together with their fault tolerance mechanisms. An essential concept for adaptive fault tolerant computing is the notion of *Separation of Concerns (SoC)*. This well-known concept implies a clear separation between the application code and the non-functional code, i.e. the FTDP instance in our case. The connection between the application code and its FTDP must be clearly defined, so that FTDPs can easily be disconnected, replaced, updated, pro-vided the connectors remains the same. However, *SoC* has some limits regarding fault tolerant computing, as FTDP implementation cannot always be application-agnostic. Some mechanisms are generic, e.g. replication mechanisms. Some are application dependent and FTDP must be parameterized by the applications.

2.2   Change Model

The choice of an appropriate FTDP for a given application depends on various assumptions and parameters:

- *FT*: the *fault model* and the effect of faults on the system behaviour, namely the failure modes, when the corresponding error has not been detected and recovered;
- *AC*: the *application characteristics* that determine the validity of a FTDP regarding determinism, state accessibility, some temporal aspects, etc.;
- *RS*: the *resources* needed to run an implementation of a FTDP, in terms of memory, bandwidth, energy, CPU nodes/cores, etc.

We denote (FT, AC, RS) as *change model*. At any point in time, the execution of a given application and its attached FTDP must match the assumptions. Some key parameters must be evaluated off-line (application characteristics, AC), some other must be monitored on-line (available resources, RS), some both off-line and on-line (fault assumptions, FT, e.g. new threats, exceptions raised, etc.). Such key parameters are used to check the validity of an FTDP during the operational life of the system.

3   Assumptions and FT Design Patterns

Assumptions enable to discriminate between several FTDPs but also several implementations of a given FTDP. A careful analysis of such assumptions enables FTDPs to be classified quite easily. Figure 1 shows an excerpt of the classification of some generic FTDP with respect to hardware faults.

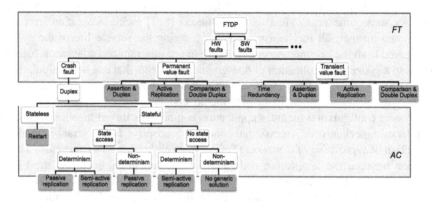

Fig. 1. Fault tolerance design patterns classification (an incomplete view)

The selection of a FTDP relies first on FT, then on AC:

- Regarding the fault model FT, and by extension the failure modes to be avoided, we rely on a classification based on well-known fault types, e.g., crash faults, value faults, development faults, undesirable events, etc.
- The application characteristics AC that we identified as having an impact on the selection of a FTDP are: application statefulness, state accessibility and code execution determinism, fail silence, etc. Control over non-deterministic decisions is almost impossible for black box applications with no access to its internal state.

Resources RS also plays a role in the selection of the adequate FTDP. They are not considered as first class assumptions like FT and AC, but as implementation constraints. The implementation of a given FTDP requires a set of resources and for each of them we can set a threshold, below which the implementation is impossible.

To illustrate our approach, we consider some conventional FTDP and briefly discuss their underlying assumptions together with some few resource needs, as shown in Fig. 2. Their definition is very much simplified, just to illustrate our approach.

Assumptions / FTDP		PBR	LFR	TR
Fault Model (FT)	crash	✓	✓	
	transient			✓
Application	Deterministic		✓	✓
Characteristics (AC)	State access	✓		✓
Resource (RS)	# CPU	2	2	1

Fig. 2. Assumptions and fault tolerance design patterns examples

We consider duplex strategies to tolerate crash faults using, passive (e.g. *Primary-Backup Replication* denoted PBR—warm redundancy variant) or active replication protocols (e.g. *Leader-Follower Replication* denoted LFR—hot redundancy variant). Each replica is considered as a perfect *fail-silent* component. At least 2 independent processing units are necessary to run these two variants.

We also consider a simple design pattern tolerating transient value faults: *Time Redundancy* (TR) tolerates transient hardware faults using repetition of the computation and comparison/voting. TR helps improving the self-checking coverage of a replica.

In summary, PBR and LFR tolerate the same fault model FT, but comply with different AC. PBR allows non-determinism of applications because only one replica computes service requests while LFR only works for deterministic applications as both replicas compute all requests. PBR requires state access for checkpointing the computation and higher network bandwidth (in general), while LFR does not require state access but generally incurs higher CPU costs (and, consequently, higher energy consumption) as both replicas perform all computations. TR requires state access to restore the initial state of the computation during the repetition of the execution. A similar analysis can be done for any other FTDP, other fault models or undesirable events. All needed FTDP during the system lifetime do not exist at initial time.

4   Adaptive Fault Tolerance and Evolution Scenarii

In this section we consider different system evolution scenarii that imply adaptation of FTDP. Any change that invalidates an assumption may call for an update of the FTDPs. Application versioning, hardware aging, physical devices loss, environmental condition and threats, evolution of both functional and non-functional specifications, have an impact on assumptions. The triggering of FTDP change can be done on-line (fault model change) or by the off-line system manager (application versioning), as explained in Sect. 5.3. Any FTDP is validated off-line before being used in the system. When a new FTDP need to be developed to comply with the assumptions, the system is in a degraded mode of operation during a maybe quite long time window, the current FTDP being inconsistent with some assumptions.

Lets define a system simply like this: a system S runs a number of applications satisfying the specs; each application is attached to a FTDP compliant with its dependability need; a number of resources have been allocated to run the implementation of FTDPs.

Let's consider a 1st evolution scenario (AC change impact):

- At **t0**, a given application **A**, a command & control application, is attached to a FTDP tolerating crash faults, say PBR to save CPU usage;
- At **t1**, the application **A** is updated, the new version **A^1** being non-deterministic whereas **A** execution was deterministic. PBR is still valid; NO IMPACT
- At **t2**, **A^1** is updated again. The new version **A^2** is deterministic but does not offers access to its internal state anymore, invalidating the PBR; IMPACT
- At **t2 + δt2**, a new FTDP is assigned to **A^2**, namely a semi active replication strategy, LFR, **A^2** being deterministic and no state access is required.

Let's consider now this simple 2nd evolution scenario (FT change impact):

- At **t3**, monitoring facilities reveal an increasing rate of transient faults detected by low-level exceptions or hardware *Error Detection Mechanisms*. IMPACT
- At **t3 + δt3**, the current FTDP implementation, LFR, is now combined with Time Redundancy becoming thus LFR + TR;
- At **t4**, $\mathbf{A^2}$ becomes *stateless* through a new update $\mathbf{A^3}$ at the application level, eliminating the persistent state of the computation: all input values are read from sensors at each beginning of the control loop; NO IMPACT

The aforementioned δt parameter in the scenarii represents the time window during which the system does not match the non-functional specifications. Obviously, this time window needs to be minimized.

5   Formal Definition of AFT

The evolution of a system S is represented by an history of timed events denoted H, H being a set of couples *(e,t)*. The event *e* corresponds to a change in the application characteristics of the fault model, *t* being the date of the event.

5.1   Notation and Definitions

An application A_i is mapped to a component C_i linked with an appropriate *Fault Tolerance Design Pattern (FT$_j$)*, following the *separation of concerns* principle. More formally, let $S = \{A_i\}$, $i \in [1..n]$ be a system where *n* is the total number of application components. For each $i \in [1..n]$, $A_i = (C_i, FT_j)$ is an application with $j \in [1..q]$, *q* being the number of FTDP that can be used by the system. By convention, $FT_j = Null$, means that no *FTDP* is attached to C_i.

In this section we illustrate the notation using simple application characteristics and the generic fault tolerance design patterns targeting physical faults given in Fig. 2.

Simple Notation for Application Components. An application component C_i has a set of non-functional characteristics, denoted $(a_{i,k})$, $k \in [1..m]$, *m* being the total number of application characteristics considered in the model. Examples of such `boolean` application characteristics are the following: `determinism, statefulness, state access, fail silence`. This list can obviously be extended according to the needs.

Application characteristics are defined as follows:

- $a_{i,1} = 1$ means that C_i is non-deterministic, $a_{i,1} = 0$ when it is deterministic;
- $a_{i,2} = 1$ means that C_i is stateful, $a_{i,2} = 0$ when it is memory less;
- $a_{i,3} = 1$ means that C_i state is not accessible, $a_{i,3} = 0$ when it is accessible.
- $a_{i,4} = 1$ means that C_i is not fail silent, $a_{i,4} = 0$ when it is fail silent.

The model is designed to offer the following property:

If a FTDP is applicable for a given application characteristic set to true ($a_{i,k} = 1$), then it is also applicable when this characteristic is false ($a_{i,k} = 0$).

For instance, a PBR strategy works for non-deterministic components, so it also works for deterministic components.

The definition of C_i also includes the types of faults it must tolerate. We use a Boolean vector to represent this set of faults, $(f_{j,k})$, $k \in [1..p]$, p being the total number of possible fault types affecting an application component in the system. Examples of such fault types are the following: value fault, omission fault, crash fault. Obviously, this list can also be extended according to the needs.

Fault tolerance requirements of an application can simply be defined as follows:

- $f_{j,1} = 1$ means that FT_j must tolerate value faults, $f_{j,1} = 0$ when not considered;
- $f_{j,2} = 1$ means that FT_j must tolerate omission faults, $f_{j,2} = 0$ when not considered;
- $f_{j,3} = 1$ means that FT_j must tolerate crash faults, $f_{j,3} = 0$ when not considered;

$$C_i = \left(\begin{pmatrix} a_{i,1} \\ a_{i,2} \\ \cdots \\ a_{i,m} \end{pmatrix}, \begin{pmatrix} f_{i,1} \\ f_{i,2} \\ \cdots \\ f_{i,p} \end{pmatrix} \right)$$

The selection of the values (0,1) is here very simple rule, just true/false. For instance, the component C_i calls for a FTDP tolerating both crash faults and value faults.

As a result, any component C_i in the system can be modelled like this:

In summary, the vector $(a_{i,k})$ represents the structural and behavioral characteristics of the application. The vector $(f_{j,k})$ represents the requested fault tolerance requirements.

Simple Notation for FTDP. An FTDP provides a solution to tolerate some types of faults, but its validity depends on some application characteristics. Given a fault model, the application characteristics represent an assumption for the selection of an FTDP.

$$FT_j = \left(\begin{pmatrix} b_{j,1} \\ b_{j,2} \\ \cdots \\ b_{j,m} \end{pmatrix}, \begin{pmatrix} ft_{j,1} \\ ft_{j,2} \\ \cdots \\ ft_{j,p} \end{pmatrix} \right)$$

In the modelling of FTDP characteristics, $b_{j,k}$ are the properties accepted by the FTDP. For example, $b_{j,1} = 1$ means that the FTDP accept non-deterministic component whereas $b_{j,1} = 0$ means it only accepts deterministic components.

In summary, the vector $(b_{j,k})$ represents application characteristics accepted by FT_j. The vector $(ft_{j,k})$ represents the type of faults tolerated by FT_j.

In the definition of C_i and FT_j, the two Boolean vectors report application characteristics and fault tolerance requirements. The design of a critical application is consistent *if and only if* FT_j assumptions match C_i characteristics and fault tolerance requirements.

5.2 Properties

Now, we can define properties enabling the consistency of a system configuration to be analysed, i.e. the validity of all application (C_i, FT_j) at any time t.

Definition of compatibility: FT_j is compatible with C_i *if and only if* FT_j accepts the application characteristics of C_i

Definition of adequacy: FT_j is adequate with C_i *if and only if* FT_j tolerates the faults requested by C_i

Definition of consistency: An application (C_i, FT_j) is consistent *if and only if* it complies with the compatibility and adequacy properties.

The notion of compatibility introduces an order relation between characteristics. For instance, handling application non-determinism is more complex that handling determinism in a fault tolerance strategy. In other words, a FTDP that accepts a non-deterministic application component also works with deterministic applications.

$$FT_j \text{ is compatible with } C_i \Longleftrightarrow \forall k \in [1..m], a_{i,k} \leq b_{j,k}$$

Adequacy is the capability of FT_j to tolerate the faults requested by C_i, namely $(f_{i,k})$. This notion introduces a simple order relation between fault models and fault tolerance design patterns, in the sense that a FT_j is adequate when $(f_{i,k}) \leq (ft_{j,k})$.

$$FT_j \text{ is adequate with } C_i \Longleftrightarrow \forall k \in [1..p], f_{i,k} \leq ft_{j,k}$$

Suppose the following example:

$$C_i = \left(\begin{pmatrix} a_{i,1} \\ a_{i,2} \\ a_{i,3} \\ a_{i,4} \end{pmatrix}, \begin{pmatrix} f_{i,1} \\ f_{i,2} \\ f_{i,3} \end{pmatrix} \right) = \left(\begin{pmatrix} 0 \\ 1 \\ 1 \\ 0 \end{pmatrix}, \begin{pmatrix} 1 \\ 0 \\ 1 \end{pmatrix} \right)$$

The component is deterministic $(a_{i,1} = 0)$, stateful $(a_{i,2} = 1)$, its state is accessible $(a_{i,3} = 1)$ and it is fail silent $(a_{i,4} = 0)$. Faults to be tolerated are random hardware faults leading to a wrong value $(f_{i,1} = 1)$ or a crash $(f_{i,3} = 1)$. Let FT_j be a FTDP such as:

$$FT_j = \left(\begin{pmatrix} b_{j,1} \\ b_{j,2} \\ b_{j,3} \\ b_{j,4} \end{pmatrix}, \begin{pmatrix} ft_{j,1} \\ ft_{j,2} \\ ft_{j,3} \end{pmatrix} \right) = \left(\begin{pmatrix} 1 \\ 1 \\ 0 \\ 0 \end{pmatrix}, \begin{pmatrix} 1 \\ 0 \\ 1 \end{pmatrix} \right)$$

FT_j tolerates both value faults and crash faults, for non-deterministic stateful applications and it requires state access and fail silent assumption on the component. This FTDP can be a combination of PBR and TR strategies.

In this example, we comply with both properties, compatibility and adequacy.

(a) Compatibility : $\forall k \in [1..4], a_{i,k} \leq b_{j,k}$
(b) Adequacy : $\forall k \in [1..3], f_{i,k} \leq ft_{j,k}$

Thus, $A_i = (C_i, FT_j)$ is consistent while no change invalidates the above inequations.

5.3   Triggers for Adaptation

In our system architecture, we assume that we have a ***monitoring engine*** responsible for collecting information on the system behaviour (e.g. rate of transient faults detected by low-level exceptions or hardware EDM obtained on-line) and changes of component version (i.e. information delivered by the off-line manager of the system). We also assume that we have an ***adaptation engine*** responsible for changing the fault tolerance strategy of applications FT_j (switch to a new mechanism, composition of several design patterns). Both engines are supervised by the off-line system manager.

The triggers for adaptation depend on some inputs, in fact the events related to changes in the application characteristics and/or in the fault model. The *sense-compute-control* paradigm is used here to define the triggers. When an event related to a change is observed (*sense*), a computation is carried out to decide whether all applications $A_{i,} = (C_i, FT_j)$, in the system need to be adapted or not, at a given instant t, to comply with their dependability requirements. The computation is simple: it simply consists in the evaluation (*compute*) of the inequations used in the definition of the compatibility and adequacy properties. The final decision (*control*) is two-fold:

- The change does not invalidate the consistency of (C_i, FT_j), and so the system is resilient (i.e. no effect, 0)
- The change invalidates compatibility or adequacy of (C_i, FT_j), and so a modification is mandatory to comply with C_i dependability requirements (i.e. update, 1)

In the later case an adaptation must be performed to maintain system dependability. A trigger signal is sent to the adaptation engine for performing a change of FT_j. It is worth noting that during the time window δt required to perform the change, the system (or at least one of its applications) does not comply with its dependability specifications. More precisely, FT_j is no more able to tolerate the faults attached to the definition of C_i, (cf. vector $(f_{j,k})$). A new FT_j must be installed.

5.4   Simple Measures

We report in this section a first attempt to measure the resilience of a system. The proposed measures rely on two simple ideas: (i) *a system is resilient when changes do not impact its current configuration while complying with its dependability specifications*; (ii) *a system is resilient when it is able to change its configuration quickly to comply with its dependability specifications*.

A statistical estimator of the first measure of resilience at time t denoted $RE(t)$ can be obtained in this way:

$$RE(t) = \frac{N - ic(t)}{N}$$

where ic(t) is the number of inconsistency periods observed since the initial time t_0 up to t, N being the total number of change events.

During the time window [t_0, t] and according to a given sequence of change events, the system S is resilient when the number of inconsistency periods observed $ic(t)$ is low. The greater $RE(t)$, the better the resilience of the system.

The second measure is related to the time duration during which the system remains consistent. We define the *Mean Time Between Inconsistency* (denoted *MTBI*) for a given period of time *t* as follows:

$$MTBI = \frac{t - \sum_{i=0}^{ic(t)} dt(i)}{ic(t)}$$

where $dt(i)$ is the time duration of the ith inconsistency period

The *MTBI* measure is pessimistic since large inconsistency periods have a bad impact on the measure of resilience. The distribution of inconsistency period durations is more interesting for deeper analysis. *MTBI* is also interesting to compare different evolution scenarii and adaptation strategies. For a given change event, several updates may be possible to comply with the dependability specifications. Thus, a sequence of change events leads to a tree of possible updates. An evaluation of the system resilience can thus be performed for each branch, using both $RE(t)$ and $MTBI(t)$, in order to compare evolution strategies for a given history H.

6 Proof of Concepts

6.1 Formalization of the Previously Defined Scenarii

In this section we formalize the scenarii given in Sect. 4. In order to keep this example clear we reduced the application to one component named C_1. This component is *deterministic*, *stateful*, we have *access to its state* and it is *fail silent* (AC). The initial objective is to tolerate *crash faults* (FT). According to FT and AC, a PBR mechanism is attached to C_1 at time **t0** (see. Figs. 3 and 4).

$$C_1(t0) = \left(\begin{pmatrix} 0 \\ 1 \\ 0 \\ 0 \end{pmatrix}, \begin{pmatrix} 0 \\ 0 \\ 1 \end{pmatrix} \right) \qquad\qquad FT_1(t0) = PBR = \left(\begin{pmatrix} 1 \\ 1 \\ 0 \\ 0 \end{pmatrix}, \begin{pmatrix} 0 \\ 0 \\ 1 \end{pmatrix} \right)$$

Fig. 3. Initial model for C_1. *AC notation reminder:* (1) Non deterministic, (1) Statefulness, (1) State not accessible, (1) Not fail silent, *FT notation reminder:* (1) Value, (1) Omission, (1) Crash

Fig. 4. Initial FT model attached to C_1. *AC notation reminder:* (1) Non deterministic, (1) Statefulness, (1) State not accessible, (1) Not fail silent, *FT notation reminder:* (1) Value, (1) Omission, (1) Crash

According to the definitions given in Sect. 5.2, $C_1(t0)$ and $FT_1(t0)$ are compatible and in adequacy. Therefore, the system S is consistent.

At time **t1** the system is updated and C_1 becomes non-deterministic. As a result, the component is now modelled as shown in Fig. 5. This modification has no impact in the system because the properties $a_{1,k} \leq b_{1,k}$ still hold, for any k.

$$C_1(t1) = \left(\begin{pmatrix} 1 \\ 1 \\ 0 \\ 0 \end{pmatrix}, \begin{pmatrix} 0 \\ 0 \\ 1 \end{pmatrix} \right)$$

$$C_1(t2) = \left(\begin{pmatrix} 0 \\ 1 \\ 1 \\ 0 \end{pmatrix}, \begin{pmatrix} 0 \\ 0 \\ 1 \end{pmatrix} \right)$$

Fig. 5. C1 update with no impact   **Fig. 6.** C_1 update with impact on FT

At **t2**, a new update is done, state access is not guaranteed anymore but the component becomes deterministic again. C_1 is now defined as show in Fig. 6. The compatibility between the component and the PBR is not verified anymore because $a_{1,3} > b_{1,3}$. The FTDP has to be modified and a LFR strategy replaces the PBR one (cf. Fig. 7)

$$FT_2(t2 + \delta t2) = LFR = \left(\begin{pmatrix} 0 \\ 1 \\ 1 \\ 0 \end{pmatrix}, \begin{pmatrix} 0 \\ 0 \\ 1 \end{pmatrix} \right)$$

Because the component C_1 is now deterministic again, after the time window denoted **δt2**, the configuration *(C₁, FT₂)* becomes consistent at time **t2 + δt2**.

At **t3**, the monitoring facility indicates that the fault model of the component has to be changed, due to an increasing rate of transient faults detected. We modify the requirements of C_1 to express the eventuality of value faults (cf. Fig. 8).

$$C_1(t3) = \left(\begin{pmatrix} 0 \\ 1 \\ 1 \\ 0 \end{pmatrix}, \begin{pmatrix} 1 \\ 0 \\ 1 \end{pmatrix} \right)$$

$$FT_3(t3 + \delta t3) = LFR + TR = \left(\begin{pmatrix} 0 \\ 1 \\ 1 \\ 0 \end{pmatrix}, \begin{pmatrix} 1 \\ 0 \\ 1 \end{pmatrix} \right)$$

Fig. 7. Change in fault model   **Fig. 8.** Composition of FTDPs: LFT + TR

The fact that $f_{1,1} > ft_{1,1}$ indicates that the component and the FTDP are not in adequacy anymore, thus a strategy combining LFR and TR is set. The new mechanism requires the component to be deterministic and protects against both value and crash faults. At **t3 + δt3**, the new system is consistent again.

$$C_1(t4) = \left(\begin{pmatrix} 0 \\ 0 \\ 1 \\ 0 \end{pmatrix}, \begin{pmatrix} 1 \\ 0 \\ 1 \end{pmatrix} \right)$$

At **t4**, a new update is done eliminating the persistent state of computation leading C_1 to become as depicted in Fig. 9.

Fig. 9. Update with no impact on consistency

This change does not introduce any incompatibility between C_1 and the LFR + TR strategy. There is no impact so the system configuration remains consistent.

6.2   Comparison, Measures and Analysis of Scenarii

The *MTBI* enables comparing several FTDP update strategies during the system lifetime. The timing values are extracted from former experimental work [13]. In our scenario, the four change events lead to two impacts (*case 1*):

$$MTBI_1 = \frac{t - \sum_{i=0}^{ic(t)} dt(i)}{ic(t)} = \frac{t4 - \delta t2 - \delta t3}{2}, \quad \text{with } \delta t2 = 1003 \, \text{ms, and } \delta t3 = 838 \, \text{ms.}$$

Therefore **MTBI$_1$** $\approx$ 732 h for a system lifetime of **t** = 2 month.

Let us consider another scenario by assuming that LFR was selected instead of PBR at **t0**. At **t1** we have now an additional impact, as the system become non deterministic. To keep consistency, PBR is selected and its installation takes **δt1**. The *MTBI* is now (*case 2*):

$$MTBI_2 = \frac{t4 - \delta t1 - \delta t2 - \delta t3}{3}, \quad \text{with } \delta t1 = 1011 \, \text{ms}, \delta t2 = 1003 \, \text{ms, and } \delta t3 = 838 \, \text{ms}$$

Therefore **MTBI$_2$** $\approx$ 488 h for a system lifetime of **t** = 2 month.

It is clear that an FTDP update at a given point in time has a side effect on the resilient behaviour of the system in the future. With this simple example, we show the side effect of such selection since the *MTBI* has decreased in **case 2**. The system remains consistent for a longer period of time in **case 1** for the same sequence of change events.

7   Conclusion

The resilience of a system encompasses architectural issues, development process issues, software technology issues, and also measures. The simple modelling approach proposed in this paper enables triggers for *Adaptive Fault Tolerance* to be easily computed. AFT follows the well-known *Sense-Compute-Control* paradigm. *Sense* involves monitoring facilities and interactions with the off-line system manager. *Compute* is based on the simple model we propose to trigger some actions when consistency is impaired. *Control* implies full or partial update of the FTDP instance attached to a given application component. Such modelling of AFT is currently used to provide triggers at runtime to the adaptation engine of a resilient system prototype on ROS [9].

The proposed measure of resilience *MTBI* is similar to *MTBF*, except that we do not speak about *Failure* but *Inconsistency*. During the inconsistency period the system is not failed but degraded with respect to its non-functional specification. It is vulnerable during a time window, a fault occurrence leading the system to fail. Another analogy can be made with the notion of *MTTR*: the *Mean Time To Update* (MTTU), mean time required to make FTDP consistent with the dependability specifications. This time window can be short when the FTDP is available, but much longer when a solution has to be design and validated off-line. Such measures help making comparisons between systems and update strategies, but also selecting a strategy for a given application context according to trade-offs between resilience and fault tolerance cost.

References

1. Laprie, J.-C., From dependability to resilience. In: 38th IEEE/IFIP International Conference on Dependable Systems and Networks (DSN) (2008)
2. Powell, D.: Failure mode assumption and assumption coverage. In: Predictably Dependable Computing Systems (1995). ISBN 3-540-59334 (First version in Proceeding of FTCS-22)
3. Kim, K.H.K., Lawrence, T.F.: Adaptive fault tolerance: issues and approaches. In: Proceedings of the Second IEEE Workshop on Future Trends of Distributed Computing Systems, pp. 38–46. IEEE (1990)
4. Krishna, C., Koren, I.: Adaptive fault-tolerance for cyber-physical systems. In: IEEE International Conference on Computing, Networking and Communications (ICNC), pp. 310–314 (2013)
5. Fraga, J., Siqueira, F., Favarim, F.: An adaptive fault-tolerant component model. In: 9th Workshop on Object- Oriented Real-Time Dependable Systems, pp. 179–186. IEEE (2003)
6. Lung, L.C., Favarim, F., Santos, G.T., Correia, M.: An infrastructure for adaptive fault tolerance on FT-CORBA. In: 9th International Symposium on Object and Component-Oriented Real-Time Distributed Computing. IEEE (2006)
7. Marin, O., Sens, P., Briot, J.-P., Guessoum, Z.: Towards adaptive fault-tolerance for distributed multi-agent systems. In: 4th European Research Seminar on Advances in Distributed Systems, pp. 195–201 (2001)
8. Stoicescu, M.: Architecting resilient computing systems: a component-based approach. Ph.D. thesis, National Polytechnic Institute of Toulouse (INP) (2013). www.theses.fr/en/2013INPT0120
9. Lauer, M., Amy, M., Fabre, J.-C., Roy, M., Excoffon, W., Stoicescu, M.: Adaptive fault tolerance mechanisms for resilient computing on ROS. In: The 17th IEEE Symposium on High Assurance Systems Engineering (HASE 2016), Orlando (FL), USA, January 2016

Automatic Invariant Selection for Online Anomaly Detection

Leonardo Aniello[1], Claudio Ciccotelli[1], Marcello Cinque[2], Flavio Frattini[2,3(✉)],
Leonardo Querzoni[1], and Stefano Russo[2]

[1] Università di Roma Sapienza, Rome, Italy
{aniello,ciccotelli,querzoni}@dis.uniroma1.it
[2] Università degli Studi di Napoli Federico II, Naples, Italy
{macinque,sterusso}@unina.it
[3] RisLab - Research and Innovation for Security Lab, Naples, Italy
flavio.frattini@rislab.it

Abstract. Invariants are stable relationships among system metrics expected to hold during normal operating conditions. The violation of such relationships can be used to detect anomalies at runtime. However, this approach does not scale to large systems, as the number of invariants quickly grows with the number of considered metrics. The resulting "background noise" for the invariant-based detection system hinders its effectiveness. In this paper we propose a general and automatic approach for identifying a subset of mined invariants that properly model system runtime behavior with a reduced amount of background noise. This translates into better overall performance (i.e., less false positives).

1 Introduction

Anomaly detection techniques based on the usage of invariants have long been introduced to discover anomalous behaviors in processing systems [1,2]. An invariant is a property of a system that is expected to hold while the system runs correctly. The idea of invariant-based anomaly detection is that it is possible to automatically analyze the evolution of the system at runtime to identify stable correlations among some monitored metrics. Such a detection process involves an initial training phase to learn invariants representing the correct behavior of the system. Then, whenever an invariant is *broken* or *violated* during operation—i.e. the underlying correlation between metrics is lost—it is considered a sign of a probable malfunction in the system.

The use of invariants is gaining interest in the field of systems where faults may have severe impacts. These systems are characterized by a great complexity that, on one side, increases the possibility of malfunctioning and, on the other side, hampers the adoption of classic fault detection techniques based on design-time modeling of normal operation conditions [3]. The practical adoption of invariants for anomaly detection is limited by their sensitivity to the number and quality of monitored system variables, however. A moderately complex system may expose hundreds of invariants, and only a subset of them stably captures

© Springer International Publishing Switzerland 2016
A. Skavhaug et al. (Eds.): SAFECOMP 2016, LNCS 9922, pp. 172–183, 2016.
DOI: 10.1007/978-3-319-45477-1_14

its correct behavior, while a large fraction are either useless (because not linked to malfunctions) or excessively unstable (e.g., they are easily broken even if the system behaves correctly). Blindly monitoring all mined invariants introduces noise and fluctuations in the detection output, which create false positives;[1] this hampers the practical usability of this technique. Currently, there is no clear approach to *"filter"* the invariants space to get rid of such unwanted effects.

In this paper we present a practical and repeatable approach to analyze a (possibly very large) set of mined invariants to automatically select a *core subset* of them that properly captures the correct runtime system behavior, while showing a good degree of insensitivity to exogenous factors not linked to malfunctions. The approach exploits information provided by both the correct and the anomalous behavior of the system.

The approach is evaluated in a testbed equipped with a real web-based application (e.g., a web-banking portal) where we inject faults (from a defined fault model), to force the anomalous behavior. Results show the effectiveness of the proposed invariant selection approach, especially in reducing false positives.

The rest of this paper is organized as follows. Section 2 discusses related works. Section 3 introduces our invariant selection approach; Sects. 4 and 5 present a case study based on a real application scenario and discuss the results of applying our approach to it. Finally, Sect. 6 concludes our work.

2   Related Work

Sharma et al. [4] proposed to use invariants to detect faults in distributed systems: a mining tool is described, and mined invariants are used for the detection. Their application can then be extended to support log analysis [2,5]. In [6] automatically mined invariants are used for online anomaly detection in a cloud-based processing system.

Invariants can be classified [7] in control-flow, execution-flow, and value-based. In this paper, we focus on an extension of value-based invariants, known as *flow intensity invariants*. They have been introduced to measure the intensity with which internal monitoring data, treated as *time series*, react to the volume of user requests. In general, time series may be mined from system/application logs and resources utilization data through common monitoring tools. Hence, the approach does not depend on the particular system under monitoring.

A flow-intensity invariant is commonly selected among all the combinations of the collected metrics by estimating its ability in describing a phenomenon. As an example, in [1] an invariant is built when two measurements are available; then, it is incrementally validated when new observations are available. If, after a certain number of measurements, a confidence score of the model is less than a threshold, the invariant is discarded. However, this approach does not scale with

---

[1] A *false positive* is an error in the detection, in which an anomaly is reported when no anomalies occurred. A *false negative* is an omission of the detector, which does not report an occurred anomaly.

the size of the system, and generates a "background noise" of broken invariants that undermines its efficiency for anomaly detection.

For these reasons, [8] introduced a filtering stage where it is estimated the probability that an invariant would have been mined when considering a random input: if this probability is larger than a certain threshold, the invariant is selected, otherwise it is filtered out. Another approach consists in considering the number of times an invariant is violated [2]. However, as discussed in the remainder, also invariants broken too often should be treated with care: if an invariant is easily violated, it may be useful for detection completeness, but it may also generate many false positives, thus negatively affecting the accuracy.

Differently from such approaches, we introduce an *automatic* filtering stage, identified as *filtering 2* hereafter. It is based on both correct and anomalous runs of the system, instead of only considering correct executions, as for the commonly adopted selection procedure, which we identify as *filtering 1*.

3   Approach

The invariant-based approach we propose (Fig. 1) is based on three steps: (1) Mining, (2) Automatic Filtering, and (3) Detection. The *invariants mining* step consists in the analysis of data characterizing the *correct system behavior* to identify invariant relationships between pairs of observed variables. Step 2 consists in the automatic *filtering* of found invariants in order to extract a subset of them that can be usefully exploited in step 3 for the *detection* of anomalies.

Existing invariant-based detection approaches, such as the ones proposed in [5,6], only consider a training dataset representing the correct behavior of a system to be used for the mining and the filtering is based on goodness of fit (*filtering 1*). This way, many invariants are mined. In this paper, we introduce a further filtering step (*filtering 2*), which also considers known faulty behaviors. To identify the invariants that are potentially good symptoms of anomalies, we consider a further dataset representative of the system when faults are activated. Thus, given the fault model for the considered system, the idea is to inject

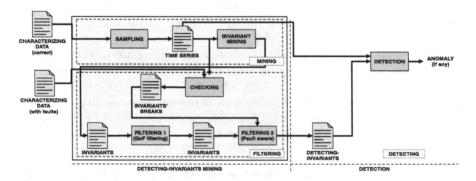

Fig. 1. Approach for invariant mining and filtering for anomaly detection.

instances of such faults in the system (for details, see Sect. 4) in order to collect the data that characterize the faulty behavior and that are then used to check when invariants are actually violated. The following sections describe the details of the three steps.

3.1 Invariant Mining

The first step consists in sampling the available data in order to have time series for mining invariants. As characterizing data, we consider data collected from the monitoring of the processing system, i.e., related to resources' utilization, such as CPU use, memory use, network packets, etc. This makes the approach generic and not dependent on the specific system workload. A time series is a sequence of values corresponding to measurements of parameters, uniformly spaced, with a certain sampling time, over a time interval. Thus, a time series is a function f over a domain of real numbers $\mathbb{R}$ and of a discrete time argument $t \in T$, $f{:}T \to \mathbb{R}$. Collected data may require some manipulation in order to have all the time series with the same sampling time. The selection of the sampling time is important for the results of the detection [5]. In our case, examples of considered time series are $f_1(t) = cpu\_system\_metric$ and $f_2(t) = proc\_run\_metric$ representing the use of the CPU in non user mode and the number of running processes, respectively. Observations of the time series at different times results in a relation as $f_2(t) + a_1 f_2(t-1) + \cdots + a_n f_2(t-n) = b_0 f_1(t-k) + \cdots + b_m f_1(t-k-m)$; by considering the vectors of coefficients and samples $\theta = [a_1, \ldots, a_n, b_0, \ldots, b_m]^T$ and $\varphi(t) = [-f_2(t-1), \ldots, -f_2(t-n), f_1(t-k), \ldots, f_1(t-k-m)]^T$, we have $f_2(t) = \varphi(t)^T \theta$. For the parameters estimation, and thus for the mining process, we use the least squares method, as described in [5].

3.2 Automatic Filtering

Filtering operations aim to improve the detection by removing redundant and/or inaccurate invariants, e.g., the ones that break either too often, leading to a large number of false positives, or too seldom, generating false negatives. They consist of three phases: *checking*, *filtering 1*, and *filtering 2*, described in the following.

Checking phase is used to verify when invariants are broken if faults are injected. Thus, apart from monitored data related to the correct behavior, also collected data of anomalous behaviors are used. In this case, as during the operational phase of the system, a set of time series is used as input. The assessment of broken invariants is discussed in Sect. 3.3.

The second part of the filtering step is made up of two phases. The goal is to filter those invariants that are not actually able to detect anomalies. Such filtering operations are performed on vectors associated to each invariant and reporting their behavior in an observation period. Considering the time lapse $t_0 \ldots t_{n-1}$, for each invariant i_j, we consider a vector v_j of size n, where n are the instants of observation, and

$$v_j[k] = \begin{cases} 0, & \text{if } i_j \text{ is not broken at } t_k \\ 1, & \text{otherwise} \end{cases}$$

Filtering 1 phase is based on the *Goodness of Fit* test. It considers only the correct behavior of the system and is also used in [5,6]. The basic idea is to remove invariants with a goodness of fit (GoF) outside a specific range. Clearly, invariants with a low GoF are invariants that do not provide a good modeling, i.e., are not able to properly describe system behavior. Conversely, invariants with a too large GoF are likely mined from too similar time series and are thus meaningless. Consider, as an instance, an invariant relating CPU use time *CPU_util* and CPU idle time *CPU_idle* ($CPU\_util = 1 - CPU\_idle$). The two time series are linearly dependent, thus, the resulting invariant has a very large GoF and is always verified, but it is useless. To discard invariants by testing the quality of their fitting, we use the Coefficient of Determination R^2, which represents the percentage of the variation that can be explained by the model. The closer the value of R^2 to 1, the better the regression.

Filtering 2 phase uses a dataset representative of the system when anomalies occur, unlike the existing approaches based only on the system correct behavior. This dataset is obtained by means of fault injection (see Sect. 4). This is the main novelty of the invariant selection strategy we propose, aiming at removing invariants that may provoke erroneous evaluations, i.e., false positives and false negatives. This phase includes the following five filtering operations.

(1) **Never-broken invariants filtering**. We remove invariants that are never broken. As a matter of fact, there could be a relation between two time series that is also able to well describe the variance of the system, but the relation always holds. Thus, it is not useful to detect anomalous events.

(2) **Correlated invariants filtering** ($Corr_{th}$). When applying the GoF filtering, invariants relating to similar time series are removed. There could still be invariants representing similar relations and that are broken at the same time. Previously, we considered the example of *CPU_util* and *CPU_idle* measurements; the invariant relating them is filtered; but, let now also consider memory utilization *Mem_util*; if there is an invariant $Mem\_util = \alpha CPU\_util$, there will also be an invariant $Mem\_util = \alpha' CPU\_idle$. Nevertheless, those invariants provide the same information, and considering both of them would be redundant. By considering the vectors v_j associated to all the invariants, we consider all the possible pairs of invariants $\langle i_i, i_j \rangle$ and compute the correlation by means of the Pearson's correlation index. If the correlation is larger than a threshold $Corr_{th}$, invariant i_j is removed and only invariant i_i is considered.

(3) **Too-often broken invariants filtering** (Oft_{all}). Some invariants may be too weak, i.e., they are broken too often and, similarly to never-broken invariants, are not useful to detect different-than-common behaviors that are likely related to anomalies' occurrence. We filter invariants that are broken more than Oft_{all} times the average number of times all the invariants are broken, in the examined lapse of time.

(4) **Invariants broken before injection filtering**. Some invariants may be broken before a fault is injected, when the system behavior is expected to be correct. Consider an invariant that is not broken too often (thus, it is not

filtered at *step 3*) but it is always broken before an injected fault is activated, i.e., before the anomaly occurs. This invariant would report not occurred anomalies, thus generating false positives, so we filter all the invariants that are broken when no anomaly is occurring in the system.

(5) **Seldom broken invariants fault-specific filtering** (Sld_{spec}). Invariants that are seldom broken for a specific fault are filtered. Even though at *step 3* invariants broken too often are filtered, the remaining ones should break often enough to detect the forced anomaly and avoid false negatives. We remove invariants that are broken less than Sld_{spec} times the average number of times the invariants are broken, in the examined lapse of time, for a specific injected fault.

3.3 Detection

A detector implements a distance function δ, which evaluates at runtime the distance of the actual system behavior from the expected one, and consider a threshold τ that, when exceeded by the value of δ, triggers an alarm.

At a time t, with respect to a specific system parameter $\hat{\theta}$ and an input $f_1(t)$, the detector has to compute the distance of the actual response of the system $f_2(t)$ from the estimated response $\hat{f}_2(t|\hat{\theta})$. As in [6], we adopt the residual function as a distance function: $R_{f_1,f_2}(t) = |f_2(t) - \hat{f}_2(t|\hat{\theta})|$. Thus, an invariant is broken at time t, if $R_{f_1,f_2}(t) > \tau$, where τ represents the tolerance of the detection system.

On the selection of the value of τ heavily depends the results of the detection, as discussed in [5]. As a matter of fact, if considering a detector with $\tau = 0$, invariants would be broken too often, generating many false positives; on the contrary, a too large τ would reduce too much the number of breaks, and too false negatives would take place. In [5], it is shown that when adopting a threshold τ which adapts to the specific prediction, the detection appears both complete and accurate. Specifically, we consider the prediction interval (p.i.) of the output with respect to the provided input [9]: the invariant is considered broken if the actual output of the system is outside the p.i. of the model's output. This happens if, for a certain value $f_1(t)$, the difference between the actual value $f_2(t)$ of the system and the estimated value $\hat{f}_2(t|\hat{\theta})$ is larger than the standard deviation of $\hat{f}_2(t|\hat{\theta})$. The standard deviation is computed as:

$$\sigma = S_{err}[1 + \frac{1}{n} + \frac{(f_{1_p} - \bar{f}_1)^2}{\sum f_1^2 - n\bar{f}_1^2}]^{1/2} \tag{1}$$

where S_{err} is the standard deviation of the model error (square root of the mean squared error), $\bar{f}_1$ is the sample mean of the predictor variable (the input of the model), and f_{1_p} a specific value of f_1.

4   Case Study

In order to evaluate the feasibility and performance of the proposed approach for invariant selection we set-up a testbed and deploy on top of it a web-based application with the aim of mimiking a typical online service offered, for example, by a bank to its customers. We monitor the system to collect time series related to several metrics. Different workloads are submitted to the system, to collect data from different load conditions. The testbed is used to produce both a *training set*, to be used for invariant mining, and a *training-test set*, for the assessment. Time series are collected for both *correct executions*, i.e., executions where no anomalies occur, and *faulty* ones, where one or more anomalies take place as a consequence of injected faults.

Testbed — The testbed is composed of 4 servers, each equipped with an Intel Xeon X5560 Quad-Core CPU clocked at 2.28 GHz and with 24 GB of RAM. The system presents a standard 3-tier architecture with one of the servers (master) hosting a centralized load balancer based on the Apache 2 Web Server and mod_cluster 2.6.0 module. The business tier hosts a JBoss AS 7.1.1. Final cluster running an instance on each machine, one master co-located with the Web Server and three slaves in execution on each of the other servers. The storage layer is based on a single instance of MySQL 5.5.38 running on the master node. On top of the JBoss cluster, we deployed a web application [10] working on both the business tier, with a front-end web application, and on the storage tier, interacting with the database. The testbed is monitored by means of the Ganglia monitoring system.

Workload — We generate workloads from a fifth machine running Tsung 1.5.0 [11]. The load consists in the number of requests per second sent to the web application. Each request involves the generation of ~400 packets in the testbed. We consider three load levels, in order to cover several operational conditions: *low*, *medium*, and *high*. By means of a preliminary analysis, we identify the *high* level, which uses almost all the resources of the system. *medium* and *low* levels are selected by considering a load that is 2/3 and 1/3 of the *high* level, respectively. The three workload levels are generated from a normal distribution by varying the mean (μ) and the standard deviation (σ) of the *connections per second*. Specifically, we consider *low* with $\mu = 5$, $\sigma = 1$, *medium* with $\mu = 10$, $\sigma = 2$ and *high* with $\mu = 15$, $\sigma = 2$.

Faultload — Candidate faults for injection are selected to include those that *(i)* are often the cause of problems in real settings, especially after changes to the deployment setup (e.g. where the deployment of a new application version or the reconfiguration of an existing one may trigger some of such faults), and *(ii)* that can not be easily detected through basic monitoring tools (e.g., a crashing process that leaves a debug trace in some log). We consider faults related to actual anomalies that can occur in processing systems and identify them on the basis of both our direct experience on real operational datacenters, and information drawn from scientific literature and online resources. The defined fault model is also compliant to the well known and widely adopted taxonomy defined by Avizienis et al. in [12]. In particular we considered the following faults:

Table 1. Invariant filtering parameters considered as *factors*.

Factor	Level 1	2	3	4	5	6	...	11	12
Oft_{all}	0.1	0.2	0.4	0.6	0.8	1.0	...	2.0	4.0
Sld_{spec}	0.1	0.2	0.4	0.6	0.8	1.0	...	2.0	4.0
$Corr_{th}$	0.70	0.75	0.80	0.85	0.90	0.95			

- *Misconfiguration faults* that derive from human errors caused by the wrong configuration of a system. Configuration errors are both common and highly detrimental, and detecting them is desirable [13]:
  - *SQL misconfiguration*: we reduce significantly the connection pool used by the application server to connect with the DB.
  - *AJP-long misconfiguration*: we reduce the thread pool for the AJP protocol (which allows the communication between the Apache web server and the JBoss slaves) to a very small size.
  - *AJP-short misconfiguration*: same as AJP-long misconfiguration, but we also reduced the length of the queue associated with the thread pool.
- *Reconfiguration faults*, representing changes of configuration during maintenance that cause unexpected failures [14,15]:
  - *Write permissions*: we revoke write permissions to one of the JBoss instances on its working directory.
- *Denials of service faults*, either malicious or not, that cause the system unavailability due to the saturation of some hardware resources:
  - *CPU stress*: we impose an abnormal CPU load on the target machine by running a strongly CPU-intensive task.
  - *Memory stress*: we impose an abnormal level of memory activity that causes high memory contention on the target machine.
  - *Disk stress*: we cause an abnormal disk access activity on the server hosting the SQL server.
  - *Full partition*: we cause the disk partition on the machine hosting Apache and the SQL server to become full.
- *Development faults* that typically produce erratic output or software aging phenomena [16]:
  - *Memory Leak*: we run a process affected by memory leak that causes the memory of the target machine to progressively saturate. The memory exhaustion in turns triggers the thrashing phenomenon.

Plan of experiments — The implemented testbed and the planned injections allow us to obtain both *correct executions*, i.e., executions where no anomaly occur, and *faulty executions*, where, from a certain time t_a, one or more of the considered faults are injected. These executions are used to produce both a **training set**, to be used for mining and filtering the invariants, and a **test set** to be used for assessing performance. Each execution for the training set lasted on average ∼9 min (time needed to reach a steady state, where metrics can be collected while excluding impact from any transient effect). For the test phase, we produced a single 90 min long test set were the system transitions among all the possible combinations of workloads and faults.

Filtering operations are performed on the training set by considering several values for the filtering parameters introduced in Sect. 3, considered as *factors*: $Corr_{th}$, for filtering correlated invariants, Oft_{all}, for removing too-often broken invariants, and Sld_{spec}, for seldom broken invariants fault-specific filtering. Table 1 shows the values used in our tests. We consider a design of experiments (DoE) [9], where the factors are the filtering parameters. The *levels* (i.e., the values assigned to the factors) are in a wide range to cover several cases. As response variables, we consider common metrics for detection assessment. *Coverage (Cov)* is the portion of kinds of anomalies that are found by a detector. If n kinds of anomalies occur, and the detector finds r of them, $Cov = r/n$. *Completeness (Cpl)* is the portion of anomalies that are found by the detector over the occurred anomalies. If o anomalies occur, the detector may find p of such anomalies, with $p \leq o$; $Cpl = p/o$. *Accuracy (Acc)* is the portion of anomalies correctly reported by a detector. A concrete detector finds s anomalies over $s' \leq s$ actual anomalies. $Acc = s'/s$. *Detection latency (Lat)* is the time required by the detector to report the occurrence of an anomaly.

5   Results

In this section, we present results related to the application of the approach to the training set and to the test set, and compare them to the common approach of invariant mining that only filters by considering the GoF (*Filtering - Goodness of Fit filtering*, discussed in Sect. 3.2). Also, we discuss how the configuration of the filtering influences detection performance.

5.1   Training

The mining and filtering steps have been applied on the training set in order to identify the invariants and find the best configuration of filtering parameters for the system at hands. As a result of the plan discussed in Sect. 4, the experimentation produces 1,176 outputs for each response variable; to evaluate the anomaly detection performance, we also consider the F-measure (F), defined as the harmonic mean of completeness and accuracy: $F\text{-}measure = (2 \cdot Cpl \cdot Acc)/(Cpl + Acc)$. The larger the completeness and accuracy (ideally, $Cpl = 1$ and $Acc = 1$), the better the detection quality of the detector, since it avoids false positives and false negatives.

To identify the values to be used for the filtering parameters $Corr_{th}$, Oft_{all}, and Sld_{spec}, we use the Pareto multi-objective optimization algorithm [17]. The algorithm returns a Pareto front with 16 combinations of the configuration parameters. Among such configurations, we consider the one allowing the detector to identify all the anomalies occurring in the system. Invariant-based detection approaches, in fact, are expected to have a large completeness given the large

Table 2. Results of the training related to the best combination of the filtering parameters. $Corr_{th} = 0.85$, $Oft_{all} = 1.8$, $Sld_{spec} = 3$.

Cpl	Acc	Lat	F-m	# inv
1.00	0.80	33.33	0.89	25

Table 3. Results of the tuned detector applied to the test set. First row: results of the proposed approach. Second row: results without the proposed filtering.

Cpl	Acc	Lat	F-m	# inv
0.99	0.76	65.55	0.86	25
1.00	0.57	47.78	0.73	265

number of invariants that can be violated when anomalies occur [5]. Results with this combination are reported in Table 2. They are achieved for $Corr_{th} = 0.85$, $Oft_{all} = 1.8$, and $Sld_{spec} = 3$.

On the training set, the invariant based approach detects all the kinds of anomalies that occur in the system, and over all the anomalies, of all the kinds, all are detected. The accuracy is 80 %; thus, there are few false positives. Anomalies are detected within 33 seconds.

We also observe a large reduction of the number of used invariants (around 90 % of reduction) after filtering. 78 metrics are monitored, thus, the possible invariants (considering all the combinations) are 3, 003. The GoF filtering selects 265 of these invariants, which involve all the 78 metrics. The proposed filtering reduces the number of used invariants by about 90 %, which involves only 19 metrics out of the 78 monitored. In practical terms, this implies a significant reduction of the monitoring overhead.

Due to space limitation, we report as examples of the mined invariants the ones that are often violated when an anomaly occurs: one relates the use of the CPU in non user mode (*cpu_system_metric*) to the number of running processes (*proc_run_metric*), another one relates the average size of incoming packets (*avg_packet_size_metric*) and CPU usage (*cpu_idle_metric*).

5.2   Test

The configuration of the filtering defines the invariants to be used by the detection module that we run on the test set. This allows us to assess the behavior of the detector in the operational stage, when ground truth is available. Achieved results are compared to the ones of the detector using not filtered invariants, and reported in Table 3. The first row of the table reports results related to the detector based on the proposed filtering approach. Results in the second row are related to the detector without filtering.

The comparison of the two detectors, with and without the *fault aware filtering*, shows that the proposed approach outperforms the detector not using the introduced filtering. When no filtering is done, coverage and completeness are maximum. In fact, having a large number of invariants implies there is a large chance that there is a violated invariant, and the anomaly is detected, whatever its kind is. Latency is small due to similar observations: the larger the number of invariants, the sooner one is violated and the anomaly detected. The chance that an anomaly is erroneously signaled is large, however. Among all the invariants, one may be broken even if there is no anomaly, generating false positives and, then, reducing the accuracy. A result of 0.57 for the accuracy implies that out of 100 anomalies reported by the detector, only 57 have been caused by faults, while the remaining 43 represent false positives.

The adoption of the proposed approach significantly improves the performance of the detector, making the approach practicable in our experimental settings. While the completeness remains high, as expected for invariant-based approaches (as also shown in [6]), the filtering approach proposed in this paper, by selecting the right subset of invariants, improves the accuracy pushing it to 0.76, i.e. reducing false positive to 24 % of the reported anomalies. Thus, the performance improves even if less than 10 % of the original invariants are adopted (from 265 to 25), hence reducing the overall monitoring overhead. On the other hand, the use of a reduced set of invariants slightly increases the latency to 65 s, i.e., the anomaly is detected within one minute from the activation of the fault causing it. Note that, since the effects of the fault may affect the system several seconds after its injection, this is an upper bound of the latency.

Analysis of variance is then used to figure out which filtering parameters mostly impact the results of the detection. Results show that detection mainly depends on Oft_{all} and Sld_{spec} parameters, while the impact of $Corr_{th}$ is not statistically significant. Specifically, the variance of coverage and completeness is explained by Oft_{all} for 55 % and by Sld_{spec} for 45 %. variance on accuracy is explained by Oft_{all} for 89 %.

6   Discussion and Conclusion

Invariant-based detectors discussed in the scientific literature present a number of false positives, given the high chance of invariants being violated, when also negligible conditions change in the system. Presented results demonstrated that the proposed invariants' filtering approach improves the performance of common invariant-based detectors, which remove invariants by only considering their capacity of properly modeling the correct system behavior. The proposed approach exploits knowledge on the faulty behavior of the system to select those invariants that are sensible enough to be violated in the case of anomaly, thus not causing false negatives, but not weak enough to break also when the system is correctly behaving, producing false positives.

The achieved detector outperforms the detector not using the introduced filtering. It covers all the anomalies of the injected kinds, and, over all the occurring anomalies, reveals 99 % of them, with an accuracy of 76 %. Clearly, reported figures are specific to the case study system, but the proposed approach is general enough to be applied to a wide range of systems. Moreover, while many invariant mining approaches consider application-specific monitored data, this one uses resources' usage information common to every processing system and collectable with any of the existing, free and open source, monitoring tools.

Acknowledgments. This work has been supported by the TENACE PRIN Project (no. 20103P34XC) funded by MIUR. The work by Cinque and Russo has also been partially supported by EU under Marie Curie IAPP grant no. 324334 CECRIS (CErtification of CRItical Systems).

References

1. Jiang, G., Chen, H., Yoshihira, K.: Discovering likely invariants of distributed transaction systems for autonomic system management. Cluster Comput. **9**(4), 385–399 (2006)
2. Lou, J.-G., et al.: Mining invariants from console logs for system problem detection. In: Proceedings of the USENIX Annual Technical Conference (2010)
3. Xu, X., Zhu, L., Weber, I., Bass, L., Sun, D.: POD-diagnosis: error diagnosis of sporadic operations on cloud applications. In: 44th Annual IEEE/IFIP International Conference on Dependable Systems and Networks (DSN) (2014)
4. Sharma, A.B., et al.: Fault detection and localization in distributed systems using invariant relationships. In: 43rd Annual IEEE/IFIP International Conference on Dependable Systems and Networks (DSN) (2013)
5. Sarkar, S., Ganesan, R., Cinque, M., Frattini, F., Russo, S., Savignano, A.: Mining invariants from SaaS application logs. In: Tenth European Dependable Computing Conference (EDCC 2014) (May 2014)
6. Frattini, F., Sarkar, S., Khasnabish, J., Russo, S.: Using invariants for anomaly detection: the case study of a SaaS application. In: IEEE International Symposium on Software Reliability Engineering Workshops (ISSREW) (2014)
7. Sahoo, S.K., et al.: Using likely program invariants to detect hardware errors. In: IEEE International Conference on Dependable Systems and Networks (DSN) (2008)
8. Ernst, M., Cockrell, J., Griswold, W.G., Notkin, D.: Dynamically discovering likely program invariants to support program evolution. IEEE Trans. Softw. Eng. **27**(2), 99–123 (2001)
9. Jain, R.: The Art of Computer Systems Performance Analysis. Wiley (1991)
10. Ticket Monster. http://www.jboss.org/ticket-monster/
11. Tsung. http://tsung.erlang-projects.org/
12. Avizienis, A., et al.: Basic concepts and taxonomy of dependable and secure computing. IEEE Trans. Dependable Secur. Comput. **1**(1), 11–33 (2004)
13. Zhang, J., et al.: Encore: exploiting system environment and correlation information for misconfiguration detection. SIGARCH Comput. Archit. News **42**(1), 687–700 (2014)
14. Rice University - Division of Information Technology, Why Are My Jobs Not Running?, April 2013. http://rcsg.rice.edu/rcsg/shared/scheduling.html
15. IGI - Italian Grid Infrastructure, Troubleshooting guide for CREAM, April 2013. https://wiki.italiangrid.it/twiki/bin/view/CREAM/TroubleshootingGuide
16. Bovenzi, A., Cotroneo, D., Pietrantuono, R., Russo, S.: Workload characterization for software aging analysis. In: IEEE 22nd International Symposium on Software Reliability Engineering (ISSRE) (2011)
17. Goldberg, D.: Genetic Algorithms in Search, Optimization, and Machine Learning. Addison-Wesley, Boston (1989)

Cyber Security

Modelling Cost-Effectiveness of Defenses in Industrial Control Systems

Andrew Fielder, Tingting Li$^{(\boxtimes)}$, and Chris Hankin

Institute for Security Science and Technology,
Imperial College London, London, UK
{andrew.fielder,tingting.li,c.hankin}@imperial.ac.uk

Abstract. Industrial Control Systems (ICS) play a critical role in controlling industrial processes. Wide use of modern IT technologies enables cyber attacks to disrupt the operation of ICS. Advanced Persistent Threats (APT) are the most threatening attacks to ICS due to their long persistence and destructive cyber-physical effects to ICS. This paper considers a simulation of attackers and defenders of an ICS, where the defender must consider the cost-effectiveness of implementing defensive measures within the system in order to create an optimal defense. The aim is to identify the appropriate deployment of a specific defensive strategy, such as defense-in-depth or critical component defense. The problem is represented as a strategic competitive optimisation problem, which is solved using a co-evolutionary particle swarm optimisation algorithm. Through the development of optimal defense strategy, it is possible to identify when each specific defensive strategies is most appropriate; where the optimal defensive strategy depends on the resources available and the relative effectiveness of those resources.

1 Introduction

Industrial Control Systems (ICS) are typically comprised of a set of supervisory control and data acquisition (SCADA) systems to control field actuators by monitoring the data of industrial processes. ICS can be found in various sectors of critical infrastructure. Disruption to such systems would lead to disastrous damage to the plants, environment and human health [26]. To promote efficient communication and high throughput, modern ICT technologies have been widely adopted into ICS, which makes them vulnerable targets for cyber criminals. ICS-CERT received 245 reports in 2014 by trusted asset owners, whilst there are still numerous incidents in critical infrastructure unreported[1].

Amongst the various cyber attacks against ICS, multi-stage Advanced Persistent Threats (APT) account for roughly 55 %[1], and these are also the most threatening ones due to their long undetected persistence, sophisticated capabilities and destructive cyber-physical effects to ICS. We show a typical ICS architecture adapted from [26] in Fig. 1(a). In an APT attack, the attackers initially

---

[1] ICS-CERT: Sept. 2014 – Feb. 2015. www.ics-cert.us-cert.gov/monitors/ICS-MM20 1502.

© Springer International Publishing Switzerland 2016
A. Skavhaug et al. (Eds.): SAFECOMP 2016, LNCS 9922, pp. 187–200, 2016.
DOI: 10.1007/978-3-319-45477-1_15

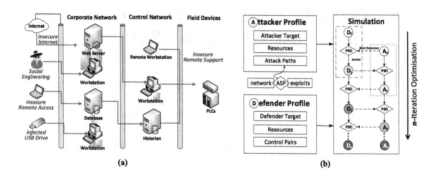

Fig. 1. (a) Typical ICS architecture threatened by APT attacks; (b) Simulation

gain access to the target network, then propagate through the network by continuously exploiting chains of vulnerabilities of hosts, and eventually compromise operational field devices. A canonical example of such an attack is Stuxnet [6] acknowledged in 2010, which enabled cyber attacks to sabotage industrial plants. Stuxnet was introduced to the network by a removable flash drive, and propagated malware through the corporate and control network by exploiting zero-day vulnerabilities of hosts. Stuxnet eventually tampered the program controlling the field PLCs and disrupted the operation of ICS. According to the report [6] by Symantec, there were approximately 100,000 infected hosts across over 155 countries by September 2010. Another more recent example was reported by the German government[2] in December 2014. A cyber attack breached a steel mill through penetrating spear-phishing emails and resulted in massive damage to the whole plant.

In the wake of the increasing cyber attacks against ICS, the notion of *Defense-in-Depth* has been highly recommended as the best practice to protect critical infrastructures by numerous reports [15,26]. Defense-in-depth provides a multilayer protection involving different security mechanisms such as a vulnerability management system, advanced firewalls with DMZ, intrusion detection, security awareness training and incident response. However, the high financial and managerial cost make defense-in-depth impractical and hard to fully implement [24]. Massive unnecessary efforts have been wasted on irrelevant attack vectors. Particularly smaller companies still struggle with finding the most cost-efficient way to deploy available controls. For this reason we look for alternative defensive strategies, and the most optimal implementation of them.

Most of the techniques involved at each stage of an APT can generally be defended by conventional security controls. A key question is how to allocate defensive resources and budget across the system to establish an effective protection against APT. In particular with limited low budget, our work here produces decision support tools to find *optimal defense strategies*, such as system-wide

---

[2] SANS ICS Defense Use Case, 2014. https://ics.sans.org/media/ICS-CPPE-case-Study-2-German-Steelworks_Facility.pdf.

evenly spreading defense (i.e. Defense-in-depth) and focused defense on critical components. Unlike conventional analysis, we novelly consider the impact of varied *cost-effectiveness* models of investments on deciding the most optimal defensive strategies, making the work more realistic and practical.

We use the notion of *attacker* to represent potential cyber attackers, and *defender* for the security manager who needs to deploy controls to protect an ICS. An attack graph is automatically generated by our logic-based reasoning engine, which chains various weaknesses of a given network that can be exploited by attackers. We model the attacker and defender as a pair of competing agents and investigate their behaviours in a co-evolutionary process. *Particle Swarm Optimisation* (PSO) [12] is adopted to aid agents in finding the most optimal strategy to attack and defend under different circumstances. From this work, we discover that with limited low budget, the defensive effort should be generally focused on the critical targets rather than spreading over the system. However, when defending the critical assets becomes very inefficient, the most optimal strategies then favour defending other less valuable assets to form a defense-in-depth style strategy. The paper starts with a related work section where the work on attack modelling and agent-based co-evolutionary approaches are presented. The approach proposed in this paper is discussed in Sect. 3, which describes the modelling of the key elements and the development of the agent-based simulation. Three case studies extracted from the CSSP Recommended Defense-In-Depth Architecture [15] are described in Sect. 4 to demonstrate the effectiveness of our proposed tools. Relevant results are presented in Sect. 5 and discussed in Sect. 6. The paper concludes with a summary and discussion of further directions of research in Sect. 7.

2   Related Work

A comprehensive introduction to the security issues of ICS is given in [26]. The generation of attack graphs has been studied extensively in the security community, and two of the most influential generators are MulVal [20] and NetSPA [17], both of which provide automatic generation of complete attack paths from scanned CVE vulnerabilities. [17] further provides a way of abstracting attack paths by classifying vulnerabilities in terms of CVE factors. Attack graphs have been widely applied to risk analysis. Noel et al. [19] measure the overall security of a network by simulating the propagation of multi-stage attacks and likelihoods of each single attack. Ma and Smith [18] provide a risk analysis for critical infrastructures to understand the impact of inter-dependency of CVE vulnerabilities on forming multi-step attack chains. This work particularly focuses on CVE vulnerabilities with effects of code execution and elevation of privileges as these vulnerabilities can serve as stepping-stone nodes to induce further attacks. In this paper, we generate attack graphs by common weaknesses of ICS, rather than specific vulnerabilities on each host. In this way, we lift our focus of defense to a more generic class of attacks, producing a more global view of deploying defense controls.

Antoine Lemay's 2013 thesis [16] presents an approach to defending SCADA components in electrical grids from APT style attacks. The author presents an Intrusion Detection System to protect ICS, with the aim of preventing the attacker from developing appropriate tools for exploiting the system. A more detailed view of the threats from APT models has been performed by Chopitea [2], and in a game theoretic manner by Pham and Cid [21]. One area of study that is of importance to this work is the concept of network hardening, which has been approached by studying vulnerabilities through attack graphs [28]. By studying the structure of networks and the vulnerabilities required to effectively exploit system, it is possible to identify the key areas where defensive measures are most effective, an approach that is taken in the representation of the problem in this work. Work undertaken by Fielder et. al. [7] uses a game theoretic approach to the optimal allocation of system administrator time to defensive tasks. The results show that a greater emphasis of the limited administrator time should be placed on the most valuable assets, consistent with a critical component defense strategy. Extensive game theoretic work has been performed by Tambe and Kiekintveld looking at optimal security decisions for real-world scenarios using Stackelberg games. The work has covered scheduling of airport security [14], allocation of air marshals to flight paths [27] and border control [13]. The work has moved into cyber security, with a study of the use of honeypots [4]. While the origins of PSO was proposed by Kennedy and Eberhart in [5], a more up to date view of the field of PSO algorithms was presented by Poli et al. in [23], which brought together many of the concepts developed over the previous 12 years. This overview was followed in a 2008 study by Poli [22], which identifies the application areas for PSO. This study identifies that very little work has gone into applying PSO algorithms to network security tasks, with only 1.3 % of the literature covering the whole security field with some work in security predictions [9], intrusion detection [25] and authentication [11].

3   Modelling and Simulation

The key components of the system are depicted in Fig. 1(b). We define *Attacker Profile* and *Defender profile* to characterise attackers and defenders' behaviours and generate attack and defense strategies respectively. Attack strategies are decided by the attacking goals, available resources of the attacker and possible attack paths to launch and deploy the attack. Given an established network and weaknesses in the network, attack paths are generated by an automatic reasoning engine using *Answer Set Programming (ASP)* [10], which works similarly as most existing attack path generators [17,20]. For defenders, defensive preference of assets and available resource are the key to the decision making, as well as a set of control pairs defining the behaviours to form defense strategies. The most important part of the system is the agent-based simulation, as shown in Fig. 1(b). Attackers and defenders are modelled as a pair of competing agents, by which their behaviours are able to co-evolve to develop an optimal solution. PSO is adopted to encode each candidate strategy as a particle of a swarm and all such particles gradually move towards the best solution during each iteration of evolution.

3.1   Modelling and Representation

In this section, we introduce the representation of the pair of competing agents – *Attackers* and *Defenders*, and other key components to establish the agent-based simulation. We first represent a typical ICS architecture as a *network graph*, where each host or asset is identified as a *target* node $t_i \in \mathcal{T}$, a valid connection between a pair of targets is an *edge* $e \in \mathcal{E}$ and $\mathcal{E} := \mathcal{T} \times \mathcal{T}$. A compromised target produces certain gains for attackers $I^a : \mathcal{T} \rightarrow \mathbb{Z}^+$, while causing certain damages for defenders $I^d : \mathcal{T} \rightarrow \mathbb{Z}^-$. A sequence of single-step attacks constitutes an effective APT attack, and each single attack exploits a weakness of a targeted host. We define all such weaknesses as a set of **attack methods** $\mathcal{M} = \{m_1, \ldots, m_n\}$. An *attack path* p is derived by attaching an applicable attack method m to an edge, indicating a possible way to progress the attack from one target to another. $O(t_i)$ has all outbound paths from t_i. Our reasoning engine can generate all such possible attack paths for a given network, which altogether render an *attack graph*. An example of such attack graph is given in Fig. 2(a). At each step of an APT, attackers probabilistically select an outbound attack path to exploit next.

Definition 1. *An* **attacker strategy** $a := \{(O(t_1), \Psi_1), \ldots, (O(t_n), \Psi_n)\}$, *where*

- $O(t_i) = [p_i^1, \ldots, p_i^k]$, *all outbound paths from the target t_i.*
- $\Psi_i = \{\psi_1, \ldots \psi_k\}$, *the probability distribution over $O(t_i)$, $\sum_{j=1}^{k} \psi_j = 1$, $\psi_j \geqslant 0$.*

The key task of *defenders* is to find a way of deploying defense controls with certain effectiveness to specifically combat APT-style attacks. Implementing a control with higher effectiveness generally requires more investment. Here we define "budget" as a general term of available resources to implement a defense control, such as system administrators' time [7], financial cost and other indirect cost [8]. We also define a cost-effectiveness function in the general form of $eff_t(x) = \frac{ax}{bx+c}$ to compute the resulting effectiveness of a control at the target t with certain investment x, where $a, b, c \in \mathbb{N}$, $ax < bx + c$. The function will be instantiated to represent various cost-efficiencies in the examples later. Given a limited budget B, defenders need to decide the most cost-efficient way to deploy controls. Unlike attackers who have specific targets to stage attacks, defenders have to protect various targets across the network from numerous possible attacks and also stop the formation of APT.

Definition 2. *A* **defender strategy** $d := \{(c_1, x_1), \ldots, (c_m, x_m)\}$ *is a set of control pairs amongst the available controls $\mathcal{C} = \{c_1, \ldots, c_m\}$, and x_i denotes the number of allocated budget units to implement c_i, and $\sum_{i=1}^{m} x_i \leqslant B$, where B is the budget limit. The effectiveness of c_i implemented at the target t is then decided by a provided cost-effectiveness function $eff_t(x_i)$.*

3.2   Simulation

We represent the problem of the calculation of optimal strategies as a competitive co-evolutionary process between an attacker and a defender. In this way we represent the problem as a system with two competing agents that aim to optimise their expected payoffs from either attacking or defending the system. In order to solve the co-evolutionary optimisation problem, we have developed a PSO algorithm. The PSO operates a number of rounds, where the attacker and defender attempt to create best response strategies to each other's actions. The PSO method creates an initial set of randomised strategies, called particles, for the attacker and the defender. The PSO algorithm explores the space of possible solutions by moving the particles to new positions in the search space aiming to find better solutions; this is done by applying a movement parameter to the particle, called a velocity. The velocity of a particle is a special form of the mixed strategy of the defender and the attacker, where the sum of all components must equal zero. Each of the particles must be evaluated to assess its performance; this is done by simulating the interactions between the two players. Considering the nature of the kinds of attacks expected, the simulation represents the interactions of the players over a given fixed number of time steps. During each time step, the players have to make a series of decisions with regards to the actions that they perform, where the outcome of those actions are scored according to the amount of damage that successful attacks cause.

For each evaluation of the defense strategy, the defender sets a defense based on the mixed strategy, to prevent damage from an attacker who attempts to breach that defense over a period of time. At the start of each evaluation, the defender assigns the whole of the available budget to the system, where each target is assigned a portion of the budget based on the distribution defined by the strategy. The amount of units assigned to each control is an amount of budget used to protect the resource, with the effectiveness of the defensive measures based on the amount invested in defending them.

An attacker attacks through the system, starting from the node labelled EXT and attempts to advance through the network exploiting subsequent nodes until they have exploited a vulnerability on a device with no further connections in the network or the attack is halted by the defender. Specifically, the attacker selects an outward path from the current node based on their strategy and attempts to exploit a vulnerability on the connected node. If there is no defense assigned, then the attack is successful, however, if the defender has assigned defense to the node, then the attacker will exploit the vulnerability with probability $p_a > \mathit{eff}_t(v)$, where p_a is distributed uniformly to represent the probability a generic attacker is able to successfully launch an attack. More advanced attacker models will be explored in the future. $\mathit{eff}_t(v)$ is the effectiveness of the defensive controls on node n, with an investment of v units from the budget.

If the attacker is successful in exploiting a vulnerability, then they continue to attack selecting a further connecting node deeper in the system. In the event that there are no further outward connections, or the attack is halted by the defensive controls, then the attacker receives the maximum reward of the nodes exploited in the attack and the defender suffers damage in line with the value of that node.

4   Case Study and Experimental Settings

The case study is adapted from the common ICS architecture in [15,26] and shown in Fig. 2(a). It is a typical three-zone architecture of ICS, with a *Corporate Network*, a *Control Network* and *Field Devices*. The node *EXT* represents the external environment. Four target nodes represent common hosts in a corporate network and a control network respectively. The node *PLC* symbolises the key control device. We collect a set of attack methods (Fig. 2(b)) from the *ICS Top 10 Threats and Countermeasures* [1] and *Common Cybersecurity Vulnerabilities in ICS* [3]. A set of controls is given in Fig. 2(c), derived from [1,15]. The attack methods countered by the controls are enumerated in the rightmost column of Fig. 2(c). An attack graph for the case study is then automatically generated by our ASP engine in Fig. 2(a). Each edge denotes a possible exploit of the system. The control stations (*ctRWs* and *ctWs*) have direct access to PLCs, and thus all attacks aiming to PLCs have to pass through them. These control workstations are not connected to any untrusted network, but can be infected by other hosts in the same network such as *ctHmi* and *ctHist*. Remote workstations (*ctRWs*) used for remote maintenance are threatened by the viruses infected by other external assets.

The cost-effectiveness functions are designed to represent a diminishing return on investment in the security of a device. Given the nature of security, the effectiveness of any control is restricted to $eff(v) < 100\%$. The implementation of the cost functions represents that as more effort is put into a control, the effectiveness of the defense that control gives is increased. At the same time the rate at which the defense is improved is reduced. This is represented by the notion, that the first unit of cost introduces a control and has the largest impact

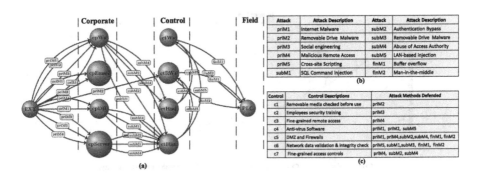

Fig. 2. Case study on ICS security management: (a) An attack graph; (b) Common ICS attack methods; (c) Common defense controls.

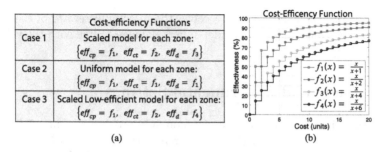

	Cost-efficiency Functions
Case 1	Scaled model for each zone: $\{eff_{cp} = f_1, \; eff_{ct} = f_2, \; eff_d = f_3\}$
Case 2	Uniform model for each zone: $\{eff_{cp} = f_1, \; eff_{ct} = f_1, \; eff_d = f_1\}$
Case 3	Scaled Low-efficient model for each zone: $\{eff_{cp} = f_1, \; eff_{ct} = f_2, \; eff_d = f_4\}$

(a)   (b)

Fig. 3. (a) Case study settings; (b) Cost-effectiveness functions of investments

on defense, but spending the same amount on the control again to either maintain or upgrade will not have the same impact. This is then logically extended to all future iterations of an increase in budget, where these diminishing increments are best represented by a form of sigmoid function. Brief introductions to the three cases are given in Fig. 3(a). The main differences amongst the three cases are the application of cost-effectiveness functions for different zones, where eff_{cp} denotes the function adopted for all targets in the *Corporate Zone*, eff_{ct} for the *Control Zone* and eff_d for the *Field Zone*. Case 1 presents a standard ICS [26] with unique characteristics in each zone, and thus variable functions are applied. An example of such ICS is Distributed Control Systems (DCS) that has high requirements on timeliness, availability and limited resource, making the defensive efforts in control and field layer less efficient. Unlike Case 1, Case 2 provides a comparative scenario where most assets are located in commercial facilities with particular emphasis on gathering data by SCADA and hence a uniform function is adopted for all zones. The last case captures a special scenario of Case 1, where most control devices can be hardly protected (e.g. isolated or remote distributed ICS) and massive effort is required to deploy controls in *Field Zone*.

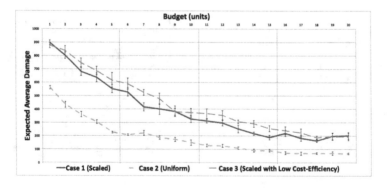

Fig. 4. Average expected system damage against the available defense budget

To run the simulations, we fixed a number of parameters that relate to the operation of the PSO Algorithm. The size of the swarm used was set at 100, which was large enough to reasonably represent the search space. This is given that the simulation happens over 50 moves per particle and for 50 generations of competition between the two agents. The weighting values for all factors contributing to the velocity were set at 0.05, this was set so as to allow for better exploration of the strategy space, by not favouring a single component. The simulation operated over 20 time steps for the attacker and defender strategies and a particle would be evaluated 30 times to reduce variance from the non-deterministic nature of the simulated environment. In the next section, we show the simulation results on the optimal defense for all three cases. We analyse the variance of the average expected damage per attack in Fig. 4 and discuss the resource assignment on the critical component PLC in Fig. 5.

5   Results

Figure 4 shows the average expected damage per attack from an indifferent attacker with the three cost-effectiveness models for defense. The most noticeable result is the difference in expected damage between the uniform cost-effectiveness and both forms of the scaled cost-effectiveness. At low budget levels the difference in expected damage between the uniform and scaled methods is approximately 300. With more than 6 units of defense, this difference is reduced to an approximate range of 150–200. This reduction in difference is representative in a change in policy, where the defender switches from a heavier focus on protecting the PLC to performing a defense-in-depth strategy. By operating a similar strategy to those with the scaled cost-effectiveness model, the difference in expected damage becomes equivalent to the difference in the efficiency. With the uniform cost-effectiveness, we see that the first 5 units provide the most benefit of defense. The first unit reduces the damage by approximately 450 units, with the next 4 units reducing the damage by an average of 84 each. After 5 units, the average net gain in defense is reduced to 10 damage per unit. In contrast, for the scaled methods, the first unit for defense has a lower benefit, providing only a reduction in average expected damage by approximately 110. For the scaled model the next 4 units have a similar impact on the defense as the uniform model, reducing the expected damage by an average of 86 each, however this reduction is only 65 for the low cost-effectiveness model. However each unit of defense after the fifth, reduces the expected damage by 24 for the normal scaled and 28 for the scaled with low cost-effectiveness.

We see this change in the reduction of damage, because the effectiveness of the defense per unit placed on a single target is lower for every unit after the first. This means that after an initial investment to protect an asset, each further investment has a lower impact. For the uniform model, the initial investment of a single unit to protect the PLC is the most significant investment, with the next 4 units able to help protect the rest of the system. Beyond this point each additional unit is used to protect a less risky component or add defense to an already defended component. For the scaled methods, this is not as consistent, since the first unit has a lower initial impact outside the assets at the corporate level. To identify the issue surrounding the type of defense that accounts for the optimal solutions, we need to identify the strategy of defense for the critical component, in this case the PLC. The graph presented in Fig. 5, shows the representation of the probability of defending PLC in the optimal solution across each of the runs.

The uniform cost-effectiveness method shows that the first unit of defense is almost always placed on the PLC, since there is no strategy that better defends the system. As the number of units increases, the probability of placing defense on the PLC decreases, but maintains the probability that at least 1 unit should be dedicated to the PLC. From 7 units, the defense tends towards a preference of defense-in-depth, with only 30 % of the budget being allocated for the PLC. The remaining 70 % budget is then split amongst all other controls, with an emphasis on the control layer. It is because with a larger budget available, it is no longer efficient to focus all the defense on the PLC, but instead spread the defense to limit not only the damage to the PLC, but protect more of the network.

Table 1. Comparison of strategies with a scaled cost-effectiveness and a budget of 2

ctWs	ctRWs	ctHist	cpDB	cpEmail	PLC	ctHmi	cpWs	cpServer
0.320	0.008	0.634	0.010	0.002	0.008	0.005	0.006	0.007
0.009	0.104	0.011	0.007	0.009	0.306	0.007	0.541	0.007

Unlike the uniform model, the scaled models initially reject placing the very limited resource in a place where it has the lower potential impact, which is at the PLC, favouring a more aggressive defense that has a higher variance. However, we see that as the budget increases, the ability to cover the PLC with some effectiveness is greatly increased, and so the scaled models adapt to this and assign resources accordingly. The low cost-effectiveness scaled model assigns on average 13 % less resources to the PLC than the standard scaled model, this is due to the lower impact that each unit has when applied to the node, with the initial uptake of non-incidental protection for the PLC occurring later. While the results may show that in general the optimal strategy for each of the cost-effectiveness strategic tested converges to $0.175 < x_{PLC} < 0.25$ with a larger budget, the variance in those results indicates that there are a number of optimal strategies. It is accounted for in the high variance of the results associated with the implementation of defense on the PLC. We compare two different solutions in Table 1, which shows two competing strategies for the defender getting the same approximate outcome of 765. In one case minimal emphasis is placed on the PLC, whereas the other strategy implements defense at the PLC with a probability of 0.306 per unit of defense.

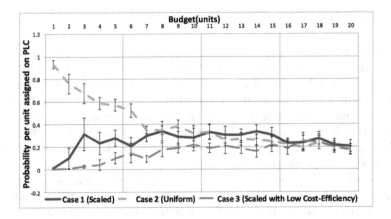

Fig. 5. Probability per unit assigned to PLC against the available budget

6   Discussion

One of the issues is what happens if the decision maker gets the cost-effectiveness model wrong. When defining the optimal defense, the cost-effectiveness model dictates how much effort should be placed onto any individual asset and so over-estimating the cost-effectiveness could prove disastrous. An overestimation could create a scenario where the defender believes they have one cost-effectiveness model, but in reality they are operating under a different model. From the per-spective of the results presented in Fig. 4, that for a budget of 4, the average expected damage for a uniform model is approximately 305, with the scaled cost-effectiveness only able to offer the same defense with a budget of 12. This means that in order to get the same coverage that was believed at a budget of 4, the defender would have to invest 3 times the amount. Additionally if the defender were to implement an optimal strategy from the uniform cost-effectiveness with a scaled cost-effectiveness model, the average expected damage would increase to 639, which is in the same range as the optimal strategy for the same budget under the correct cost-effectiveness model. However, we see that there is a 109 % increase in damage from the expected damage using the uniform model.

While we have considered the impact of not as strongly defending the PLCs through a reduction in cost-effectiveness, the results show that the defender should still place some emphasis on the PLC. However we know that there are some systems that have very restricted operational capacity, mainly concerning field controllers. To represent this within the model, we ran a special case of the variable cost-effectiveness, where the cost-effectiveness was set at $\frac{x}{x+14}$. With this low cost-effectiveness, we see that the emphasis on protecting the PLC at high levels has an average probability of 0.08, where the emphasis of the defense is split across the rest of the devices with a higher emphasis placed on those in the more valuable control layer.

7   Conclusions

In this work, we have developed a model studying the cost-effectiveness of investments for defending components on a network. The model simulates an attacker attempting to breach a system against a probabilistic defense assignment of the defender. Using a particle swarm optimisation algorithm to simulate the behaviour of two agents, we have been able to identify the optimal strategy of a system defender in an ICS environment. The results show that as the cost-effectiveness of protecting the most vulnerable node in a network decreases, the uptake of defense-in-depth style defenses increases.

To extend this work, we want to better represent the resources and decision making of the attacker. In this current model, we focus on the defender and the defense decisions, but in an APT style attack, the attacker is a more active player than currently considered. The attacker needs to better consider the paths and methods of defense utilised, where exploring the system is an action that is constrained by time. To represent this a proposed extension would be to view the transitions between nodes as an event that occurs over time, creating a scenario, where the attacker must balance attacking the quickest paths against the defender's optimal strategy.

The biggest issue for further study is the real world applicability of the model. At this stage the model has been focussed on the possibilities within a generic architecture. This limits the usefulness of the outputs, since it is difficult to define if the strategies are true to an actual system, as they are dependent on the cost functions and the rewards. By extending the study to consider a real case, we are able to better implement the payoffs and cost-effectiveness functions, raising the reliability of the results and the advice.

Acknowledgement. This work is funded by the EPSRC project RITICS: Trustworthy Industrial Control Systems (EP/L021013/1).

References

1. BSI: Industrial control system security top 10 threats and countermeasures 2014, March 2014. www.allianz-fuer-cybersicherheit.de/ACS/DE/_downloads/ techniker/hardware/BSI-CS_005E.pdf
2. Chopitea, T.: Threat modelling of hacktivist groups organization, chain of command, and attack methods (2012). http://publications.lib.chalmers.se/records/ fulltext/173222/173222.pdf
3. U.S. Department of Homeland Security: Common cybersecurity vulnerabilities in industrial control systems (2011). www.ics-cert.us-cert.gov/sites/default/files/ documents/DHS_Common_Cybersecurity_Vulnerabilities_ICS_20110523.pdf
4. Durkota, K., Lisy, V., Kiekintveld, C., Bosansky, B.: Game-theoretic algorithms for optimal network security hardening using attack graphs. In: Proceedings of International Conference on Autonomous Agents and Multiagent Systems, pp. 1773–1774 (2015)

5. Eberhart, R.C., Kennedy, J.: A new optimizer using particle swarm theory. In: Proceedings of 6th International Symposium on Micro Machine and Human Science, New York, vol. 1, pp. 39–43 (1995)
6. Falliere, N., Murchu, L.O., Chien, E.: W32. Stuxnet dossier. White paper, Symantec Corp., Security. Response 5 (2011)
7. Fielder, A., Panaousis, E., Malacaria, P., Hankin, C., Smeraldi, F.: Game theory meets information security management. In: Cuppens-Boulahia, N., Cuppens, F., Jajodia, S., Abou El Kalam, A., Sans, T. (eds.) SEC 2014. IFIP AICT, vol. 428, pp. 15–29. Springer, Heidelberg (2014)
8. Fielder, A., Panaousis, E., Malacaria, P., Hankin, C., Smeraldi, F.: Decision support approaches for cyber security investment. Decis. Support Syst. **86**, 13–23 (2016)
9. Gao, K., Jianming, L., Xu, R., Wang, Y., Li, Y.: A hybrid security situation prediction model for information network based on support vector machine and particle swarm optimization. Power Syst. Technol. **4**, 033 (2011)
10. Gebser, M., Kaminski, R., Kaufmann, B., Ostrowski, M., Schaub, T., Schneider, M.: Potassco: the Potsdam answer set solving collection. AI Commun. **24**(2), 107–124 (2011)
11. Karnan, M., Akila, M.: Personal authentication based on keystroke dynamics using soft computing techniques. In: 2nd International Conference on Communication Software and Networks, ICCSN 2010, pp. 334–338. IEEE (2010)
12. Kennedy, J.: Particle swarm optimization. In: Sammut, C., Webb, G.I. (eds.) Encyclopedia of Machine Learning, pp. 760–766. Springer, Berlin (2010)
13. Klíma, R., Lisý, V., Kiekintveld, C.: Combining online learning and equilibrium computation in security games. In: Khouzani, M.H.R., Panaousis, E., Theodorakopoulos, G. (eds.) GameSec 2015. LNCS, vol. 9406, pp. 130–149. Springer, Heidelberg (2015). doi:10.1007/978-3-319-25594-1_8
14. Korzhyk, D., Conitzer, V., Parr, R.: Complexity of computing optimal Stackelberg strategies in security resource allocation games. In: AAAI (2010)
15. Kuipers, D., Fabro, M.: Control Systems Cyber Security: Defense in Depth Strategies. Department of Energy, United States (2006)
16. Lemay, A.: Defending the SCADA network controlling the electrical grid from advanced persistent threats. Ph.D. thesis, École Polytechnique de Montréal (2013)
17. Lippmann, R.P., Ingols, K.W., Scott, C., Piwowarski, K., Kratkiewicz, K.J., Artz, M., Cunningham, R.: Evaluating and Strengthening Enterprise Network Security Using Attack Graphs. Defense Technical Information Center, Fort Belvoir (2005)
18. Ma, Z., Smith, P.: Determining Risks from advanced multi-step attacks to critical information infrastructures. In: Luiijf, E., Hartel, P. (eds.) CRITIS 2013. LNCS, vol. 8328, pp. 142–154. Springer, Heidelberg (2013)
19. Noel, S., Jajodia, S., Wang, L., Singhal, A.: Measuring security risk of networks using attack graphs. Int. J. Next-Gener. Comput. **1**(1), 135–147 (2010)
20. Ou, X., Boyer, W.F., McQueen, M.A.: A scalable approach to attack graph generation. In: Proceedings of 13th ACM Conference on Computer and Communications Security, pp. 336–345. ACM (2006)
21. Pham, V., Cid, C.: Are we compromised? Modelling security assessment games. In: Grossklags, J., Walrand, J. (eds.) GameSec 2012. LNCS, vol. 7638, pp. 234–247. Springer, Heidelberg (2012)
22. Poli, R.: Analysis of the publications on the applications of particle swarm optimisation. J. Artif. Evol. Appl. **2008**, 3 (2008)
23. Poli, R., Kennedy, J., Blackwell, T.: Particle swarm optimization. Swarm Intell. **1**(1), 33–57 (2007)

24. Small, P.E.: Defense in Depth: An Impractical Strategy for a Cyber World. SANS Institute, Bethesda (2011)
25. Srinoy, S.: Intrusion detection model based on particle swarm optimization and support vector machine. In: IEEE Symposium on Computational Intelligence in Security and Defense Applications, CISDA, pp. 186–192. IEEE (2007)
26. Stouffer, K., Falco, J., Scarfone, K.: Guide to industrial control systems (ICS) security. NIST Special Publication (2011). http://csrc.nist.gov/publications/nistpubs/800-82/SP800-82-final.pdf
27. Tsai, J., Rathi, S., Kiekintveld, C., Ordez, F., Tambe, M.: IRIS - A tool for strategic security allocation in transportation networks, vol. 2, pp. 1327–1334. International Foundation for Autonomous Agents and Multiagent Systems (IFAAMAS), 1 (2009)
28. Wang, L., Noel, S., Jajodia, S.: Minimum-cost network hardening using attack graphs. Comput. Commun. 29(18), 3812–3824 (2006)

Your Industrial Facility and Its IP Address: A First Approach for Cyber-Physical Attack Modeling

Robert Clausing[1(✉)], Robert Fischer[2], Jana Dittmann[2], and Yongjian Ding[1]

[1] Department of Electrical Engineering,
Magdeburg-Stendal University of Applied Sciences,
PO Box 3655, 39011 Magdeburg, Germany
{robert.clausing,yongjian.ding}@hs-magdeburg.de
[2] Department of Computer Science, AMSL Research Group,
Otto-Von-Guericke University of Magdeburg,
PO Box 4120, 39016 Magdeburg, Germany
robert.fischer@ovgu.de,
jana.dittmann@iti.cs.uni-magdeburg

Abstract. In the last decade, the amount of cyber-attacks targeting industrial facilities with specialized knowledge, tools and malware increased dramatically. The wide variety of industrial IT-systems and various required expertise for cyber-physical attack modeling is currently a challenge for interdisciplinary research. To address the variety of systems and get a point of reference, we merged architecture descriptions from available resources. Based on this reference architecture, we introduce attack scopes and provide exemplary attack scenarios per scope. As modeling strategy for the introduced scopes and to realize abstracted representations of particular industrial facility architectures, a component-based modeling approach is proposed. The main contribution of the presented work is a first generic attack modeling technique facilitating the required interdisciplinary collaboration in this important field of research.

Keywords: Cybersecurity · Interdisciplinary security modeling · Attack modeling · Industrial control systems · Supervisory control and data acquisition

1 Introduction

Stuxnet brought cyber-attacks against Industrial Control Systems (ICS) into focus of security research and public debate. Recently a power outage was achieved by attacks against various Ukrainian power companies impacting approximately 225,000 customers [1]. Due to extensive reconnaissance, the attackers were well prepared and executed the attack within 30 min. Even after restoration procedure, the workflow of affected companies remained constrained.

Referring to a survey report from the SANS institute regarding the state of security in control systems [2], 32 % of interviewed participants indicated that their control system assets or network had been infiltrated. At least 44 % of them were unable to identify the source of the infiltration. Breaches were not detected for more than a week,

© Springer International Publishing Switzerland 2016
A. Skavhaug et al. (Eds.): SAFECOMP 2016, LNCS 9922, pp. 201–212, 2016.
DOI: 10.1007/978-3-319-45477-1_16

as stated by 20 % of the participants. This leads to the implication that better security controls are strongly required for ICS. Regardless whether industrial facility or traditional enterprise, common security goals should be taken into account. Security goals like confidentiality, integrity, availability, authenticity, non-repudiation and privacy [3] have to be considered on a facility or company-wide level.

ICS security is an interdisciplinary research field, because cyber-physical attacks are based on traditional cyber-attacks, but influence the real world. Due to this fact, harm to production, process flow, industrial hardware and even human beings are possible impacts. Interdisciplinary knowledge of involved processes is needed for protection and prevention. Beside computer scientists, different parties like automation engineers, electrical engineers or chemists need to work together. Generic modeling of attacks, which is understood from all parties, might be a help for collaboration.

This paper is oriented on [4], which makes Car-to-Car communication a subject of discussion for security considerations. We adapt the concept of assuming various attack scenarios, subsequently analyzing them and presenting an application of selected examples. In this context, the main contributions of this paper are: (1) a first fusion of identified architectures in Sect. 3, (2) a 3-fold scope for attacks in Sect. 4, (3) a generic modeling approach to describe industrial infrastructures in Sect. 5 and (4) the exemplary application of the suggested generic modeling approach in Sect. 6. The overall objective of this paper is a generic attack modeling approach for industrial facilities.

2   Related Work

We identified guidelines as resource for industrial architectures from U.S. Department of Homeland Security [5] and National Institute of Standards and Technology (NIST) [6]. Additionally scientific papers like [7, 8] give a rudimentary overview.

The "Computer and Network Incident Taxonomy" [9] serves as a basis for a high-level perspective to model architectures and attacks. This includes definitions for incident, attack and event. On the contrary, attack trees are a common approach to model attack actions [10]. Attack trees usually do not consider architectures respectively specific targets and therefore may lack of completeness or become complex.

Approaches that closely related to this modeling challenge are: AutomationML [11] and the Cyber Security Modeling Language (CySeMoL) [12]. AutomationML is a format for data exchange to represent communication systems. Logical and physical representations of a communication system are provided. Communications system models are intended to exchange relevant engineering information, but are not focused on security. However, CySeMoL is used to determine the probability that attacks on systems will succeed. It is based on a metamodel mainly consisting of logical components to describe computer systems. Linked attack steps and corresponding Bayesian networks are considered for probability calculations. Since the backend of the corresponding tool is not intuitive, modifications are difficult to apply for interdisciplinary researchers. While addressing the well-structured exchange of engineering information and the determination of attack successes, both techniques do not focus on an exchange of attack information across specialist fields. Furthermore, CySeMoL might be too complex in its application for the direct modeling of industrial attacks and testing purposes.

3 Industrial Facility Architecture

Facilities are built with different purposes, environmental requirements, financial investment, equipment vendors and possibly other design influences. Hence the architecture of one facility might differ from another facility. A reference architecture that includes a common design is needed as a starting point for generic modeling of attacks. We analyzed different information sources [5–8] to obtain a merged architecture that addresses the variety. Based on these documents, we created a reference architecture for networked industrial facilities (see Fig. 1).

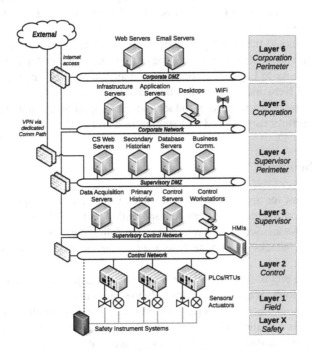

Fig. 1. Reference architecture for networked industrial facility; fusion of architectures in [5–8]

The facility is accessed through the internet or other external, dedicated communication paths. The external zone has the highest variety of risk [5].

Layer 6 and 5 represent a common enterprise network. These layers are used for corporate communication and services. Common systems are e.g. E-mail servers, DNS servers and IT business system infrastructure. External accessible servers are placed in the Demilitarized Zone (DMZ) to protect inner layers. The network segmentation is often achieved by firewalls. Typically two firewalls from different vendors are deployed for higher security requirements.

The segmentation of Layers 6 and 5 is similar for Supervisory Control Network and its DMZ. Layer 3 is important for continuous monitoring and managing of the Control

Network. Operational support devices, engineering management devices, data acquisition servers and historians are located here.

Layer 2 consists of Programmable Logic Controllers (PLCs), Remote Terminal Units (RTUs) and Human Machine Interfaces (HMIs) which are connected to sensors and actuators of Layer 1. Sensors and actuators are basic input/output devices that are reading data from physical processes and affecting these physical processes based on control decisions of controllers (e.g. PLCs). Modern control network devices support TCP/IP and other common protocols [5].

Layer X is only described in [5]. Devices such as Safety Instrument Systems are placed here. These devices are able to automatically control the safety level of sensors/actuators. This layer is conceptually air-gapped, but due to TCP/IP support of new devices, a connection to Layer 2 is possible for purposes like remote monitoring and redundancy support.

It should be noted that the layer model (also zone model) of a facility might be violated through various design issues. Some of them are illustrated in Fig. 1 like direct external connectivity to Layer 4, an optional connection of Safety Instrument Systems with the Control Network or the connection of HMIs to Layer 2 and 3.

In Sects. 5 and 6, we want to introduce modeling approaches to model attacks on complex architectures as proposed and summarized in Fig. 1.

4   Attack Scopes

As a starting point for a classification of attacks, we divide the scope of attacks into facility-centered, communication-centered and entity-centered. Exemplary attack scenarios (AS) per Attack Scope are presented in the following subsections. Thereby, we demonstrate that attacks of similar type may occur on each scope with different characteristics.

Related to the proposed scopes, the terms intra-structural and inter-structural impact are defined as follows: If an attack affects only the target itself, it has an intra-structural impact. Therefore no other scope is part of the impact. For an inter-structural impact the attack target needs a relation with other parts of a scope or another scope. The relation leads to at least one additional target (passively attacked).

4.1   Facility-Centered Scope

The first scope represents the "big picture" and covers the overall functionality of a facility. A systematical description of the facility structure in its design, implementation and configuration including possible entry points, network connections, installed devices and control flows is considered. Expertise about the facility and its processes is needed to spot possible vulnerabilities. Exploitation leads to either intra-structural or inter-structural impact.

Intra-structural impact depends on attacks on communication and entities (see Sects. 4.2 and 4.3) respectively their related relevance for processes. The impact is limited to the facility itself. However, inter-structural impact depends on the role of the specific facility. Due to the assigned role, inter-structural impact arises for external processes and infrastructures (outside world).

The role of a facility is assigned by its economic and societal importance. If the correct function of a facility is essential, the term critical infrastructure is used. In [13] multi-order dependencies between multiple critical infrastructures are examined. Examples for attacks scenarios in scope of a facility are described below.

- AS1: By synchronizing attacks on multiple power plants the attackers achieve a cascading power outage (inter-structural impact). For this result, the attackers make use of the remote access of plants. In the next step they infect selected systems and execute malicious operations on Layers 2–4. The attacks lead to malfunction of the plants (intra-structural impact) [1].
- AS2: By using public information, like the website of a facility owner, the attackers create a spear-fishing campaign which looks almost like the corporate design. They are running the campaign against public available Email addresses (Layer 5) to get credentials for remote access.
- AS3: Attackers are limited to on-site information like visible doors/gates, public areas and their usage through observed behavior. An attacker recons the used public transports to the facility or commissioned service companies. This information is used for Social Engineering.

4.2 Communication-Centered Scope

A facility contains various communication relations as shown in Fig. 1. Communication is either bidirectional or unidirectional. Unidirectional communication is realized by software (e.g. firewall) or hardware (e.g. data diodes [14]). The communication needs a medium as physical base. Protocols define how communication takes place, typically divided into the protocol specification and a particular implementation.

Impact arises due to malicious interactions on communication and control channels. Typically, the terms Alice and Bob are used to represent sender/recipient and Malory is used for the attacker. Exemplary attack scenarios are accordingly described as follows.

- AS4: After getting access to the Supervisory Control Network (Layer 3), Malory causes a denial of service by sending a STOP command to PLCs (Layer 2) [15].
- AS5: After getting access to Layer 3, Malory uses the IP address of Alice to send TCP/IP packets to Bob (spoofing). The reset-flag of TCP is set for these packets. Thereby every TCP connection between Alice and Bob is interrupted [16].
- AS6: After getting access to Control Network (Layer 2), Malory sends out bits with value 0. Without knowing what he/she is doing asynchronous transmissions between PLCs are disturbed. This may happen because synchronization time of 33 bits with the idle-bit value 1 shall be needed at minimum before new telegrams are accepted [17].

4.3   Entity-Centered Scope

The third scope is focused on single entities and the control flow/processing inside of an individual entity. Processing entities are for instance servers, workstations, network devices, PLCs and actuators. Rooms and areas are considered as housing entities, which host processing entities. Processing entities are composed of multiple hardware components, an operating environment and running applications. Processing entities are communicating with each other (see Sect. 4.2). Exemplary attack scenarios that are targeting entities are described below.

- AS7: The attacker knows that the engineering software at control workstations determines user privileges based on project-file fields that lack integrity protection. After gaining access to a project-file, the attacker modifies the permissions for device users. A user is tricked to upload the project file to the device to activate new permissions [18].
- AS8: The engineering and control software utilize pre-defined credentials that allow administrative access to the database server at Supervisory Control Network. An attacker uses this knowledge to gain illegitimate access [19].
- AS9: Due to missing integrity control, the attacker is able to write arbitrary bits to random storage positions. This leads to a malfunction of the entity.

5   Component-Based Modeling

The modeling of an entire infrastructure like the one proposed in Sect. 3, which allows the mapping of complex attacks (see Sect. 4) is a challenge for the cyber-physical security community. A uniform modeling approach for all parties is needed. We propose an approach that is derived from Components that are used as part of the Unified Modeling Language (UML) [20]. The concept was extended by influences of Computer and Network Incident Taxonomy (CNIT) which was proposed in [9] and also used in [4]. CNIT differentiates between physical and logical attacks. We are adapting this for Component-based Modeling. Formal notion is also utilizable for modeling by using UML as a base. The basic elements for Component-based Modeling are introduced in this section.

An **Entity** is an organizational unity for the Entity-centered Scope. Therefore an Entity is either physical (e.g. room, hardware) or logical (e.g. operating system, services). The initial Entity constitutes the root Entity. It cannot be part of any other Entity. A facility itself might be the root Entity. A Physical Entity may contain other Logical Entities, but not vice versa. Logical Entities can contain other Logical Entities. The same goes for Physical Entities. An example is given in Fig. 2.

An **Interface** is needed for communication with other Entities. Each Entity may have none, one or multiple Interfaces. Each Physical Interface is assigned to a Physical Entity. The same goes for Logical Interfaces. Interfaces are limited to either transmit (OUT) or receive (IN) data for a unidirectional communication. Atomic operations independently from context are used for uniform naming: read and write. For bidirectional communication INOUT interfaces are used. Signal transformation ability might be implemented for analog to digital or digital to analog. Interfaces are connected

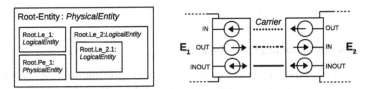

Fig. 2. Physical Entity with capsuled Logical/Physical Entities (left) and interfaces of Entities E_i connected via Carriers (right)

by **Carrier** (transmission medium) to other interfaces. Figure 2 visualizes the connections between two interfaces.

A **Protocol** is a processing specification on how to use Interfaces and Carriers. It consists of two parts: a specification and its concrete implementation. Protocol implementations are encapsulating the access to interfaces. The simplified interaction of a user program with a protocol implementation is shown in Fig. 3.

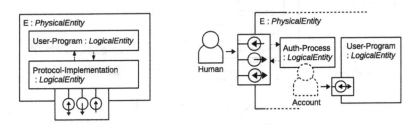

Fig. 3. Utilization of Protocol (left) and Human with its logical representation (right)

Furthermore, we take into account that **Humans** are interacting with Entities. Humans read/write on Physical Interfaces or interact remotely via other Humans with Physical Interfaces (e.g. Social Engineering). Physical Interfaces are linked to Logical Interfaces to access Logical Entities.

Considering all introduced components **Data** is stored on Physical Entities, processed by Logical Entities, transmitted via Carriers in an encapsulated format or directly exchanged on interfaces. Accounts are special types of Data due to their meaning for authenticity. By processing account Data a logical representation of a Human is temporary created (see Fig. 3).

6 Application of Component-Based Modeling

In order to demonstrate the modeling capabilities of the introduced approach, this section is subdivided into the modeling of single computer systems, connections between systems and connections between facilities. Finally, a simplified application on an exemplary attack scenario is provided.

6.1 Modeling of Computerized Systems

First, we want to give a modeling example for a generic Entity to demonstrate the applicability of the introduced Component-based Modeling. For this purpose the nesting of multiple Physical and Logical Entities (PE, LE) is shown in Fig. 4. For the sake of simplicity the internal communication is not visualized. Implicit communication takes place vertically – from Application-Environment to Hardware-Assembly and vice versa.

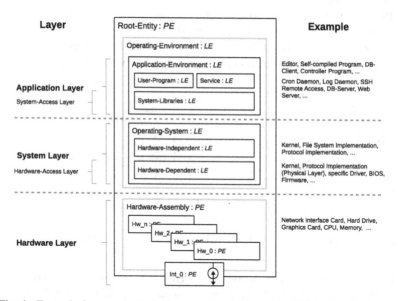

Fig. 4. Example for generic Entity (e.g. workstation, server, PLC or related systems)

In Fig. 4 common components of a computer system are consolidated. The structure is oriented on the design of Linux [21] and the model for computer systems by Tanenbaum [22]. The figure is outlined bottom-up as follows: Starting with basic hardware assembly like CPU, memory and network interface card. Hardware-dependent implementations are used to initialize and access the hardware (e.g. BIOS). Hardware-independent programs (e.g. TCP/IP) are installed to use hardware on an abstracted level. User programs and services access system libraries for processing at application layer respectively for accessing of hardware through the layers. A root Entity comprises all Physical and Logical Entities.

While the given example might be correct for office desktops and regular servers (Layers 4–6), specialized industrial systems might look different in practice. For instance, Siemens SIMATIC PLCs are composed of modular hardware. The setup consists of a CPU module and an optional CP module as an external network interface. The CPU module itself consists of an internal network interface as well [23, p. 33].

6.2 Modeling of Systems Interconnection

The communication between two systems, represented by Physical Entities, requires an Interface per Physical Entity and a Carrier connected to these Interfaces. Humans might control these Entities directly via equipment like displays (OUT), keyboards (IN) or touchscreens (INOUT). Accounts are the logical representation within Physical Entities and might be used for communication as well. This context is illustrated in Fig. 5.

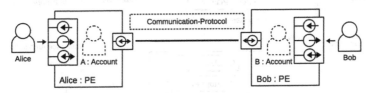

Fig. 5. Example for a communication between two Humans/Physical Entities

According to the Open Systems Interconnection model (ISO OSI model) [24], a Protocol for the communication consists of 7 layers. For instance, web browsing is subdivided into HTTP (OSI layers 5–7), TCP (OSI layer 4), IP (OSI layer 3) and Ethernet (OSI layer 1–2). Values that are specified for these layers are encapsulated in Data, which is transferred over the Carrier.

6.3 Modeling of Facilities Interrelationship

In case of an attack, attackers might execute malicious operations through existing Carriers. These operations influence Entities within industrial facilities. For physical impact, a change of actuators behavior, and thereby the controlled processes, are the objective of an attack. Figure 6 depicts this relation.

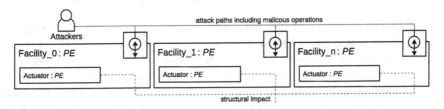

Fig. 6. Example for relationships between industrial facilities and external world

A change of actuators behavior might lead to intra-structural impact within particular facilities, if actuators influence other actuators, e.g. they explode. However, malfunctions might lead to inter-structural impact between multiple facilities as well.

6.4   Modeling of Selected Attack Scenario

For the demonstration of applicability of the modeling approach, the attack scenario
AS1 was selected (see Sect. 4.1). The attack scenario is based on an alert notification
from Industrial Control System Cyber Emergency Response Team (ICS-CERT) [1].
Public vulnerability or alert notifications usually are not detailed, among other things,
to avoid copy-cats. Due to that, some intermediate attack steps are missing in the
modeled attack scenario. We used the published information in context with the proposed reference architecture in Fig. 7. Due to the complexity of individual Entities (see
Fig. 4), we limited the modeling to relevant Entities, that were part of the attack.

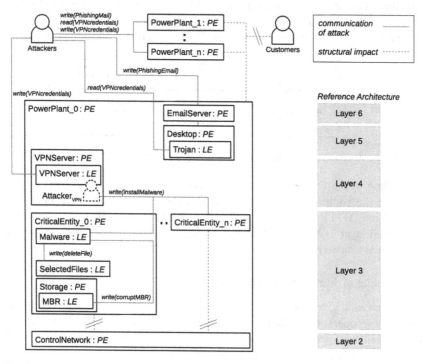

Fig. 7. Example of component-based modeling using attack scenario AS1 (see Sect. 4.1)

Initially the attackers executed a phishing attack with available Email addresses.
A Trojan horse was embedded in an attachment. Hence desktop computers at Layer 5
were infected to spy out credentials for VPN access to Layer 4. Subsequently, the
credentials were used to connect to Layer 3 (Supervisory Control Network) as
authorized user. Next, unspecified critical Entities were infected by malware. The
malware was used to delete selected files and corrupt the master boot record (MBR).
Thus these critical Entities went inoperable. As a consequence essential supervisory
control needed for Layer 2 was interfered (intra-structural impact). The incident happened at multiple power plants in parallel. This caused a power outage impacting
customers (inter-structural impact). The given model characterizes the selected attack
scenario. An abstraction is realized to support interdisciplinary collaboration.

7 Conclusion

The overall objective of this paper is to enable the generic modeling of attacks against industrial facilities. We introduced 3 scopes of attacks (facility, communication, entity) and presented exemplary attacks scenarios within these scopes. In consideration of the scopes and common industrial architectures, we also presented a first generic modeling approach. An incident, which recently took place, was used to demonstrate the application of the suggested approaches.

The modeled attack scenario highlights the importance of inter-structural and intra-structural impact. While Component-based Modeling might help to trace back vulnerabilities and facilitates collaboration between specialist fields, more evaluation needs to be done to ensure sufficient modeling capabilities. At this stage, it was found that interactions with Entities are not specific enough, e.g. missing chronology of individual attack operations. A notation to describe individual read and write operations is needed. Furthermore, physical impact of Entities like PLCs is unspecified, e.g. status of actuators. Linked states of Entities could lead to statements about the overall facility status, which is especially important for the analysis of inter-structural impacts.

Models are also further improvable by considering attack contexts and the knowledge of attackers per attack scope, since this is directly related to the required skill, capabilities and the outcome of an attack. A partitioning of the attackers knowledge and the context of attacks are proposed in [25].

Due to the overall achieved capability for a generic architectural modeling, Component-based modeling is a starting point for potential improvement. This approach outlines the possibility to make use of engineering information, e.g. AutomationML, and a supportive role for more complex approaches, e.g. CySeMoL.

Acknowledgements. The presented work is funded by the German Federal Ministry of Economic Affairs and Energy (BMWi, project no. 1501502A, 1501502B) in the framework of the German reactor safety research program. The authors thank all project partners and reviewers for their helpful comments.

References

1. ICS-CERT: IR-ALERT-H-16-056-01 Cyber-Attack Against Ukrainian Critical Infrastructure. https://ics-cert.us-cert.gov/alerts/IR-ALERT-H-16-056-01 (2016)
2. Harp, D., Gregory-Brown, B.: The State of Security in Control Systems Today. https://www.sans.org/reading-room/whitepapers/analyst/state-security-control-systems-today-36042 (2015)
3. Cherdantseva, Y., Hilton, J.: A reference model of information assurance & security. In: Eighth International Conference on Availability, Reliability and Security (ARES), pp. 546–555. IEEE (2013)
4. Lang, A., Dittmann, J., Kiltz, S., Hoppe, T.: Future perspectives: the car and its IP-address – a potential safety and security risk assessment. In: Saglietti, F., Oster, N. (eds.) SAFECOMP 2007. LNCS, vol. 4680, pp. 40–53. Springer, Heidelberg (2007)

5. U.S. Department of Homeland Security: Recommended Practice: Improving Industrial Control Systems Cybersecurity with Defense-In-Depth Strategies. https://ics-cert.us-cert.gov/sites/default/files/recommended_practices/Defense_in_Depth_Oct09.pdf (2009)

6. Stouffer, K., Pillitteri, V., Lightman, S., Abrams, M., Hahn, A.: Guide to Industrial Control Systems (ICS) Security. National Institute of Standards and Technology (2015)

7. Krotofil, M., Gollmann, D.: Industrial control systems security: what is happening? In: 2013 11th IEEE International Conference on Industrial Informatics (INDIN), pp. 670–675. IEEE (2013)

8. Ahmed, I., Obermeier, S., Naedele, M., Richard III, G.G.: SCADA systems: challenges for forensic investigators. Computer **45**, 44–51 (2012)

9. Howard, J.D., Longstaff, T.A.: A common language for computer security incidents. Sandia National Laboratories (1998)

10. Kordy, B., Piètre-Cambacédès, L., Schweitzer, P.: DAG-based attack and defense modeling: don't miss the forest for the attack trees. Comput. Sci. Rev. **13–14**, 1–38 (2014)

11. Bendik, F., Schmidt, N.: Exchange of engineering data for communication systems based on AutomationML using an EtherNet/IP example. Presented at the ODVA Industry Conference and 17th Annual Meeting, Friso, Texas, USA (2015)

12. Sommestad, T., Ekstedt, M., Holm, H.: The cyber security modeling language: a tool for assessing the vulnerability of enterprise system architectures. Syst. J. IEEE **7**, 363–373 (2013)

13. Kotzanikolaou, P., Theoharidou, M., Gritzalis, D.: Assessing n-order dependencies between critical infrastructures. Int. J. Crit. Infrastruct. **9**, 93–110 (2013)

14. U.S. Department of Homeland Security: Seven Steps to Effectively Defend Industrial Control Systems. https://ics-cert.us-cert.gov/sites/default/files/documents/Seven%20Steps%20to%20Effectively%20Defend%20Industrial%20Control%20Systems_S508C.pdf (2016)

15. The MITRE Corporation: CVE-2016-2200 (2016)

16. Floyd, S.: RFC 3360 Inappropriate TCP Resets Considered Harmful. https://tools.ietf.org/html/rfc3360 (2002)

17. CENELEC: EN 61158-4-3:2014: Industrial communication networks - Fieldbus specifications - Part 4-3: Data-link layer protocol specification - Type 3 elements (IEC 61158-4-3:2014) (2014)

18. The MITRE Corporation: CVE-2015-1356 (2015)

19. The MITRE Corporation: CVE-2010-2772 (2010)

20. Object Management Group: OMG Unified Modeling Language (OMG UML) Version 2.5. http://www.omg.org/spec/UML/2.5 (2015)

21. Mauerer, W.: Professional Linux Kernel Architecture. Wiley, Indianapolis (2008)

22. Tanenbaum, A.S.: Modern Operating Systems. Pearson Education, Upper Saddle River (2009)

23. Siemens AG: CPU-CPU Communication with SIMATIC Controllers (SIMATIC S7) Version 2.1. https://cache.industry.siemens.com/dl/files/908/78028908/att_32073/v1/78028908_SIMATIC_Comm_DOKU_v21_e.pdf (2013)

24. ISO/IEC: ISO/IEC 7498-1:1994(E) Information technology - Open Systems Interconnection - Basic Reference Model (1994)

25. Fischer, R., Clausing, R., Dittmann, J., Ding, Y.: Industrie 4.0 Schwachstellen: Basisangriffe und Szenarien. In: Proceedings of DACH Security 2016 (2016, to appear)

Towards Security-Explicit Formal Modelling of Safety-Critical Systems

Elena Troubitsyna[1], Linas Laibinis[1(✉)], Inna Pereverzeva[1], Tuomas Kuismin[2], Dubravka Ilic[2], and Timo Latvala[2]

[1] Åbo Akademi University, Turku, Finland
{elena.troubitsyna,linas.laibinis,inna.pereverzeva}@abo.fi
[2] Space Systems Finland, Espoo, Finland
{tuomas.kuismin,dubravka.ilic,timo.latvala}@ssf.fi

Abstract. Modern industrial control systems become increasingly interconnected and rely on external networks to provide their services. Hence they become vulnerable to security attacks that might directly jeopardise their safety. The growing understanding that if the system is not secure then it is not safe calls for novel development and verification techniques weaving security consideration into the safety-driven design. In this paper, we demonstrate how to make explicit the relationships between safety and security in the formal system development by refinement. The proposed approach allows the designers to identify at early design states mutual interdependencies between the mechanisms ensuring safety and security and build robust system architecture.

1 Introduction

Modern industrial systems rely on novel information and communication technologies to supervise complex control systems and infrastructures. Increasing reliance on networking not only offers a wide range of business and technological benefits but also brings in imminent security threats. Exploiting security vulnerabilities might result in loss of control and situation awareness directly threatening safety of human lives. Therefore, we need to create the techniques that facilitate systematic analysis of safety and security interdependencies.

In this paper, we propose a formal approach to integrating security consideration into formal development of safety-critical systems in Event-B [1]. Event-B is a rigorous approach to correct-by-construction system development by refinement. Development typically starts from an abstract model of most essential system functionality and properties, e.g., safety. In the refinement process, the abstract model is transformed into a detailed specification explicitly representing the behaviour of system components, occurrence of faults, and fault tolerance mechanisms introduced to cope with components failures and ensure safety.

The refinement process allows us also explicitly represent the impact of security failures and identify their impact on safety. Proofs – the main verification mechanism of Event-B – may be used to guide the process of identifying the security requirements derived from the system safety goals.

© Springer International Publishing Switzerland 2016
A. Skavhaug et al. (Eds.): SAFECOMP 2016, LNCS 9922, pp. 213–225, 2016.
DOI: 10.1007/978-3-319-45477-1_17

In this paper, we generalise the experience gained in two modelling experiments. Both developments aim at supporting an integrated reasoning about safety and security in the Event-B refinement process. While arriving at the same result, the approaches adopt different refinement strategies. In the first case, refinement and constraints derivation is driven by the safety case construction. In the second case, the refinement process focusses on explicitly representing the data flow ad deriving the required constraints from verification of a closed-loop system model. In the industrial practice, the strategy that better fits the adopted development process can be chosen.

The approach helps us to perform an integrated analysis of system safety and security at a rather detailed architectural level and hence allows to capture the dynamic nature of safety and security interplay, i.e., analyse the impact of deploying the fault tolerance and security mechanisms on safety assurance.

The paper is structured as follows. In Sect. 2 we briefly describe our formal framework – Event-B. Section 3 introduces the general idea behind our formal reasoning about safety – formal derivation of the safety and security constraints from the safety goals. In Sects. 4 and 5 we present two different approaches allowing us to derive these constraints by refinement in Event-B. In Sect. 6 we discuss our achieved results and overview the related work.

2   Background: Event-B

Event-B [1] is a state-based framework that promotes the correct-by-construction approach to system development and formal verification by theorem proving. In Event-B, a system model is specified as an *abstract state machine* [1]. An abstract state machine encapsulates the model state, represented as a collection of variables, and defines operations on the state, i.e., it describes the dynamic system behaviour. A machine also has an accompanying component, called *context*, defining user sets, constants and their properties given as model axioms.

A general form for Event-B models is given in Fig. 1. The machine is uniquely identified by its name M. The state variables, v, are declared in the **Variables** clause and initialised in the *Initialisation* event. The variables are strongly typed by the constraining predicates I given in the **Invariants** clause.

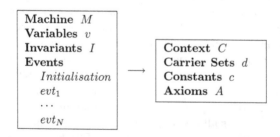

Fig. 1. Event-B machine and context

The invariant clause might also contain other predicates defining essential properties (e.g., safety invariants) that should be preserved during system execution.

The dynamic behaviour of the system is defined by a set of atomic *events*. Generally, an event has the following form:

$$e \mathrel{\widehat{=}} \textbf{any } a \textbf{ where } G_e \textbf{ then } R_e \textbf{ end},$$

where e is the event's name, a is a list of the local event variables, and the *guard* G_e is a state predicate. The body of an event is defined by a *multiple* assignment over the system variables, semantically represented by the next-state relation R_e. Later on, we will rely on two kinds of concrete assignment statements: deterministic ones, in the standard form $x := E(x, y)$, and non-deterministic ones, represented as $x :\mid Pred(x, y, x')$. In the latter case, the variable x gets updated by some value x' related to the initial values of x and y by the condition *Pred*.

The guard defines the conditions under which the event is *enabled*, i.e., its body can be executed. If several events are enabled at the same time, any of them can be chosen for execution nondeterministically.

If an event does not have local variables, it can be described simply as:

$$e \mathrel{\widehat{=}} \textbf{when } G_e \textbf{ then } R_e \textbf{ end}.$$

Event-B employs a top-down refinement-based approach to system development. Development typically starts from an abstract specification that nondeterministically models essential functional requirements. In a sequence of refinement steps, we gradually reduce nondeterminism and introduce detailed design decisions. In particular, we can add new events, split events as well as replace abstract variables by their concrete counterparts, i.e., perform *data refinement*.

The consistency of Event-B models, i.e., verification of well-formedness and invariant preservation as well as correctness of refinement steps, is demonstrated by discharging a number of verification conditions – proof obligations. For instance, to verify *invariant preservation*, we should prove the following formula:

$$A(d, c), \; I(d, c, v), \; G_e(d, c, x, v), \; R_e(d, c, x, v, v') \; \vdash \; I(d, c, v'), \quad \text{(INV)}$$

where A are the model axioms, I are the model invariants, d and c are the model constants and sets, x are the event's local variables and v, v' are the variable values before and after event execution. For more information, see [1].

The Rodin platform [8] provides an automated support for formal modelling and verification in Event-B. In particular, it generates the required proof obligations and attempts to (automatically or interactively) discharge them.

3   Formal Reasoning About Safety

The top-level safety goal of many safety-critical systems is to keep some safety parameter within the predefined boundaries. Let *p_real* correspond to the physical value of such a parameter. Then the safety invariant can be formulated as

$$p\_crit\_low \leq p\_real \leq p\_crit\_high.$$

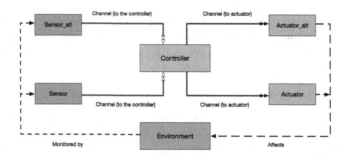

Fig. 2. Generic control system

The safety goal is usually achieved by changing the state of the actuator that influences the value of *p_real*. A typical architecture of a control system is shown in Fig. 2. The controlled parameter can be directly measured by the sensor *Sensor* or computed on the basis of the alternative (probably indirect) measurements obtained from *Sensor_alt*. The parameter is controlled by changing the state of the actuator *Actuator* or its spare *Actuator_alt*.

We are considering a networked control system. It means that both sensors and actuators are linked with the controller by the corresponding communication channels that could be possibly vulnerable to security attacks.

Let *act* be a variable modelling the state of the actuator. It can be assigned the values *decreasing* and *increasing* reflecting the status of the controlled parameter. For instance, if the parameter *p* is a temperature and the actuator is a heater, the values *decreasing* and *increasing* correspond to the heater being switched off and on correspondingly. Such a behaviour is abstractly modelled by the specification Controller given in Fig. 3.

Machine Controller **Sees** contx_C
Variables *phase, act, p, p_real*
Invariants *phase* ∈ PHASE ∧ *act* ∈ ACT ∧ *p* ∈ N ∧ *p_real* ∈ N ∧
　　　　　　phase = *est* ∧ *p* ≥ *p_high* ⇒ *act* = *decreasing* ∧
　　　　　　phase = *est* ∧ *p* ≤ *p_low* ⇒ *act* = *increasing*
Events
Initialisation *phase* := *est* || *act* := *none* || *p* := *p0* || *p_real* := *p_real0* **end**
est ≙
　　where *phase* = *est* **then** *p* :∈ *estim(p_real)* || *phase* := *cont* **end**
act_dec ≙
　　where *phase* = *cont* ∧ *p* ≥ *p_high* **then** *act* := *decreasing* || *phase* := *env* **end**
act_inc ≙
　　where *phase* = *cont* ∧ *p* ≤ *p_low* **then** *act* := *increasing* || *phase* := *env* **end**
act_skip ≙
　　where *phase* = *cont* ∧ *p* < *p_high* ∧ *p* > *p_low* **then** *phase* := *env* **end**
env ≙
　　where *phase* = *env* **then** *p_real* :∈ N || *phase* := *est* **end**

Fig. 3. Specification of Controller

The variable *phase* defines the interleaving between the events env, modelling the changes in the environment, est, modelling the controller estimation of the

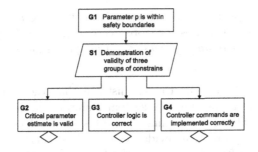

Fig. 4. Decomposition of the top level safety goal

parameter p using the abstract relation *estim*, and the events modelling the control actions – act_dec, act_inc, or act_skip. When the variable *phase* obtains the value *cont*, one of the events act_dec, act_inc, or act_skip becomes enabled. They represent the commands issued by the controller to the actuator.

Note that the estimated value p is not necessarily equal to the measurements produced by the sensor that monitors *p_real*. In our model, p is an abstraction representing the controller's "perception" of the environment that depends on the presence of accidental and malicious failures. The model invariant postulates that the actuator is set to the decreasing state when the parameter p is approaching the critically high value and vice versa for the lower limit.

Our specification relies on three groups of constraints:

Group 1: Validity of the critical parameter estimate
A1. The value p used by the controller at each cycle as an estimate of the value of the critical parameter is sufficiently close to the real physical value *p_real* of the parameter, i.e., $|p - p\_real| \leq \Delta$ for some fixed constant Δ;

Group 2: Correctness of the controller logic
A2. *p_high* is calculated so that $p\_high + \Delta + max\_increase\_per\_cycle \leq p\_crit\_high$;
A3. *p_low* is calculated so that $p\_low - \Delta - max\_decrease\_per\_cycle \leq p\_crit\_low$;
A4. When p is greater than *p_high* then the controller always sets the actuator to the state *decreasing*;
A5. When p is less than *p_low* then the controller always sets the actuator to the state *increasing*;

Group 3: Correctness of controller command implementation
A6. The actuator receives the command from the controller once per *cycle* (period);
A7. When the controller sets the actuator to the state *decreasing* then the value of *p_real* decreases (or stops increasing) with the passage of time, i.e., $act = decreasing \Rightarrow p\_real_c \geq p\_real_{c+1}$, for any system cycles c and $c + 1$;

A8. When the controller sets the actuator is in the state *increasing* then the value of *p_real* increases (or stops decreasing) with the passage of time, i.e., $act = increasing \Rightarrow p\_real_c \leq p\_real_{c+1}$, for any system cycles c and $c + 1$.

These constraints allow us to demonstrate that the controller invariant implies the safety invariant, i.e., the system maintains *p_real* within the given safety boundaries. Therefore, argument about system safety – a safety case – can be constructed by supplying evidences that these constraints are satisfied.

A safety case is often described in the Goal Structuring Notation [6] – a graphical notation explicitly representing how goals (the claims about system safety) are decomposed into subgoals until the claims can be supported by the direct evidences. A fragment of the safety case depicting the decomposition of the top goal according to the proposed groups of constraints is shown in Fig. 4. Here rectangles depict goals, while parallelograms contain decomposition strategies.

In this paper, we aim at demonstrating how formal refinement-based development allows us to systematically construct the evidences justifying safety subgoals *G2*–*G4*, shown in Fig. 4. Indeed, Event-B allows us to introduce the constraints on the constants as the axioms, while proofs of the invariant preservation guarantees the correctness of the controller actions.

The specification Controller and the associated proofs allow us to justify achieving the goal *G3*, as shown in Fig. 5. To justify *G2*, we need to explicitly define a procedure for computing p estimates in the presence of non-malicious and malicious faults. To address *G4*, we should investigate how faults might cause deviations in implementing of the controller actions. In both cases, we need to explicitly represent the system architecture and investigate the impact of security failures on system safety.

In this paper, we describe two experiments with formal development. Both approaches can be used to arrive at a detailed model of the system by refinement, with all the necessary system and environment constraints and assumptions

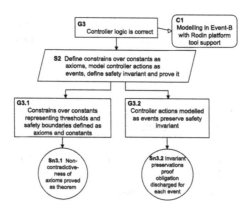

Fig. 5. Decomposition of the goal *G3*

explicitly defined. The first approach relies on incremental derivation of the networked architecture by refinement. The development of the model proceeds simultaneously with that of the safety case. Verification of refinement allows us to derive safety and security constraints required to justify the safety goals.

The second approach starts by introducing the entire networked system architecture. Due to non-deterministic modelling of the component behaviour, the initial model is severely under-constrained. The subsequent chain of the refinement steps introduces the explicit restrictions on the component behaviour as well as new assumptions (axioms) about the environment for specific system operating modes. The final refinement step produces the model sufficiently constrained to prove the system safety invariant. In the next sections we outline both approaches and then discuss the lessons learnt from our experiments.

4   Incremental Derivation of Safety and Security Constraints by Refinement

In our first approach, we start from the abstract specification given in Fig. 3 and unfold the system architecture together with the associated communication links by refinement. To explicitly represent communication between the system components, we have to explicitly define the states of the communicating components at different stages of data transmission. Such a modelling approach allows us to represent the impact of the security failures by their effect on the components.

Let us present a generic pattern for modelling two communicating components called *data producer* and *data consumer*. If the components are connected by a reliable non-compromised communication channel then data transmission results in copying the data from the output buffer of the producer to the input buffer of the consumer. If a security failure occurs during transmission, the produced data would typically differ from the consumed data. In the context of the control systems, it is relevant to consider the effect of a spoofing producer, data tampering and DOS (or, in general, channel unavailability). The specification of the producer-consumer arrangement under different conditions is given in Fig. 6.

Machine ProducerConsumer **Sees** contx_PC
Variables $trans, state, c\_in, p\_out$
Invariants $trans \in TRANS \land state \in STATES \land p\_out \in DATA \land c\_in \in DATA \land$
$\quad (trans = idle \land state = OK \Rightarrow p\_out = c\_in)$
Events
Initialisation $trans := idle \,||\, state := OK \,||\, p\_out := NIL \,||\, c\_in := NIL$ **end**
to_progr $\triangleq$
$\quad$ **where** $trans = idle$ **then** $p\_out :\in DATA \,||\, trans := progr$ **end**
to_idle $\triangleq$
$\quad$ **any** c_in_new
$\quad$ **when** $trans = progr \land c\_in\_new \in DATA \land ((state = OK \land c\_in\_new := p\_out) \lor$
$\quad\quad (state = DOS \land c\_in\_new := NIL) \lor (state = compromised \land c\_in\_new \neq p\_out))$
$\quad$ **then** $c\_in := c\_in\_new \,||\, trans := idle$ **end**
change_state $\triangleq$
$\quad$ **where** $trans = progr$ **then** $state :\in STATES$ **end**

Fig. 6. Specification of the ProducerConsumer model

The variables p_out and c_in model the output buffer of the producer and the input buffer of the data consumer respectively. The constant NIL represents an empty buffer. The variable *state* indicates whether the system is under attack.

Since we prevent overwriting the data by the producer before they are consumed, the invariant states that, if the system is not under attack, the data received by the consumer is not altered by the channel, i.e., our invariant abstractly defines the properties of the authenticated link.[1]

In the cases of spoofing and tampering, upon completion of the data transmission, the value stored in the input buffer of the consumer differs from the one in the output buffer of the producer. Finally, in the case of the channel unavailability, the input buffer of the consumer does not receive any data.

In our specification, the variable *state* represents the outcome of security monitoring. If the system resources permit, encryption or message-authentication codes are used to ensure security of critical communication. In general, security monitoring relies on anomaly detection including checks of well-formedness of data packets, deviations in response time or periodicity, etc.

Our ProducerConsumer model defines a generic specification pattern that can be instantiated to model communication in networked control systems. We will rely on it to derive the constraints allowing us to justify the goals $G2$ and $G4$.

Let us first focus on the goal $G2$ and consider a simple case – the sensor monitoring p is fault free and the controller uses the measurements produced by the sensor as the estimate of p. The sensor plays the role of the data producer and the controller is the data consumer.

By refinement, we introduce a model of the sensor and sensor-actuator communication link. To prove the required safety properties, we need the constraint explicitly stating that the sensor imprecision is acceptable, i.e., $sen\_\delta \leq \Delta$. Also, we should guarantee that the introduced channel security monitor detects security failures and the controller does not use corrupted data as a p estimate. Finally, we have to ensure that the controller does not ignore a corrupted value but triggers error recovery and switches to an alternative mode of estimating p.

The formal modelling allows us to formulate a strengthened version (refinement) of the general condition for ensuring data validity: for data used in calculating the critical parameter p, the source of data should be authenticated, the channel should guarantee data integrity (no data alternation) and high availability. Moreover, error detection is triggered if a security failure is suspected. The generic pattern of the corresponding safety case fragment is shown in Fig. 7.

Similarly to a security failure, a (non-malicious) sensor failure should be detected and error recovery triggered. The detection of a sensor failure relies on finding a discrepancy between the expected and received measurements of p. In case the link between the sensor and the controller is authenticated, the controller can assume that the deviation is caused by a sensor failure. In another case, both accidental and malicious faults could be assumed. For instance, if the sensor readings are accompanied by the time stamp, the outdated time stamp

---

[1] Due to a lack of space we present a simple model of communication. A more elaborated model similar to [5] can also be used.

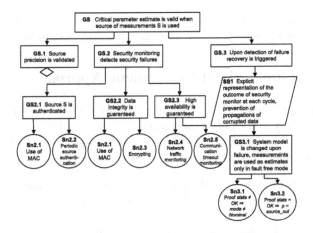

Fig. 7. Decomposition of the safety goal

would signal about a sensor or communication failure; if the value is outside of the feasible range, either the sensor failed or data were tampered.

Upon detection of a failure, the controller ignores the obtained measurement and relies on the (retained) last good sensor value to compute p. The failure is initially considered transient. If within a certain interval of time the controller starts to receive correct readings, the normal system operation is resumed.

In the next refinement step we introduce the additional abstract function *last_good_estim* to model this procedure. The constraints imposed on this function require that the imprecision associated with the function after k cycles does not exceed Δ. Essentially, this restricts the number of cycles for which it is safe to treat the failure as a transient one.

If the system fails to recovery within the predefined number of cycles then the failure is considered permanent. In this case, the system should reconfigure, e.g., the controller should start to rely on the measurements produced by *Sensor_alt*.

To ensure validity of the estimate in this mode, we recursively apply the safety case pattern shown in Fig. 7. Essentially, we should verify that the imprecision of measurements obtained by reliance on *Sensor_alt* is less than Δ and the data link between the controller and *Sensor_alt* is reliable and non-compromised.

Finally, let us discuss the fault tolerance and security constraints that should be introduced to justify achieving the goal $G4$. A similar type of reasoning demonstrates that spoofing identity of the controller or tampering the controller commands can directly lead to a violation of safety. The absence of controller commands due to a communication failure or an actuator failure would also breach safety invariant. Therefore, we should guarantee that the communication link between the controller and the actuator is secure and reliable and, in case of an actuator or a communication failure, the system switches to *Actuator_alt*.

For each of the considered modes, we build the corresponding fragment of the safety case and derive constraints justifying $G2$ and $G4$. Our modelling allows to explicitly demonstrate the interplay between safety and security requirements: whenever the mode is changing and system switches to the use of different components in the assessment and control of the critical parameter p, higher security requirements should be imposed on the corresponding communication links.

5 A Data Flow Driven Refinement Approach

In the second experiment, we introduce an abstract representation of the system architecture already in the initial specification. To achieve this, we define the data flow in the control cycle and specify how the value of the controlled parameter is "perceived" by different components. Thus we consider its four distinct values:

- p_env – the current value of the parameter p in the environment;
- p_sensed – the value of p as read by *Sensor*. It can be affected by the sensor imprecision and sensor or security failures;
- p_sensed_alt – the value of p as read by *Sensor_alt*;
- p_cont – the value of p as received by *Controller*. It can be additionally affected by the communication channel corruption, message loss or other failures as well as security attacks such as tampering.

The abstract system model enforces the control and information flow between the system components. While the control flow is quite strict, the data transformations within the system components are very loose, i.e., non-deterministic. Such a style of modelling allows us to specify the effect of accidental and malicious failures on the data flow quite easily. In the refinement process, we will focus on specific system components and consider different cases of their behaviour – the nominal fault-free behaviour as well as the behaviour in the presence of failures or attacks. As a result, more and more assumptions and constraints on the environment will be explicitly formulated.

Once sufficient knowledge is added into the refined models, we can introduce the notion of operational modes to model particular combinations of component states and system reactions. This also allows us to formulate and prove safety invariants that hold in particular modes and with specific, explicitly stated system constraints and assumptions. Below we briefly outline the refinement process.

In the initial model we create an abstract architecture of the modelled system according to Fig. 2. The model structure is given on Fig. 8. The variable *phase* is used to enforce the pre-defined cyclic execution order Env → Sensor or Sensor_alt → Transfer_to_cont → Controller → Transfer_to_act → Actuator or Actuator_alt → Env. Here Transfer_to_cont and Transfer_to_act model the respective communication channels to the controller and actuators.

In the first refinement step, we model the nominal and abnormal behaviour of sensors and actuators. As a result, each of the abstract events Sensor, Sensor_alt and Actuator, Actuator_alt gets refined by several different versions, reflecting the cases when, e.g., a sensor works as nominally intended or fails thus producing possibly arbitrary values. Then we refine the model of the communication channels by considering the cases when the sent value is successfully transferred,

```
MACHINE M0 Sees Data
    VARIABLES p_env, p_sensed, p_sensed_alt, p_cont, act_cont, act_received,
                act_status, act_status_alt, phase
    INVARIANT
        p_env ∈ N  ∧  p_sensed ∈ N  ∧  p_sensed_alt ∈ N  ∧  p_cont ∈ N ∧
        act_cont ∈ ACT_STATUS ∧ act_received ∈ ACT_STATUS ∧
        act_status ∈ ACT_STATUS ∧ act_status_alt ∈ ACT_STATUS  ∧  phase ∈ BOOL
    EVENTS
        Env  = ...            Controller  = ...         Actuator  = ...
        Sensor  = ...         Transfer_to_act  = ...    Actuator_alt  = ...
        Sensor_alt  = ...     Transfer_to_cont  = ...
END
```

Fig. 8. The machine M0

tampered or lost. As a result, the abstract Transfer_to_cont and Transfer_to_act events are refined by the respective three concrete versions.

Our further refinement steps introduce the controller logic and model how the environment is subsequently affected by the actuator value(s), i.e., define dependencies between the actuator state and the expected range of p_env value.

Our next goal is to show that, under the defined constraints and conditions, the system functions properly (by reacting to the environment changes according to the controller logic), consequently satisfying the essential system property of maintaining the environment parameter(s) within the given safe boundaries $p\_low\_crit..p\_high\_crit$. Since we are modelling all possible combinations of nominal and abnormal system conditions to achieve this, we structure the system behaviour using the operational modes an derive the conditions and constraints that are sufficient to guarantee the aforementioned properties in each mode.

For instance, in the nominal mode, we can rely on the communication channels and the absence of failures in sensors and actuators. This allows us to actually prove a number of system properties as system invariants, e.g., we can show that in this mode the difference between p_env and p_cont never exceeds sen_delta within the same cycle. We prove the following system invariant:

$$phase \in \{CONT, TO\_ACT, ACT, ENV\} \land mode = NOMINAL \Rightarrow$$
$$p\_cont \in p\_env - sen\_delta..p\_env + sen\_delta$$

Also, we can prove correctness of the controller logic by the following invariants:

$$mode = NOMINAL \land p\_cont > p\_high \land phase = ENV \Rightarrow act\_status = decreasing$$
$$mode = NOMINAL \land p\_cont < p\_low \land phase = ENV \Rightarrow act\_status = increasing$$

With several additional constraints on the environment model and system behaviour for the nominal mode, we can finally prove the system safety invariant

$$mode = NOMINAL \Rightarrow p\_env \in p\_low\_crit..p\_high\_crit.$$

In a similar way, in the next refinement steps we derive the constraints for the other modes, e.g., formulate the constraints for the cases when the controller relies on the last good reading or uses the alternative sensor.

6   Overview of Related Work and Conclusions

Discussion. Our experiments have aimed at studying how to cope with complexity of integrated safety-security requirements modelling in Event-B. The first presented approach starts with a very concise system model, focusing primarily on the controller component. It immediately introduces the system safety invariant and formulates the model assumptions and constraints under which this invariant holds. In a sense, these constraints are very "wide", since they should account for many factors that are still hidden. In the refinement process, the system details are gradually unfolded, which also requires to strengthen the formulated earlier constraints. Simultaneously, the associated safety case is gradually built, reflecting the discovered system constraints. The proving effort is evenly distributed, however, additional care should be taken about validation of system assumptions and constraints belonging to quite different levels of abstraction.

The second approach starts with modelling a full system architecture with the intended control and data flow between system components. However, data transformations in the initial model are under-constrained, thus making it impossible to prove the system safety invariant. In a number of refinement steps, different safety/security-related details are revealed. Once sufficient knowledge of the system behaviour is introduced, the system functionality is further structured using the notion of operational modes. For specific modes, safety invariants are formulated and proved, by explicitly defining the necessary constraints about the involved data. The verification effort is much higher in the later refinement steps, however, it is partially alleviated by the fact that the system constraints in the specific operational modes are more concrete.

Related Work. The issue of safety and security interaction has recently received a significant research attention by recognising that there is a clear need for the approaches facilitating an integrated analysis of safety and security [9,10].

This issue has been addressed by several techniques demonstrating how to adapt traditional safety techniques like FMECA and fault trees to perform a security-informed safety analysis [4,9]. The techniques aim at providing the engineers with a structured way to discover and analyse security vulnerabilities with safety implications. Since the use of such techniques facilitate a systematic analysis of failure modes and results in discovering safety and security requirements, the proposed approaches provide a valuable input for our modelling.

There are several works that address formal analysis of safety and security requirements interactions, in particular, conflicts between them [2,7]. A typical scenario used to demonstrate this is a contradiction between the access control rules and safety measures. In our approach, we look at safety-security interplay at a more detailed level, i.e., we analyse the system architecture, investigate the impact of security failures on system functions, and demonstrate how fault tolerance required for safety leads to discovery of additional security requirements.

The distributed MILS approach [3] employs a number of advanced modelling techniques to create a platform for formal architectural analysis of safety and security. The approach supports a powerful analysis of the system data flow using model checking and facilitates derivation of security contracts. Since our approach enables incremental construction of complex distributed architectures, it would be interesting to combine these techniques to support an integrated safety-security analysis throughout the entire model-based system development.

Conclusions. In this paper, we have experimented with the security-aware development of safety-critical systems in Event-B. We have demonstrated how the formal construction of evidences for a system safety case results in derivation of both safety and security requirements. In our work, we considered safety and security as the interdependent constraints required for building a robust system.

This paper generalises the results of two experiments with refinement-based development in Event-B. The experiments have demonstrated that formal development significantly facilitates derivation of safety and security requirements. The integrated safety-security modelling in Event-B could be further facilitated by the use of tools for constraint solving and continuous behaviour simulation.

Acknowledgements. This work is partially funded by the TEKES project Cyber Trust.

References

1. Abrial, J.R.: Modeling in Event-B. Cambridge University Press, Cambridge (2010)
2. Brunel, J., Rioux, L., Paul, S., Faucogney, A., Vallée, F.: Formal safety and security assessment of an avionic architecture with alloy. In: ESSS 2014, EPTCS, vol. 150, pp. 8–19 (2014)
3. Cimatti, A., DeLong, R., Marcantonio, D., Tonetta, S.: Combining MILS with contract-based design for safety and security requirements. In: Koornnee, F., van Gulijk, C. (eds.) SAFECOMP 2015 Workshops. LNCS, vol. 9338, pp. 264–276. Springer, Heidelberg (2015). doi:10.1007/978-3-319-24249-1_23
4. Fovino, I.N., Masera, M., Cian, A.D.: Integrating cyber attacks within fault trees. Reliab. Eng. Syst. Safety **94**(9), 1394–1402 (2009)
5. Iliasov, A., Laibinis, L., Troubitsyna, E., Romanovsky, A.: Formal derivation of a distributed program in Event B. In: Qin, S., Qiu, Z. (eds.) ICFEM 2011. LNCS, vol. 6991, pp. 420–436. Springer, Heidelberg (2011)
6. Kelly, T.P.: Arguing safety - a systematic approach to managing safety cases. Ph.D. thesis (1998)
7. Kriaa, S., Bouissou, M., Colin, F., Halgand, Y., Pietre-Cambacedes, L.: Safety and security interactions modeling using the BDMP formalism: case study of a pipeline. In: Bondavalli, A., Di Giandomenico, F. (eds.) SAFECOMP 2014. LNCS, vol. 8666, pp. 326–341. Springer, Heidelberg (2014)
8. Rodin: Event-B platform. http://www.event-b.org/
9. Schmittner, C., Gruber, T., Puschner, P., Schoitsch, E.: Security application of failure mode and effect analysis (FMEA). In: Bondavalli, A., Di Giandomenico, F. (eds.) SAFECOMP 2014. LNCS, vol. 8666, pp. 310–325. Springer, Heidelberg (2014)
10. Young, W., Leveson, N.G.: An integrated approach to safety and security based on systems theory. Commun. ACM **57**(2), 31–35 (2014)

A New SVM-Based Fraud Detection Model for AMI

Marcelo Zanetti, Edgard Jamhour$^{(\boxtimes)}$, Marcelo Pellenz, and Manoel Penna

Pontifical Catholic University of Parana, Curitiba, Brazil
marcelo.zanetti11@gmail.com, ejamhour@gmail.com,
marcelopellenz@gmail.com, camillo.penna@gmail.com

Abstract. This paper presents a new strategy for fraud detection in Advanced Metering Infrastructure (AMI) based on the analysis of disturbances in the pattern consumption of end-customers. The proposed strategy is based on the use of SVM (Supported Vector Machine). SVM requires labeled training data in order to define a classification function. The need of labeled data is a serious limitation for practical implementation of fraud detection systems in AMI. To work around this problem, we propose a new strategy for training SVM classifiers that requires only normal consumption patterns in the training phase. The anomalous consumption is generated by simulating attacks on the normal consumption patterns.

Keywords: AMI · Fraud detection · Energy theft · Smart grid · SVM

1 Introduction

In power systems, losses refer to the amounts of electricity injected into the transmission and distribution grids that are not paid by the end users. There are two types of losses: technical and non-technical [13]. Technical losses are inherent to the transmission of energy and consist mainly of power dissipation. Non-technical losses (NTL) consist primarily of electricity theft, non-payment by customers, and errors in accounting and record-keeping. Non-technical losses (NTL) are small in developed countries [13]. In contrast, the situation tends to be significantly different in developing countries, and can commonly exceed 10 %. NTL may be very difficult and costly to identify in grids based on monthly manual measures of consumption [14]. However, with the introduction of Advanced Metering Infrastructure (AMI) in Smart Grids new automated approaches are possible. A promising approach consists to generate consumption patterns for the end users and monitor significantly divergences from these patterns. According to [7], with the large amount of data obtained with AMI, to determine user profiles using statistical techniques may be very difficult. However, machine learning techniques are a very promising and suitable approach.

In this paper, we presented a new method for detecting energy theft in grids monitored by AMI. The method uses a SVM (Supported Vector Machine) learning approach to generate a fraud detection model (FDM) capable of detecting

© Springer International Publishing Switzerland 2016
A. Skavhaug et al. (Eds.): SAFECOMP 2016, LNCS 9922, pp. 226–237, 2016.
DOI: 10.1007/978-3-319-45477-1_18

disturbances in the pattern of consumption of end-users. SVM is a supervised learning model that requires labeled training data in order to define a classification function. The need of labeled data is a serious limitation for practical implementation of fraud detection systems in AMI. To work around this problem, we propose a new strategy for training SVM classifiers that requires only normal consumption patterns in the training phase. The anomalous consumption is generated by simulating attacks on the normal consumption patterns.

The main contribution of this paper is not the use of a specific machine learning technique. Instead, the innovation of our approach is to build individual consumer profiles, while most proposals in the literature builds profiles to classes or groups of users (see Sect. 2). Also, we have defined and formalized a strategy to simulate several types of false data injection into consumer patterns (defined in Sect. 3), which permits a robust training of the proposed machine learning detection model (presented in Sect. 4) and also works as an accurate test-bed to evaluate the performance of any other fraud detection model for AMI (presented in Sect. 5). Our evaluation (Sect. 6) shows that this approach is very promising, as it permits to detect the most common types of frauds.

2 Related Works

In this section we review some works that also address the problem of detecting energy theft by customers. The authors in [2] uses a fuzzy-based clustering algorithm to identify subgroups of users with similar profiles. Suspect profiles are identified by measuring the distance between the client consumption and the regular (normal) profile. The fraud detection model proposed by the authors is unsupervised and independent of rules. A SVM based approach that uses customer load profile information and additional attributes to expose abnormal behavior that is known to be highly correlated with NTL activities is proposed by [8]. The authors dispose of profile information of two types of users: normal and anomalous. That permits to generate a labeled training dataset, and use SVM to generate a decision function that can classify new users into the classes normal or anomalous.

An intrusion detection system (IDS) that combines meter audit logs of physical and cyber events with consumption data to more accurately model and detect theft-related behavior is proposed by [7]. The authors evaluate that smart meters are more vulnerable than mechanical meters. The IDS uses an attack graph based information fusion technique to combine evidences of three types: network and host-based IDS, on-meter anti-tampering sensors and anomalous consumption detectors.

A non-repudiation technique to detect frauds that employs two meters for each individual wire connecting the subscriber and the provider is proposed by [15]. The readings of the two meters are continuously compared and if a certain threshold is exceeded a fraud alarm is generated. The same approach is used in [14], but in this case, instead of using a redundant meter for each subscriber, a single meter is used for a group of subscribers. The authors proposes a set of techniques to detect frauds by comparing the reading from the collective meter with the summation for the reading from the subscriber meters. A framework for training and testing customer energy consumption datasets in order to separate and group illegal consumers is proposed by [5]. The authors use a SVM algorithm to classify consumption patterns with respect to geographical location, type of customer (residential, commercial, etc.) and season of the year. A set of rules is used to classify customers into different classes that represents how suspect the user profile is. The authors in [11] also conclude that the introduction of AMI may increase the risk of frauds because smart meters are subject to more types of attacks than mechanical meters. The authors are concerned about proposing a fraud detection model that preserve the privacy of consumption information from the end users. To address this problem the authors proposed a distributed technique that identifies the honesty of users by solving a linear system of equations that takes into account the consumption of users in a neighborhood and the total energy consumption of this neighborhood measured at a local data collector.

The method proposed in this paper have some similarities with [2,5,8]. However, these works generate profiles based on group of users. On the other hand, our approach consists to generate a different profile for each user. In the evaluation section we show the superiority of our approach by comparing with the method proposed by [8]. Another important difference is that our approach uses a dataset with measures obtained from a real AMI deployment. Therefore, the method developed in this paper uses unique information about the consumption patterns that have been ignored by most of the other studies.

3 Non-Technical Losses

Non-technical losses (NTL) in power systems refers mainly to energy theft, but also may include losses due to poor equipment maintenance, calculation errors and accounting mistakes. Usually, NTL related to energy theft are located in the "last mile" of the power distribution system. Traditionally, consumers are the primary source of NTL [6]. Some common methods used by consumers to generate NTL in non-AMI grids are discussed in [1,4]. With the use of smart meters and deployment of AMI, some NTL threads may be avoided. However, the introduction of networking elements and digital communication offers new possibilities for malicious users. Figure 1 illustrates a typical AMI topology [9]. In AMI, malicious users may generate false measures of consumption by modifying the meter, the communication from the meter to the utility billing system or by tapping energy illegally from the grid in order to bypass meters. According to [12], three levels of vulnerability can be considered in Smart Grids: from smart meters to concentrator nodes (HAN), from concentrator nodes to data centers (NAN) and on application level and community networks that use gathered meter data (WAN). In this paper we consider the frauds generated by modifying the meter or its communication in the HAN, which are usually referred as false data injection (FDI). The authors in [7] enumerate the following types of FDI

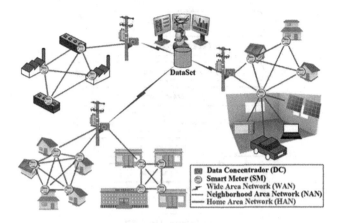

Fig. 1. Advanced Meter Infrastructure (AMI)

generated by malicious users: (i) Zero consumption: report zero consumption; (ii) Act as generator: report negative consumption; (iii) Percentage: cut the report by a given percentage; (iv) Cut-off point: alter the load profile to hide large loads. In this paper we consider two additional types of FDI: (v) Offset: cut report by a constant value and (vi) Low profile: report a low profile to simulate vacancy;

4   SVM-Based Fraud Detection System

Supported Vector Machine is a supervised learning method that generates classification functions [3]. A classification function defines a mapping $V \mapsto Y$ where $v \in V$ is some object and $y \in Y$ is a class label. Let's assume a binary SVM, and objects corresponding to a vector of real numbers. So: $v \in R^n$, $y \in \{-1, 1\}$. If the elements in V are linearly separable, SVM produces a decision function $g(v)$ as a hyperplane in R^n that permits to classify each element v into -1 or $+1$.

In this paper, we employ a linear (binary) SVM algorithm to construct a fraud detection model (FDM) for individual consumption profiles. To generate a decision function, SVM requires a training dataset with labeled data that includes both normal and anomalous measures. In this section, we explain how to generate the training dataset using only normal measures.

Figure 2 shows the main steps used to generate the SVM-based FDM. Usually, data is acquired regularly by the AMI system in intervals of an hour or less. We assume that a dataset without frauds is available for SVM training (a). Normal profiles can be obtained by assuring that the sum of the consumption reported by a group of users match collective meters placed in the low power distribution grid. This approach is not trivial, as it requires taking into account technical losses, but it is feasible [11,16]. In order to generate a successful classification model, the training dataset must include enough number of normal and anomalous samples. In our method, anomalous samples are generated by injecting false measures in the normal profile dataset (b). Assuming that $x \in X$ are the normal

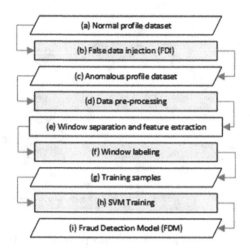

Fig. 2. Fraud Detection Model (FDM) generation

measures, the anomalous dataset X' is generated by replacing x by x' according to Table 1. In this paper we have not considered frauds in energy production because there is still not enough public data with this type of profile available. In the table, P represents a parameter that controls the amount of energy stolen and $\bar{x}$ is the average value of $x \in X$. The cut-off point FDI replaces all measures above the threshold A by a random value $\in (A_{min}, A)$. For the purpose of the tests presented in this paper, A and A_{min} are adjusted to match the amount of energy stolen defined by P. The zero consumption and the low profile FDIs are not controlled by P. In the low profile FDI, X_{low} represents a subset of the lower measures in X. In our tests, X_{low} is lower third part of the measures in X.

Table 1. FDI definitions

FDI	Measure modification
Offset	$x' \leftarrow x - P \cdot \bar{x}$
Percentage	$x' \leftarrow (1 - P) \cdot x$
Cut-off point	$x' \leftarrow \begin{cases} x & \text{if } x \leq A \\ \text{rand}\,(A_{min}, A) & \text{if } x > A \end{cases}$
Zero consumption	$x' \leftarrow 0$
Low profile	$x' \leftarrow \text{rand}\,(a \in X_{low})$

During the training, the offset, cut-off point and percentage FDIs are applied to the normal dataset in order to generate an anomalous dataset as illustrated in Fig. 3 (c). The other types of FDI are not used because they are easier to detect. They can be considered extreme cases of the other FDIs. The sensitivity

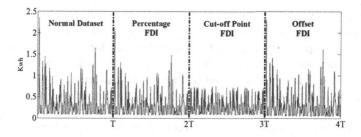

Fig. 3. Training dataset example

of the training procedure is controlled by the parameter P. An excessive small P can cause the system to generate many false alarms. Conversely, a large P may cause the system to neglect small frauds.

When the measurement interval is small, the incremental consumption may variate significantly. The incremental variations of consumption are not very useful to typify the behavior of a consumer. Indeed, our tests indicate that SVM generate poor classifiers when raw data is used for training. We have observed that it is more useful to smooth the consumption data by using a simple or exponential moving average, which is performed in step (d). In our tests we have employed a simple moving average where each measure is the mean of the measures within the last two-hours.

The samples used to train the SVM classifier must correspond to vectors $v = (x_1 \cdots x_w)$ of same dimension. In step (e), the training dataset is divided in windows with w measures. We have also observed that using all measures in a window as training samples results in bad classifiers. Therefore, we propose to use only a fraction of the data in a window, extracted in accordance to a heuristic that depends on the type of fraud we want to detect. The measures from a windows of size w are ordered and divide into three subsets of equal size $(v_{min}, v_{avg}, v_{max})$. The subset v_{max} is used to generate FDM for detecting frauds of type "cut-off point" and "low profile". The subset v_{min} is used for all other types of frauds. The same feature extraction strategy is used during the training and evaluation phases.

In step (f), each window v is labeled as normal (1) or anomalous (-1) by tracking the measures to determine if they came from a normal or anomalous dataset. The labeled features extracted from the windows correspond to the samples used by the SVM (g). Finally, the SVM algorithm (h) is used to generate the fraud detection model (i).

5   Dataset Preparation and Metric Definition

The dataset used in this paper was obtained from the Project Smart City from the City of Newcastle, Australia [10]. The dataset contains the consumption information of 31 houses, monitored for about one year. The energy consumption (kwh) is measured in intervals of 30 min, generating 48 daily records per house.

In our experiments, only 28 houses were considered. Three houses were excluded because they are energy producers. To evaluate our system, we have divided the dataset into two parts: training data and evaluation data. Because the original dataset contains only normal data, we have injected frauds in the dataset using the algorithm 1. The variables used by the algorithm are explained in Table 2. Basically, the algorithm uses two exponentially distributed variables to control the fraction of measures from the original dataset that are replaced by frauds. In average, the fraction of measures replaced is given by: $\frac{A}{A+N}$, where A and N are the means of the random variables a and n, respectively. Figure 4 shows how the measures of a consumer are affected by the fraud injections. We can also observe that periods with very low consumption are common in the dataset, as residents may be in vacancy (narrowest rectangle in Fig. 4). Except when the size of the evaluation window is very large, these periods tend to generate false alarms.

Table 2. Symbols in the algorithm used to contaminate the dataset

Symbol	Meaning
T	Number of measures used for training
D	Number of measures in the dataset
n	Random variable that controls a normal period (mean N)
a	Random variable that controls a FDI (mean A)
f	FDI function

Algorithm 1. Contaminate the dataset with FDI

```
 1: i ← T                                          ▷ i measure index
 2: repeat
 3:     n ← Floor (Random (N))
 4:     i ← i + n                                   ▷ jumps normal period
 5:     a ← Floor (Random (A))
 6:     f ← Randomly selected FDI function
 7:     while i < Min (i + a, D) do                 ▷ applies FDI
 8:         xᵢ ← f (xᵢ)
 9:         i ← i + 1
10:     end while
11: until i < D
```

In the evaluation section we have used the following metrics to measure the performance of the fraud detection system: tpr (true positive rate), fpr (false positive rate) and F-measure (F). The F-measure definition requires the definition of an intermediate metric called precision (p). These metrics are defined as follows: $tpr = \frac{tp}{tp+fn}$; $fpr = \frac{fp}{fp+tn}$; $p = \frac{tp}{tp+fp}$ e $F = 2 \cdot \frac{p.tpr}{p+ptr}$, where: tp (true positive): a corrupted window was detected; fp (false positive): a normal window was pointed as fraud; fn (false negative): a corrupted window was not detected and tn (true negative): a normal window was pointed as legitimate.

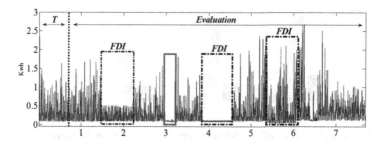

Fig. 4. Dataset preparation

6   Fraud Detection System (FDS) Evaluation

The evaluation presented in this section has the following purposes: (i) Determine the best configuration of the parameters: T (training period), w (window size) and the training distribution approach used to account for the effect of seasons; (ii) Determine the performance under different attack conditions expressed in terms of the amount of energy stolen: P and (iii) Compare our strategy with the group-based profile generation approach defined in [8].

According to our method, a window is the minimum set of measures that can be reported as a fraud. Figure 5 shows the influence of the windows size (w) on the FDS performance. This evaluation was performed considering only FDIs of type cut-off point, percentage and offset, randomly applied to 30 % of the dataset. The average FDI duration was $A = 1008$ measures (21 days). The other types of FDI were not used in this test because they are easier to detect and may masquerade the results. The test was repeated with three different amounts of energy theft: $P = 10\%$, 20 % and 30 %. The SVM classifier was trained with a dataset injected with the same frauds, but only $P = 10\%$ of energy theft. All tests in this section have used $P = 10\%$ for training. It is important to note that neither the type of FDI nor the amount of energy theft need to be known beforehand.

The figure shows the average result obtained considering all houses and all amounts of energy theft. The best metric to evaluate the performance of the FDS is the F-Measure, because it can balance the ability of the system to detect frauds without generating excessive false positives. Using this metric as reference, the best overall result was obtained with $w = 144$ measures per window (or 3 days).

The effect of the training period on the performance of the FDS is shows in Fig. 6. This test was executed with $w = 144$ (3 days). The performance increases up to $T = 3024$ (63 days). After this point increasing the training period does not increase the performance of the system.

In the previous tests the training period was placed in the beginning of the database. However, the consumption profile of a customer is heavily influence by the season. Therefore, we have evaluated if distributing the training period among different seasons can improve the FDS performance. We have considered four different techniques with respect to how the training period was distributed: Technique 1: one training period $T = 3024$ (63 days) in the beginning of

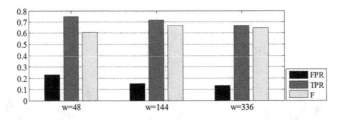

Fig. 5. Effect of the window size on the FDS performance

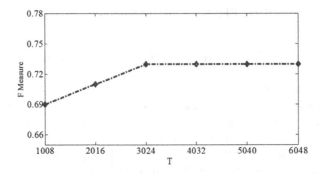

Fig. 6. Effect of the training period on the FDS performance.

the dataset; Technique 2: one training period in the beginning of each season ($T = 756$ for each period); Technique 3: one training period in the beginning of each month ($T = 252$ for each period) and Technique 4: one different model for each season ($T = 756$). Techniques 1 to 3 generate a single model that is applied to the remaining of the dataset. Technique 4 generates a distinct model for each season, and the model is shifted accordingly when the season changes. Figure 7 shows the performance of these techniques with respect to the FDIs of type off-set, cut-off point, percentage and the average result considering all three types of FDI.

In Fig. 7, techniques 1 and 4 presented similar results. Figures 8 and 9 present a more detailed comparison between these techniques. Both techniques were evaluated with the same dataset, where 30 % of the measures were randomly contaminated with all types of FDI. One can observe that both techniques have similar detection rates, but technique 4 generates far less false positives. Normal seasonal variations of consumption are misinterpreted as attacks by technique 1, but not by technique 4 that employs a shifting model.

We have used the same dataset [10] to evaluate the SVM-based FDS presented by [8]. The FDS proposed in [8] follows a different approach, as a fraud detection model is generated by using data gathered from group of users. Because the number of houses is small, we have selected 10 houses to generate the anomalous profile and the remaining 18 houses to generate the normal profile. We have modified 30 % of the measures available for the anomalous houses with the

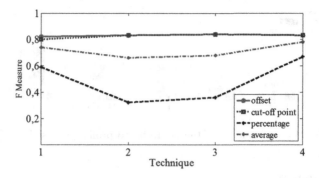

Fig. 7. Effect of the training distribution on the FDS performance.

five types of FDI defined in Table 1. To approximate the conditions suggested by the authors, we have used a window size of 1440 measures (1 month) and used 50 % of the dataset for training and 50 % for evaluation of the resulting SVM classifier. Figure 10 shows the average result obtained for all houses with respect to different amounts of energy stolen. Given the diversity of profiles used for training, the resulting classifier is very conservative, and generates a very low rate of false positives. However, it is also inaccurate to detect true attacks. For $P = 30\%$, our approach achieves $F = 0.66$ with $TPR = 0.95$ (technique 1) and $F = 0.76$ with $TPR = 0.95$ (technique 4), while [8] achieves only $F = 0.5$ with $TPR = 0.45$. As pointed by the authors, their method is expected to perform well only for large amounts of energy stolen.

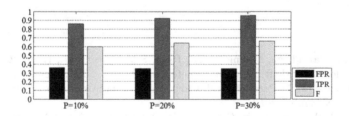

Fig. 8. Evaluation of technique 1 with respect to the amount of energy stolen

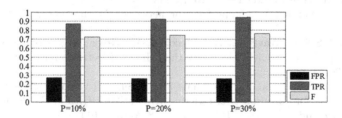

Fig. 9. Evaluation of technique 4 with respect to the amount of energy stolen

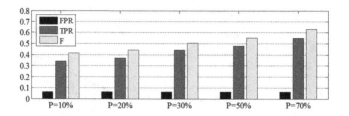

Fig. 10. Performance of the group based profile proposed in [8].

7 Conclusion

We have presented a fraud detected system (FDS) for detecting energy theft in grids monitored by AMI. In the literature, the most common approach consists to generate a fraud detection model (FDM) using information gathered from a group of users. Our evaluation with a dataset based on measures obtained from an actual AMI deployment indicates that a neighborhood with similar economical conditions presents significant differences on their consumption profiles. Therefore, a FDM based on information of a group of users tends to be very inaccurate to hold significant consumption discrepancies. We have addressed this issue by generating a different FDM for each consumer, greatly improving the accuracy of the FDS. As a future research, we intend to integrate the information from meters that measure the total consumption of a neighborhood. That approach will permit to update the consumption profile of the users whenever the comparison between the neighborhood meter and the individual meters indicate no fraud.

References

1. Anas, M., Javaid, N., Mahmood, A., Raza, S.M., Qasim, U., Khan, Z.A.: Minimizing electricity theft using smart meters in AMI. In: 2012 Seventh International Conference on P2P, Parallel, Grid, Cloud and Internet Computing (3PGCIC), pp. 176–182, November 2012
2. Angelos, E.W.S., Saavedra, O.R., Cortés, O.A.C., de Souza, A.N.: Detection and identification of abnormalities in customer consumptions in power distribution systems. IEEE Trans. Power Deliv. **26**(4), 2436–2442 (2011)
3. Cortes, C., Vapnik, V.: Support-vector networks. Mach. Learn. **20**(3), 273–297 (1995)
4. Depuru, S.S.S.R., Wang, L., Devabhaktuni, V., Green, R.C.: High performance computing for detection of electricity theft. Int. J. Electr. Power Energy Syst. **47**, 21–30 (2013)
5. Depuru, S.S.S.R., Wang, L., Devabhaktuni, V.: Support vector machine based data classification for detection of electricity theft. In: 2011 IEEE/PES Power Systems Conference and Exposition (PSCE), pp. 1–8, March 2011
6. Jiang, R., Lu, R., Wang, Y., Luo, J., Shen, C., Shen, X.S.: Energy-theft detection issues for advanced metering infrastructure in smart grid. Tsinghua Sci. Technol. **19**(2), 105–120 (2014)

7. McLaughlin, S., Holbert, B., Fawaz, A., Berthier, R., Zonouz, S.: A multi-sensor energy theft detection framework for advanced metering infrastructures. IEEE J. Sel. Areas Commun. **31**(7), 1319–1330 (2013)
8. Nagi, J., Yap, K.S., Tiong, S.K., Ahmed, S.K., Mohamad, M.: Nontechnical loss detection for metered customers in power utility using support vector machines. IEEE Trans. Power Deliv. **25**(2), 1162–1171 (2010)
9. NIST. Nist framework and roadmap for smart grid interoperatibility satandards, release 3. Technical report, U.S. Department of Commerce (2014)
10. Department of Industry and Science. Sample household electricity time of use data, July 2014
11. Salinas, S., Li, M., Li, P.: Privacy-preserving energy theft detection in smart grids. In: 2012 9th Annual IEEE Communications Society Conference on Sensor, Mesh and Ad Hoc Communications and Networks (SECON), pp. 605–613, June 2012
12. Skopik, F., Ma, Z.: Attack vectors to metering data in smart grids under security constraints. In: 2012 IEEE 36th Annual Computer Software and Applications Conference Workshops (COMPSACW), pp. 134–139, July 2012
13. World Bank. Reducing technical and non-technical losses in the power sector. World Bank Group, Washington, DC (2009)
14. Xiao, Z., Xiao, Y., Du, D.H.: Exploring malicious meter inspection in neighborhood area smart grids. IEEE Trans. Smart Grid **4**(1), 214–226 (2013)
15. Xiao, Z., Xiao, Y., Du, D.H.-C.: Building accountable smart grids in neighborhood area networks. In: 2011 IEEE Global Telecommunications Conference (GLOBECOM 2011), pp. 1–5, December 2011
16. Xiao, Z., Xiao, Y., Du, D.H.-C.: Non-repudiation in neighborhood area networks for smart grid. IEEE Commun. Mag. **51**(1), 18–26 (2013)

Exploiting Trust in Deterministic Builds

Christopher Jämthagen[1(✉)], Patrik Lantz[1,2(✉)], and Martin Hell[1]

[1] Department of Electrical and Information Technology, Lund University,
Lund, Sweden
{christopher.jamthagen,martin.hell}@eit.lth.se
[2] Ericsson Research, Lund, Sweden
patrik.lantz@ericsson.com

Abstract. Deterministic builds, where the compile and build processes are reproducible, can be used to achieve increased trust in distributed binaries. As the trust can be distributed across a set of builders, where all provide their own signature of a byte-to-byte identical binary, all have to cooperate in order to introduce unwanted code in the binary. On the other hand, if an attacker manages to incorporate malicious code in the source, and make this remain undetected during code reviews, the deterministic build provides additional opportunities to introduce e.g., a backdoor. The impact of such a successful attack would be serious since the actual trust model is exploited. In this paper, the problem of crafting such hidden code that is difficult to detect, both during code reviews of the source code as well as static analysis of the binary executable is addressed. It is shown that the displacement and immediate fields of an instruction can be used the embed hidden code directly from the C programming language.

Keywords: Backdoor · Overlapping code · Deterministic builds · Malware

1 Introduction

Throughout the years there have been numerous attempts by adversaries to plant backdoors in software projects [1–5]. The main goal of backdoors is to gain unauthorized access by circumventing the authentication step or simply by gaining access to a system remotely. These are often very subtle modifications of the source code that can easily go unnoticed by code reviewers or static analysis tools. Developers often rely on static tools that inspect the source code for any programming flaws [6–8]. These tools have a difficulty of identifying logical flaws and manual review must be conducted to identify potential backdoors. Reviewers rely on manual reading of code, supported by checklists and coding standards. This consists of identifying certain unsafe functions that can be the cause of security vulnerabilities or if input is being sanitized [9]. This type of scan for security vulnerabilities may not be sufficient for identifying potential backdoors, instead the reviewer may have to read and understand each line of code in a project which is time-consuming and costly. The more mature open source

© Springer International Publishing Switzerland 2016
A. Skavhaug et al. (Eds.): SAFECOMP 2016, LNCS 9922, pp. 238–249, 2016.
DOI: 10.1007/978-3-319-45477-1_19

projects have adopted peer reviewing as an important quality assurance [10, 11]. In some cases a code commit must first be reviewed before it is accepted. Depending on how trusted the developer is, i.e., the better reputation he has, it is more likely that the developer will get code changes accepted [12]. There is also a lack of extensive results and research on how peer reviewing reduces security vulnerabilities and backdoors in open source community. Still, there is research addressing these questions that have been initiated [13].

A backdoor can be seen as trigger-based code which is executed when specific inputs are received, denoted as trigger conditions. Discovering the trigger conditions can be difficult [14,15] to automated analysis. The actual problem of identifying trigger-based code has made recent advances, introducing tools for automatic detection of backdoors [16] for detecting rarely exercised code paths. As a response to this, Andriesse and Bos [17] show how one can hide the backdoor via instruction-level steganography by modifying the final binary.

In order to thwart tampering of binaries, the code can be signed by the compiler or the person in hand of publishing the binary. Lately some initiatives have been taken to introduce secure software distribution that would enable trusted binaries to be downloaded and verified by multiple users. This is denoted as deterministic, reproducible or verifiable builds [18–20] in which the build process will generate identical binaries.

In this paper we investigate the problem of adding hidden machine code via the source code instead of directly modifying the binary. Such hidden code, if undetected, would result in hashes and code signatures that are correctly verified as genuine. We address the problem of keeping the semantics of such instructions hidden in the source code as well as in the binary so that both a code review of the source code and static analysis of the binary will not easily reveal the hidden code. This is accomplished by carefully constructing data structures where the offset to a base address can be used to interpret machine instructions. In the binary, these instructions will be hidden from the main execution path and not visible in a disassembly listing.

2   Background

In this section we provide the necessary background required for the remain of this paper. We will be presenting details related to the x86 architecture instruction set along with an introduction to determinstic builds.

2.1   x86 ISA

The x86 architecture pioneered by Intel remains one of the most widely used ISAs today. It is a Complex Instruction Set Computing (CISC) architecture meaning that it provides instructions that themselves may execute several low-level operations as one. Instructions may be between 1 and 15 bytes [21]. CISC instructions can be executed from any byte alignment, with the possibility of executing an instruction from a byte never meant to be the starting byte of an instruction, also denoted as unintended instructions.

2.2 Anatomy of an x86 Instruction

An x86 instruction, as illustrated in Fig. 1 is divided into six fields where the opcode is the only mandatory field.

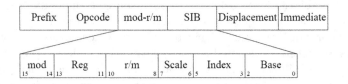

Fig. 1. Illustration of a x86 instruction

An instruction can have up to four **prefixes**. A prefix changes the behavior of the instruction it is applied to by e.g., changing or overriding the operand or address size.

The **Opcode** is the instruction code that defines the main behaviour of the instruction. Most opcodes are one byte long, but can be extended.

The **mod-r/m** byte defines the addressing mode and operands of the instruction. It is divided into the 2-bit mod field and two 3-bit fields called Reg and r/m. The mod field specifies direct or indirect addressing, i.e., directly register to register or if one of the registers are to be dereferenced. The mod field also specifies if there is a displacement field or SIB-byte for this instruction.

The **Scale-Index-Base** byte (SIB-byte) is used for indexed addressing, e.g., in arrays. It is illustrated as [Base + Index*Scale] where Base and Index are registers and Scale can assume the value 1, 2, 4 or 8.

The **Displacement** field specifies an offset for a memory dereferencing instruction. The address displacement can be of 0, 1, 2 or 4 bytes.

The **Immediate** field contains any constants used in instructions and can be 0, 1, 2 or 4 bytes.

2.3 Overlapping Instructions

Overlapping instructions exist in all compiled x86 code. The variable-length instructions accommodates different interpretations of the code depending on which byte decoding starts from. An example of this phenomenon is shown below where the jmp instruction will jump to the latter half (0xff) of its own instruction and execute from that point.

```
eb ff        jmp -1
c0 c3 00     rol bl, 0x0
;The jump will execute
ff c0        inc eax
c3           retn
```

This can be used in application exploitation attacks based on return-oriented programming (ROP). In order to find more useful instructions for the gadgets used in this attack, unintended instructions can be discovered using this overlapping technique by decoding instructions at different offsets.

2.4   Deterministic Builds

Distributing compiled binaries of open source software does not guarantee that the binaries are in fact compiled from the referenced source code. There is nothing stopping an attacker from adding malicious code, producing the binaries from the modified source code and claim that it was the result of compilation of the unmodified source code. This poses security issues for people who do not have the knowledge or do not want to compile the source code themselves. They must trust the single entity who compiled the binary.

Deterministically built binaries allows multiple builders to produce the same byte-by-byte binary such that a hash value of the binary is the same for all builders. This removes the single point of failure whereby trust needs to be put into a single builder. Instead trust is now distributed between multiple builders, whereby each builder individually publishes a signature of the hash digest of the binary. This allows anyone who wishes to install the binary directly to verify that multiple builders have compiled the binaries from the referenced source code and that there are no discrepancies between the hashes of the different builders. Unless all builders are conspiring or are all controlled by another attacker, the binary can be deemed safe from manipulation before compilation.

Examples of security critical applications that use deterministic building for their binaries are the Tor projects Tor Browser Bundle [20] and the reference implementation of the cryptocurrency Bitcoin, called Bitcoin Core [22].

It is important to note that just because some application has been deterministically built, it does not guarantee that there is no malicious code. It merely solves the need of trusting a single builder.

3   Hiding Instructions in Binary Code

In this section we show how to inject instructions in a program and have its semantics hidden from an analyst in both the source code and the compiled binaries. It can be implemented entirely within the source code.

The requirements to make this work is for the attacker to have complete control over the part of the source code where the injected instructions are implemented. The project should also be compiled in a reproducible way to ensure that produced binaries are byte-for-byte identical between builders.

The examples in this section are based on a 32-bit Linux system with the compiler GCC 4.9.1 with no optimizations enabled. Some of the examples may not be applicable to other compilers or other versions of GCC. It should be straightforward to adapt the techniques explained here for other compilers and configurations.

For the remain of this paper we also assume that the trigger condition used to execute the hidden instructions is chosen and designed in such way that it is sufficiently hard for an automated analysis to identify it [14,15]. Therefore, we regard this topic as out of scope and focus on hiding the trigger-based code.

3.1 Main and Hidden Execution Paths

We begin by defining the Hidden Execution Path (HEP) and the Main Execution Path (MEP) in the binary. The HEP is defined as a sequence of assembly instructions hidden implicitly in the source code, i.e., the semantics of those hidden instructions can not be seen in the source code. It is also explicitly hidden in the compiled source code's disassembly listing. This is true for both static and dynamic analysis scenarios, as long as the HEP is not executed. The MEP is defined as a sequence of assembly instructions that is implicitly visible in the source code, i.e., the source code seen generates the expected assembly instructions. The generated assembly instructions are clearly visible in the disassembly listing of the compiled source code. The MEP shows the functionality that we want to show the user and the HEP is the malicious code. Outside the MEP and the HEP are the normal instructions that are as visible as the assembly instructions in the MEP, but ones that do not contain any intended malicious hidden instructions.

The HEP can include any instruction that is valid. The MEP is limited to what instructions the utilized compiler and associated configurations can generate from the source code.

3.2 Basic Design

Our approach of inserting hidden instructions in the source code relies on having the compiler generate instructions in the MEP in such a way that overlapping instructions are formed to a semantically correct, predetermined HEP. One limitation is the self-synchronizing nature of x86 instructions due to the Kruskal Count [23], i.e., beginning decoding instructions from different byte offsets will soon result in a merge of the different execution paths. Designing the HEP in one continuous set of bytes would result in limited functionality. In [24] this was circumvented with unusually formatted nop instructions which are not prevalent in compiled code and thus cannot be used here. Instead, we scatter fragments of the HEP throughout the application, ending each fragment with a branch instruction pointing to the next fragment. A HEP fragment includes one or more HEP instructions and a branch instruction, see Fig. 2.

In Sect. 3.3 we will show how mappings between MEP instruction fields and HEP instructions fields are made with ease of implementation in mind.

3.3 MEP-to-HEP Mappings

MEP instruction fields must be mapped to HEP instruction fields in a way that keep MEP instructions relevant for the program in general and its surrounding

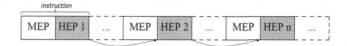

Fig. 2. Control flow of the HEPs

instructions. It must also be formed so the relevant HEP instructions are decoded correctly.

To achieve this, we analyze the different MEP instruction fields.

- Prefixes are very limited in the number of values they can take and will depend heavily on the rest of the fields. One prefix value can take 11 out of 256 values.
- Opcodes can assume a larger number of bytes, more precisely one-byte opcodes can take 244 out of 256 values (excluding prefixes and the 0x0f two-byte opcode extension code). The compiler may not be able to generate all of them. Many of the opcodes are redundant, which is why it is likely that compilers are just using a subset of all opcodes.
- The mod-r/m byte is only one byte and also limited by the compiler in what values it can take.
- The same applies for the SIB byte as for the mod-r/m byte, in that it is difficult to make the compiler use the specific source and destination operands we want.
- The displacement field can be 0,1,2 or 4 bytes long and is relatively easy to use to make the compiler generate desired values. Accessing a stack variable will make the compiler generate an instruction that dereferences memory from an offset to the base pointer ebp. This offset is the displacement field, and depending on how we design the stack layout and which variables we use, these values can be controlled. When using a 32-bit displacement field, there is a trade-off between the size of a data structure allocated in memory and how much of the displacement field we can control. Using only the three least significant bytes of the 32-bit displacement field, the maximum amount of allocated memory is 16777216 bytes.
- The immediate field is ideal to work with, because we can set it to whatever we want without any practical consequences. It can be 0, 1, 2 or 4 bytes in size by using the types char, short and int respectively.

Based on this analysis the displacement and immediate fields of a MEP instruction will be used to create the HEP, see Fig. 3. Since the fields are adjacent they can be combined to create HEP instructions.

4   Constructing the HEP from Source Code

In this section we describe how to write code that generates the desired hidden code fragments. This is illustrated in Fig. 4 where the hidden code fragment is introduced at the source code level to be compiled and later invoked as unintended instructions.

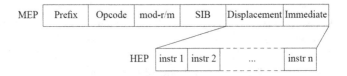

Fig. 3. Illustration of MEP and HEP layout in an x86 instruction

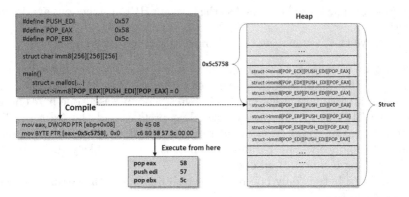

Fig. 4. Introducing a HEP in the source code. Compilation of the source code will generate unintended instructions which are executed by decoding at certain offsets in the compiled code

We start by defining two different structs.

```
struct imm8_t {
    char imm8[256][256][256];
};
struct imm32_t {
    int imm32[256][256][64];
};
```

We assume the structs are allocated on the heap, and when dereferencing any elements in a struct, this is done with an offset from the base address of that struct located in register `eax`.

4.1 Hiding Code in Immediate Fields

The `imm8_t` struct provides a simple way to assign MEP instruction `displacement` fields with the desired values coupled with an 8-bit `immediate` field. As we use struct member 'imm8' which is of type char, the compiler will generate assembly instructions with an 8-bit `immediate` field. Likewise, the `imm32_t` will generate instructions with 32-bit `immediate` fields when assigning struct member 'imm32' a value. As an example, assigning a value to the first position in the 'imm8' member in the `imm8_t` struct and the first position in the 'imm32' member of the `imm32_t` struct will generate the following assembly instructions respectively.

```
c6 00 0a              mov    BYTE PTR [eax],0xa
c7 00 0a 00 00 00     mov    DWORD PTR [eax],0xa
```

The first instruction only includes an 8-bit `immediate` field (0x0a) since the variable assigned is of type `char` and the second instruction includes a 32-bit `immediate` field (0x0000000a) because the type is `int`.

4.2 Hiding Code in Displacement Fields

In order to generate 8-bit `displacement` fields with these structs the last two indices of either struct member would have to be set to zero. Since the struct is allocated on the heap, the first index of the struct member is restricted to values between 0x00 and 0x7f. The reason is that when referencing an element in the struct on the heap, we will do so by using a positive offset from `eax`. If the `displacement` value exceeds 0x7f the compiler will put the value in a 32-bit `displacement` field in order to not get the incorrect sign.

The design of the 3-dimensional matrix corresponding to the struct allows the HEP designer to set the exact bytes of the `displacement` field directly in the source code. For example, the following assignment of the 'imm8' member in the `imm8_t` struct illustrates the process.

```
imm8_t *a = malloc(...);
a->imm8[0x10][0x20][0x30] = 0xa;
```

This will generate the following machine code.

```
c6 80 30 20 10 00 0a  mov  BYTE PTR [eax+0x102030],0xa
```

The indices chosen are seen directly in the decoding of the instruction.

When referencing an element on struct member 'imm8', the `displacement` value is derived in the following way.

```
imm8[x][y][z] -> displacement = x<<16 + y<<8 + z
```

Thus, index positions will result in bytes in the `displacement` field.

Note that the most significant byte will always be 0x00 since we use a 3-dimensional matrix.

The first index of the `imm32_t` member 'imm32' is set to 64 because it stores integer type values which take up four bytes of memory per element. This means that for each index increment, there will be an increment of four for the least significant byte of the `displacement` value. Thus, any value put into the first index position must be divided by four in order to get the correct value representation in the `displacement` field. One drawback of using `imm32_t` for encoding HEP instructions is that the first index position cannot assume values not divisible by four, thus limiting its use to only 25 % of all byte values. Should this one byte not be useful in the HEP fragment, it could simply be skipped and the HEP fragment's first byte be what is specified in the second index. Below is an example of how the assignment of `imm8[0][0][4]` with `0x0a` is represented in the `displacement` field.

```
c7 40 10 0a 00 00 00    mov    DWORD PTR [eax+0x10],0xa
```

The `displacement` is a single byte with value `0x10` and in order to get the desired value, which is 4, we have to code the assignment statement as `[0][0][4>>2]`. This will generate the following assembly instruction.

```
c7 40 04 0a 00 00 00    mov    DWORD PTR [eax+0x4],0xa
```

Here we can see that the value of the `displacement` field is now 4.

4.3 Tying It All Together

To simplify the procedure, a set of macros can be used to define all one-byte opcodes and prefixes needed to program the HEP. If we want to create the following HEP fragment

```
58          pop eax
57          push edi
c3          retn
```

we would define the following.

```
#define POP_EAX     0x58
#define PUSH_EDI    0x57
#define RETN        0xC3

struct imm8_t *a = malloc(...);
a->imm8[RETN][PUSH_EDI][POP_EAX] = 0;
```

This fragment generates the following machine code for the assignment statement.

```
mov eax, DWORD PTR [ebp+0x08]       8b 45 08
mov BYTE PTR [eax+0xc35758],0x0     c6 80 58 57 c3 00 00
```

If execution starts from the third byte in the second instruction, our desired HEP instructions will be executed. Assuming that register `edi` holds an address to the next HEP fragment, the `retn` instruction will pop that value and continue execution from there. In this example the `immediate` value can be set to anything as it will not be a part of the HEP, allowing for some flexibility in designing the MEP.

4.4 Proof-of-Concept Backdoor

We have implemented and released a proof-of-concept backdoor [25] which utilizes the technique described. The backdoor opens up a listening tcp port and gives shell access to whoever connects to that port. The HEP fragments are scattered throughout multiple functions of the application. No other functionality is implemented, and the program consists only of dummy statements to make the backdoor work.

The backdoor is a modified variant of the one found in [26]. It was modified to make the number of bytes for each instruction as small as possible in order to simplify encoding them in the `displacement` and `immediate` fields of the MEP instructions. We also reduced the total number of instructions used by placing some sequences of instructions inside functions that could be called multiple times.

5 Related Work

Jamthagen et al. [24] shows how to hide instructions inside multi-byte NOPs and provide with an algorithm to detect hidden code. The paper shows how to construct HEPs and MEPs in assembly code and which instructions are best suited for connecting two hidden instructions, so called wrapping instructions. In addition to having one segment with multiple-byte NOPs, the authors describe how to split it into multiple segments across a binary. Main difference with this paper is that we introduce the HEPs and MEPs in the source code of a high-level language such as C/C++.

Andriesse and Bos [17] describe instruction-level steganography in order hide the backdoor code and to evade binary analysis. When disassembling a binary, the trigger-based code is hidden inside other instructions by utilizing instruction overlapping. The backdoor code is triggered by introducing a bug in the source code of the target application and modifying the resulting binary in order to embed the hidden code. As our described approach addresses deterministic builds, it is not possible to modify the binary, therefore we have to rely on implementing the hidden functionality at the source code level.

In [27], the inside threat of an evil developer is described. Wang et al. present an attack where iOS applications are released with a deliberately injected vulnerability by the developer that can be remotely exploited. The vulnerability is placed in such way that it should pass the review and vetting process of Apple. The application is introduced with a bug and when triggered, a ROP attack is performed. In the attack they still have to send the attack payload, i.e., the gadget addresses/offsets to the vulnerable application while our technique triggers the backdoor directly in the code without any information required on how to locate the attack payload. In our case only the trigger condition must be fulfilled which can be done via a specially crafted network packet for example. This is the main strength of our method compared to an ordinary ROP attack. The size of the payload necessary to trigger the exploit can be much smaller for our attack than with a ROP attack, which requires gadget addresses and additional data to be sent on the network. With the hidden code technique we could more easily bypass IDSes and other security technologies [28] that tries to detect exploitation traffic. Additionally, even though the set of ROP gadgets in a binary often are Turing-complete [29], our method introduces a flexibility in what the trigger code actually executes.

6   Conclusion and Future Work

In this paper we have presented a technique that allows an attacker to craft malicious code in an application's source code and have its semantics hidden in both the source code and compiled binaries. One requirement to achieve this is that the software is compiled on a CISC architecture and in a reproducible manner. Our proof-of-concept backdoor shows that the technique is feasible and that a determined attacker could utilize it to compromise a software project.

Future work should study the feasability of utilizing this technique on existing projects. The stealth of the source code hiding instructions may also have room for optimizations. How maintainable code like this is would also be an interesting research topic considering compilers and build processes gets updated.

References

1. Edge, J.: A backdoor in UnrealIRCd (2010). https://lwn.net/Articles/392201/
2. Posted by corbet. An attempt to backdoor the kernel (2003). https://lwn.net/Articles/57135/
3. Evans, C.: Alert: vsftpd download backdoored (2011). http://scarybeastsecurity.blogspot.com/2011/07/alert-vsftpd-download-backdoored.html
4. SecurityFocus.com. ProFTPD Backdoor Unauthorized Access Vulnerability (2010). http://www.securityfocus.com/bid/45150
5. welivesecurity.com. Linux/SSHDoor.A Backdoored SSH daemon that steals passwords (2013). http://www.welivesecurity.com/2013/01/24/linux-sshdoor-a-backdoored-ssh-daemon-that-steals-passwords/
6. Coverity: Software Testing and Static Analysis Tools. http://www.coverity.com/
7. Flawfinder. http://www.dwheeler.com/flawfinder/
8. Splint. http://www.splint.org/
9. Howard, M.A.: A process for performing security code reviews. IEEE Secur. Priv. 4(4), 74–79 (2006)
10. Asundi, J., Jayant, R.: Patch review processes in open source software development communities: a comparative case study. In: Proceedings of the 40th Annual Hawaii International Conference on System Sciences, HICSS 2007, p. 166c. IEEE Computer Society, Washington, DC (2007)
11. Rigby, P.C., Storey, M.-A.: Understanding broadcast based peer review on open source software projects. In: Proceedings of the 33rd International Conference on Software Engineering, ICSE 2011, pp. 541–550. ACM, New York (2011)
12. Bosu, A., Carver, J.C.: Impact of developer reputation on code review outcomes in OSS projects: an empirical investigation. In: Proceedings of the 8th ACM/IEEE International Symposium on Empirical Software Engineering and Measurement, ESEM 2014, pp. 33:1–33:10. ACM, New York (2014)

13. Bosu, A., Carver, J.C.: Peer code review to prevent security vulnerabilities: an empirical evaluation. In: 2013 IEEE 7th International Conference on Software Security and Reliability-Companion (SERE-C), pp. 229–230, June 2013

14. Wang, Z., Ming, J., Jia, C., Gao, D.: Linear obfuscation to combat symbolic execution. In: Atluri, V., Diaz, C. (eds.) ESORICS 2011. LNCS, vol. 6879, pp. 210–226. Springer, Heidelberg (2011)

15. Sharif, M., Lanzi, A., Giffin, J., Lee, W.: Impeding malware analysis using conditional code obfuscation. In: Proceedings of the 15th Annual Network and Distributed System Security Symposium (NDSS) (2008)

16. Schuster, F., Holz, T.: Towards reducing the attack surface of software backdoors. In: Proceedings of the ACM SIGSAC Conference on Computer Communications Security, CCS 2013, pp. 851–862. ACM, New York (2013)

17. Andriesse, D., Bos, H.: Instruction-level steganography for covert trigger-based malware. In: Dietrich, S. (ed.) DIMVA 2014. LNCS, vol. 8550, pp. 41–50. Springer, Heidelberg (2014)

18. Gitian. https://gitian.org/

19. Debian: Reproducible builds. https://wiki.debian.org/ReproducibleBuilds

20. Tor: Deterministic builds. https://blog.torproject.org/category/tags/deterministic-builds

21. Intel 64 and IA-32 Architectures Software Developer's Manual. https://www-ssl.intel.com/content/dam/www/public/us/en/documents/manuals/64-ia-32-architectures-software-developer-manual-325462.pdf

22. Bitcoin core. https://bitcoincore.org

23. Lagarias, J.C., Rains, E., Vanderbei, R.J.: The Kruskal Count (2001). http://arxiv.org/abs/math/0110143

24. Jamthagen, C., Lantz, P., Hell, M.: A new instruction overlapping technique for anti-disassembly and obfuscation of x86 binaries. In: 2013 Workshop on Anti-malware Testing Research (WATeR), pp. 1–9, October 2013

25. Hiding code in deterministically built binaries - Proof-of-Concept - Linux/x86. https://github.com/cjamthagen/backdoor_deterministic_code

26. shell_bind_tcp.asm. https://github.com/geyslan/SLAE/blob/master/1st.assignment/shell_bind_tcp.asm

27. Wang, T., Lu, K., Lu, L., Chung, S., Lee, W.: Jekyll on iOS: when benign apps become evil. In: Proceedings of the 22nd USENIX Conference on Security, SEC 2013, pp. 559–572. USENIX Association, Berkeley (2013)

28. Jamthagen, C., Karlsson, L., Stankovski, P., Hell, M.: eavesROP: listening for ROP Payloads in data streams. In: Chow, S.S.M., Camenisch, J., Hui, L.C.K., Yiu, S.M. (eds.) ISC 2014. LNCS, vol. 8783, pp. 413–424. Springer International Publishing, Heidelberg (2014)

29. Shacham, H.: The geometry of innocent flesh on the bone: Return-into-libc without function calls (on the x86). In: Proceedings of the 14th ACM Conference on Computer and Communications Security, CCS 2007, pp. 552–561. ACM, New York (2007)

Fault Trees

Advancing Dynamic Fault Tree Analysis - Get Succinct State Spaces Fast and Synthesise Failure Rates

Matthias Volk[(✉)], Sebastian Junges, and Joost-Pieter Katoen

Software Modeling and Verification, RWTH Aachen University, Aachen, Germany
`matthias.volk@cs.rwth-aachen.de`

Abstract. This paper presents a new state space generation approach for dynamic fault trees (DFTs) together with a technique to synthesise allowed failures rates in DFTs. Our state space generation technique aggressively exploits the DFT structure — detecting symmetries, spurious non-determinism, and don't cares. Benchmarks show a gain of more than two orders of magnitude in terms of state space generation and analysis time. Our approach supports DFTs with symbolic failure rates and is complemented by parameter synthesis. This enables determining the maximal tolerable failure rate of a system component while ensuring that the mean time of failure stays below a threshold.

1 Introduction

Fault tree analysis is a prominent technique in reliability engineering. Dynamic fault trees (DFTs) [1,2] are an expressive model catering for common dependability patterns, such as spare management, functional dependencies, and sequencing. The *state space generation* process is one of the main bottlenecks in DFT analysis. DFT analysis mainly focuses on the mean time to failure — what is the expected time of the failure? — and reliability — how likely is the system operational up to time t? These analyses require DFTs where all component failure rates are known. In practice, this rarely holds. Thus, a relevant question is to *synthesise* the allowed component failure rates ensuring a given mean time.

This paper presents three main advances to state-of-the-art DFT analysis: (1) fast generation of succinct state spaces, (2) the analysis of several measures-of-interest that go beyond mean time and reliability, and (3) the synthesis of (possibly partially) unknown failure rates in DFTs for mean time and more.

Fast Generation of Succinct State Spaces. Our approach is a modern version of one of the first DFT semantics [3] as used in the `Galileo` tool [4] that caters for possible *non-determinism*, as in [5]. In all these approaches, a state space, i.e., a Markov model, is built. This leads to a precise representation of the DFT and allows for off-the-shelf analysis tools. The major drawback is the typically huge state space involved – which has lead to some state-space

© Springer International Publishing Switzerland 2016
A. Skavhaug et al. (Eds.): SAFECOMP 2016, LNCS 9922, pp. 253–265, 2016.
DOI: 10.1007/978-3-319-45477-1_20

free approximation techniques, an overview is given in [6]. To obtain succinct
state spaces, we tailor two successful techniques from the field of model checking — symmetry reduction [7] and partial-order reduction [8, Chap. 8] — to
DFTs, and combine this with don't care detection. We *aggressively exploit the
DFT structure*: detect symmetries, i.e., isomorphic sub-DFTs and stochastic
independencies while pruning sub-DFTs that become obsolete (don't care) after
the occurrence of some faults. This is combined with *detecting superfluous non-
determinism* such that certain failure orderings are irrelevant yielding a simpler
and cheaper analysis.

Beyond Reliability and Availability. By exploiting powerful state-of-the-art
quantitative model checking techniques [8, Chap. 10] we support a broad range of
measures-of-interest. This includes reliability and mean time to failure (MTTF),
the probability to reach a certain DFT configuration e.g., where certain subDFTs
have failed and others have not, conditional MTTF — what is the MTTF given
that certain DFT elements failed? — and the variance of the time to failure.

Failure Rate Synthesis. We support DFTs whose failure rates are (possibly partially) unknown. These unknown (or: symbolic) rates are represented by
parameters, or functions thereof; e.g., components may fail with rate λ, 2λ, etc.,
where λ is unknown. Our slim state space generation techniques support symbolic rates. We complement this by a sound and complete technique to *synthesise*
all values of symbolic rates that ensure the MTTF (and various other measures)
to be below a given threshold. To the best of our knowledge, this is the first failure rate synthesis technique for DFTs. In addition, the *sensitivity* of the MTTF
on the symbolic rates can be determined, as in alternative techniques [9].

Experimentation. We have realised a prototypical implementation of the
aforementioned techniques. In addition to the original DFT elements in `Galileo`,
we support probabilistic dependencies [10], nested spares [5] and priority or-
gates [11]. Experiments have been conducted on all benchmark DFTs from [12];
a rich collection of DFTs gathered from the literature and from industrial case
studies. The experiments reveal that our slim state space generation technique
significantly outperforms the best competitor for DFTs, the tool `DFTCalc` [13].
For a majority of the benchmarks, our approach yields a speed-up of two to
four orders of magnitude. Failure rate synthesis works for the moderately-sized
models in the literature (up to 20 basic events) with up to three unknown rates.

2   Dynamic Fault Trees

Fault trees (FTs) are directed acyclic graphs with typed nodes. The leaves, i.e.,
nodes without successors (or: *children*), are *basic events* (BEs). All other nodes
are *gates*. The *top event* (or: root) is a specifically identified node. An FT fails,
if its top event fails. For the sake of simplicity, we assume that BEs represent

(a) BE (b) VOT$_k$ (c) OR (d) AND (e) PAND (f) POR (g) PDEP (h) SEQ (i) SPARE

Fig. 1. Node types in ((a)–(d)) static and (all) dynamic fault trees.

component failures. Initially, every BE is *operational*; it *fails* if the event occurs. A gate fails if its *failure condition* over its children is fulfilled. The key gate for static fault trees (SFTs) is the *voting* gate (denoted VOT$_k$) with *threshold k*. The failure condition for a node x of type VOT$_k$ is given by "x fails, if k of its children have failed". A VOT$_1$ gate equals an OR-gate, while a VOT$_k$ with k children equals an AND-gate. These gates are shown in Fig. 1(b)–(d).

2.1   Dynamic Nodes

To overcome the limitations [6] of SFTs, several extensions commonly referred to as *Dynamic Fault Trees* (DFTs) have been introduced. A main feature of these extensions is that they feature an internal state, e.g., the order in which events fail influences the internal state, and thus whether the top event has failed. The extensions introduce several new node types; we categorise them as *priority gates*, *dependencies*, *restrictions*, and *spare gates*.

Priority Gates. Priority gates extend static gates by imposing a condition on the ordering of failing children. A *priority-and* (PAND) node fails if all its children have failed in the order from left to right. Figure 2(a) depicts a PAND with children A and B. It fails if A fails first and then (or simultaneously) B fails. If B fails first, the PAND becomes *fail-safe*. The *priority-or* (POR) node [11] only fails if the left-most child fails before any of the other children does. Priority-gates allow for order dependent failure propagation.

Dependencies. Dependencies do not propagate a fault to their parents but are triggered by their first child. Upon triggering, they affect some BEs, the dependent events. We consider *probabilistic dependencies* (PDEPs) [10]. Once the trigger of a PDEP fails, its dependent events fail with probability p. Figure 2(b) shows a PDEP where the failure of trigger A causes a failure of BE B with probability 0.8 (provided it has not failed before). *Functional dependencies* (FDEPs) are PDEPs with probability one.

Restrictions. Restrictions do not propagate failures but rather limit possible failure propagations. *Sequence enforcers* (SEQs) assure that their children only fail from left to right. This differs from priority-gates that do not prevent certain orderings, but only propagate if an ordering is met. The DFT in Fig. 2(c) fails if A and B have failed (in any order) but the SEQ enforces that A fails prior to B. This DFT is never fail-safe.

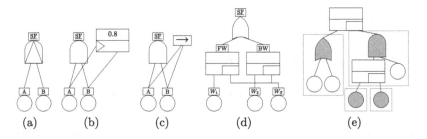

Fig. 2. Simple examples of dynamic nodes.

Spare Gates. Spare-gates (SPAREs) are the most complex gates in DFTs. Consider the DFT in Fig. 2(d) modelling (part of) a motor bike with a spare wheel. If either wheel fails, the motor bike fails. Both wheels can be replaced by the spare wheel but not both. The spare wheel is less likely to fail as long as it isn't used (warm). Assume the front wheel fails. The spare wheel is available and used, and its failure rate is increased (hot). If any other wheel fails, then no spare wheels are available anymore, and the SPARE and the DFT fails.

SPAREs have a child they use. If this child fails, the SPARE tries to use a spare child (left to right) — a process we call *claiming*. Only operational children that are not used by another SPARE can be claimed. If claiming fails, the SPARE fails. This behaviour is extended by an *activation mechanism*. As in [5], SPAREs may have (independent) subDFTs as children. This includes nested SPAREs. A *spare module* is a set of nodes linked to a child of a SPARE via a path without an intermediate SPARE. Every leaf of a spare module is either a BE or a SPARE. Each child of a SPARE thus represents a spare module, cf. Fig. 2(e) where boxes are spare modules and shaded nodes are the representatives. SPAREs which are not nested are *active*. For each active SPARE, all nodes in the spare module of the used child are also active. BEs which are active fail with their active failure rate, BEs which are passive fail with their passive failure rate (warm events) or cannot fail (cold events). More details can be found in [6].

2.2 Syntactic Restrictions

We are rather liberal w.r.t. dynamic gates, but have to impose syntactic restrictions as in [13] to exclude DFTs with undefined behaviour. These restrictions are: (a) VOT_k have at least k children; (b) the top level event is a gate or a BE; PDEPs and restrictions have no parents; (d) all dependent events are BEs; (e) spare modules, i.e., subDFTs under a SPARE, do not overlap; (f) primary spare modules are not shared between SPAREs.

3   State Space Generation

The goal for our state space generation is to produce a Markov model which is subject to further analysis. As operational model, we use *Markov Automata*.

3.1   Markov Automata

Markov Automata (MA) [14] extend continuous-time Markov chains (CTMCs) with non-determinism. MA are state transition systems whose transitions between states are either labeled with rates (i.e., non-negative real numbers), or with actions. The former transitions specify a random delay and correspond to the failures in DFTs; the latter are used to select the handling of a triggered PDEP. Delay transitions relate a source state with a target state; action transitions relate a state to a probability distribution over states. An action transition thus yields a new state with a given likelihood. MA are a slight variant of the operational model for DFTs used in [5]; they differ in allowing discrete probabilistic branching which are used to model PDEPs. We introduce MAs by example.

Figure 3 shows an MA for a coffee machine, used by inhabitants of room A (IoA) and B (IoB). IoA (IoB) arrive at the machine at a rate of 5 IoA/hour (3 IoB/hour). They can either have coffee or espresso. All IoA want espresso (action we), while IoB non-deterministically want coffee (action wc) or espresso. IoB wanting espresso are with probability 0.1 too sleepy and select coffee. Users always get their selected product (ge, gc). In state s_0, either an IoA or an IoB arrives at the machine (evolving into s_1, s_2). In state s_1 espresso is selected, whereas in s_2 a choice between actions we and wc is made. Selecting we in s_2 results in s_3 with probability 0.9 and in s_4 with probability 0.1. The user then gets the product and the automaton returns to initial s_0. For simplicity, the products' preparation time is not modelled.

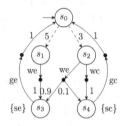

Fig. 3. Example MA.

3.2   State Space Generation

As in Galileo, we construct a *fault tree automaton* (FTAut) from a DFT. We then translate the FTAut to an MA, which we further simplify and analyse. The FTAut consists of states and labelled transitions.

States. We give each node in the DFT a unique id. A state in the FTAut is a mapping from ids to its status: *operational* (OP), *failed* (F), *fail-safe* (FS), or *don't care* (X). Additionally, we store the *currently used child* (CUC) of operational SPAREs and for spare module representatives their *activity*, i.e. whether the module is active (A) or passive (P). We initialise all nodes as operational, the CUCs and activate modules as described in Sect. 2.

Transitions. State changes originate from the failure of BEs. As the probability of two rate-governed BEs to fail simultaneously is zero, BEs never fail simultaneously. When considering dependencies, this assumption no longer has to hold. To avoid problems with causalities as described in [6], and to directly resolve spare

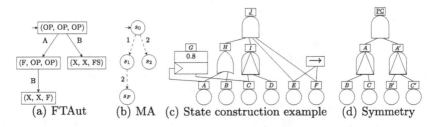

(a) FTAut   (b) MA   (c) State construction example   (d) Symmetry

Fig. 4. Dedicated examples.

races [6], we assume that dependent events fail immediately after the triggering BE. W.l.o.g. we assume that PDEPs have a single dependent event.

Given a source state and an operational BE x that fails, we copy the source state and additionally mark x with F, and compute the target state. In a bottom-up fashion, we iterate over the gates. For each gate, we check the failure condition. If the failure condition holds, we mark the gate as failed. If a CUC of a SPARE fails, we iterate over its remaining children and check whether they are not listed as the CUC of any of their parents and whether they are still operational. If so, we update the CUC, otherwise, we mark the SPARE as failed. We iterate over all restrictions, and check whether any of their failure conditions hold; if so, we skip the transition at hand. We then reiterate over all gates, and check if the fail-safe condition holds (i.e. if it cannot fail in the future), we mark the gate FS. We then iterate top-down over all nodes. If all parents of a node are either failed or fail-safe, we mark the node as don't care (DC-propagation).

Example 1. The FTAut of the DFT in Fig. 2(a) is given in Fig. 4(a). Initially, all nodes are operational. If B initially fails, the PAND becomes fail-safe, and thus A and B both become don't care. The resulting state is (X, X, FS). If A however initially fails, B and the PAND remain operational. An additional failure of B then causes the top event to fail. DC-propagation yields the state (X, X, F).

Now consider Fig. 4(c). Initially, every node is operational. A's failure causes H to fail and makes B don't care. This yields a transition from the initial state to state (F, X, OP, OP, OP, OP, OP, F, OP, OP). In this state, the PDEP is triggered, yielding a state (with probability 0.8) in which C failed, and the same state (with probability 0.2) as C does not fail. A failure of D in the initial state does not trigger a failure of the PAND I; in fact I becomes fail-safe, and this is propagated to J, i.e., DC-propagation marks all children (and their children) X. This together yields a transition from the initial state to a state in which all nodes are marked X. Finally, from the initial state, propagating a failure of node F is discarded as the restriction fails (by F failing before E.)

The initial state for nodes $(W_1, W_2, W_S, \text{FW}, \text{BW}, \text{SF})$ in Fig. 2(d) is (OP, OP, OP, W_1, W_2, OP) where W_1, W_2 are the CUCs and as initially the CUCs are active, the activity for W_1, W_2, W_S is given as (A, A, P). A failure of W_1 is propagated to FW. As its CUC fails, it checks further children. W_S is operational and not a CUC, therefore, the resulting state is (F, OP, OP, W_S, W_2, OP) and

(A, A, A). From that state, W_2's failure yields (F, F, OP, W_S, F, F) after failure propagation, as the only remaining child of BW is already claimed. DC-propagation yields the state (F, X, OP, W_S, X, F) and (A, A, A).

As rate-governed transitions have probability 0 to fire at time 0, we either have immediate transitions or rate transitions. Thus, for each state, we check if any PDEPs are triggered. If so, we mark the state as *immediate* and add two outgoing transitions for each triggered PDEP: One where the PDEP transmits the failure and one where it doesn't. Otherwise, we mark the state as *Markovian*, and add transitions for each BE which has (in the given state) a failure rate $\neq 0$.

Translation. The translation from the FTAut to the MA is straightforward, cf. Fig. 4(b). The state spaces of the FTAut and the MA are equal. Each MA state is labeled with the status of the DFT nodes. For Markovian states, each transition labelled with a BE x is translated into a delay transition with the failure rate of x as its rate. For BEs in passive spare modules, we take their passive failure rate. Each immediate state has a non-deterministic choice over triggered PDEPs in the DFT. Each PDEP leads to a probabilistic branching, where with probability p the PDEP propagates the failure, whereas with $1-p$ it does not.

3.3   Optimisations

Technical Aspects. We use a selection of well-known techniques to reduce the overhead of propagation: The states are encoded as bit-vectors, and during exploration, we use an expanded state representation. By exploiting depth-first search, we keep the set of states that we explore later on small. Work lists keep only track of the nodes we need to consider. Overriding failed and fail-safe nodes by don't care, we merge states which differ only in their past behaviour, but not in their future behaviour. Afterwards, the state space is reduced by bisimulation.

Partial-Order Reduction. In many DFTs, the actual order in which subsets of BEs fail is not crucial. We exploit this for dependencies, where — instead of exploring all interleavings over the triggered events — we aim to only explore a single order. We adapt a technique called (static) *partial order reduction* [8] to DFTs. Based on a static analysis, we identify which dependencies can be executed in arbitrary order, and expand only a canonical order.

State Elimination. In MA, we can eliminate probabilistic branching by adopting a *state elimination* technique as used in [15]. In particular, this allows us to reduce MA without non-deterministic branching to CTMCs, which can be analysed much faster as non-determinism is absent.

Modularisation. The use of modularisation in FTs has been proposed in [16]. It identifies independent subtrees in the DFT, analyses them separately, and combines the results to a final result. If applicable, it is extremely powerful.

Symmetry Reduction. Many parts in DFTs are symmetric. This can be exploited (cf. [7]) as follows. Given a successfully detected symmetry, we use the fact that a fault has an analogous effect in symmetric parts. Moreover for isolated symmetric parts, if the node identities are not used in the analysis and the parts are only connected to the remaining DFT via the same node, we *exchange* the states of the parts, and thus assume that a fault in a symmetric part happened in an equivalent DFT. In the DFT in Fig. 4(d), we find two symmetric parts (the subtrees of A and A'), which are independent. If we are only interested in the top level, we can use the exchange technique. That is, if both symmetric parts are in equivalent states (e.g., the initial state) and A' fails, we assume that A failed instead. Now, the two parts are not in an equivalent state. However, after the additional failure of A', the two parts are in an equivalent state again.

4   Measures of Interest

Several quantitative measures can be determined on the generated state space.

Measures and Importance Factors. Various measures are based on the *reliability function*, the cdf for the probability of a failure after a given time t. Another prominent measure is the *mean time to failure* (MTTF), the expected time until a system failure. The *variance* of the time to failure (VTTF) is obtained by $\mathrm{Var}(X) = E[X^2] - E[X]^2$ for random variable X, the time to failure. The *probability of failure* considers the limit probability of the reliability function for t to ∞. This is of interest as in DFTs not all events fail eventually, cf. Fig. 2(a). These measures can be used for single events in the DFT, and also for Boolean combinations of failed and operational gates, such as e.g., the expected time to a DFT state where events A and C have failed. Another measure-of-interest is the *expected number of faults before the DFT fails*; if this is high, it indicates that are various possibilities to take countermeasures. The *Fussell-Vesely importance factor* is the probability that a BE has failed when the DFT fails [17]. An exemplary *criticality importance factor* is the probability that a BE causes the DFT to fail. The measures above are analysed using efficient algorithms to verify temporal properties on CTMCs [18] or MA [19].

Conditional Measures. All measures except $R_F(t)$ can be conditioned on the occurrence of events, cf. the first column of Table 1. For example, as $\mathrm{Pr}_F \neq 1$ for some fault trees, the MTTF is not always defined. For this case a reasonable alternative is to condition the MTTF, assuming the DFT eventually fails.

Measure Preservation Under Optimisations. Techniques such as modularisation, DC-propagation and symmetry reduction are not applicable to all measures. Their robustness w.r.t. the measures is indicated in the last columns of Table 1, where * means support of a light version. Modularisation is powerful

Table 1. Supported measures and importance factors

Symbol	Name	Cond.	Par.syn.	Mod.	dc.	Sym.red
$R_F(t)$	Reliability at t	✗	✗	✓	✓	✓
Pr_F	Probability of failure	✓	✓	✓	✓	✓
MTTF_F	Mean time to failure	✓	✓	✗	✓	✓
VTTF_F	Variance of time to failure	✓	✓	✗	✓	✓
	Expected faults before failure	✓	✓	✗	✗	✓
	FV importance factor	✓	✓	✗	✗	*
	Criticality importance factor	✓	✓	✗	✓	*

if a partial state space suffices, e.g., if the measure is compositional –meaning that the measure can be obtained from its subDFTs' measures. This holds e.g., for reliability but not for MTTF. Symmetry reduction requires a lack of identity (of DFT nodes), which does not hold for some measures, including many conditional statements. If the lack of identity is not given, only a light version is applicable.

5   Parameter Synthesis

Problem. The analysis discussed so far has two drawbacks: It requires all failure rates in the DFT to be given and does not guarantee any robustness w.r.t. perturbations. The latter has been addressed by *sensitivity analysis* [9]. These deficiencies inspired us to treat *symbolic* failure rates, i.e. DFTs where failure rates and propagation probabilities in PDEPs are given as polynomials over a set of parameters (pDFTs). Our state space construction technique is largely unaffected by this. Our focus is on the failure rate synthesis in DFTs for any measure in Table 1, second column, i.e., *determine all values (of the symbolic rates) such that the DFT satisfies a given desired threshold on a measure.* For simplicity, we focus on DFTs that (after our reductions) obey no non-determinism, which applies to the vast majority of the DFTs in the literature. Thus, the underlying state space of pDFTs can be reduced to a *parametric* CTMC, i.e. a CTMC whose rates are polynomials over the DFT parameters.

Approach. To enable the synthesis in pDFTs we exploit the parameter synthesis tool PROPhESY [20]. Based on ideas in [15], it computes a closed form (precisely: a rational function) for a parametric CTMC and the measure of interest. To enable sensitivity analysis, it provides the derivative w.r.t. the parameters. On top of obtaining these functions, PROPhESY allows for parameter space partitioning — using satisfiability-modulo-theory (SMT) techniques for non-linear arithmetic. That is, given a pDFT, we can synthesise for which parameter values the measure (e.g., MTTF) is above a threshold. An example output is depicted

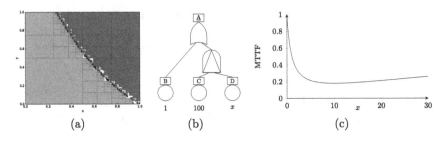

Fig. 5. (a) Sample output, (b) a sample parametric DFT, and (c) its MTTF. (Color figure online)

in Fig. 5(a). This plot was obtained for the DFT of Fig. 2(d) where W_1, W_2 and W_S have failure rates x, 1 and y respectively for unknown x, y.

The green boxes represent areas in which *all* failure rates of W_1 and W_S give rise to an MTTF that exceeds 1.5, while the red boxes guarantee *all* rates yield an MTTF below 1.5. For the white areas, none of the above statements can be made. Note that this output is extremely valuable as it provides information about many (in fact uncountably many) failure rate combinations for which the MTTF is below or above the threshold. We like to point out that obtaining this information is far from trivial, and intrinsically more involved than analysing a DFT where all failure rates are given. Consider the small example DFT from Fig. 5(b), where D has a symbolic failure rate. The MTTF of the DFT is given by the plot in Fig. 5(c). As the MTTF is not monotonic, the parameter synthesis is not straightforward.

6   Experiments

Set-Up. To evaluate our approach, we tested the performance of our tool on reliability and the MTTF assessment. We compare with the state-of-the-art tool DFTCalc [13] and assess the effect of our abstraction techniques. The experiments were conducted on an HP BL685C G7 restricted to 8 GB RAM and used a single 2.0 GHz core and a time-out of 1 h. We use the benchmark suite from [12]. Besides the smaller HCAS and SAP sets, it contains the following benchmarks:

HECS. The *Hypothetical Example Computer System (HECS)* stems from the NASA handbook on FTs [2]. It features a computer system consisting of a processor, a memory unit (MU) and an interface consisting of hard- and software.

MCS. The *Multiprocessor Computing System (MCS)* contains computing modules consisting of a processor, a MU and two disks, the DFT was given in [10].

RC. The *Railway Crossing (RC)* is an industrial case modelling a level crossing which fails whenever any of the sensor-sets, barriers or controller fail [21].

SF. The *Sensor Filter (SF)* benchmark is a DFT that is automatically generated from an AADL (Architecture Analysis & Design Language) system model [22].

We used the simplified DFTs as produced in [12], as this is shown to be beneficial for DFTCalc. For each instance, we tested reliability for $t = 100$ and the MTTF. Further features were tested on a range of > 100 crafted instances.

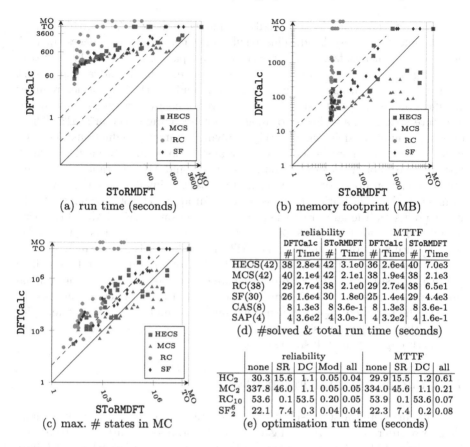

(a) run time (seconds)

(b) memory footprint (MB)

(c) max. # states in MC

	reliability		MTTF	
	DFTCalc	SToRMDFT	DFTCalc	SToRMDFT
	#	Time	#	Time	#	Time	#	Time
HECS(42)	38	2.8e4	42	3.1e0	36	2.6e4	40	7.0e3
MCS(42)	40	2.1e4	42	2.1e1	38	1.9e4	38	2.1e3
RC(38)	29	2.7e4	38	2.1e0	29	2.7e4	38	6.5e1
SF(30)	26	1.6e4	30	1.8e0	25	1.4e4	29	4.4e3
CAS(8)	8	1.3e3	8	3.6e-1	8	1.3e3	8	3.6e-1
SAP(4)	4	3.6e2	4	3.0e-1	4	3.2e2	4	1.6e-1

(d) #solved & total run time (seconds)

	reliability				MTTF			
	none	SR	DC	Mod	all	none	SR	DC	all
HC_2	30.3	15.6	1.1	0.05	0.04	29.9	15.5	1.2	0.61
MC_2	337.8	46.0	1.1	0.05	0.05	334.0	45.6	1.1	0.21
RC_{10}	53.6	0.1	53.5	0.20	0.05	53.9	0.1	53.6	0.07
SF_2^6	22.1	7.4	0.3	0.04	0.04	22.3	7.4	0.2	0.08

(e) optimisation run time (seconds)

Fig. 6. Overview of the experimental results on four different benchmark sets.

Results. Figures 6(a-c) compare the performance of our tool (referred to as SToRMDFT) with DFTCalc on MTTF (where modularisation is not applicable). All plots use a log-log-scale. Figure 6(a) presents the analysis time of a DFT. This includes state space generation. The lower dashed line indicates an advantage of our tool by a factor ten, the upper of a factor 100. The outer lines indicate TOs and MOs, respectively. Figure 6(b) indicates the peak memory consumption as given by the operating system. Figure 6(c) shows the peak intermediate state size. Figure 6(d) summarises the performance on the benchmark sets — it lists the number of benchmarks solved and the cumulative time needed for the solved benchmarks. Figure 6(e) shows the effect of the individual optimisation techniques (symmetry reduction, DC-propagation, modularisation) versus using all of them.

Observations. For non-parametric DFTs the performance is dominated by the state space construction. SToRMDFT creates intermediate state spaces that are often ten times smaller; especially for moderately-sized DFTs, this is done with a much lower overhead. This results in generating state spaces up to 5 orders of magnitudes faster. The informed state space generation allows to stop exploring states where the measure of interest is settled. This advantage is best observed by comparing top events typed OR and AND. The former requires significantly smaller state spaces, which is reflected by the smaller intermediate state spaces — and leads to a significant advantage over DFTCalc. These effects are multiplied by aggressively applying symmetry reductions and DC-propagation. For many benchmarks, our abstractions directly yield the small bisimulation quotient. However, on some HECS and MCS instances, our symmetry reduction does not yet suffice and DFTCalc gains an advantage in terms of memory. Modularisation remains a powerful approach for assessing reliability. It profits additionally from the performance on small DFTs. Model-checking for reliability is for both SToRMDFT and DFTCalc so fast that our slightly better performance is hardly significant. For MTTF, SToRMDFT is significantly faster.

For parametric instances, the original DFTs from literature can be handled: For, e.g., the standard HECS from literature it takes 5 s to compute the rational function with more than 400 terms in the numerator. Parameter synthesis for 90 % of the parameter space finishes within four minutes. However, scalability beyond these moderately-sized DFTs remains an open issue, as the parameters appear throughout the full state space.

7   Conclusions and Future Work

We have presented a state space generation technique for DFTs that is more than two orders of magnitude faster than the state-of-the-art. The technique is complemented with a new feature in DFT analysis — the synthesis of failure rates for measures such as MTTF. Future work includes the failure rate synthesis for reliability (e.g., using [23]) and improve scalability for parameterised MTTF.

Acknowledgement. We thank Christian Dehnert for fruitful discussions. This work was supported by the Excellence Initiative of the German federal and state government, the CDZ project CAP (GZ 1023), and the BMBF project HODRIAN.

References

1. Dugan, J.B., Bavuso, S.J., Boyd, M.: Fault trees and sequence dependencies. In: Proceedings of RAMS, pp. 286–293 (1990)
2. Stamatelatos, M., Vesely, W., Dugan, J.B., Fragola, J., Minarick, J., Railsback, J.: Fault Tree Handbook with Aerospace Applications. NASA Headquarters, Washington, D.C. (2002)
3. Coppit, D., Sullivan, K.J., Dugan, J.B.: Formal semantics of models for computational engineering: a case study on dynamic fault trees. In: Proceedings of ISSRE, pp. 270–282 (2000)
4. Sullivan, K., Dugan, J.B., Coppit, D.: The Galileo fault tree analysis tool. In: Proceedings of FTCS, pp. 232–235 (1999)

5. Boudali, H., Crouzen, P., Stoelinga, M.I.A.: A rigorous, compositional, and extensible framework for dynamic fault tree analysis. IEEE Trans. Dependable Secure Comput. **7**(2), 128–143 (2010)

6. Junges, S., Guck, D., Katoen, J.P., Stoelinga, M.: Uncovering dynamic fault trees. In: Proceedings of DSN (2016, to appear)

7. Clarke, E.M., Emerson, E.A., Jha, S., Sistla, A.P.: Symmetry reductions in model checking. In: Hu, A.J., Vardi, M.Y. (eds.) CAV 1998. LNCS, vol. 1427, pp. 147–158. Springer, Heidelberg (1998)

8. Baier, C., Katoen, J.P.: Principles of Model Checking. MIT Press, Cambridge (2008)

9. Ou, Y., Dugan, J.B.: Sensitivity analysis of modular dynamic fault trees. In: Proceedings of IPDS, pp. 35–43 (2000)

10. Montani, S., Portinale, L., Bobbio, A., Codetta-Raiteri, D.: Automatically translating dynamic fault trees into dynamic Bayesian networks by means of a software tool. In: Proceedings of ARES, pp. 804–809 (2006)

11. Walker, M., Papadopoulos, Y.: Qualitative temporal analysis: towards a full implementation of the Fault Tree Handbook. Control Eng. Pract. **17**(10), 1115–1125 (2009)

12. Junges, S., Guck, D., Katoen, J.P., Rensink, A., Stoelinga, M.: Fault trees on a diet - automated reduction by graph rewriting. In: Li, X., Liu, Z., Yi, W. (eds.) SETTA 2015. LNCS, vol. 9409, pp. 3–18. Springer, Heidelberg (2015)

13. Arnold, F., Belinfante, A., Van der Berg, F., Guck, D., Stoelinga, M.: DFTCALC: a tool for efficient fault tree analysis. In: Bitsch, F., Guiochet, J., Kaâniche, M. (eds.) SAFECOMP. LNCS, vol. 8153, pp. 293–301. Springer, Heidelberg (2013)

14. Eisentraut, C., Hermanns, H., Zhang, L.: On probabilistic automata in continuous time. In: Proc. of LICS, pp. 342–351. IEEE Computer Society (2010)

15. Daws, C.: Symbolic and parametric model checking of discrete-time Markov chains. In: Liu, Z., Araki, K. (eds.) ICTAC 2004. LNCS, vol. 3407, pp. 280–294. Springer, Heidelberg (2005)

16. Gulati, R., Dugan, J.B.: A modular approach for analyzing static and dynamic fault trees. In: Proceedings of RAMS, pp. 57–63 (1997)

17. Ruijters, E., Stoelinga, M.: Fault tree analysis: a survey of the state-of-the-art in modeling, analysis and tools. Comput. Sci. Rev. **15–16**, 29–62 (2015)

18. Baier, C., Haverkort, B.R., Hermanns, H., Katoen, J.P.: Model-checking algorithms for continuous-time Markov chains. IEEE Trans. Softw. Eng. **29**(6), 524–541 (2003)

19. Guck, D., Hatefi, H., Hermanns, H., Katoen, J.P., Timmer, M.: Analysis of timed and long-run objectives for Markov automata. LMCS **10**(3), 17 (2014)

20. Dehnert, C., Junges, S., Jansen, N., Corzilius, F., Volk, M., Bruintjes, H., Katoen, J.-P., Ábrahám, E.: PROPhESY: a PRObabilistic ParamEter SYnthesis tool. In: Kroening, D., Păsăreanu, C.S. (eds.) CAV 2015. LNCS, vol. 9206, pp. 214–231. Springer, Heidelberg (2015)

21. Guck, D., Katoen, J.P., Stoelinga, M., Luiten, T., Romijn, J.: Smart railroad maintenance engineering with stochastic model checking. In: Proceedings of RAILWAYS, Civil-Comp Proceedings, Civil-Comp Press, vol. 104, pp. 299–314 (2014)

22. Bozzano, M., Cimatti, A., Katoen, J.P., Nguyen, V.Y., Noll, T., Roveri, M.: Safety, dependability and performance analysis of extended AADL models. Comput. J. **54**, 754–775 (2011)

23. Češka, M., Dannenberg, F., Kwiatkowska, M., Paoletti, N.: Precise parameter synthesis for stochastic biochemical systems. In: Mendes, P., Dada, J.O., Smallbone, K. (eds.) CMSB 2014. LNCS, vol. 8859, pp. 86–98. Springer, Heidelberg (2014)

Effective Static and Dynamic Fault Tree Analysis

Ola Bäckström[1], Yuliya Butkova[2(✉)], Holger Hermanns[2], Jan Krčál[2],
and Pavel Krčál[1(✉)]

[1] Lloyd's Register Consulting, Stockholm, Sweden
Pavel.Krcal@lr.org
[2] Computer Science, Saarland University, Saarbrücken, Germany
{butkova,hermanns}@cs.uni-saarland.de

Abstract. Fault trees constitute one of the essential formalisms for static safety analysis of various industrial systems. Dynamic fault trees (DFT) enrich the formalism by support for time-dependent behaviour, e.g., repairs or dynamic dependencies. This enables more realistic and more precise modelling, and can thereby avoid overly pessimistic analysis results. But analysis of DFT is so far limited to substantially smaller models than those required for instance in the domain of nuclear power safety. This paper considers so called *SD fault trees*, where the user is free to express each equipment failure either statically, without modelling temporal information, or dynamically, allowing repairs and other timed interdependencies. We introduce an analysis algorithm for an important subclass of SD fault trees. The algorithm employs automatic abstraction techniques effectively, and thereby scales similarly to static analysis algorithms, albeit allowing for a more realistic modelling and analysis. We demonstrate the applicability of the method by an experimental evaluation on fault trees of nuclear power plants.

1 Introduction

Fault trees are a very prominent formalism for inductive failure modelling. They underly safety assessments in a wide spectrum of technical systems, ranging from nuclear power production [9,17], over chemical and process industry [7] to automotive and aerospace [14] systems.

A fault tree decomposes the failure potential of a complete system into failures of its subcomponents, sub-sub-components, and sub-sub-subcomponents, up to the level of so-called *basic events*. The latter represent individual equipments, atomic external events, operator errors, etc. These are assumed to be quantifiable wrt. estimates of failure frequencies or probabilities, achieved by statistical methods from operation history or simulations or even by engineering computations. Originally, fault trees describe a static view on a system, we thus call them static fault trees (SFTs). Static fault trees pair simplicity in modelling with efficiency in analysis techniques.

A particularly effective analysis technique characterises all fault combinations leading to the complete failure of an SFT, and returns their minimal-sized

© Springer International Publishing Switzerland 2016
A. Skavhaug et al. (Eds.): SAFECOMP 2016, LNCS 9922, pp. 266–280, 2016.
DOI: 10.1007/978-3-319-45477-1_21

representation, in the form of so called *minimal cutsets*. Even though the number of minimal cutsets can be exponential in the number of basic events, it is possible to appropriately employ the cutoff on low probability cutsets to reduce the size of the problem. This minimal cutset analysis is in daily use for instance in the safety analyses of nuclear power plants [9,17], where SFTs with several thousands of basic events are routinely processed, supported by tools such as SAPHIRE [18] or RISKSPECTRUM [13].

It has been argued [2–4,11,14] that the static system view supported by SFTs is often very rough (though conservative), in the sense that a more precise analysis is possible if the fault tree formalism provides support for representation and analysis of the changes in state of the system in operation. In the nuclear safety domain, this means that the dynamics of an accident and possible countermeasures can be detailed. The promised gain in precision is of industrial relevance, for instance for analyses with longer mission time, such as probabilistic Level 2 [10] (and consequently Level 3) studies in nuclear power plants. After the Fukushima accident, the interest in analyses studying 'safe state' rather than a fixed mission time has increased. This will increase the need to properly treat long mission times also within Level 1 [9] probabilistic safety assessment.

Over the years, several kinds of dynamic fault trees have been proposed, starting with the work of Dugan [2]. However, dynamic analysis techniques need to implicitly or explicitly explore the state space spanned by the system dynamics. This space tends to be prohibitively large; often it is of exponential size, relative to the number of basic events. With previous techniques, models with more than a few hundred basic events are impossible to process. This means that these approaches cannot be directly applied to large scale industrial fault tree models such as those of nuclear power plants.

SD fault trees [11] (SD-FTs) have lately been proposed to provide a potential way forward. They extend SFTs with features to model *some* parts of the system dynamically, without the need to construct the induced state space of the entire fault tree. This means that it remains possible to utilize efficient solver technology for SFTs, and combine this with less efficient, but focused analysis for the dynamic parts. The new features can capture (1) *sequential* application of elementary safety functions and (2) *repairs* of failed components. Basic events can be considered either static or dynamic. Dynamic dependencies are expressed via a triggering mechanism, whereby a safety function failure may *activate* other safety functions and failed components can be repaired (and thus continue to perform their function).

In this paper, we build on the SD-FT concept. We attack the problem that the focused analysis needed for the dynamic parts may still suffer from state space explosion, exponential in the amount of dynamic basic events. Indeed, the algorithm originally developed for the SD-FT formalism [11] is efficient only if restricting the triggering logic severely in expressiveness. This is rooted in the fact that the algorithm calculates the dynamic failure probability exactly, which in turn requires considering all possible accident progression scenarios, including consecutive failures and repairs of components. This becomes quickly infeasible for increasingly intricate triggering patterns induced by a richer triggering logic.

However, our analysis of real-life safety analysis models has made apparent that most of these scenarios turn out to be rather unrealistic. This is reflected by their relatively low probability compared to a few dominating simple scenarios. The present paper exploits this observation to leap to a generally applicable method. The crux of this leap lies in abstracting away from unrealistic event sequences in a controlled manner. This allows us to obtain an over- and under-approximation, safely bounding the exact value. As a result, the present work lifts the triggering restrictions in their entirety, enabling efficient analysis of SD-FTs with arbitrary triggering logic. We present this approach on a mildly restricted subclass of SD-FTs that limits the shape of dynamic basic events, in contrast to restrictions on the triggering logic.

As we will demonstrate by means of several examples, the resulting method scales very well to industrial-size systems, even from the nuclear power domain, and with high precision guarantees. The restrictions we need to impose on SD-FTs do not affect their adequacy for the application context as they cover all standardly used reliability models of basic events.

2   Static and Dynamic Fault Trees

We focus our work on a class of *static and dynamic (SD) fault trees*, introduced in [11]. It allows the modelling of components of the system either statically or dynamically. The behaviour of dynamic components are modelled via *continuous-time Markov chains*.

Definition 1. *A failure continuous-time Markov chain (failure CTMC, or fCTMC) is a tuple $\mathcal{C} = (S, R, \nu, F)$ where S is a finite state space, ν is the initial distribution over S, $R : S \times S \to \mathbb{R}_{\geq 0}$ is the rate matrix, and $F \subseteq S$ is the set of failed states.*

At initialisation time, the system chooses a state according to initial distribution ν. The amount of time the system spends in some state s is distributed exponentially (with the *rate* parameter of the distribution $\lambda = \sum_{s' \in S} R(s, s')$). After this delay the system moves from the current state to successor s' with probability $R(s, s') / \sum_{s'' \in S} R(s, s'')$.

The set F of states of a fCTMC $\mathcal{C}$ corresponds to failed states of a component. The complement set represents properly functioning ones. Failure of the component is modelled by transitions from functioning to failed states, and repair - from failed to functioning. An example fCTMC is depicted in Fig. 1.

The SD-FT formalism allows one to model redundant back-up components as well. Whenever a component is failed, its back-up substitute can be used by the system until the main component gets fixed. This feature is modelled with the help of *triggered CTMCs*:

Definition 2. *A triggered CTMC (tCTMC) is a fCTMC with states partitioned into $S^{off} \uplus S^{on}$ and with total functions on $: S^{off} \to S^{on}$ and off $: S^{on} \to S^{off}$. We require $F \subseteq S^{on}$ and $\{s \in S \mid \nu(s) > 0\} \subseteq S^{off}$, i.e. only an on state can be considered failed, and only at off states the system can be initialized.*

A component represented by a tCTMC can be either *switched on* or *off*. Figure 1 displays an example of a tCTMC. Dashed transitions, representing the effect of functions *on* and *off*, are called *triggering transitions*. Being currently in an *on* or *off* state, a tCTMC behaves in the same way as an fCTMC. Triggering transitions are ignored unless an external event

Fig. 1. An example fCTMC (left) and tCTMC (right). Double circles indicate F states. States *ok* (left) and off_1 (right) are initial.

arrives (e.g. failure of another component). In this case the tCTMC takes *instantaneously* the corresponding triggering *off* or *on* transition.

Definition 3 (SD fault trees [11]). *A static and dynamic fault tree (SD-FT) is a finite directed acyclic graph where its leaves are partitioned into sets B_s, called static basic events, and B_d, called dynamic basic events. Its inner nodes G are called gates where a distinguished root node is denoted g_{top}. Additionally,*

- *each gate is either of type* AND *or of type* OR,
- *each gate g has a set of dynamic basic events* trig(g) *that are triggered by g,*
- *each static basic event a is specified by its probability of failing $p(a)$,*
- *each dynamic basic event a is specified by $T(a)$ which is a tCTMC iff a is triggered by some gate, and an ordinary fCTMC, otherwise.*

SD-FT can be considered as a specific subclass of BDMPs [4], albeit at the price of dropping the distinction between static and dynamic events. In fact it is this distinction that we exploit to conquer and intertwine static and dynamic analysis steps effectively.

Without loss of generality, we assume that each dynamic basic event is triggered by at most one gate. The case of multiple triggering gates $g_1, g_2, \ldots g_k$ can be reduced to only one by adding an OR gate over

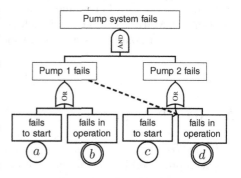

Fig. 2. An example of a SD fault tree.

$g_1, g_2, \ldots, g_k$, and making only this OR gate triggering. We also require that there are no cyclic dependencies in the triggering structure. Scenarios excluded by this requirement are exactly "deadlocks" situations where none from a group of several dynamic events can fail before all others have failed.

Example 1. Figure 2 depicts an example SD-FT. Dynamic basic events b and d are denoted by double circles, and their CTMCs are given in Fig. 1 (non-triggered for b and triggered for d). Failure of pump 1 triggers the event d from the pump 2, depicted by the dashed edge.

Behaviour of a SD-FT. At time zero each static event a either fails with probability $p(a)$ or succeeds with probability $1 - p(a)$. Dynamic events randomly choose their initial states according to their initial distributions and proceed as described above. Failures and repairs of basic events instantaneously propagate up through the SD fault tree according to the rules of Boolean logic. We call a gate *failed* or *functioning*, if the logic beneath the gate is failed or functioning. Whenever a triggering gate becomes failed, or gets repaired, it instantaneously triggers the corresponding triggered basic events, which each instantaneously take a transition labelled by *on* or *off*, respectively.

Semantics. For the formal definition of the SD-FT semantics we refer to [11]. Informally, it is given in terms of a product Markov chain $\mathcal{C}_{FT} = (S, R, \nu, \mathbf{F})$. To this end, first, each static basic event a is represented as an equivalent Markov chain. It consists of only two states *ok* and *fail*, has no transitions between them, and $\nu(fail) = p(a)$. Then, the product Markov chain is built over the product state space of all its basic events. Transitions between states occur according to parallel interleaving, i.e. only one basic event can transit at a time. The failure state set $\mathbf{F}$ of the $\mathcal{C}_{FT}$ is formed by those states in which failures of the respective components jointly induce a failure of the top gate.

Probability of Failure. We are interested in the probability of the top gate of the fault tree FT to fail within some fixed time horizon t. We will denote this value as $p(FT)$. This value corresponds to the reachability property [1] of the product Markov chain $\mathcal{C}_{FT}$, which is the probability of the Markov chain to reach the set of goal states $\mathbf{F}$ within time t. Thus

$$p(FT) = \Pr\nolimits_{\mathcal{C}_{FT}} \left[\text{Reach}^{\leqslant t} \mathbf{F} \right]$$

3   SD-FT Analysis

Existing Techniques. An effective computational method for SD-FT analysis has been proposed in [11], albeit with restrictions: The price of the computation speed is paid by severe constraints on the triggering logic. These constraints exclude, for instance, multiple dynamic basic events in different subtrees below OR gates or any occurrence of dynamic basic events in subtrees of AND gates. Furthermore, for nested triggering, they enforce that all dynamic events under a (nested) triggering gate are triggered by the same trigger. Relinquishing any of these constraints makes the algorithm not scale well. For regular industrial systems the application of this algorithm is therefore limited. However, the algorithm will be our natural reference for comparison in the experimental evaluation in Sect. 4.

A More General and More Efficient Approach. In order to successfully apply SD-FTs to real world applications we thus need a more general and more efficient approach. In this section we present a new simple and efficient algorithm for solving SD-FTs. The approach overcomes constraints on the triggering logic in their entirety. It uses abstractions so as to cope with the state space explosion problem. In doing so, it introduces a reasonable and controllable error margin, and comes at the price of mildly restricting tCTMCs appearing as triggered basic event behaviours. These restrictions are not prohibitive at all with respect to models currently used in practice. This is rooted in the lack of available statistical data. Models of basic events that are used in real world application need the data of failure and/or repair rates for a specific component. These values are gathered statistically and so far are mostly available for very simple basic events, like those depicted in Fig. 1. Due to this, designing a finer model of a basic event is in most cases not possible.

Our algorithm is built upon the ideas of static fault tree analysis and is centred around the notion of *minimal cutsets*. A set of basic events C is a *cutset* if whenever all of the basic events in C are simultaneously in a failed state then the top gate is failed as well. A cutset C is *minimal* if there is no smaller cutset contained in C. For instance, in Example 1 the set $C = \{a, b, c\}$ is a cutset, while $C = \{a, c\}$ is a minimal cutset (MCS). A *failure probability* of a cutset $p(C) :=$ $\Pr_{\mathcal{C}_{FT}}\left[\text{Reach}^{\leqslant t}\mathbf{F}(C)\right]$, where $\mathbf{F}(C)$ are those states of the product CTMC $\mathcal{C}_{FT}$ in which all events from C are failed. The set of minimal cutsets $L(FT)$ of a tree FT represents exactly the failure scenarios of a system, i.e. $\text{Reach}^{\leqslant t}\mathbf{F} = \bigcup_{C \in L(FT)} \text{Reach}^{\leqslant t}\mathbf{F}(C)$. Thus, $p(FT) = \Pr_{\mathcal{C}_{FT}}\left[\bigcup_{C \in L(FT)} \text{Reach}^{\leqslant t}\mathbf{F}(C)\right]$ and can be computed via minimal cutsets and the inclusion-exclusion principle.

Due to the scale of systems, computation of the failure probability of a fault tree becomes rarely feasible. Instead, a value called *rare event approximation* [14] *with a cutoff* is usually targeted. This quantity is defined by $p_{rea}(FT) := \sum_{p(C)>c^*} p(C)$. Here c^* is called a *cutoff* constant. In static fault tree analysis it is usually set to values in the order of 10^{-10}. We call a MCS C *relevant* if $p(C) > c^*$. Following the best practices, we as well approximate the value $p_{rea}(FT)$ rather than $p(FT)$ in our analysis.

We will introduce now a subclass of triggered CTMCs that allows efficient analysis. It mildly restricts the structure of tCTMCs without sacrificing expressiveness.

Definition 4 (Simple SD-FT). *A SD fault tree is simple if the tCTMC of each triggered dynamic basic events satisfies the following:*

- $R(s, s') > 0 \Leftrightarrow s, s' \in S^{on}$ *or* $s, s' \in S^{off}$;
- *both on ∘ off and off ∘ on are identities;*

– *the projection of the tCTMC on S^{on} (or equivalently S^{off}) has one of the shapes depicted in Fig. 3 with $k \geqslant 0$ and $l \geqslant 1$;*
– *for any two states s_{off} and s_{on}, such that $s_{off} = off(s_{on})$ (or equivalently $s_{on} = on(s_{off})$):*

$$s_{off}, s_{on} \in S \backslash F \to R(s_{off}, succ(s_{off})) \leqslant R(s_{on}, succ(s_{on}))$$
$$s_{off}, s_{on} \in F \quad \to R(s_{off}, succ(s_{off})) \geqslant R(s_{on}, succ(s_{on})),$$

i.e. the rate of failing is higher when the component is turned on, than when it is off, and, analogously, the rate of repair is lower.

This definition in particular naturally allows for models that return to a stable configuration (on repair or similar). An example of a simple SD-FT is the tCTMC depicted in Fig. 1.

Remark. The correctness of our algorithm is rooted in properties of *open Interactive Markov Chains* (oIMCs) [5]. Nowadays, oIMC analysis has scalability issues, but it might benefit from recent advances in the field of *Continuous Time Markov Decision Processes* [6]. In this way, our approach can be lifted to the general class of tCTMCs, possibly retaining its effectiveness.

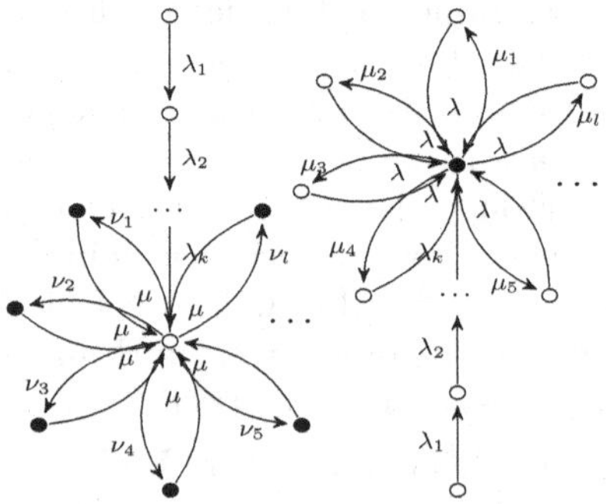

Fig. 3. Two possible shapes of CTMCs of triggered BE of a simple SD-FT. States filled with black denote failed states and the non-filled ones are functioning.

3.1 Quantification of a SD-FT

Let FT be a simple SD-FT and c^* be our cutoff constant. As mentioned before, we target the approximation of the value $p_{rea}(FT) := \sum_{p(C) > c^*} p(C)$. To quantify this value we need a list of relevant cutsets and a procedure to quantify the value $p(C)$ for each relevant cutset C. To efficiently obtain the list of relevant cutsets we can proceed in the same way as presented in [11]. To this end we use the MOCUS algorithm [8], which returns the set of relevant cutsets L_{c^*} as well as the bound ε on the error introduced by the cutoff c^*. We will thus skip this step and in the following concentrate on the algorithm to quantify each relevant cutset.

Quantification of Failure Probability of a MCS. As observed in [11], the failure probability $p(C)$ of a MCS C can be *exactly* expressed by the failure probability of a smaller SD-FT FT_C, which we will call *representative tree for* C. It is constructed as follows:

  BuildRepTree(C)
1. Add to FT_C a new top AND gate with all basic events from C as inputs.

2. To track which gates we model in FT_C, label all gates of FT as *missing*.
3. While FT_C has a basic event that is in FT triggered by a *missing* gate g:
   (a) Calculate minimal cutsets $C_1, \ldots, C_k$ of the subtree of g.
   (b) Model in FT_C the gate g by a new OR gate that has as inputs new gates $g_1, \ldots, g_k$ where each g_i is an AND gate over basic events from C_i. (In this process, copy to FT_C all the newly referred basic events.)
   (c) Label g as *not missing*.
4. Finally, having modelled all triggering gates, add to FT_C all the trigger edges, i.e. between a basic event b and gate g if g triggers b in FT.

Lemma 1. $p(C) = p(FT_C)$

In order to quantify $p(C)$ one can construct the semantical CTMC of the fault tree FT_C and apply a numerical algorithm for the reachability analysis on it [1]. However, the size of the fault tree FT_C depends on the triggering structure of FT and in the worst-case can be as large as FT, rendering the direct analysis of the semantical CTMC infeasible. For comparison, 100 dynamic basic events translates into 2^{100} states of the product CTMC, when modern tools for CTMC analysis (e.g. PRISM) can handle up to 2^{40} states at most. We will later show in the experimental evaluation section that this growth problem is not an exotic corner case, but is a real problem even for simple real world models. Our approach instead avoids the explosion by building conservative over- and under-approximations of the value $p(C)$. In this way we sacrifice precision but retain expressiveness and efficiency.

Over- and Under-Approximations of the MCS Failure Probability. We aim at decreasing the size of the state space by reducing the amount of basic events of FT_C and simplifying its triggering structure. Intuitively, we shall replace some of the dynamic basic events with trivial *static* ones, which are failed either always or never (for over- and under-approximations respectively). This will allow us to cancel out not only a number of dynamic basic events, but also some of the triggering gates completely, thereby significantly simplifying the analysis. We do so in a way that controls the error introduced by this replacement.

We need to differentiate between *immediate* and *nested* triggering gates, with respect to a cutset C. Immediate gates are those that trigger some BE from C directly, while nested gates trigger basic events indirectly through a sequence of failures and triggering of other gates. We will also introduce two new static basic events: e_{slow} with probability 0 and e_{fast} with probability 1. Intuitively, e_{slow} never fails, while e_{fast} is failed from the beginning.

We will now define the procedure that allows us to obtain an abstraction of the representative tree of a cutset. Let C be a cutset, the variable $dir \in \{over, under\}$ denotes the direction of abstraction (over- or under-approximation). The list of basic events to be cancelled out is called an *abstraction sequence*. The procedure we present is applicable for an arbitrary abstraction sequence. Later in this section we will present heuristics for obtaining abstraction sequences for over and under-approximations, that we used in our experiments. In the following, whenever we perform an operation on a cutset (or a list of cutsets) we assume an equivalent operation to be performed on its representative tree and vice versa.

AbstractTree(C, c^*)

1. Using the BuildRepTree procedure, build the representative tree of C. In step 3(a) of BuildRepTree instead of using the set of cutsets of a gate g, use the set of relevant cutsets $L_{c^*}(g)$. The value $L_{c^*}(g)$ and the cutoff error bound ε_g can be obtained in the same way as described above using the MOCUS algorithm;
2. If $dir = over$ add to $L_{c^*}(g)$ the set $\{b_{\varepsilon_g}, e_{fast}\}$ where b_{ε_g} is a new static basic event with probability ε_g[1];
3. Choose an *abstraction sequence* $A = (b_1, G_1)(b_2, G_2)\ldots(b_n, G_n)$, where b_i is a non-triggered basic event of FT_C and G_i is a set of gates;
4. Repeatedly for $i = 1..n$:
   (a) for each gate $g \in G_i$, for each cutset $C_g \in L_{c^*}(g)$ replace all occurrences of b_i by e_{slow} if $dir = under$, and by e_{fast} if $dir = over$[2];
   (b) remove from $L_{c^*}(g)$ cutsets that have become non-minimal (propagate these changes into the tree by removing respective gates);

Remark. Notably, after step 4(b) one can still perform a number of further reductions of the state-space of FT_C. For instance whenever an event b is replaced with e_{slow}, all the cutsets containing b can be immediately removed, since they will never fail. As a result of this procedure we obtain new trees $\overline{FT_C}$ and $\underline{FT_C}$ for over- and under-approximations.

Lemma 2. $p(\underline{FT_C}) \leqslant p(C) \leqslant p(\overline{FT_C})$

Depending on the chosen abstraction sequence, $\overline{FT_C}$ and $\underline{FT_C}$ can be of a much smaller size than the original FT_C, making it possible to apply the efficient CTMC analysis we discussed above directly to product CTMCs constructed separately for $\underline{FT_C}$ and $\overline{FT_C}$. Let $\underline{\mathbf{F}}$ and $\overline{\mathbf{F}}$ be failed states of $\underline{FT_C}$ and $\overline{FT_C}$, and let ε' be the error bound used by the CTMC algorithm. We thus define the over- and under-approximations as follows:

$$\underline{p}_{c^*}(C) := p(\underline{FT_C}) \qquad = \mathrm{Pr}_{C_{\underline{FT_C}}}\left[Reach^{\leqslant t}(\underline{\mathbf{F}})\right]$$
$$\overline{p}_{c^*}(C) := p(\overline{FT_C}) + \varepsilon' = \mathrm{Pr}_{C_{\overline{FT_C}}}\left[Reach^{\leqslant t}(\overline{\mathbf{F}})\right] + \varepsilon'$$

---

[1] This is to compensate for the cutoff error bound ε_g.

[2] Whenever the event b_i belongs to a cutset of a gate $g \notin G_i$, we create a copy of b_i and direct all the transitions from gates g to b_i to the new basic event. Thus whenever b_i is abstracted in gates $g \in G_i$, it is not abstracted away in gates $g \notin G_i$.

The Abstraction Sequence Heuristic. The abstraction sequence that one decides to use in the above procedure affects directly the error introduced by the approximation. We will now describe the heuristics for selecting an abstraction sequence that we find reasonable in practice and that we used for the experiments.

For nested gates, we abstract all basic events in an arbitrary order yielding $\overline{L_{c^*}}(g) = \{\{e_{fast}\}\}$ and $\underline{L_{c^*}}(g) = \{\{e_{slow}\}\}$[3]. As regards immediate gates, we use different heuristics for over- and under-approximations. We first introduce two new measures $\varepsilon^U(b_i) \geqslant 1$ and $\varepsilon^O(b_i) \geqslant 1$ of the impact of abstracting event b_i away. These measures are based on the notions of *risk increase(decrease) factor* [16]. The closer these values are to 1 the smaller is the loss of precision due to reduction of the respective event. We therefore aim at abstracting such events.

Let $err \geqslant 0$ be an allowed error parameter, $x \in \{O, U\}$. We assign each G_i to be the set of all immediate triggering gates. The following procedure applies to both over- and under-approximation (by using respective x):

1. Enumerate all the basic events b from FT_C except for those in C by their ascending $\varepsilon^x(b)$. The $\varepsilon^x(b)$ needs to be re-evaluated for every element in the sequence as abstracting all previous events changes the FT_C;
2. Stop once reducing the next basic event according to the given order would make the error $\prod\limits_{reduced\ b} \varepsilon^x(b)$ exceed $err + 1$;

Remark. As a result of applying these abstraction sequences one may obtain a lot of cutsets of a specific shape. Those are either singleton cutsets, or pairs of the form $\{b, b_i\}, \{b, b_j\}$. In order to further reduce the state space one can add another abstraction step that lumps such cutsets together, while preserving the property of being an over- or under-approximation. We indeed defined such a lumping procedure for the class of dynamic basic events whose CTMC has one of the shapes depicted in Fig. 3, and used it in our experiments

4   Experimental Evaluation

This section presents the empirical evaluation of our approach. Since our focus is on an efficient approach that integrates well with the *industrial practice*, we do not consider small or medium-size synthetic examples whose homogeneous structure would enable to study model size vs. solution time tradeoffs. Instead we prefer to present results for realistic models from industrial practice, therefore serving as a proof of concept.

As an implementation of the MOCUS algorithm we use RISKSPECTRUM [13], and resort to the PRISM tool [12] for the reachability analysis of the CTMCs. All the intermediate processing, mainly reductions and conversions, were implemented as Python scripts. All experiments are carried out on a single Intel Core

---

[3] Reduction of a triggered basic event is possible due to reduction of its triggering gate.

i7-4790 with 32 GB of RAM. The following abbreviations will appear throughout the section: *BE*, *DynE* and *TrigE* denote the overall number of basic events, dynamic basic events, respectively triggered events in a given SD-FT. The number of relevant minimal cutsets is denoted as *RelMCS*.

Models. We evaluate our approach on four simple and two larger reactor models. These are derived from models representing analyses built by safety engineering experts with all the modelling power that *static fault trees* offer. For each of these original models, a static top value p_{stat} can be computed (by RISKSPECTRUM) characterizing the state-of-the-art failure frequency estimate of the analysed scenario. We obtained SD-FT models from these static ones by adding dynamic features offered by SD-FT formalism in a realistic manner. For all the dynamic basic events we use repair rate 0.1, which is approximately in the order of magnitude of real component repair rates. We use the static values p_{stat} as reference values for comparison in our experiments.

Simple Reactor Models. These models are variations of a toy example of a probabilistic safety assessment model of a boiling water reactor. We always calculate a core damage consequence, which is a typical Level 1 analysis with a 24 h

Table 1. Model characteristics.

	BE	DynE	TrigE	RelMCS
Simple reactor	40	13	7	Various
IND-1	3000	220	168	3164
IND-2	2215	599	12	96042

time horizon. The size of these models is tiny relative to real-life models. Their common characteristics are presented in Table 1 (first row), the variants differ in the triggering logic:

TwoTrains models a system with two redundant trains of separate equipment, such as pumps, diesel engines, SWS (Service Water System), and CCW (Component Cooling Water System). The second train is triggered whenever the first pump fails;

Diesel is a system where the two diesel engines are redundant per train. One diesel engine is enough to make the respective train function properly;

SWS+Diesel adds redundancy for SWS systems in addition and similar to the diesel engine redundancy;

CCW+SWS+Diesel supports redundancy for CCW, SWS, and diesel engines.

Industrial-size Reactor Models. These are two slightly adapted core damage consequence analysis cases from two different real-life probabilistic safety assessment models. We will further refer to them as IND-1 and IND-2. Table 1 shows some of the core characteristics of the models. The most significant adaptations concern (1) switching off the common cause failure treatment and (2) updating failure data for some static basic events. We have added dynamic dependencies between components which in reality represent redundant systems (such as pumps) where only a subset of components has to run in order to guarantee the safety function. Triggering gates were chosen in a way that can be considered induced by

Table 2. Runtime experiments for simple reactor models performed with $err = 1$.

	T	T_{PRISM}	$RelMCS$	$AvDynE$	$AvTrigE$	$AvAdd$	$MaxSet$	$\#Set_{>8}$	[11]
TwoTrains	07:01	06:49	15061	4.8	0.1	0.2	15	818	>4 h
Diesel	30:04	29:53	10389	4.8	0.09	0.21	27	586	>4 h
SWS+Diesel	23:16	23:07	8007	4.8	0.09	0.20	27	501	>4 h
CCW+SWS+Diesel	15:42	15:34	5145	4.9	0.1	0.23	27	456	>4 h

a convenient modelling methodology. We chose gates corresponding to failures of complete systems and we did not simplify the logic under triggering gates by remodelling. All basic events with the mission time reliability model under the gates corresponding to the triggered systems were considered dynamic and triggered. Such a modelling requires only a high level understanding of dynamic relations between systems and components and knowledge about which gates model failures of these systems.

Experiments. In all the experiments we analyse a mission time of 24 h. The precision of time bounded reachability (computed by the PRISM tool) is set to 10^{-7}. In the tables presented, $AvDynE$ (respectively $AvTrigE$) denotes the average amount of dynamic (respectively immediately triggered) events per cutset. When we report runtime, we use, unless otherwise stated, *min:sec* as format, and use T for overall runtime, and T_{PRISM} for the fragment thereof needed by PRISM. Value $AvAdd$ denotes the average amount (over all cutsets C) of basic events, both static and dynamic, that have not been abstracted from FT_C (excluding the events from C itself). $MaxSet$ refers to the maximum (over all cutsets) amount of basic events in a cutset tree that have been left after all abstractions, and $\#Set_{>8}$ shows the amount of cutsets, whose representative trees contain more than 8 basic events.

In order to evaluate our approach we use three measures: runtime, achieved accuracy and accuracy gain compared to a static analysis. To estimate the latter, we use the ratio of over-approximation $\overline{p}_{rea}$ to the value p_{stat} described above. This ratio can be expected to be lower than 1, since modelling the dynamics brings more accuracy and thus less pessimism. The runtime of the static analysis step is not reported. It was in the order of seconds for all experiments performed, given that the cutsets were precomputed by RiskSpectrum.

Influence of Model Parameters. We first want to estimate the effect of different parameters of the model itself on the running time of our algorithm. To do this we performed experiments on all the simple reactor models. These models share the same value of parameters BE, $DynE$ and $TrigE$ and differ mainly in their triggering logic. Each of the relevant cutsets contains at least one dynamic event. Table 2 summarizes the results of this experiment. As we can see, the existing algorithm from [11] is not competitive. The runtime of our algorithm is influenced by the maximum size of cutsets as well as the amount of large cutsets. More concretely, even though the amount of relevant cutsets for the

Table 3. Experiments with varying parameter err on TwoTrains, where $p_{stat} = 5.836344 \cdot 10^{-5}$.

err	T	$\underline{p}_{rea} \times 10^5$	$\overline{p}_{rea} \times 10^5$	$AvAdd$	$MaxSet$	$\#Set_{>8}$	$\overline{p}_{rea}/p_{stat}$
3	06:46	4.5747	4.6017	0.19	15	755	0.78
2	06:52	4.5769	4.6017	0.20	15	764	0.78
1	07:01	4.5848	4.6017	0.20	15	818	0.78
0.1	12:05	4.5927	4.6016	0.21	15	818	0.78
0.01	24:30	4.5961	4.6012	0.27	15	818	0.78
10^{-3}	38:10	4.5966	4.6012	0.34	15	818	0.78
10^{-4}	38:47	4.5966	4.6012	0.34	15	818	0.78
10^{-5}	38:46	4.5966	4.6012	0.34	15	818	0.78

Table 4. Experiments with varying parameter err for Ind-1, where $p_{stat} = 3.037881 \cdot 10^{-8}$.

err	T	$\underline{p}_{rea} \times 10^8$	$\overline{p}_{rea} \times 10^8$	$AvAdd$	$MaxSet$	$\#Set_{>8}$	$\overline{p}_{rea}/p_{stat}$
20	05:50	2.4790	2.5760	0.26	16	306	0.84
10	06:58	2.4790	2.4915	0.34	16	531	0.82
5	07:01	2.4790	2.4915	0.35	16	589	0.82
2	27:54	2.4798	2.4847	0.43	23	846	0.81
1	>6 h	2.4802	N/A	0.58	63	870	N/A

Table 5. Experiments with varying parameter err for Ind-2, where $p_{stat} = 7.342436 \cdot 10^{-7}$.

err	T (hrs:min:sec)	$\underline{p}_{rea} \times 10^7$	$\overline{p}_{rea} \times 10^7$	$AvAdd$	$MaxSet$	$\#Set_{>8}$	$\overline{p}_{rea}/p_{stat}$
20	02:16:10	4.8934	6.0541	0.05	14	103561	0.82
10	02:16:06	4.8934	6.0541	0.05	14	103561	0.82
5	03:01:27	4.8934	4.9301	0.1	14	107249	0.67
2	03:01:25	4.8934	4.9301	0.1	14	107249	0.67
1	03:01:27	4.8934	4.9301	0.1	14	107249	0.67

model TwoTrains is higher than for Diesel, the runtime on the latter model is notably higher due to the values $MaxSet$ and $\#Set_{>8}$. As apparent from Table 2, the dominant portion of runtime is taken by the Prism processing. In further experiments we therefore do not report this value separately, and instead show only the overall running time of the algorithm.

Influence of Parameter err. Parameter err is the only parameter of the heuristic that we use for reductions. We performed various experiments to evaluate the effect of it on the running time and accuracy of our algorithm. Tables 3, 4 and 5 show results of the experiments on one of the simple models and on both the industrial-size models. One can see that, as expected, with the increase of accuracy (decrease of err) the amount of added basic events increases as well. This in turn enlarges the state space of the product CTMC, what explains the increase of the running time. On the other hand, the abstractions become more and more precise. We achieved a gain of 22 % on the simple model, 19 % on IND-1 and 33 % on IND-2 compared to the static value p_{stat}. In some cases higher precision seems to come with slightly lower running time, e.g. in Table 5. This however is an artefact of runtime measurement inaccuracy, the actual computations performed are identical.

5   Concluding Comparison with Related Work

We have presented a generic analysis and approximation scheme for fault trees combining static and dynamic features. The key innovation is the use of bounding approximations for the underlying dynamic behaviour. The method enables to trade precision against runtime in an effective manner, so as to make it an industrial-scale dynamic safety analysis method.

Other available methods for solving fault trees with dynamic features suffer from either scalability or expressiveness issues [11,15]. Approaches with comparable expressiveness include Dynamic Fault Trees [2,3], Boolean Driven Markov Processes [4] and others. Analysis support for these models is limited to fault trees with at most 300 dynamic basic events, which is far from the sizes that one usually encounters in the nuclear safety domain. We have reported here on successful experiments for models with up to 600 dynamic basic events contained inside SD-FTs with several thousands of basic events in total.

Acknowledgments. This work is partly supported by the ERC Advanced Investigators Grant 695614 (POWVER), by the EU 7th Framework Programme under grant agreement no. 318490 (SENSATION) and 288175 (CERTAINTY), by the DFG Transregional Collaborative Research Centre SFB/TR 14 AVACS, by the CDZ project 1023 (CAP), and by the Czech Science Foundation, grant No. P202/12/G061.

References

1. Baier, C., Haverkort, B.R., Hermanns, H., Katoen, J.: Model-checking algorithms for continuous-time Markov chains. IEEE Trans. Softw. Eng. **29**(6), 524–541 (2003)
2. Dugan, B.J., Bavuso, S.J., Boyd, M.: Dynamic fault-tree models for fault-tolerant computer systems. IEEE Trans. Reliab. **41**(3), 363–377 (1992)
3. Boudali, H., Crouzen, P., Stoelinga, M.: A rigorous, compositional, and extensible framework for dynamic fault tree analysis. IEEE Trans. Dependable Sec. Compt. **7**(2), 128–143 (2010)
4. Bouissou, M., Bon, J.L.: A new formalism that combines advantages of fault-trees and Markov models: Boolean logic driven Markov processes. Reliab. Eng. Syst. Saf. **82**(2), 149–163 (2003)

5. Brázdil, T., Hermanns, H., Krčál, J., Křetínský, J., Řehák, V.: Verification of open interactive Markov chains. In: FSTTCS. LIPIcs, vol. 18, pp. 474–485 (2012)
6. Butkova, Y., Hatefi, H., Hermanns, H., Krcál, J.: Optimal continuous time Markov decisions. In: Finkbeiner, B., et al. (eds.) ATVA 2015. LNCS, vol. 9364, pp. 166–182. Springer, Heidelberg (2015). doi:10.1007/978-3-319-24953-7_12
7. Center for Chemical Process Safety: Guidelines for Hazard Evaluation Procedures, 3rd edn. Wiley, Hoboken (2008)
8. Fussell, J.B., Vesely, W.E.: A new methodology for obtaining cut sets for fault trees. Trans. Am. Nucl. Soc. **15**, 262–263 (1972)
9. IAEA: Development and Application of Level 1 Probabilistic Safety Assessment for Nuclear Power Plants, IAEA Safety Standards Series No. SSG-3 (2010)
10. IAEA: Development and Application of Level 2 Probabilistic Safety Assessment for Nuclear Power Plants, IAEA Safety Standards Series No. SSG-4 (2010)
11. Krčál, J., Krčál, P.: Scalable analysis of fault trees with dynamic features. In: DSN 2015, pp. 89–100 (2015)
12. Kwiatkowska, M., Norman, G., Parker, D.: PRISM 4.0: verification of probabilistic real-time systems. In: Gopalakrishnan, G., Qadeer, S. (eds.) CAV 2011. LNCS, vol. 6806, pp. 585–591. Springer, Heidelberg (2011)
13. Lloyd's Register Consulting: RiskSpectrum, Theory Manual (2013)
14. NASA: Fault Tree Handbook with Aerospace Applications (2002)
15. Ruijters, E.J.J., Stoelinga, M.I.A.: Fault tree analysis: a survey of the state of the art in modeling, analysis and tools. Comput. Sci. Rev. **15**, 29–62 (2015)
16. Vesely, W., Davis, T., Denning, R., Saltos, N.: Measures of risk importance and their application (NUREG/CR-3385). US Nuclear Regulatory Commission (1983)
17. Vesely, W., Goldberg, F., Roberts, N., Haasl, D.: Fault Tree Handbook(NUREG/CR-0492). US Nuclear Regulatory Commission (1981)
18. Wood, S., Smith, C.L., Kvarfordt, K.J., Beck, S.: Systems Analysis Programs for Hands-on Integrated Reliability Evaluations (SAPHIRE): Summary Manual (NUREG/CR-6952, vol. 1). US Nuclear Regulatory Commission (2008)

Safety Analysis

SAFER-HRC: Safety Analysis Through Formal vERification in Human-Robot Collaboration

Mehrnoosh Askarpour[1(✉)], Dino Mandrioli[1], Matteo Rossi[1],
and Federico Vicentini[2]

[1] Dipartimento di Elettronica, Informazione e Bioingegneria, Politecnico di Milano,
Piazza Leonardo da Vinci 32, 20133 Milan, Italy
{mehrnoosh.askarpour,dino.mandrioli,matteo.rossi}@polimi.it
[2] Istituto di Tecnologie Industriali e Automazione,
Consiglio Nazionale delle Ricerche, via Bassini 15, 20133 Milan, Italy
federico.vicentini@cnr.itia.it

Abstract. Whereas in classic robotic applications there is a clear segregation between robots and operators, novel robotic and cyber-physical systems have evolved in size and functionality to include the collaboration with human operators within common workspaces. This new application field, often referred to as Human-Robot Collaboration (HRC), raises new challenges to guarantee system safety, due to the presence of operators. We present an innovative methodology, called SAFER-HRC, centered around our logic language TRIO and the companion bounded satisfiability checker Zot, to assess the safety risks in an HRC application. The methodology starts from a generic modular model and customizes it for the target system; it then analyses hazards according to known standards, to study the safety of the collaborative environment.

Keywords: Safety analysis · Formal verification · Safety rules · Human-robot collaboration

1 Introduction

In Human-Robot Collaboration (HRC) applications, close proximity and direct interaction between robot and operator are unavoidable, so providing safety for the operator requires more effort and a more rigorous approach. Thus, the safety of machinery community has published several standards [11,15], which include a list of significant *hazards* in HRC applications, potential sources of harms for the operator, their likely origins, and safety regulations for guiding the design and deployment of robotic solutions. In particular, ISO standard 10218-2 [11] identifies four possible collaborative modes between humans and industrial robots. Of these, Power and Force Limitation (PFL) is the one involving actual physical contact, and it is associated with strict safety requirements in terms of pressure and force thresholds, in order to limit the effects on the human body. Our focus in this work is on collaborative robots that are considered in the PFL category.

© Springer International Publishing Switzerland 2016
A. Skavhaug et al. (Eds.): SAFECOMP 2016, LNCS 9922, pp. 283–295, 2016.
DOI: 10.1007/978-3-319-45477-1_22

HRC applications must be evaluated through the analysis laid out in ISO standard 12100 [12], to identify existing hazards and unwanted situations due to intentional *misuses* or unconscious *errors* of the operator; and to prevent their consequences, which are measured in terms of quantified *risk* values.

Figure 1(a) shows the stages of a standard iterative risk analysis (resulting in the C€ marking in the case of European directives).

(i) **Limits of Machinery**: The desired tasks of the robot and its machinery regulations and constraints are determined.

(ii) **Hazards Identification**: The existence of hazards (and combinations thereof) listed in product-specific standards such as ISO 10218-2 is identified.

(iii) **Risk Estimation**: The risk values associated with hazards identified in the previous step are measured. Many risk-scoring methods are introduced in [14], all of which combine the severity of a harm with its likelihood.

(iv) **Risk Evaluation**: The significance of each hazard is evaluated. The methods reported in [14] help determine the range of acceptability for the risk scores.

(v) **Risk Reduction**: If the risk value is not negligible, appropriate measures are (iteratively) introduced to reduce each risk, either by redesigning the system to eliminate the hazard, or through the introduction of a safety function (e.g. "full stop in case of a signal from a protection sensor"), which needs to be verified against suitable requirements of reliability and availability. We refer the reader to [13] for a complete discussion about functional safety.

The process continues iteratively until no new risk is identified and the residual risk value is acceptable. New risks may appear due to hazards related to risk reduction measures, or to operator behaviors in reaction to such measures. Devices and protection measures can alter the course of actions (use and misuse).

In this paper we introduce the SAFER-HRC (Safety Analysis through Formal vERification in HRC applications) methodology, which provides a technique to comprehensively identify hazards through the exhaustive exploration, rooted in formal methods, of the behavior of the target system. Among the different types of hazards (e.g., electrical, ergonomic, ...), this work addresses operational hazards with a specific focus on those that are caused by human-robot interactions. Although we do not claim that SAFER-HRC guarantees that all possible hazards in a system are found, we argue that the exhaustive exploration on which the methodology is based helps increase the confidence that no significant hazardous situations are left unconsidered. To achieve an exhaustive analysis of the system model, we rely on the state-space exploration capabilities of formal verification techniques. Due to the impossibility of foreseeing all possible behaviors of the operator, it cannot be claimed that all possible interactions of operator and system are taken into account; nevertheless, an iterative methodology based on formal verification techniques can eventually provide a thorough analysis of all significant ones. At each iteration, if the design fails to satisfy the desired safety requirements, it is improved by adding new risk

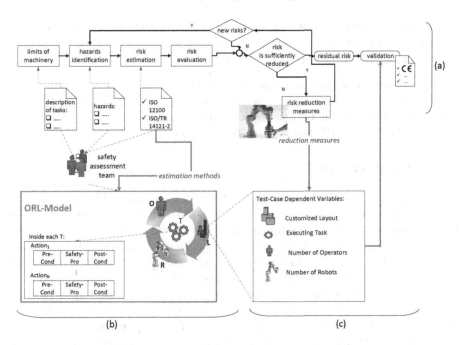

Fig. 1. Overview of the safety analysis methodology: (a) standard procedure; (b) principal model of SAFER-HRC; (c) scenario refinement.

reduction measures. This methodology relies on a "human-in-the-loop" approach [6] and it does not automatically select risk reduction measures. As shown in Fig. 1(b), the safety strategy is designed and acknowledged by a pool of experts and users of the application under assessment (the safety assessment team). The essential aspect of the proposed methodology is the systematic validation of the constraints and their possible violations at all steps of the application. The thoroughness of the validation ensures that the selected safety strategy is failsafe. SAFER-HRC starts from informal, goal-oriented descriptions of collaborative tasks, and converts them into formal models built upon logical formulae, on which formal verification techniques are applied to check whether the safety requirements are satisfied or not. The model includes separate formalizations for operator and robot; hence, the verification phase also checks their interactions, taking into account how they are affected by the physical environment. After the principal model has been thoroughly analyzed, it can be modified and re-used to study different scenarios for the HRC application (e.g., combinations of different safety functions, uncommon actions by the operator).

The main contributions of the methodology presented in this paper are:

1. Applying formal methods to the safety assessment of HRC applications, where the presence of the operator negatively impacts on the predictability of the system behavior, but also imposes demanding safety standards that must be rigorously studied.

2. Providing a flexible approach that supports the safety assessment team in throughly exploring different design assumptions, thus complementing the human insight with the power of formal verification.

The paper is structured as follows: Sect. 2 discusses related works, and Sect. 3 gives a brief formal background. Section 4 introduces the essential aspects of the SAFER-HRC methodology. Section 5 illustrates our approach through an example of a collaborative assembling task. Section 6 concludes.

2   Related Works

Classic hazard identification approaches such as FTA and FMECA [4] are not well-suited for HRC applications, as they cannot deal with unpredictable human interactions with robots. We use formal verification methods as a means to improve hazard identification in robotic applications. These methods can be applied to complement informal techniques such as Hazop [10], which consists of a set of meetings and brainstorming sessions to identify and evaluate potential hazards concerning operators, equipment or efficiency. Its aim is to exploit as much information as possible from expert users and experienced safety engineers. Another informal hazard analysis technique is STPA [16], which builds a model of the control structure of the system to identify control-related flaws.

There are recent works tackling safety issues in robotic applications with human intervention using semi-formal solutions, or a combination of semi-formal and formal solutions. For example, in [9,19] State-charts are first used to describe the behavior of the robot, and then HAZOP is employed using UML models to identify potential hazards, their causes and their severity. In [17] hazards are identified by a combination of UML and HAZOP, then they are formalized in CTL (Computation Tree Logic). The same authors in a later work [18] compute a set of if-then-else safety constraints, and then add them to the logical model of the system to avoid predicted hazards. However, their application domain consists of assistive, rather than collaborative robots, and so the operator is a passive element whose on-the-fly decisions or errors are not considered as a determinative fact. A recent work [8] systematizes the pairing of HAZOP and UML, and presents results also for collaborative scenarios, excluding the formal point of view and focusing on an informal solution. As we aim at combining the two aspects, this approach could be used to define the first informal description of the system from which to derive the principal model discussed in Sect. 4.

In building our logical model, we use a contract-based approach similar to the one in [2]. Such an approach allows us to break down the overall task description into small components, to specify the requirements of each component separately, and to have a modular, clean formal description of collaborative tasks.

3   Preliminaries

Our approach is rooted in TRIO, a logical language which assumes an underlying linear temporal structure and features a quantitative notion of time [7].

Table 1. List of derived TRIO operators.

Operator	Definition	Meaning
$\text{Futr}(\phi, d)$	$d > 0 \wedge \text{Dist}(\phi, d)$	ϕ occurs exactly at d time units in the future
$\text{Past}(\phi, d)$	$d > 0 \wedge \text{Dist}(\phi, -d)$	ϕ occurred exactly at d time units in the past
$\text{AlwF}(\phi)$	$\forall t(t > 0 \Rightarrow \text{Dist}(\phi, t))$	ϕ holds always in the future
$\text{Until}(\phi, \psi)$	$\exists t(\text{Futr}(\{\}\psi, t\} \wedge \\ \forall t'(0 < t' < t \Rightarrow Dist(\phi, t')))$	ψ Will occur in the future and ϕ will hold until then
$\text{SomF}(\phi)$	$\exists t(t > 0 \wedge Dist(\phi, t))$	ϕ occurs sometimes in the future
$\text{SomP}(\phi)$	$\exists t(t > 0 \wedge Dist(\phi, -t))$	ϕ occurred sometimes in the past

TRIO formulae are built out of the usual first-order connectives, operators, and quantifiers, as well as a single basic modal operator, called Dist, that relates the *current time*, which is left implicit in the formula, to another time instant: given a time-dependent formula ϕ (i.e., a term representing a mapping from the time domain to truth values) and a (arithmetic) term t indicating a time distance (either positive or negative), formula $\text{Dist}(\phi, t)$ specifies that ϕ holds at a time instant at a distance of exactly t time units from the current one.

While TRIO can exploit both discrete and dense sets as time domains, in this work we assume the standard model of the nonnegative integers $\mathbb{N}$ as discrete time domain. For convenience in the writing of specification formulae, TRIO defines a number of *derived* temporal operators from the basic Dist, through propositional composition and first-order logic quantification. Table 1 defines some of the most significant ones, including those used in this work.

The satisfiability of TRIO formulae is in general undecidable. However, in this paper we consider a decidable subset of the language, that can be handled by automated tools, to build the system model and to express its properties. In particular, Zot [1] is a bounded satisfiability checker for TRIO formulae [20]. We use Zot in this work to check the model of the system against desired safety properties. In case the property is not satisfied, Zot provides a counterexample witnessing a system execution that violates the property.

4   Overview of the SAFER-HRC Methodology

This section introduces SAFER-HRC, a semi-automated verification methodology which benefits from formal verification techniques to extract the violation of safety requirements mentioned in ISO10218 [11] during the design of collaborative robotic systems. As depicted in Fig. 1(b), at the core of SAFER-HRC lies a safety assessment team (SATeam). SATeam, which includes robotic and formal methods experts, studies the limitations of the machinery and the tasks of the target robot, and predicts possible human-robot interactions. They also determine which of the hazards listed in ISO 12100 can occur, and evaluate the risk level based techniques defined in ISO standard 14121 [14]. In SAFER-HRC, SATeam relies on a formal model of the HRC application to support and systematize these activities. More precisely, SATeam starts from the informal, textual definitions of the tasks, and then builds UML diagrams as a bridge towards the formal representation.

General O-R-L Model. The formal model captures the dynamics of the interactions occurring in the system in terms of the relationships among three main elements, O, R and L, which formally describe, respectively, operator, robot and layout through logic formulae. O is a formal model of the operator's body parts, each with critical safety requirements as described in standard ISO/TC 184/SC. R models the robot by describing the edges that have some degree of freedom in their movements; the nature of this model depends heavily on robot type and shape. O and R contain constraints to avoid considering unrealistic body shapes or robot structures (e.g., the head of the operator is in one corner of the workspace, while her hand is in the opposite one). L provides a representation of the layout of the system that allows us to describe the position of the physical features of O and R at any time instant. The O-R-L model contains some elements and constraints that are common to all HRC applications (e.g., the description of body parts); other parts of it (e.g., the features of the robot) are instead instantiated depending on the specific HRC application.

The O-R-L Model includes also a part related to the pool of tasks that the robot modeled in R is supposed to perform. Each task and its requirements and regulations are modeled in an element called T. The definition of each task T determines the type and frequency of interactions among O-R-L elements. The execution of a task involves a functional relationship between each pair of O-R-L elements. These relationships can be physical ones (e.g., contact between the robot arm and the operator, presence of the operator and robot in a common area in the layout) or informational (e.g., inputs given to the robot by the operator). For example, consider the following safety requirement: "operator's head should not be close to the robot end-effector while it is drilling". The model defines a value (L_{drill}) corresponding to the area in the layout where drilling is done, a variable (EF) capturing the position of the end-effector, and another one ($OpHead$) for the operator's head position; then, T contains the following constraint associated with the drilling task, stating that $OPHead$ cannot be in L_{drill} while drilling is executing: $Drilling_{state} = exe \Rightarrow \neg(OPHead = L_{drill}) \wedge (EF = L_{drill})$.

Usually the definition of a task has a goal-oriented view and contains multiple smaller units of execution. Breaking down a task into the smallest possible functional units, i.e., into *elementary actions* [5], enables SATeam to extract the previously mentioned relationships among O-R-L elements and also helps to identify the hazards that might otherwise be overlooked if one only stayed at a higher level of analysis. Another benefit of distinguishing single actions is that, in case it is possible to achieve the same goal with different sequences of actions, and the operator has the ability to decide on-the-fly what sequence to use, different sets of hazards caused by each sequence are identified. Further, the human body parts that are in contact with or close to the robot end-effector can differ for separate actions within a task, and this in turn can affect the possibility and criticality of hazards. SAFER-HRC characterizes each of the elementary actions within model T of the corresponding task by three main features: its pre-conditions, post-conditions, and safety properties (Fig. 1(b)). These features are formalized as TRIO formulae that have to hold respectively before, after and during execution of each action. In addition, each action has a property called *priority*, which defines its execution preference over other actions. More precisely, if at a time instant the pre-conditions of both $action_i$ and $action_j$ are satisfied, the one with higher priority starts to execute. The current model considers that systems operate at their maximum level of parallelism; that is, all actions that have the highest priority among those that are enabled start executing in parallel. Each action can also have additional constraints and timing requirements that are included in its formalization. At each instant, an action is in one of the following states:

1. *ns (not started)*: pre-conditions are not yet satisfied.
2. *wait*: pre-conditions are satisfied, but there is another action with higher priority in execution or waiting mode.
3. *exe (executing)*: under execution (solo, or concurrently with other actions).
4. *pause (ps)*: at some point in the execution, safety properties are violated and execution is paused.
5. *dn(done)*: the execution is terminated.

Model Tailoring. When applying SAFER-HRC to perform the safety analysis for a system, SATeam first needs to tailor the O-R-L model to the target HRC application, by selecting the appropriate robot model and application parameters, which corresponds to carrying out the following activities (see Fig. 1):

- Choose the tasks that the robot will be executing.
- Set the number of operators and robots. In case the application requires more than one element for each category, SAFER-HRC creates multiple, separate instances of elements R and O.
- Define the configuration of the layout, in terms of the number of regions, reachability of each region for robot(s) and operator(s), and specification of obstacles or other physical features.

At this point, SAFER-HRC checks through the Zot formal verification tool whether the model so tailored satisfies the desired safety requirements. If a safety property is violated, Zot produces a counterexample, signaling the presence of one or more hazards in the system. A violation can be due to: (i) the system still includes hazardous situations, or allows for operator errors or on-purpose misuses; or (ii) the system does not have proper reduction measures for identified hazards. Then, the designer should improve the system model: by adding proper risk reduction measures, which correspond to TRIO formulae that should avoid the violation; or by including new formulae to capture hazards that were undetected in the previous analysis. Next, a new validation is carried out on the improved model. The model is refined iteratively until no more violations occur.

The next section shows an example of using SAFER-HRC to design an assembly application for a KUKA Light Weight Robot (LWR).

5   Applying SAFER-HRC in Practice

In this section we illustrate how SAFER-HRC works in practice. We used a test-case with a KUKA robot, performing an assembly task with one operator in the layout depicted in Fig. 2. The scenario is the following:

> The operator fetches a workpiece from a bin and moves to the assembly position, where the robot screw-drives the workpiece to the pallet using N fixtures. Before the robot starts screw-driving each fixture, the operator must prepare it and put it in the right position. As soon as the screw-driving of all of the fixtures for the workpiece is finished, the operator can release the workpiece and leave the assembly position.

The execution of this task has a loop whose index spans the number of fixtures N to be screw-driven. It means that for example, if $N = 2$, then SAFER-HRC defines 2 instances of each action in the loop. For brevity, we provide only a simplified formalization of the test-case. Figure 3 shows the complete list of actions of the task. As explained in Sect. 4, each action is formalized through its pre/post-conditions and safety properties according to a contract-based approach. We present as an example a snippet of the formalization of $action_9$ "screwing the workpiece".

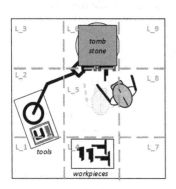

Fig. 2. Layout of the test system with nine areas. The assembly pallet board is in L_6 and the area blocked by the workpiece bin is L_4.

Pre-condition: There should be at least a prepared fixture. This property is captured by a Boolean predicate $prepared_{Fixture}$, which is set by data coming from visual sensors configured in the layout.

Safety property 1: Only the hands of the operator are allowed on the pallet. Since the O-R-L model includes in O an array to capture the position of the various body parts, and its seventh element refers to the hands, this corresponds to condition $Bodypart_7 = pallet$.

Safety property 2: The robot end-effector should be on the pallet. Model R captures the position of the end-effector through predicate EF, so this property simply corresponds to formula $EF = pallet$.

Safety property 3: The workpiece must be held. This simply corresponds to predicate $wpHeld$ being true.

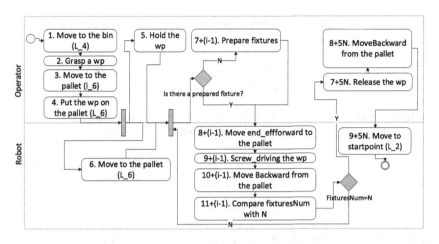

Fig. 3. Activity Diagram of the example task. The names of the actions in the loop are indexed by the current loop iteration i. There are 14 actions for $N = 1$.

Post-condition: End-effector and operator hands are still on the pallet: $Bodypart_7 = pallet \land EF = pallet$.

Other formulae in T are dedicated to formalizing different allowed sequences of actions to execute in order to achieve the goal of the task. One way to achieve this is by setting suitable values for the *priority* property of different actions. For example, $action_5$ "hold the workpiece" has higher priority than $action_7$ "prepare fixtures" in the definition of the task, since the operator must choose to give precedence to the former, even if he is ready to execute the latter. On the other hand, the robot must execute $action_6$ "move to the pallet" strictly before $action_8$ "move end-effector forward to the pallet", independent of the operator's choices; then, $action_6 = dn$ is defined as a pre-condition of $action_8$. Let us now provide some examples of formulae that are defined in T for this task. They are defined for each element $action_i$ of the set A_T of actions of the task.

(i) If an action has not started, it was never executing or done in the past:

$$action_{i,\text{state}} = \text{ns} \Rightarrow \neg\text{SomP}(action_{i,\text{state}} = \text{exe} \lor action_i = \text{dn})$$

(ii) If an action is waiting, it was never executing or done in the past, and it was in the "not started" state previously:

$$action_{i,\text{state}} = \text{wait} \Rightarrow \text{SomP}(action_{i,\text{state}} = \text{ns} \land$$
$$\neg\text{SomP}(action_{i,\text{state}} = \text{exe} \lor action_i = \text{dn}))$$

(iii) If an action is executing (solo or concurrently with other actions), it has started in the past, it will never be starting or waiting again in the future, and it has not been done previously:

$$action_{i,\text{state}} = \text{exe} \Rightarrow \text{SomP}(action_{i,\text{state}} = \text{ns} \land action_i = \text{wait}) \land$$
$$\neg\text{SomF}(action_{i,\text{state}} = \text{ns} \lor action_i = \text{wait}) \land \neg\text{SomP}(action_{i,\text{state}} = \text{dn})$$

(iv) If an action is paused, it was executing before that, and at some point it will restart its execution:

$$action_{i,\text{state}} = \text{ps} \Rightarrow \text{SomP}(action_{i,\text{state}} = \text{exe}) \wedge \text{SomF}(action_{i,\text{state}} = \text{exe}) \wedge$$
$$\neg\text{SomF}(action_{i,\text{state}} = \text{ns} \wedge action_i = \text{wait})$$

(v) If an action is waiting, the next time unit it will start executing if there is no other waiting or executing action with higher priority:

$$action_{i,\text{state}} = \text{wait} \ \wedge \bigwedge_{j \in A_T, j \neq i} \left(\begin{array}{l} action_{j,\text{state}} = \text{wait} \vee action_{j,\text{state}} = \text{exe} \\ \Rightarrow action_{i,\text{priority}} \geq action_{j,\text{priority}} \end{array} \right)$$
$$\Rightarrow Futr(action_{i,\text{state}} = \text{exe}, 1)$$

(vi) If multiple actions are waiting, those with higher priority will start to execute at the next time unit, whereas the others will remain waiting or go back to "not started" status (this can happen if their pre-condition stops holding):

$$action_{i,\text{state}} = \text{wait} \ \wedge \bigvee_{j \in A_T, j \neq i} \left(\begin{array}{l} action_{j,\text{state}} = \text{wait} \wedge \\ action_{i,\text{priority}} < action_{j,\text{priority}} \end{array} \right)$$
$$\Rightarrow Futr(action_{i,\text{state}} = \text{ns} \vee action_i = \text{wait}, 1)$$

(vii) When execution of an action is done, it means that it was being executed in the past, and its state will not change in the future:

$$action_{i,\text{state}} = \text{dn} \Rightarrow \text{AlwF}(action_{i,\text{state}} = \text{dn}) \wedge \text{SomP}(action_{i,\text{state}} = \text{exe})$$

(viii) Each action must eventually terminate:

$$\bigwedge_{i \in A_T} \text{Som}(action_{i,\text{state}} = \text{dn})$$

Model Tailoring. At this step, SATeam provides the details to instantiate the O-R-L model with the information specific to the target application, such as the actual layout of the common workspace. In the case study it is enough to introduce one instance each of O and R. Also, L is customized as follows. As Fig. 3(a) shows, the layout of the cell is divided in nine regions. The positions of the pallet and of the workpiece bin are L_6 and L_4, respectively. Regions L_1 to L_6 are reachable by the operator, except for region L_4, where the bin is located. The adjacency of areas is defined through a matrix given by SATeam. After these configurations are carried out for the model, safety properties 2 and 3 mentioned above for $action_9$ become $Bodypart[7] = L_6$ and $EF = L_6$, respectively.[1]

---

[1] The complete O-R-L Model can be found at https://github.com/Askarpour/ORL-Model.

Safety Analysis of the Tailored O-R-L Model. In this step of the SAFER-HRC methodology, the SATeam carries out an iterative analysis, to find the operator errors that can cause serious problems (if they have not been taken into account in the initial model), or possible incompatibilities between layout and task execution. The analysis is done by formally verifying the O-R-L model described above against the safety properties of each action. The execution time for the verification activities is not a concern in this case study, since verification is completed in a few seconds using a modified plug-in [3] of the Zot bounded satisfiability checker. The verification bound (i.e., the maximum length of analyzed traces) was 100, which is over the completeness bound.

The following are examples of problems that SAFER-HRC found in the O-R-L model of the case study.

(a) While $action_9$ is executing, the operator mistakenly gets close to the pallet with her face (for example, she might want to see the screw-driving action better) and when $action_{10}$ starts to execute the robot hits her face. This can cause serious injuries in the face and eye area, so we modified the safety property package of $action_9$. More precisely, we added the following formula, which states that no other body part other than the hand is allowed in the area close to the pallet, and in case the operator makes such mistake the execution is paused (in fact, whenever a safety property of an action is violated, the execution of that action is paused):
$\bigwedge_{i \in BodyIndexes \wedge i \neq 7} \neg(Bodypart[i] = pallet)$.

(b) As mentioned above, the concurrency of actions depends on the values of their priorities. In some cases, the inconsistencies that might happen during the concurrent execution of actions have been avoided by design, through the definition of suitable pre/post-conditions. However, this issue has not been addressed in the initial model between $action_9$ and $action_5$. In fact, the safety property of $action_5$ is not satisfied, and according to the counterexample returned by Zot, there are system configurations where $action_9$ is executing, but the workpiece is not held by the operator. This highlights two issues: (i) the operator could make an error and release the workpiece before the screw-driving action terminates; (ii) $action_9$ should always execute concurrently with $action_5$. To circumvent this, the safety properties of $action_9$ are updated by adding formula $action_5 = $ exe to them. The modification is applied also to $action_8$, $action_{10}$, and $action_{11}$.

6 Conclusions

This paper introduced the SAFER-HRC methodology for the semi-automated safety analysis of HRC applications. The methodology is based on formal verification techniques to explore foreseeable wanted and unwanted interactions (errors and misuses) between operators and robots. We have applied the methodology to a realistic case study consisting of a KUKA robot performing an assembly task. Our approach allows a team of system safety experts to: (i) create formal models of HRC applications that can be flexibly modified to take into account different layout configurations and safety requirements; (ii) identify operational hazards caused by the relations and interactions among operators, robots, layouts and tasks; and (iii) introduce and validate suitable reduction measures to counter them. Unlike other approaches, our methodology emphasizes the effects of the presence of operators in the system and their choices in the execution order of the actions within a task.

As future work, we will include risk estimation techniques into the methodology to evaluate the level of risk associated with different possible execution orders of actions within a task. This will allow us to compare the criticality of each ordering and to help the operator to choose the one with the lowest risk value. We also aim to develop a framework based on the presented methodology to support safety engineers from the early design phases—e.g., semi-formal descriptions of tasks—to the introduction of risk reduction measures mitigating identified hazards.

References

1. The Zot bounded satisfiability checker. http://github.com/fm-polimi/zot
2. Baracchi, L., Cimatti, A., Garcia, G., Mazzini, S., Puri, S., Tonetta, S.: Requirements refinement and component reuse: the FoReVer contract-based approach. In: Handbook of Research on Embedded Systems Design (2014)
3. Baresi, L., Kallehbasti, M.M.P., Rossi, M.: How bit-vector logic can help improve the verification of LTL specifications over infinite domains. In: Proceedings of SAC, pp. 1666–1673 (2016)
4. Dhillon, B.S., Fashandi, A.R.M.: Safety and reliability assessment techniques in robotics. Robotica 15(6), 701–708 (1997)
5. Espiau, B., Kapellos, K., Jourdan, M.: Formal verification in robotics: why and how? In: Giralt, G., Hirzinger, G. (eds.) Robotics Research, pp. 225–236. Springer, London (1996)
6. Fung, P., Norgate, G., Dilts, T., Jones, A., Ravindran, R.: Human-in-the-loop machine control loop. Patent nr. US 5116180 A (1992)
7. Furia, C.A., Mandrioli, D., Morzenti, A., Rossi, M.: Modeling Time in Computing. Monographs in Theoretical Computer Science. An EATCS Series. Springer, Heidelberg (2012)
8. Guiochet, J.: Hazard analysis of human-robot interactions with HAZOP-UML. Saf. Sci. 84, 225–237 (2016)
9. Guiochet, J., Do Hoang, Q.A., Kaaniche, M., Powell, D.: Model-based safety analysis of human-robot interactions: the MIRAS walking assistance robot. In: Proceedings of the International Conference on Rehabilitation Robotics (ICORR), pp. 1–7 (2013)
10. International Electrotechnical Commission: IEC 61882, Hazard and operability studies (HAZOP studies) Application guide (2001)
11. International Standard Organisation: ISO10218-2:2011, Robots and robotic devices - Safety requirements for industrial robots - Part 2: Robot Systems and Integration
12. International Standard Organisation: ISO12100:2010, Safety of machinery - General principles for design - Risk assessment and risk reduction

13. International Standard Organisation: ISO13849-1:2015, Safety of machinery - Safety-related parts of control systems - Part 1: General principles for design
14. International Standard Organisation: ISO14121-2:2007, Safety of machinery - Risk assessment - Part 2
15. International Standard Organisation: ISO/TS15066:2015, Robots and robotic devices - Collaborative robots
16. Leveson, N.: Engineering a Safer World: Systems Thinking Applied to Safety. MIT Press, Cambridge (2011)
17. Machin, M., Dufossé, F., Blanquart, J.-P., Guiochet, J., Powell, D., Waeselynck, H.: Specifying safety monitors for autonomous systems using model-checking. In: Bondavalli, A., Di Giandomenico, F. (eds.) SAFECOMP 2014. LNCS, vol. 8666, pp. 262–277. Springer, Heidelberg (2014)
18. Machin, M., Dufossé, F., Guiochet, J., Powell, D., Roy, M., Waeselynck, H.: Model-checking and game theory for synthesis of safety rules. In: Proceedings of HASE (2015)
19. Martin-Guillerez, D., Guiochet, J., Powell, D., Zanon, C.: A UML-based method for risk analysis of human-robot interactions. In: Proceedings of SERENE, pp. 32–41. ACM (2010)
20. Pradella, M., Morzenti, A., San Pietro, P.: Bounded satisfiability checking of metric temporal logic specifications. ACM TOSEM **22**(3), 1–54 (2013)

Adapting the Orthogonal Defect Classification Taxonomy to the Space Domain

Nuno Silva[1,2(✉)] and Marco Vieira[2]

[1] CRITICAL Software S.A., Coimbra, Portugal
nsilva@criticalsoftware.com
[2] DEI/CISUC, University of Coimbra, Coimbra, Portugal
{npsilva,mvieira}@dei.uc.pt

Abstract. Space systems are developed using conservative technologies and processes and respecting requirements and restrictions imposed by specific standards, domain policies, and design and optimization constraints. However, the artefacts produced at each lifecycle phase are not perfect. To overcome this, Independent Software Verification and Validation (ISVV) represents a valuable asset to detect issues, but, a proper and efficient issue classification system is necessary to analyze the root causes, identify the development processes to improve, and assess the efficiency of verification activities. The Orthogonal Defect Classification (ODC) is the most commonly used and adopted classification scheme, but was not originally targeted to engineering issues in critical systems. In this paper we present an empirical study where ODC has been used to classify space domain issues and propose an adaptation of the taxonomy for space systems.

Keywords: Defect · Safety critical · Quality · Dependability · Root cause analysis

1 Introduction

Following a standard is not enough to guarantee defect free software, thus complementary processes such as Independent Software Verification and Validation (ISVV) are required. The objective of ISVV is to provide complementary and independent assessments of the software artefacts to find remaining defects and allow their correction in a timely manner. Independence is the most important concept of ISVV and it has been referred to and used in safety-critical domains such as civil aviation (DO-178B [1]), railway signalling systems (CENELEC [2]), and space (ECSS working groups (e.g. [3, 4])). However, these systems are still far from being perfect, and it is common to hear about software bugs in aeronautics, car accidents caused by software problems, a satellite system that needs to be patched (for corrections or updates) after launch and so on. Defects can impact important properties of the system: functionality, performance, maintainability, safety and cause system degradation.

Consolidated ISVV metrics [18] works show that standards and engineering practices are not enough to guarantee the required levels of safety and dependability of critical

© Springer International Publishing Switzerland 2016
A. Skavhaug et al. (Eds.): SAFECOMP 2016, LNCS 9922, pp. 296–308, 2016.
DOI: 10.1007/978-3-319-45477-1_23

systems (CS), thus we have applied the Orthogonal Defect Classification (ODC) [6] to issues identified by ISVV to study their classification (type, trigger and impact).

In practice, we classified ISVV issues from space systems using ODC (a total of 1070 ISVV issues). The conclusions are that most of the defect types are related to documentation issues, functionality issues, and defective implementations of the planned functions. The main defect triggers are related to document consistency, traceability activities, and test activities. The principal defect impacts include capability, reliability, maintainability, and documentation quality. However, as mentioned before, ODC was not specifically developed nor even intended to target critical systems, thus almost one third of the issues in our dataset could not be adequately classified.

In order to enhance ODC for better applicability to critical systems and support to root cause analysis, this paper proposes specific adaptations of the Type, Trigger and Impact taxonomies. The adaptation has been defined after conducting the classification of the 1070 issues with the original ODC and by carefully analysing the classification gaps. To validate the modifications, the adapted ODC was used to reclassify the entire dataset in a simple and unequivocal way. This work should help engineering in tackling the main problems and the more common ones first, and not one by one (as is done now and traditionally). This larger picture of results will help addressing the causes that lead to more problems, in a way that future corrections and recommendations right away affect most of the issues. Also, problems related to technologies, tools, methods, standards and culture will be easily identifiable and corrected/improved. Currently in industry there are no generic nor commonly accepted classification and root cause techniques (these are done mostly ad hoc) and such processes are required to help determining the procedures to change or improve, the training required by the different teams, the changes on application of the standards, the tools to apply and so on. We intend to take a step forward towards defining such a process.

This paper presents background and related work in Sect. 2. Section 3 describes the analysis procedure. An overview of the case studies is presented in Sect. 4. The ODC taxonomy adaptations are listed in Sect. 5. The results of applying the improved taxonomy are summarized in Sect. 6 with threats to the validity in Sect. 7. Finally, conclusions and future work are presented in Sect. 8.

2 Background and Related Work

ODC is one of the more adopted defect classification approaches originally proposed by IBM (Chillarege et al. [6]). ODC is quite generic but it is mostly oriented to design, code and testing defects. The goal of ODC is to support the analysis and feedback of defect data targeting quality issues mostly in software design, code and documentation. Other classification taxonomies have been studied before selecting ODC[1], namely (a) Beizer's [25], (b) Kaner, Falk and Nguyen's [25], (c) Robert Binder's [25],

---

[1] ODC was selected since it was the only taxonomy claiming to be orthogonal, quite mature and widely used (several academic and industrial publications refer to and use ODC).

(d) Whittaker's "How to Break Software" [25], (e) Vijayaraghavan's eCommerce [25], (f) Hewlett Packard [26], and (g) IEEE Standard Classification for Software Anomalies [27]. The current ODC specification is at version 5.2 and defines eight attributes for defect classification, divided into two main groups, depending on the defect phase in which they are classified: (a) opener, and (b) closer. Three attributes (Activity, Trigger and Impact) are used to classify when the defect is discovered and so they are part of the opener group. The other five attributes (Target, Type, Qualifier, Age and Source) are used when the defect is resolved, being part of the closer group. The values for each attribute can be obtained from the ODC v5.2 specification. Section 5 presents the tailoring performed to the ODC specification to better comply with the needs of space critical systems.

ODC has been used as a starting point for developing new and focused defect taxonomies for particular domains. A few examples of this were presented by Leszak et al. [10] and Margarido et al. [12], which used ODC for studying, building and validating defect categorization schemes.

ISVV is a set of structured engineering activities and tools that allow independent analysts to evaluate the quality of the software engineering artefacts produced at each phase. ISVV provides an additional layer of confidence and is not expected to find a large number of severe issues. In practice, ISVV produces evidences that can support measuring the quality of the software and is referenced in several international standards, the ISVV guide [5], ISO/IEC 12207 [8] and formalized in IEEE 1012 [7].

ISVV is usually composed of six main phases that can be executed sequentially or selected/adapted as the result of a tailoring process [5]:

- **ISVV Planning:** planning of the activities and selection of the appropriate methods and tools to be applied.
- **Specification/Requirements Verification:** verification for completeness, correctness, consistency, testability. Maps to ODC activity 'Requirements Verification'.
- **Architectural/Design Verification:** adequacy and conformance to requirements and interfaces, the internal and external consistency checks and the verification of feasibility and maintenance. Maps to the ODC activity 'Design Verification'.
- **Source Code Verification:** verification of completeness, correctness, consistency and traceability through inspections, metrics analysis, standards compliance verification and static analysis. Maps to the ODC activity 'Code Verification'.
- **Test Specification/Results Verification:** verification of the test artefacts, including test specs, procedures, results and reports, traceability verifications and completion of test areas. This phase maps to the ODC activity 'Test Verification'.
- **Independent Validation:** based on the identification of unstable components/ functionalities and missing testing areas to promote validation on Error-Handling. Includes test execution, and maps to the ODC activity 'Test execution'.

Typically, ISVV classifies issues according to three severity levels: (a) *Major* – a significant impact in the system dependability, quality or safety; (b) *Minor* – a minimum impact; and (c) *Comment* – an improvement suggestion (not really a defect).

Previous studies have been performed for critical systems analysis, but mostly from the perspective of metrics, efficiency and efficacy of the techniques used to identify the defects and issues [18–21], and not from point-of-view of the suitability of classification of issues to improve the development processes, techniques, tools, and standards, nor for issues from mission- and safety-critical systems, nor an extensive and complete classification and root cause analysis for embedded systems. Li et al. [13] performed a study and ODC adaptation for black box testing results only. Although they effectively made a detailed analysis for those types of tests, our study covers the full spectrum of the development lifecycle defects and is thus intended to be more general while applicable to critical systems.

The objective of our work is to provide a classification method to support correlation of defects and the development properties (quality model), and to classify orthogonally the defects. The ODC approach is mostly applicable from the design to the coding and testing phases and for defects detected during those phases. ODC is commonly used as a starting point for developing new and focused defect taxonomies for particular domains but, as far as we know, not for critical embedded systems (as we are doing).

Several researchers have looked at the analysis of failures in safety-critical systems during different life-cycle phases (from requirements to operations) and performed empirical studies and root-cause analysis [11, 14–16]. For example, Seaman et al. [17] used historical datasets with inspection defect data and applied different categorization schemes to the defects. M. Jones has also provided an interesting study about space failures in the frame of the European Space Agency missions [9], but simply concluded that the main cause for all the accidents was lack of testing.

Wagner [23] has presented work using ODC and questioning the taxonomies and the applicability of the classification types. Other works also agree that it is not an easy task to create a one size fits all solution for appropriate defect classification and evaluation [22–24]. In summary, no classification is commonly agreed nor widely used to organize in classes the defects properties and allow defects analysis. Our paper considers a large set of Critical Systems (CS) issues, covering CS properties, and applying ODC as a promising start point, now in the context of embedded critical systems, and empirically determining the best classification taxonomy.

3   Analysis Procedure

The procedure followed for the analysis, classification and adaptation of the ODC taxonomy for ISVV issues in critical systems is as follows:

(1) **ISVV Issues Selection** – selection of the ISVV issues. In order to have representative data for the engineering processes, the selection was based on several criteria, namely confirmed issues (1070 issues), different missions (4 missions), diverse prime contractors (3) and software development entities (a dozen), several types and sizes of systems or sub-systems (more than 10), issues from all the software development lifecycle phases (specification: 199; architecture: 189; implementation: 297; testing: 381) and issues identified after system deployment (4 issues). In practice, a significant amount of issues is considered in order to allow a statistical analysis of the observations.

(2) **Data Clean-Up/Anonymization** – anonymization of the data to avoid passing sensitive information such as mission, system and customer/software developer information, which are obviously ruled by non-disclosure agreements. This is the reason why we do not present a more detailed characterization of the datasets used in the study.

(3) **Data Classification (ODC)** – application of ODC (v5.2 [6]) to the issues selected and identification of the issues that could not be classified. ODC identifies a limited number of defect types, impacts and the relevant triggers (assessment techniques, testing, analysis methods, etc.) for each defect. In addition to supporting our study, the results can be used for statistical quality control (e.g. measuring improvements), as well as for in-process monitoring and reliability assessment (required for critical systems). They are also frequently used to promote specific process and resources improvements by tackling the identified issues directly. The main contributions of step (3) are: (i) application of the ODC approach to critical issues datasets; (ii) identification of classification difficulties; and (iii) the classified issues themselves. A summary of the overall results of this work is presented in Sect. 5. The results indicate the need of adaptation for critical systems, as stated in step (4).

(4) **Results Analysis [ODC Adaptation]** – analysis of the classification results and definition of a new classification taxonomy. Once the classification work has been performed (in step (3)), the obtained classifications have been analysed and the results used for the adaptation of the ODC taxonomy (type, trigger and impact) in order to align with the critical systems issues. In practice, we used data analysis to identify classification patterns. Results of this step are presented in Sect. 5.

(5) **Recommendations** – validate the ODC adaptation by using it to re-classify the issues. See Sect. 6 for the results of this step.

4 Case Studies

The case studies are in the space domain (satellite systems), and cover different types of systems (start-up or boot software, on-board application software, payload software, full system), the data comes from 2 control systems, several payload systems boot software and one overall system. The data are from Earth Observation and Science satellites. The engineering processes used for the selected missions followed the ECSS standards [3] (E-40, the engineering standard) and [4] (Q-80, the quality standard) and thus had a quite similar lifecycle and similar strict requirements imposed by the European Space Agency (ESA). An independent team has identified the issues after the development teams have performed their own required verification and validation activities. The issues (called Review Item Discrepancies) are defects detected in the development artefacts with major or minor impact, or comments to improve the engineering.

These subsystems needs/objectives/requirements, common to space systems, have been collected from the ECCS standards [3, 4] and engineering interpretation of mission specifications documents and characterize the case studies of the data, including:

Table 1. ISVV issues quantification

Severity	Req. Verification	Design verif.	Code verif.	Test verif.	Operations	Total
Major	27	14	43	62	2	**148**
Minor	98	84	185	294	18	**679**
Improv.	37	14	150	42	0	**243**
Total	162	112	378	398	20	**1070**

- No crash or hang shall happen at any time;
- No dynamic memory allocation is allowed;
- Communications must always be possible between ground and the satellite;
- A Safe Mode (basic communications, patch and dump) must exist;
- A very simple and stable start-up software (also called boot software);
- There must be a watchdog (Hardware and/or Software) or an alive signal;
- Systems are built with redundancy (at least for Hardware);
- Most systems must include FDIR (Fault Detection Isolation and Recovery);
- These systems must have high autonomy and some self-correction procedures;
- Systems are categorized with a criticality level (consequences of system failures).

The projects analysed are also characterized by:

- Requirements written in natural language (structured), highly based on documentation and non-formal processes and languages;
- Documentation in UML/SysML and PDF;
- Programming languages such as C, Ada and Assembly, that are quite mature and low level languages;
- Unit tests performed in commercial tools (e.g. Cantata ++, VectorCast, LDRA), commonly adapted for the specific projects embedded systems and environments;
- Integration and system testing performed in specific validation environment (Software Validation Facility - SVF) developed for the purpose on a case by case situation, with HW emulation and HW in-the-loop, simulated instruments, etc.

The types of issues are presented in Table 1. A large amount of Major issues is still caught during ISVV. With this dataset we are covering all phases and severities, with emphasis on the phases that traditionally identify more issues (code and test analysis).

The issues come from different ISVV activities (requirements, design, code and test verification) and post-launch corrections (called Operation Monitoring). The dataset includes issues from 16 different systems or subsystems, and 14 % have been classified as Major issues, 66 % as Minor, and 20 % as Improvements. They originated from the analysis of more than 10,000 Software requirements, more than 1 million lines of code, and over 3,000 tests, and were not caught by the original V&V activities.

In all the case studies, the objective of the ISVV team was to find issues in the project artefacts and report and classify them in a clear and consistent way for the customer to act upon. The issues were originally classified using the classification adopted by the ISVV team, which is composed of the following types:

- **External consistency:** inconsistencies among artefacts from one phase to the next or with other applicable or reference artefacts (e.g. inconsistent documentation);
- **Internal consistency:** inconsistency within the same artefact (e.g. different code for same purpose, differences within a document or architectural components);
- **Correctness:** item incorrectly implemented or with technical issues (e.g. erroneous implementation, wrong documentation description, bad architectural definition);
- **Technical feasibility:** item not technically feasible with the actual constraints (e.g. unattainable or impossible requirement, architecture nor viable);
- **Readability and Maintainability:** item hard to understand and/or maintain (e.g. lack of comments or no description, requirements too complex or too generic);
- **Completeness:** item not completely defined or insufficient details provided (e.g. missing details, insufficient requirements, not all requirements coded);
- **Superfluous:** item that is a repetition or brings no added value to the artefact (e.g. repeated requirements, copy-pasted code doing the same actions);
- **Improvement:** suggestion to improve an artefact usually not related to one of the other classification types (e.g. efficiency, simplicity, readability);
- **Accuracy:** the item does not describe with precision or follows the applicable standard (e.g. measurement precision, calculation precision, exact implementation).

The main types of issues, as classified by the ISVV engineers, are external consistency (differences between the implementation of artefacts between phases), completeness (missing information/implementations), and correctness (wrong implementation/design). These three types account for 75 % of the total of issues.

In what concerns the issues that have been totally classified with ODC and the issues that had at least one attribute (type, trigger or impact) that could not be mapped, about 1/3 of the issues could not be completely classified (e.g. some traceability issues were partially classified as Backward or Lateral Compatibility, the Internal Document trigger that was replaced by Consistency/Completeness a more used terminology for the engineers, or some configuration defects that could not be properly classified as HW or SW only), which supports our argument about the need for adapting ODC for CS (out of the non-classified issues, 27 % were comments, 59 % minor issues, and 14 % major issues, compared to 21 %, 66 % and 14 %, for the ones classified). An important aspect is that the new classification of the issues shall support the identification of the most common problem types, their triggers and their impacts in order to act upon the causes and improve the software processes and find gaps in the applied standards, techniques and processes. For example, in some cases where requirements were repeated or redundant, we had difficulties in using ODC for specifying the defect type and impact, as it could be documentation and maintenance, but also function and documentation. On the opposite, the use of magic numbers in code was easily classified in the documentation type and maintenance impact.

5   ODC Adaptation for Space Critical Systems

This section proposes modifications to ODC taking into account our findings while classifying the issues presented in Sect. 4 using the original ODC (v5.2).

Three main activities have been performed to contribute to the proposed taxonomy: (a) **data analysis** to identify the missing classification types, triggers and impacts, in order to properly cover the classifications; (b) **expert judgement** on the non-classified issues, trying to understand why they could not be properly classified (e.g., why there were difficulties and doubts when deciding between a rare situation trigger and a side effects trigger, as they appeared similar); and (c) **proposal of adaptations** to ODC and re-classification of the issues that could not be classified with the original taxonomy to validate the proposed adaptations. The modifications to the ODC taxonomy were based on: (a) an analysis of a significant number of defects that could not clearly be classified during the first round (more than 300); (b) the grouping of the classification difficulties by generic types/triggers/impacts; (c) a comparison and mapping of the groups to ODC existing taxonomy; (d) the suggestions for additional taxonomy elements from experts; and (e) the merging of classification elements to promote an easier classification.

5.1 ODC Attributes – Trigger

Triggers classify what actions or checks may uncover the defect. Some changes to the triggers were made from the standard ODC specification in order to simplify and streamline it as much as possible (for each trigger a small description provides the rationale in order to better clarify when to use it):

- **Design conformance, Logic/Flow, Concurrency, Test coverage, Test variation, Test sequencing, Test interaction, Workload/Stress, Start-up/Restart, Recovery/Exception, Blocked test** – same meaning as ODC v5.2.
- **Standards conformance** – replaces the original 'Language Dependency' trigger, broadening the scope to better suit issues in critical systems. It is applicable to defects that arise when checking items for standards compliance (which typically do not exist for the systems for which ODC was originally defined). This includes requirements not written according to specific rules, deviation from best practices.
- **Traceability/Compatibility** – replaces both 'Backward Compatibility' and 'Lateral Compatibility' in the ODC v5.2 specification. It is applicable in cases where traceability is unclear or missing, or system blocks have compatibility issues. This merge and adaption was deemed necessary to cover specific requirements related to CS (where traceability is a strong quality assurance and safety assurance requirement) and requirements imposed by standards that extensively use traceability.
- **Consistency/Completeness** – replaces the 'Internal Document' trigger, providing a more appropriate terminology, such as the one CS engineers are used to. Defects related to incorrect information, inconsistency or incompleteness are mapped here.
- **Rare situation** – this trigger is the result of the merge of both 'Side Effects' and 'Rare Situation' from the ODC v5.2 specification. We did not find it relevant to separate the two in our case studies due to their frequency and similarity. Also, it was very difficult to specifically map to one or another in several cases.
- **White box path coverage** – merged 'Simple path coverage' and 'Complex path coverage', applicable in unit testing when the tester is exercising specific paths, as both are required and demand the same level of attention in CS testing strategies.

- **HW/SW configuration** – merged 'Hardware configuration' and 'Software configuration' to cover configuration issues at large, as no major difference was found that require to keep them separate. Also, hardware and software in embedded systems are strongly coupled, thus making such distinction while classifying issues may lead to many doubts without relevant added value.

5.2   ODC Attributes – Impact

This attribute depicts the impact that the defect would have had upon the end user if it was not detected during ISVV, or in the case of operation monitoring reported defects, what was the impact of the failure. The proposed adaptations are:

- **Capability, Documentation, Installibility, Integrity/Security, Migration, Performance, Reliability, Requirements, Standards, Usability**– same as ODC v5.2.
- **Maintenance** – merged with 'Serviceability', as for CS the definition of the two is similar and refer to diagnosing issues and applying corrective/preventive actions.
- **Safety** – added for the cases where defects in CS can directly impact the safety of humans or of the environment (these are specific requirements for many CS).
- **Testability/Verifiability** – added to fulfil the need to classify defects with an impact in testability/verifiability of the systems. This is important to the applicable standards conformance in critical systems since testability and verifiability are commonly strict requirements that need to be part of the system.

5.3   ODC Attributes – Type

The type attribute represents where the defect was actually fixed. We adapted the ODC v5.2 classification and extended it when appropriate for our needs, as follows:

- **Algorithm/Method, Checking, Function/Class/Object, Timing/Serialization, Documentation** – same as ODC v5.2.
- **Assignment/Initialization** – similar to ODC v5.2, but extendable to cases where, for instance, variable names are changed to be in compliance with coding standards (frequently required for critical systems).
- **Build/Package/Environment** – applied in defects related to the build process, packaging of data/functionality, and environment setup. Includes libraries that are never used, or large dead code. Several issues couldn't be classified exactly into one of these types, and merging them simplifies the classifier job (and improves the orthogonality of the taxonomy).
- **Interface** – merged 'Interface' and 'Relationship' into one single type, as both relate to interfaces (internal or external) and the classification was not always obvious due to the interface specificities of embedded CS.

An overview of the initial classification using ODC is shown Table 2, together with the results of re-classification using the adapted ODC taxonomy.

Table 2. Top 5 ODC classifications

Defect type	AR (%)	BR (%)	Defect trigger	AR (%)	BR (%)	Defect impact	AR (%)	BR (%)
Documentation	48.1	36.1	Traceability/Compatibility	28.9	19.3	Capability	28.8	30.2
Function/Class/Object	19.0	21.3	Test coverage	21.2	19.8	Maintenance	24.7	18.7
Algorithm/Method	9.0	11.4	Consistency/Completeness	19.3	22.3	Reliability	23.6	24.8
Checking	6.4	6.6	Logic/Flow	11.1	13.0	Documentation	14.7	18.6
Interface	5.2	6.6	Design conformance	11.1	11.8	Performance	3.6	3.8
Total	**87.7**	**82.0**	**Total**	**91.6**	**86.2**	**Total**	**95.4**	**96.1**

AR: Values after the reclassification (100 % of the issues with the adapted taxonomy)
BR: Values before the reclassification (covering the classification of 68.3 % of the issues)

6 Reclassification with the Adapted ODC Taxonomy

The application of the adapted taxonomy to the dataset produced the results depicted in Table 2. In addition to the important facts that no issue was left unclassified and that most of the issues were classified in a much easier way (for example, about 30 h to reclassify 100 issues, when compared to the 75 h per 100 issues in the initial classification), the results highlight the following:

- More 'Documentation' defect types were observed (12 % increase). This can be justified by the fact that critical systems highly depend on documentation and documented evidences to prove the accomplishment of requirements and standards.
- 'Traceability/Compatibility' is the more frequent trigger and even 'Test Coverage' became a trigger which lead to the identification of more defects than 'Consistency and Completeness'. This suggests that the best defect triggers are the simplest.
- The 'Maintenance' defect impact became more frequent than 'Reliability', and the 'Documentation' impact frequency has been reduced. In fact, maintainability is an important property (more than reliability) for the systems in our dataset. Most of the new Documentation type defects lead to Maintenance impact and not Documentation impact (which was the default before re-classification).

The effort for re-classification included: (1) understanding (reading) of the defect text; (2) classification of the defect type (according to corrective action type); (3) classification of the defect trigger (how was the defect found); and (4) classification of the defect impact. Furthermore, in order to clarify some issues about the classification we consulted the original documentation (specifications, design, code, test artefacts) to make a more precise and educated decision on the classification. Finally, a confirmation was performed on the classification between the classification engineer and the author of this paper. The end result was **18 min per defect** for the rec-classification. The reduction in the classification effort is partly due to the knowledge acquired during the first classification attempt, where the non-classified defects have been assessed. Most of the re-classification was however performed by an experienced engineer together with the main author while the first classification round was performed by the main author together with another engineer.

A practical observation of the results in Table 2 shows that the 5 main types, triggers and impacts cover about 90 % of the issues analysed showing that with 5 taxonomy elements we are covering the large majority of the issues. This observation suggests that actions can be taken to quickly improve the quality of systems.

7 Threats to Validity

The fact that the issues data cannot be shared nor publicized, as no company wants their issues exposed, makes this work harder and a great effort of anonymization had to be performed. Also, the acceptance of the results may be challenged.

The space systems involved cover most of the development activities performed for those systems, and involve different companies (at geographic, size and management level), thus we consider these results to be quite general for this domain. A similar study for other domains (e.g. railway) is undergoing, but existing data is not as structured as for space systems. Again, data confidentiality will be a challenging issue.

The classification is done based on the opinion and knowledge of experts. However, it is important to note that the initial ODC (the one that could not classify all the issues) was performed by two engineers, whose work was also checked by a third space domain expert. This domain expert also performed the reclassification himself (verified and discussed with another space domain expert engineer).

Finally, the adaptations were performed based on the 31.7 % of the issues that could not be classified with the initial ODC. This required several rounds of discussion, and the majority of changes are merges where terms were not well distinguishable for these systems. Also, details about the systems requirements (namely non-functional, safety and dependability, etc.) originated doubts about the initial ODC classification. The justifications are briefly stated in Sect. 5.

8 Conclusions and Future Work

The classification issues identified by the ISVV teams using ODC allowed the classification of 739 issues (out of 1070). The remaining $\sim$ 32 % could not be fully classified and required an improved taxonomy, which is proposed and applied in this paper. In addition to the analysis of a large dataset of real issues in space critical systems, this work proposes an adaptation or extension of ODC that allows a more complete classification and thus a better analysis of the results. The initial classification effort for the 1070 issues consumed approximately 800 h. The new taxonomy is appropriate for our dataset as all the issues are classified. The proposed new taxonomy is currently supporting root cause and defects analysis and prioritization allowing actions to be taken on the most important (major) issues, the most frequent ones, the ones with common root causes or with the more severe impacts (such as safety). This taxonomy can suffer adjustments in order to cope with technology or specific domain needs.

The results presented in this paper can help the space industrial community in focusing on the weakest points of the engineering process to improve them (e.g. review process application, test planning and strategy). Also, by using the adapted ODC, ISVV teams can work much more efficiently with the triggers that catch more problems and even develop appropriate and more precise V&V tools (e.g. logic & dataflow analysis, fault injection, traceability verification). This way, we propose several improvements and topics that should be tackled as future work. Firstly, we need to test the completeness and effectiveness of this new adapted classification taxonomy with other datasets (currently being applied to hundreds of railway systems defects with no hassle demonstrating its applicability – suggesting that the adapted ODC is not only specific to space but can be general to other critical systems). Secondly, we need to enlarge the analysis to include more and larger datasets (covering all activities for each dataset, for example). Thirdly, the analysis of the results should be also done per defect removal activity (requirements, design, implementation, testing, operations). Then, we need to perform root cause analysis on the ODC resulting classification. Finally, it is important to measure the impact of the proposed changes in the engineering processes, especially in terms of the reduction of the number of issues found during ISVV analysis.

Acknowledgements. This work has been partially supported by the European Project FP7-2012-324334-CECRIS (CErtification of CRItical Systems).

References

1. RTCA DO-178B (EUROCAE ED-12B), Software Considerations in Airborne Systems and Equipment Certification, RTCA Inc., Washington, DC, December 1992
2. CENELEC EN 50128: Railway applications - Communication, signalling and processing systems - Software for railway control and protection systems
3. ECSS-E-ST-40C, Space engineering - Software, ECSS, 06/03/2009
4. ECSS-Q-ST-80, Space Product Assurance - Software Product Assurance, ECSS, 06/03/2009
5. ESA ISVV Guide, issue 2.0, 29/12/2008, European Space Agency
6. Orthogonal Defect Classification v 5.2 for Software Design and Code, IBM, 12 September 2013
7. IEEE 1012-2004 - IEEE Standard for Software Verification and Validation. IEEE Computer Society
8. ISO/IEC 12207:2008 Systems and software engineering – Software life cycle processes
9. Jones, M.: Software Engineering: Are we getting better at it? ESA Bulletin **121**, 52–57 (2005)
10. Leszak, M., Perry, D.E., Stoll, D.: Classification and evaluation of defects in a project retrospective. J. Syst. Softw. **61**, 173–187 (2002)
11. Leszak, M., Perry, D.E., Stoll, D.: A case study in root cause defect analysis. In: Proceedings of 22nd International Conference SW Engineering (ICSE'00), pp. 428–437. IEEE CS Press, Los Alamitos (2002)
12. Margarido, L., João Pascoal, I., Raul, F., Vidal, M., Vieira, M.: Classification of defect types in requirements specifications: literature review, proposal and assessment. In: 2011 6th Iberian Conference on Information Systems and Technologies (CISTI), pp. 1–6. IEEE (2011). http://ieeexplore.ieee.org/xpls/abs_all.jsp?arnumber=5974237
13. Li, N., Li, Z., Sun, X.: Classification of software defect detected by black-box testing: an empirical study. In: 2010 Second World Congress on Software Engineering (WCSE), Wuhan, pp. 234–240 (2010). doi:10.1109/WCSE.2010.28

14. Lutz, R.R., Mikulski, I.C.: Empirical analysis of safety-critical anomalies during operations. IEEE Trans. Softw. Eng. **30**(3), 172–180 (2004)
15. Lutz, R.: Analyzing software requirements errors in safety-critical, embedded systems. In: Proceedings of IEEE International Symposium Requirements Engineering, pp. 126–133. IEEE CS Press (1993)
16. Lutz, R., Mikulski, I.C.: Operational anomalies as a cause of safety-critical requirements evolution. J. Syst. Softw. **65**, 155–161 (2003)
17. Seaman, C.B., Shull, F., Regardie, M., Elbert, D., Feldmann, R.L., Guo, Y., Godfrey, S.: Defect categorization: making use of a decade of widely varying historical data. In: Proceedings of the Second ACM-IEEE International Symposium on Empirical Software Engineering and Measurement, pp. 149–57. ACM (2008). http://dl.acm.org/citation.cfm?id=1414030
18. Silva, N., Rui, L.: Independent test verification: what metrics have a word to say. In: 1st International Workshop on Software Certification (WoSoCER), ISSRE, Hiroshima, Japan, 30 November 2011
19. Silva, N.; Lopes, R.: Overview of 10 years of ISVV findings in safety-critical systems. In: 2012 IEEE 23rd International Symposium on Software Reliability Engineering Work-shops (ISSREW), p. 83, 27–30 November 2012
20. Silva, N.; Lopes, R.: Independent assessment of safety-critical systems: we bring data!. In: 2012 IEEE 23rd International Symposium on Software Reliability Engineering Workshops (ISSREW), p. 84, 27–30 November 2012
21. Silva, N., Lopes, R.: 10 years of ISVV: what's next? In: 2012 IEEE 23rd International Symposium on Software Reliability Engineering Workshops (ISSREW), pp. 361–366, 27–30 November 2012
22. Diego, V., Grazioli, F., Herbert, J.: A framework to evaluate defect taxonomies. In: XV Congreso Argentino de Ciencias de La Computación (2009). http://sedici.unlp.edu.ar/handle/10915/20983
23. Stefan, W.: Defect classification and defect types revisited. In: Proceedings of the 2008 Workshop on Defects in Large Software Systems, pp. 39–40. ACM (2008). http://dl.acm.org/citation.cfm?id=1390829
24. Wagner, S.: A model and sensitivity analysis of the quality economics of defect-detection techniques. In: Proceedings of ISSTA 2006, pp. 73–83. ACM Press (2006)
25. Copeland L.: Software Defect Taxonomies. http://flylib.com/books/en/2.156.1.108/1/
26. Grady, R.B.: Practical Software Metrics For Project Management and Process Improvement. HP (1992)
27. IEEE: IEEE 1044-2009 Standard Classification for Software Anomalies. Institute of Electrical and Electronics Engineers, 7 January 2010

Towards Cloud-Based Enactment
of Safety-Related Processes

Sami Alajrami[1(✉)], Barbara Gallina[2], Irfan Sljivo[2], Alexander Romanovsky[1],
and Petter Isberg[2]

[1] Newcastle University, Newcastle upon Tyne, UK
{s.h.alajrami,alexander.romanovsky}@newcastle.ac.uk
[2] Mälardalen University, Västerås, Sweden
{barbara.gallina,irfan.sljivo,petter.isberg}@mdh.se

Abstract. Engineering safety-critical systems is a complex task which involves multiple stakeholders. It requires shared and scalable computation to systematically involve geographically distributed teams. The paper proposes a model-driven cloud-based enactment architecture automating safety-critical processes. This work adapts our previous work on cloud-based software engineering by enriching the architecture with an automatic support for generation of both, product-based safety arguments from failure logic analysis results and process-based arguments from the process model and the enactment data. The approach is demonstrated using a fragment of a process adapted from the aerospace domain.

Keywords: Safety process enactment · Argumentation · Cloud computing

1 Introduction

The malfunctioning of safety-critical systems may lead to catastrophic consequences to the environment and people. Safety-critical systems are identified as complex systems and their engineering has to follow best practices. More specifically, (safety) standards provide guidance in terms of reference process models for the development and assessment of such systems. The complexity of such systems is reflected in their supply chain, which consists of a complex, geographically-distributed and heterogeneous supply network. The suppliers provide software/hardware components or automation of certain activities during the production. This compositional nature is reflected in software-specific, hardware-specific, tool qualification-specific, system-specific and method-specific guidance and/or reference processes recommended by standards. To be released on the market, the integrated systems must be certified. The certification process in various domains is conducted by scrutinizing an argument supporting system safety [16]. In the automotive and rail domains, such argument is known as *safety case*. In the aerospace domain, an explicit safety case is not required however as discussed by Holloway [13] an implicit safety case request is contained within

© Springer International Publishing Switzerland 2016
A. Skavhaug et al. (Eds.): SAFECOMP 2016, LNCS 9922, pp. 309–321, 2016.
DOI: 10.1007/978-3-319-45477-1_24

the standards. While the considerations listed in this paper hold for several complex safety-critical systems, we focus on aircraft as an example of such systems. In particular, we use the Preliminary System Safety Assessment (PSSA) from ARP4761 [1] as an example which demonstrates safety process-related requirements. Aircrafts must be accompanied by a safety case that provides assurance about their behaviour as well as about the set of processes that were adopted to develop them. Safety cases can/should also reflect the compositional nature of the systems under examination. The provision of a safety case may follow a reference process [3]. The planning and execution of all the recommended reference processes is a time consuming and costly activity. Moreover, given the compositional and geographically distributed nature of the supply network, different interpretations of the processes may coexist resulting in conflicts and ultimately risk of low-quality products. To reduce time, cost as well as conflicting interpretations we propose to adapt a model-driven, cloud-based process enactment architecture for safety-critical systems. Using cloud computing not only reduces cost (through the pay-as-you-go and on-demand acquisition models), but also provides an accessible platform for the distributed teams involved in the system engineering process. In addition, artefacts from across the different geographical locations can be maintained centrally. Along with the use of a standardized process modelling language, this can reduce the conflicting interpretations. Our vision is that a manufacturer enforces the execution of the planned safety lifecycle as well as of the corresponding argumentation process. To achieve that vision, the paper provides the following contributions: (a) an extension of our cloud-based process enactment architecture from [4] for safety-critical systems (Sect. 3.1), (b) automation of product-based safety argument generation from failure logic analysis results and automation of evidence gathering, in particular, detecting sources of failures (if exist) or finding full and partial mitigators (Sect. 3.2), and (c) automation of the generation of process-based arguments directly from the process model and enactment-related provenance data (Sect. 3.2). We demonstrate the usability and effectiveness of this approach on a portion of a safety process (from PSSA) which we enact on the cloud and generate product and process based safety arguments fragments. These fragments are manually integrated within a single safety case.

The paper is structured as follows: Sect. 2 provides a background foundation. Section 3 describes our approach to enacting safety processes followed by a case study in Sect. 4. Section 5 discusses related work and finally, Sect. 6 draws our conclusions and highlights our future work.

2   Background

In this section, we recall essential information on our previous work and on safety-critical systems engineering and certification.

2.1   General Architecture on the Cloud

To enact software processes on the cloud and ease global software engineering, we proposed a model-driven cloud-based architectural solution [4]. Our solution consists of three layers: (a) the modelling layer where processes along with their enactment requirements are modelled, (b) the enactment service layer which orchestrates the process enactment on the cloud and (c) the workflow engines which are deployed on the cloud and host the enactment of individual activities. We implemented a prototype of this architecture consisting of two main components: **The Enactment Service** which consists of subcomponents for: scheduling activities execution, monitoring executions, managing artefacts and monitoring and registering workflow engines. The enactment service maintains a document-oriented database where all artefacts, activities and their meta-data are stored. Interactions with the enactment service are done through a RESTful API. **The Workflow Engine** is where the individual process activities are executed. The execution on the workflow engine is black-boxed: a workflow engine executing an activity of a process does not have information about the rest of the process execution. These two components of the prototype are decoupled (they communicate through asynchronous message queues) and are platform-independent (i.e. they can be deployed on any physical/virtual machine).

2.2   EXE-SPEM

To model the software processes and their enactment requirements, we proposed EXE-SPEM [5] which is an extension of the OMG standard Software and Systems Process Engineering Meta-model (SPEM2.0). EXE-SPEM permits process engineers to model important information needed for enabling the enactment such as: control flow of process enactment (i.e., order, conditions and loops), the responsible person for enacting each activity (task), and the cloud-specific enactment information such as: the choice of cloud deployment model (private vs. public) and the amount of computational resources required.

Table 1. Subset of EXE-SPEM modelling elements

Process	TaskUse	Activity	WorkProduct

Table 1 shows the icons of a subset of EXE-SPEM concrete syntax, obtained by decorating the SPEM2.0 icons with the symbol of the cloud. Via model-to-text transformational rules, EXE-SPEM models are mapped onto XML-based textual representations, compliant with our enactment-oriented XML-meta-model.

2.3   Aircraft Engineering and Certification

To engineer and certify safety-critical systems, various standards are at disposal. Typically, these standards provide requirements that should be followed to define the process to be used during the development and assessment of the aircraft and the software and hardware to be integrated within the aircraft. A document aimed at showing process compliance by providing a process-based argument is typically required. Besides the process requirements, safety standards also include product requirements aimed at assessing the level of a product's safety. Additional requirements target the assessment process, which, as mentioned, in many application domains is conducted by scrutinising an explicit or implicit safety case. A complete safety case as the final output of the assessment process should contain both the process and the product-based arguments. ARP4761 [1] defines Airworthiness Safety Assessment Process to handle hazardous events (system and equipment failure or malfunction that may lead to hazard). This process includes: Functional Hazard Assessment (FHA), Preliminary Aircraft Safety Assessment (PASA) and PSSA. PSSA consists of a systematic examination of a proposed system architecture(s). It takes in input the system FHA and the aircraft Fault Tree Analysis. PSSA tasks include: identifying the derived safety requirements, associating them with Development Assurance Levels (DALs) and allocating them to architectural elements. For certification purposes, both process- and product-related behavioural evidence constitute the basis for supporting safety claims. Thus, additional tasks that should be considered are: creation of arguments fragments explaining why the safety claim can be supported. PSSA is conducted according to guidelines contained in Appendix B3 of ARP4761. In this paper, we use GSN [3] and SACM [15] for representing safety case arguments. We refer the readers to [3,15] for details about these notations.

2.4   Process and Product-Based Arguments Fragments Generation

The product-based argument aims at showing that the product behaves as it should. To automate the generation of such arguments, the analysis and verification results can be exploited. For example, information about the failure behaviour of the system, extracted from the Fault Propagation and Transformation Calculus (FPTC) results, is used to generate an argument that the unacceptable failures have been successfully mitigated [17]. FPTC is a failure logic analysis allowing for the calculation of the system level failure behaviour based on the failure behaviour of the individual components. The propagation of failures from the inputs to the outputs of a component is captured via FPTC rules. The process-based argument aims at showing that the process mandated by the corresponding standard has been followed. To automate the generation of such arguments, MDSafeCer (Model-driven Safety Certification) [8] is at disposal. Via MDSafeCer, process models compliant with e.g., SPEM 2.0 are transformed into composable process-based argumentation models compliant with e.g., SACM and presented via e.g., GSN. The top level claim of the MDSafeCer generated arguments states that "the process is in compliance with the required standard and integrity level". This claim is decomposed by showing that all the activities have been executed and that in turn for each activity all the tasks have been executed and so on until an atomic work-unit is reached.

3   Cloud-Based Engineering of Safety-Critical Systems

Through the introduction and background, we have learnt that safety-critical systems engineering is a complex task which needs to comply with standards and involves heterogeneous and geographically-distributed stakeholders. Undertaking such a complex engineering task requires extensive support. In this paper, we identify some requirements that a development environment/platform should satisfy to fit for safety-critical systems engineering. These are: **R1. Process Enforcement and Reuse:** Despite the dynamicity of safety-critical processes, they still need to be enforced (including enforcing change as it happens) to maintain consistency and compliance. To avoid misinterpretations of the process (and its changes) in a distributed setting, the process should be executable. Process customization and reuse across similar projects should also be supported to save time and cost. **R2. Distribution Management:** The distribution of stakeholders not only bring communication and time difference challenges, but also brings cultural and language hindrances which might lead to misinterpretations and lack of trust between collaborating teams. This raises the need for synchronization and mutual understanding of the development process in order to minimize failure propagation between sub-systems built by different teams. **R3. Safety Artefacts Management:** Safety artefacts range from safety requirements to safety cases and safety arguments. In a dynamic and global environment, manually managing safety artefacts and continuously ensuring their consistency and compliance is an expensive task. Artefacts can be physically distributed and co-authored by multiple distributed teams. Capturing artefacts and their meta-data is also related to capturing safety evidence that is used to support safety cases.

This list is not comprehensive and other necessary requirements may exist. Therefore, the development platform should be extensible. In this paper we focus on supporting the ones mentioned above.

3.1   Extended Architecture for Safety-Critical Systems Engineering

In a previous work [4], we focused on supporting global software development using a model-driven cloud-based architecture. In this work, we extend that architecture to fully satisfy the requirements identified in Sect. 3. The extension affects the following: **Artefacts:** we introduce versioning of artefacts in which each change introduced to an artefact is treated as a new version. The versions (and meta-data) are kept in a central repository on the cloud. This satisfies requirement *R3* as artefacts are unified and versions capture their change. **Execution Scheduler:** we enable parallel execution of activities which are ready to execute (i.e. their input artefacts are ready). **EXE-SPEM:** we enable

```
S: the set of system components; HE: the set of undesired hazardous events
M: list of mitigators; PM: list of partial mitigators
for each he in HE {
        if(he.criticality > negligible)
                if(he exists on the system output)
                        trace_failure_to_the_source();
                else
                        for each component s in S
                          if(he is present on s.input)
                                  if(he is not on s.output){
                                      M.add(s);
                                      find_the_mitigating_rule();
                                  }else
                                          if(the source of he on s.output != s.input)
                                              PM.add(s);}
```

Fig. 1. The pseudo code for analysing the FPTC results.

```
R1: Make CLAIM "All causes of hazardous Failure Modes are acceptable"
R2: For each hazardous event {he} in the set HE, apply the following:
  R2.1: If {he} is negligible, make a CLAIM "Hazardous Failure Mode {he} is negligible"
  R2.2: If {he} is not negligible, make a CLAIM "Hazardous Failure Mode of type {he} absent
        in contributory software functionality" and attach CONTEXT "Known causes of {he}
        failure mode"
  R2.2.1: If {he} is present on the output, make COUNTER-EVIDENCE "The {he} Hazardous
          Failure Mode present in the contributory software functionality. Check traces."
  R2.2.2: If {he} is not present on the system output, make a STRATEGY "Argument over
          failure mechanisms" and attach a JUSTIFICATION "Identified failure mechanisms
          describe all known causes of {he} hazardous Failure Mode"
    R2.2.2.1: make a CLAIM "The known causes of secondary failures of other components are
              acceptably handled" and leave it undeveloped.
    R2.2.2.2: make a CLAIM about the mitigators "Hazardous event {he} has been mitigated by
              {mitigators}" and attach an EVIDENCE "Mitigation details in the textual argument"
```

Fig. 2. Rules for product-based argument generation.

capturing some safety-related elements in the process model. Those elements are: certification information for roles, the qualification of activities and the guidance and standard each activity adheres to. The executability of models ensures that a process is enforced, which satisfies requirement *R1*. As models can be edited/re-enacted, reuse of processes and activities becomes possible. In addition, *R2* is satisfied since a single process model with its enactment semantics is centrally shared between stakeholders. This gives each stakeholder a global awareness of the progress. **Argument Generation Support:** we extended the enactment service to support generating safety arguments from process models. This is done by capturing artefacts and activities execution meta-data and extract safety cases content from it.

3.2   Argument Generation

Product-Based Argument: We generate product-based arguments from FPTC analysis results. By analysing if certain failures/hazardous events (HEs) occur or not, we can argue about how the system handles HEs. The analysis starts by parsing the FPTC results and following the pseudo code in Fig. 1. Then

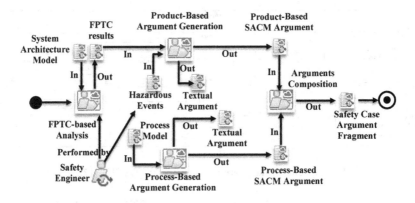

Fig. 3. PSSA augmented with the argument generation process.

the argument is formulated by constructing *Claims* and *Strategies* and supporting them by *Evidences/Counter-Evidences* following the rules in Fig. 2. These
rules are adapted from [17] where the generation of product-based argument-
fragments is made from contracts translated from FPTC analysis. In this work
we provide rules for generation of argument-fragments directly from the FPTC
analysis, thus skipping the translation of FPTC specification to contracts. Moreover, we provide more fine-grained analysis of how the system handles HE based
on the FPTC specification. If the HE is present in the system, we produce a
counter-evidence in the form of a trace to the source(s) of the HE. If it is not,
we find the component(s) that mitigated it. We distinguish between partial or
full mitigation. Full mitigation is when the failure does not propagate from a
component's input to its output, while partial mitigation is when the failure is
present on the output, but at least one of the input causes of the output failure
has been mitigated by the component.

Process-Based Argument: We use the rules explained in MDSafeCer [8] to
structure a process-based safety argument fragment. As explained in Sect. 2.4,
the fragment argues about: the tools used, the roles involved, the guid-
ances/standards followed and the work products generated/consumed in the
process. Information about these aspects is extracted from both the process
model and provenance data about the process enactment.

Once the product and process-based argument fragments are generated, they
are joined with a top claim arguing about the overall system safety to compose
the overall safety case argument fragment.

4   Case Study

The purpose of this case study is to demonstrate the cloud-based execution of
the augmented PSSA process. Fig. 3 shows the EXE-SPEM model of the PSSA
augmented with the argument generation process. It consists of four activities

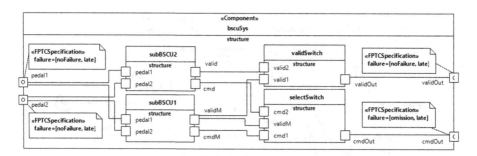

Fig. 4. The brake system control unit (BSCU) [17].

and involves creation of multiple artefacts. The *FPTC-based Analysis* activity analyses the failure behaviour of a system. It takes as an input the system architecture model and generates as an output the failure behaviour of the system. As mentioned in Sect. 3.2 this failure behaviour can be used by the next activity (*Product-based Argument Generation*) to verify if the *undesired hazardous events* (identified after performing FHA) have been mitigated. The *Process-based Argument Generation* activity uses the process model and provenance data about the process enactment to populate the process-based safety argument. Finally, the *Arguments Composition* activity combines both the product and the process based arguments into one safety argument fragment.

In this case study, we used the airplane Wheel Braking System (WBS) adopted from ARP4761 [1]. The WBS consists of the Brake System Control Unit (BSCU) and the hydraulics system which is connected to the wheels of the airplane. We limit our attention to the portion of the architecture that comprises the BSCU (shown in Fig. 4). Since the FHA process for the WBS system is out of the scope of this case study, we have randomly selected the *undesired hazardous events* that the system should mitigate and provided them as an input to the *Product-based Argument Generation* activity.

4.1   Implementation

After modelling the PSSA augmented with the argument generation process (Fig. 3), the model is mapped onto XML to be enacted on the cloud-based architecture. Below, we describe the implementation of each of the activities used in the safety argument generation process. **FPTC-Based Analysis:** This activity uses Concerto-FLA (the extended FPTC implementation from the CONCERTO project[1]) to perform the FPTC analysis. The CONCERTO toolset allows: creating UML-based architectural models of the system; performing FPTC analysis (using Concerto-FLA) including back-propagation of the results on the models. The architectural model is transformed to the *flamm* format (an XML-like format) on which the analysis takes place. The *flamm* model consists of composite components (systems) containing atomic components. The (atomic) components

---

[1] www.concerto-project.org/.

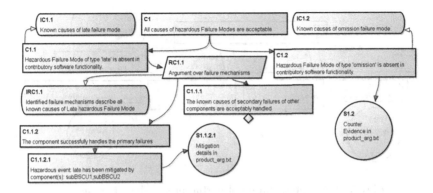

Fig. 5. GSN representation of the generated product-based argument.

```
...
CLAIM 1.1: HAZARDOUS FAILURE MODE OF TYPE 'OMISSION' IS ABSENT IN
    CONTRIBUTORY SOFTWARE FUNCTIONALITY.
        CONTEXT 1.1: Known causes of omission failure mode.
        COUNTER_EVIDENCE 1.1: The omission Hazardous Failure Mode is present
    in the contributory software functionality. Check the traces.
        CONTEXT 1.1: omission CAUSED BY:
        Failure: 'omission' On Output Port: 'cmd' of Component: 'selectSwitch
    '. CAUSED BY: {Failure: 'omission' On Input Port: 'cmd2' of Component: '
    selectSwitch'. CAUSED BY: Failure: 'omission' On Output Port: 'cmd' of
    Component: 'subSCU2'. CAUSED BY: ...
```

Fig. 6. The product-based argument represented in text.

have input and output ports where failures are attached. In addition, each component has a set of rules defining its failure behaviour. For this case study, we have extracted the FPTC analysis part from Concerto-FLA into this standalone activity which embed the analysed failure behaviour of the system into the *flamm* model. **Product-Based Argument Generation:** This activity uses the FPTC analysis results to construct the argument concerning the BSCU. Each undesired HE is accompanied by a definition of its criticality level. These levels are mapped to a five-level numerical criticality scale ranging from 1 (lowest criticality) to 5 (highest criticality). For instance, in ARP4754A [2], the levels are 1: *negligible*, 2: *minor*, 3: *major*, 4: *hazardous*, 5: *catastrophic*. The tracing and mitigation details are presented in an extended textual argument following the *Argument Outline* format [12] and is referenced in the SACM/GSN arguments. Figure 5 shows the generated product-based GSN argument for the BSCU while Fig. 6 shows a snippet of the textual argument. It is worth noting that we use the GSN *solution* notation to represent counter evidences (as in *S1.2* in Fig. 5).

Process-Based Argument Generation: This activity generates the argument arguing about compliance with PSSA. Figure 7 shows an argument for *FPTC-based Analysis* activity from the safety argument generation process we used in this case study. The tools and roles we used, are not qualified. Therefore, undeveloped goal is attached for them. The *failures_list* artefact corresponds to the result of the FTA analysis as required by Appendix B4.1 of ARP4761.

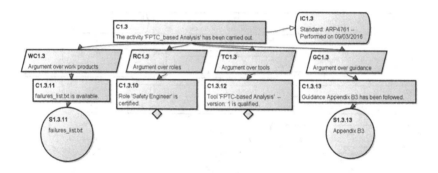

Fig. 7. GSN representation of partial process-based argument.

Arguments Composition: This activity combines the process and product-based arguments into one arguing about the overall system safety.

4.2   Execution

We enacted the safety argument generation process model (shown in Fig. 3) in the prototype of our extended cloud-based enactment architecture. We deployed the *Enactment Service* and one *Workflow Engine* on two different Amazon EC2"t2.small" machines. Using a web browser, we were able to enact the process and retrieve the generated artefacts containing the FPTC analysis results and the safety arguments (separate and combined) in both SACM/ARM XMI and text formats. The SACM/ARM XMI formats were then converted into GSN diagrams (Figs. 5 and 7) using the Astah GSN editor[2].

4.3   Discussion

By enacting the safety argument generation process on the cloud we demonstrated the application of our cloud-based enactment architecture for safety-critical processes. While we have used a process from an aerospace domain standard, processes from other standards can be modelled and enacted similarly. The enactment architecture is our target platform for modelling/development of safety processes. It is a service-oriented architecture and can be deployed into any cloud deployment model (public, private or hybrid). It can also be interfaced with existing platforms as a service call. This flexibility can address security and privacy concerns when using the cloud, i.e. one can use a private cloud to host the process enactment (partially or fully as each activity can be configured differently) and the generated artefacts. Furthermore, the architecture can be extended to support new rising requirements other than the three mentioned in Sect. 3. In this paper we showed how we extended our initial architecture [4] as detailed in Sect. 3.1. This involved extending the modelling language (EXE-SPEM) to model new requirements and extending the architecture components to incorporate the new required behaviours.

---

[2] http://astah.net/editions/gsn.

However, there are some limitations to the type of activities that can be supported. Software processes are often long-running and typically would involve human-intensive activities. The implemented prototype of the architecture does not yet support intensive interactions with humans during process execution. Capturing those interactions provides more data that could be integrated into safety arguments. Furthermore, a failure/exception during a long-running process will break the execution and in the current prototype, the process will need to be restarted. It is essential to have support to pause/resume processes in such situations. Since we do not have support to resume process enactment in case of failures, we recommend splitting processes into short-living sub-processes. Sub-processing also means better separation of concerns between teams. Finally, not all activities within a process can be automated and the borders between what can/cannot be automated is not defined yet. The benefits from automation remain, however. The automation of arguments generation saves time and cost and utilizes the enactment architecture to capture and generate supporting evidences for the arguments. The approach we propose does not address the issue of completeness of requirements, hazards etc. As Leveson [14] points out, there will be always hazards that are not considered and that depends on assumptions, the uncertainties and limitations of the used methods.

5   Related Work

As already pointed out by Sljivo et al. [17], there has been extensive research of safety case argumentation management and argument generation. For example, Hawkins et al. [11] propose a model-based approach for automated generation of assurance cases from automatically extracted information from the system design, analysis and development models. The approach uses model weaving to capture the dependencies between the reference information models and the assurance argument patterns. The Model Based Assurance Case (MBAC) program is in the heart of the prototype tool that implements the approach [10]. MBAC takes the argument pattern, reference information and weaving models as its input together with the corresponding metamodels, and provides an instantiated argument model as the output. While the weaving approach represents a more generic solution idea, our approach complements that work by looking at the specific information and argumentation pattern models and providing the corresponding model transformation rules. Most of the related approaches to argumentation management (e.g., [6,7]), however, lack support for distributed and remote safety case development for distributed teams. Moreover, these approaches do not address the potential need for scalable computational power needed for certain tasks in the overall safety certification enactment process. Our work offers a cloud-based solution that allows integrated coproduction of the safety case by geographically distributed teams. Furthermore, we do not only support the product, but also the process-based side of the argument. Gorski et al. [9] present an evidence-based argument management methodology TRUST-IT and a cloud-based software-as-a-service platform called NOR-STA supporting the application of this methodology. Similarly to GSN-goal structures, the TRUST-IT argumentation model represents evidence-based arguments in a tree-like structure. In contrast to NOR-STA, we aim at providing a complete process enactment service on the cloud where argumentation management is not treated as an activity separated from the activities mandated by the standards. Producing the evidence and managing the argumentation on the same platform allows us to automate the creation of the argument fragments that can be later combined in the overall safety case. Furthermore, by generating the argument fragments in a standardised format we support portability.

6   Conclusion and Future Work

This paper starts with listing a set of requirements for a development environment that supports the enactment of safety-critical processes. To meet such requirements we extend our previous model-driven cloud-based software process enactment architecture [4] to support the safety critical processes. We present a fragment of a process adapted from the aerospace domain and demonstrate its executability on the cloud. While our proposal brings the economical benefits of the cloud to safety-critical systems engineering, empirical studies and industrial collaborations are still needed to study the impacts of our proposal at both the organizational and individual levels and on the quality and safety of the produced systems.

To take this work further, we plan to develop a support for continuous compliance modelling and checking, for enabling extensive human interactions and off-line activities, as well as for sub-processing to allow long-lived processes typical for the aerospace domain.

References

1. ARP4761: Guidelines and Methods for Conducting the Safety Assessment Process on Civil Airborne Systems and Equipment. (1996)
2. ARP4754A: Guidelines for Development of Civil Aircraft and Systems. SAE International (2010)
3. GSN: Community Standard Version 1. Origin Consulting (York) Limited (2011)
4. Alajrami, S., Gallina, B., Romanovsky, A.: Enabling global software development via cloud-based software process enactment. Tech. Rep. TR-1494, Newcastle University, School of Computing Science (03 2016)
5. Alajrami, S., Gallina, B., Romanovsky, A.: Exe-spem: Towards cloud-based executable software process models. In: Proceedings of the 4th International Conference on Model-Driven Engineering and Software Development (2016)
6. Armengaud, E.: Automated Safety Case Compilation for Product-based Argumentation. In: Embedded Real Time Software and Systems (2014)
7. Denney, E., Pai, G.J.: Automating the Assembly of Aviation Safety Cases. IEEE Transactions on Reliability 63(4), 830–849 (2014)
8. Gallina, B.: A Model-driven Safety Certification Method for Process Compliance. In: 2nd International Workshop on Assurance Cases for Software-intensive Systems. pp. 204–209. IEEE (2014)

9. Górski, J., Jarzebowicz, A., Miler, J., Witkowicz, M., Czyznikiewicz, J., Jar, P.: Supporting Assurance by Evidence-Based Argument Services. In: 1st Workshop on Next Generation of System Assurance Approaches for Safety-Critical Systems. LNCS, vol. 7613, pp. 417–426. Springer (2012)

10. Hawkins, R., Habli, I., Kelly, T.P.: The Need for a Weaving Model in Assurance Case Automation. Ada User Journal **36**(3), 187–191 (2015)

11. Hawkins, R., Habli, I., Kolovos, D., Paige, R., Kelly, T.P.: Weaving an Assurance Case from Design: A Model-Based Approach. In: 16th International Symposium on High Assurance Systems Engineering. pp. 110–117. IEEE (Jan 2015)

12. Holloway, C.M.: Safety case notations: Alternatives for the non-graphically inclined? In: 3rd IET International Conference on System Safety. pp. 1–6 (2008)

13. Holloway, C.M.: Explicate '78: Uncovering the implicit assurance case in do-178c. Tech. Repp. 20150009473, NASA Langley Research Center (2015)

14. Leveson, N.: White paper on the use of safety cases in certification and regulation. Technical report. MIT (May 2012)

15. (OMG), O.M.G.: SACM: Structured Assurance Case Metamodel (2013)

16. Rushby, J.: New challenges in certification for aircraft software. In: 9th ACM International Conference on Embedded Software. pp. 211–218. EMSOFT (2011)

17. Sljivo, I., Gallina, B., Carlson, J., Hansson, H., Puri, S.: A Method to Generate Reusable Safety Case Fragments from Compositional Safety Analysis. In: 14th International Conference on Software Reuse. pp. 253–268. LNCS, Springer (2015)

Author Index

Printed in the United States
By Bookmasters